UNDESIRABLE IMMIGRANTS

PRINCETON STUDIES IN INTERNATIONAL HISTORY AND POLITICS

Tanisha M. Fazal, G. John Ikenberry, William C. Wohlforth, and Keren Yarhi-Milo, Series Editors

Undesirable Immigrants: Why Racism Persists in International Migration, Andrew S. Rosenberg

Human Rights for Pragmatists: Social Power in Modern Times, Jack L. Snyder

Seeking the Bomb: Strategies of Nuclear Proliferation, Vipin Narang

The Spectre of War: International Communism and the Origins of World War II, Jonathan Haslam

Strategic Instincts: The Adaptive Advantages of Cognitive Biases in International Politics, Dominic D. P. Johnson

Divided Armies: Inequality and Battlefield Performance in Modern War, Jason Lyall

Active Defense: China's Military Strategy since 1949, M. Taylor Fravel

After Victory: Institutions, Strategic Restraint, and the Rebuilding of Order after Major Wars, New Edition, G. John Ikenberry

Cult of the Irrelevant: The Waning Influence of Social Science on National Security, Michael C. Desch

Secret Wars: Covert Conflict in International Politics, Austin Carson

Who Fights for Reputation: The Psychology of Leaders in International Conflict, Keren Yarhi-Milo

Aftershocks: Great Powers and Domestic Reforms in the Twentieth Century, Seva Gunitsky

Why Wilson Matters: The Origin of American Liberal Internationalism and Its Crisis Today, Tony Smith

Powerplay: The Origins of the American Alliance System in Asia, Victor D. Cha

Economic Interdependence and War, Dale C. Copeland

Knowing the Adversary: Leaders, Intelligence, and Assessment of Intentions in International Relations, Keren Yarhi-Milo

Nuclear Strategy in the Modern Era: Regional Powers and International Conflict, Vipin Narang

Undesirable Immigrants

WHY RACISM PERSISTS IN INTERNATIONAL MIGRATION

ANDREW S. ROSENBERG

PRINCETON UNIVERSITY PRESS
PRINCETON & OXFORD

Published by Princeton University Press
41 William Street, Princeton, New Jersey 08540
6 Oxford Street, Woodstock, Oxfordshire OX20 1TR

press.princeton.edu

ISBN 9780691238739
ISBN (pbk.) 9780691238746
ISBN (e-book) 9780691238753

British Library Cataloging-in-Publication Data is available

Editorial: Bridget Flannery-McCoy and Alena Chekhanov
Production Editorial: Natalie Baan
Cover Design: Pamela L. Schnitter
Production: Lauren Reese and Erin Suydam
Publicity: Charlotte Coyne and Kate Hensley
Copyeditor: Jennifer McClain

Cover art: Shutterstock

This book has been composed in Arno

10 9 8 7 6 5 4 3 2 1

For my family,
who made everything possible

Memory says, "I did that." Pride replies, "I could not have done that." Eventually, memory yields.

—FRIEDRICH NIETZSCHE, *BEYOND GOOD AND EVIL*, EPIGRAM 68

You shall not wrong a stranger or oppress him, for you were strangers in the land of Egypt.

—EXODUS 22:20

CONTENTS

List of Illustrations xi
Preface xv
Acknowledgments xix

1 Introduction: A Ruinous, Residual Racism 1

2 The State, Sovereignty, and Migration Policy 30

3 Colonialism, Immigrant Desirability, and the Persistence of Inequality 60

4 A Forensic Approach to Racial Inequality 93

5 Unmasking Racial Bias in a "Color-Blind" World 116

6 Colonialism and the Construction of Undesirability 174

7 The Expansion of Closure in the Modern International Order 218

8 Conclusion: Reflections on the Future 268

Appendix A: Baseline Model Details 295
Appendix B: Graded Response Model 298
Appendix C: Immigration Policy Analysis 300

Bibliography 309
Index 345

LIST OF ILLUSTRATIONS

Figures

3.1 The expansion of border fence construction, 1965–2016 87

5.1 Estimated total global migration flow from 1960 to 2015 125

5.2 Logged global migration flows by period, 1960–2015 126

5.3 Emigration underflows have increased from 1960 to 2015 133

5.4 Low-income countries have the largest emigration underflows 135

5.5 The gap between OECD and sub-Saharan African countries 138

5.6 Racial bias in international migration flows 141

5.7 Simulated differences in migration bias between White and Black states, 1960–2015 143

5.8 Border and land control policies have increased over time 149

5.9 Bordering and legal entry policies pull in opposite directions across all countries in the DEMIG dataset 154

5.10 Latent policy restrictiveness increases over time and varies by country 156–157

5.11 The moderating effect of liberal democracy? 168

6.1 Liberal democracy moderates the effect of postcolonial inflows on restrictive policies 208

6.2 Postcolonial immigration inflows moderate the effect of being a colonizer on policy restrictiveness 212

6.3 Comparing a former colonial power to a noncolonial power 214

7.1 IO membership and the proliferation of border fences 251

7.2 Interaction between colonial history and IOs 263

7.3 Comparing the probability of fence construction between former colonies and colonizers 265

A.1 Distribution of migration flows, 1960–2015 296

C.1 Distribution of aggregate immigration policy restrictiveness, 1960–2015 301
C.2 Distribution of measures of racially different immigration flows 302
C.3 Linear-additive test 303

Tables

3.1 Shares of world GDP, 1700–1952 75
5.1 Example of dyadic migration deviations 122
5.2 Example of sending-state migration deviations 123
5.3 Average migration bias by world region 136
5.4 Country-years included in the DEMIG policy database 147
5.5 An excerpt from the DEMIG policy dataset 148
5.6 United States immigration policy changes, 2005 152
5.7 Association between inflows and increased policy restrictiveness (1960–2013) by three measures 162
5.8 Regression models of immigration policy restrictiveness, 1960–2013 163
5.9 Countries with the largest positive effect of average ancestral distance of immigration population 169
6.1 Are immigration flows from former colonies associated with greater migration policy restrictiveness? (1960–2013) 206
6.2 Effect of colonial histories 210
6.3 Countries with the largest positive effect of postcolonial inflows on immigration policy 213
7.1 Raw count of border fences by region, 2014 255
7.2 Regression models of new border fence construction 259
7.3 Regional random intercepts for baseline likelihood of building a border fence 261
A.1 Baseline model results 297
C.1 Distribution of racially different immigration measures by region 302

C.2 Model specification with lagged dependent variable 304
C.3 Regression models of immigration policy restrictiveness with postcolonial variable 305
C.4 Logistic regressions with time trend 306
C.5 Logistic regressions with lagged dependent variable 307

PREFACE

MY GRANDMOTHER Audrey's mother was named Bluma Slapak.[1] Her grandchildren called her Nannie, and she was born and raised in Knyszyn, Poland, which was then a part of the Russian Empire. Like many Polish Jews, Nannie wanted to immigrate to the United States because she feared persecution and violence. Her parents and extended family helped her cobble together enough money to afford passage, and she left Poland on October 31, 1922, bound for New York via Antwerp. She embarked from Antwerp on November 22 on the Red Star Line ship, the *S. S. Zeeland*.

Nannie's story reflects the experience of many Jewish immigrants of the day. She arrived in New York harbor, passed through Ellis Island (changing her name to Beatrice in the process), lived in the Bronx, worked in a garment factory, and eventually headed west, where she met my great-grandfather. They settled in Omaha, Nebraska, where my grandmother and her sister were born, moved to Des Moines, Iowa, in the 1940s, and the rest is history.

When Jews speak about those who made it out of Europe during this period, they tend to cite the horrors that their family members were running from: pogroms, fascism, indiscriminate violence, and so on. However, they almost always neglect the horrors that their family members ran *toward*: pervasive Jew hatred. Such hatred—typically known as *anti-Semitism*[2]—ran rampant throughout the United States during this period because it fit nicely within the "scientific" racist and eugenicist ideologies of the day, the goals of

1. I am indebted to my cousin Suzy Weber for dutifully compiling our family's genealogy. She keeps the family flame alive and is a top-class historian!

2. With others, I use the term *Jew hatred* over *antisemitism* because Wilhelm Marr coined the latter in Germany in the 19th century to provide an air of legitimacy to discrimination toward Jews. "Earlier Germans were blunter: They called it *Judenhaas*, liberally Jew-Hatred. [Marr] sought a pseudo-scientific and therefore more palatable word. He knew the term 'Semitic' had historically referred to a family of languages that originated in the Middle East. So he refashioned the word to mean prejudice against Jews alone" (S. D. Smith 2020).

which were to prevent the pollution of American society with "feebleminded-ness, insanity, criminality, and dependency."[3] Many Americans thought Jews were "filthy, un-American, and often dangerous in their habits. . .lacking any conception of patriotism or national spirit."[4] They were racial undesirables who would refuse to assimilate, corrupt society's morals, and leech off the public purse.

This commonplace Jew hatred in part spurred the United States' infamous Immigration Act of 1924, which Congress passed just two years after my great-grandmother arrived in New York.[5] The act imposed strict immigration quotas that favored the "Nordic" races of northern and western Europe at the expense of the "undesirable" races of eastern and southern Europe.[6] These restrictions combined with existing anti-Asian restrictions to maintain the US's racial homogeneity. These laws were so successful at "safeguarding" its "Nordic character" that they received Adolf Hitler's vehement praise in *Mein Kampf* and elsewhere as "the prime, and indeed only, example of *völkisch* citizenship legislation in the 1920s:"[7]

> *Es gibt zur Zeit einen Staat, in dem wenigstens schwache Ansätze für eine bessere Auffassung bemerkbar sind. Natürlich ist dies nicht unsere vorbildliche deutsche Republik, sondern die amerikanische Union, in der man sich bemüht, wenigstens teilweise wieder die Vernunft zu Rate zu ziehen. Indem die amerikanische Union gesundheitlich schlechten Elementen die Einwanderung grundsätzlich verweigert, von der Einbürgerung aber bestimmte Rassen einfach ausschließt, bekennt sie sich in leisen Anfängen bereits zu einer Auffassung, die dem völkischen Staatsbegriff zu eigen ist.*

> There is currently one state in which one can observe at least weak beginnings of a better conception. This is of course not our exemplary German Republic, but the American Union, in which an effort is being made to consider the dictates of reason to at least some extent. The American Union categorically refuses the immigration of physically unhealthy elements, and simply excludes the immigration of certain races. In these

3. P. K. Wilson 2002.

4. Neuringer 1980 [1969], 134.

5. The Immigration Act of 1924 codified the National Origins Formula originally set out in the Emergency Quotas Act of 1921.

6. Ngai 1999.

7. Whitman 2017, 46.

respects America already pays obeisance, at least in tentative first steps, to the characteristic *völkisch* conception of the state.[8]

This praise would become darkly ironic, and it epitomizes the deep alliance between the US's intentions to use immigration law to ensure the racial desirability of its population and the twentieth century's most insidious ideology of Jew hatred.[9] Naturally, President Calvin Coolidge refused to veto the Immigration Act of 1924 because, "America must be kept American."[10]

Nannie was lucky; she left Poland at exactly the right time. She avoided the pogroms. She avoided the Immigration Act of 1924. She avoided being executed by the Nazi gestapo on the Knyszyn courthouse steps like her family that remained behind. But there was nothing special about her, and there is nothing special about my family. Nannie did not have to make it; in fact, many throughout the world would have preferred her story end differently. They assumed that Jewish immigrants were inferior and would make undesirable members of their political community. To use the jargon of social science, the Anglo-European world used racist, pseudoscientific reasoning to *construct* Jews as unfit for membership in American society because of their undesirable, immutable traits.

I begin with my great-grandmother's story because nearly all research has an autobiographical quality. But also, the purpose of this book is to show that the exclusionary politics of international migration that plagued the lives of many of my ancestors and other "undesirable" groups remain in the present day. Many politicians and citizens throughout the world marshal the same arguments about desirability, danger, and fiscal cost to warrant increasingly restrictive immigration policies, much like the Congress that passed the Immigration Act of 1924. There are two principal differences between the two eras: 1) most laypersons presume that today's restrictions are "objective" or "color-blind;"[11] and 2) the majority of the world's immigrants now come from

8. Hitler 2016, 1117. This is James Q. Whitman's translation of the German, cited in Whitman 2017, 45–46.

9. I describe how this ideology pervaded the rest of the Anglo-European world in chapters 2 and 3.

10. Calvin Coolidge, "First Annual Message," December 6, 1923, https://millercenter.org/the-presidency/presidential-speeches/december-6-1923-first-annual-message.

11. In this book, there are dozens of instances where I use language like "objectively" or "color-blind" or "undesirable." In most, if not all, of these instances, the implication is that the people using this language are doing so under false pretenses, with mistaken confidence, or

formerly colonized regions of the global South.[12] But many still perceive certain immigrants to be dangerous or undesirable on the basis of supposedly objective characteristics that actually are products of historical events and contexts that those immigrants cannot control. It bears repeating that Americans thought Jews would refuse to assimilate because they lived in shtetls and ghettos in Europe,[13] but they ignored that this segregation was not by choice. Facts and nuance rarely emerge in public discourse about immigration.

To be sure, many will disagree with me and the arguments that I make in this book. They might even think these ideas are dangerous or naive. Be that as it may, I ask those who immediately recoil at mentions of race, racism, or immigration to read with an open mind and appreciate that there is a fine line between being a member of a "desirable" or an "undesirable" group. We cannot control who our ancestors were, but we can all control our appreciation of this fact.

---

some other problematic circumstance. To avoid visual and cognitive overload, I eschew the quotation marks in most cases.

12. Abel 2018.

13. Blood libels about Jews killing Christian children and other racist conspiracy theories also spurred European pogroms during this period (see, e.g. Bemporad 2019; Brustein 2003).

ACKNOWLEDGMENTS

WRITING THIS BOOK has been a very rewarding experience, and I have many people to thank. However, I must first acknowledge that nearly all the writing and editing of this book took place during the ongoing COVID-19 pandemic. While living through a once-in-a-century global health crisis was certainly bleak and disorienting, I have been very fortunate to have stable academic employment and ample resources to complete this project. Reliance on precarious labor is one of the great stains on higher education (and society in general), and the pandemic has only exacerbated these circumstances. No words can adequately express my gratitude for those in our society who make things work.

This project began as a doctoral dissertation at the Ohio State University. In that undertaking, I accumulated many debts, beginning with my coadvisers, Chris Gelpi and Alex Wendt. Chris and Alex encouraged me to pursue a project that was politically important, provocative, and that would have real stakes. They both bore the brunt of my one thousand earlier, worse ideas and never wavered in their support of this project. Thank you for letting me gamble.

William Minozzi, Bear Braumoeller, and Inés Valdez also served on the committee, and each provided guidance that greatly enhanced this book. William was the first faculty member I met when I arrived in Columbus. He has been a mentor, adviser, but most of all, a great friend, and he has always generously made the time to be there for me whenever needed. Bear was the person who convinced me to come to Ohio State, and he has always been more generous with his time and feedback than he needed to be. Coauthoring with Bear taught me the ropes of doing academic work, and I am grateful for that opportunity. Finally, this book would not exist without Inés. She implored me to read Du Bois, and I cannot overemphasize how much I benefited from her careful eye, her insightful comments, and her advice on book writing and professional development.

This project also gained from many others' insights and support, including Bentley Allan, Larry Baum, Rob Bond, Philippe Bourbeau, Aisha Bradshaw, Ben Campbell, Austin Carson, Skyler Cranmer, Raphael Cunha, Marina Duque, Errol Henderson, Rick Herrmann, Dan Kent, Ben Kenzer, Vlad Kogan, Marcus Kurtz, Kyle Larson, Adam Lauretig, Michael Lopate, Will Massengill, Ben McKean, Jennifer Mitzen, Carolyn Morgan, John Mueller, Lauren Muscott, Michael Neblo, Irfan Nooruddin, Tom Nelson, Ruthie Pertsis, Jan Pierskalla, Amanda Robinson, Randy Schweller, Greg Smith, Alex Thompson, Leyla Tosun, Pete Tunkis, Linnea Turco, Daniel Verdier, and Iku Yoshimoto. Special thanks go to several members of my small-but-mighty graduate school cohort: Jose Fortou, Austin Knuppe, Reed Kurtz, Anna Meyerrose, and Avery White. They are great friends who have all been instrumental to this project in many ways, from its conception to the final manuscript.

In addition, this book would not have been possible without the training I received at Johns Hopkins and the London School of Economics. I went to college expecting to study history, but the guidance of Steven David, Dan Deudney, Joel Grossman, Siba Grovogui, Hitomi Koyama, and Khalid Kurji convinced me that I should study political science. It was also a stroke of fortune that I ended up at the LSE for a master's degree because without Iver Neumann I certainly would not have gotten a PhD in IR. But most of all, I must acknowledge the incredible education I received in the West Des Moines Community School District. My teachers provided a peerless foundation for success that highlights the importance of investing in public education.

I presented earlier versions of parts of this project at the following institutions: Georgetown University; George Washington University; Harvard University; Merton College, Oxford; Université Laval; and the Universities of Florida and Minnesota, as well as at various meetings of the American Political Science Association, the European Political Science Association, the International Studies Association, the Midwest Political Science Association, and the Millennium Journal Conference. I am grateful for the opportunities and for all the valuable, incisive feedback that participants provided.

Turning to the present, I wrote this book at the University of Florida, and the Department of Political Science has been a wonderful academic home since 2019. I have benefited greatly from sharing a genuinely pluralist department with such a talented group of scholars across the subfields of political science. I want to specifically highlight the influence of Hannah Alarian, Badredine Arfi, Michael Bernhard, Aida Hozić, and Ben Smith on this project. As department chair, Dan Smith has also provided generous support and advice. Nicole Figueroa, Ellie Schauer, and Eve Vanagas also provided essential research and administrative support.

At Princeton University Press, I am indebted to Bridget Flannery-McCoy, who has been enthusiastic about this project ever since our first conversation. Bridget's guidance has been instrumental in making the manuscript better. I also must thank Alena Chekanov and Natalie Baan, who were decisive in seeing the project through to the finish line. I am also appreciative of Jennifer McClain for copyediting the manuscript and Enid Zafran for compiling the index. Despite its remaining faults, this project also benefited immensely from the remarkable feedback of two anonymous reviewers and Errol Henderson (again). Errol's comments left an immeasurable impact, and I cannot thank him enough for his critical eye and support.

This book is dedicated to my family. Sadly, my grandmother Audrey Rosenberg and grandfather Stanley Engman passed away while the manuscript was going through the review and production processes. While I'm devastated that they will never get to read it, I take comfort from remembering all the time we spent together and their unfailing love and encouragement, even when I was skeptical that things would work out. Embarrassingly, I was mortified that my grandmother found out that the manuscript was under consideration—I'm too superstitious for my own good—but I often go back and read the text message she sent after I explained that there was "probably a million-to-one chance" that Princeton would publish it: "We won't say anything—just always proud of each step along the way."

The rest of my family has also been a source of support throughout this process. Unfortunately, there are far too many members to acknowledge individually, but I will highlight a few notables. I struggle to find the words to express my love and admiration for Shari Engman and Harlan Rosenberg (the original Dr. Rosenberg). They continue to give me so much for which I am thankful, and I look forward to sharing many more Iowa football Saturdays with them. Ken and Denise Coyne are relatively new additions to the family, but they continue to love me like their own son. My stepparents, Jeff Chapman, Keely Rosenberg, and Randy Cain, also provided immeasurable encouragement throughout the years, and I appreciate all they have done for me. I am also fortunate to have two wonderful parents, Kim and Steve, whose faith in me has always outstripped my own. They have provided a foundation of support, inspiration, and understanding throughout my life that I could never possibly repay. I can only hope to pay it forward and try to live up to their example. Thank you for believing in me and letting me follow my own path.

Finally, my wife and partner, Colleen, has been my truest companion for nearly a decade. I met Colleen the first week I moved to Columbus for graduate school, and she has been my closest confidante this entire time (along with our dog, Quigby, of course). Quite frankly, I could not have written this book without her. She tolerated, to varying degrees, my penchant for obsessive work during the spring/summer of 2020, but she never let me forget what was important in life and rightfully pushed me to relax once in a while. I am eternally grateful for her insights, intellect, support, and sacrifices, and I cannot imagine spending life with anyone else.

Andrew S. Rosenberg
Gainesville, FL
January 2022

UNDESIRABLE IMMIGRANTS

1

Introduction
A Ruinous, Residual Racism

FROM 1901 TO 1973, Australia had the world's most racist immigration policies. These policies were called "White Australia," and their purpose was to "guard the last part of the world in which the higher races can live and increase freely for the higher civilization."[1] Indeed, the parliamentary debate over these laws exuded an incontrovertible racism, as Australian policymakers feared that the White race would soon face an overwhelming economic, social, and political threat from non-Whites.[2] Too much racial mixing, after all, would dilute and denigrate the White race,[3] and the Australians were willing to face the imperial and international consequences of their actions.[4]

This government-sponsored racism began to change in 1966. Over the next few years, the Holt government passed several new laws that shifted Australia's policies away from selecting immigrants on the basis of race and toward selecting them on the basis of skill, expertise, and race-blind desirability. Accordingly, ever since the Whitlam government abolished the last remnants of White Australia in 1973, many Australians have praised their immigration policy as fair and nondiscriminatory. By the letter of the law, Australia's transformation from racist to "color-blind" is a remarkable achievement.

1. Pearson 1893, 15–16.

2. Many throughout the Anglo-European world shared similar fears of a "Great Replacement" or "race suicide" that would threaten world White supremacy. See, e.g., Barder 2019.

3. For example: "We have more to fear from the educated coloured people than from the ignorant coloured people, because the latter will not attempt to mingle or associate with the white race." Commonwealth of Australia, Parliamentary debates, session 1901–02, IV, 4633, 1 September 1907.

4. Lake and Reynolds 2008, 75–94.

However, recent events cast doubt on the reality of this transformation. In 2018, the Australian government introduced a special humanitarian program to allow immigration from White South African farmers who, proponents exclaimed, faced increased violence and unlawful land seizures from the country's Black majority. Although no data support the claim that White South Africans face excessive violence,[5] Australia was eager to give the farmers special dispensation in the immigration process. To justify this initiative, Peter Dutton, the Minister for Home Affairs, argued that the farmers were hard-working, would not need welfare, and would integrate and contribute to Australian society.[6] In other words, these South Africans were the ideal beneficiaries of an immigration policy designed to rescue victims of persecution and bring in the best and brightest from abroad. Prime Minister Malcolm Turnbull lauded this "generous" policy as "non-discriminatory," implicitly associating it with Australia's post–White Australia, egalitarian Renaissance.[7]

During the same period, the Rohingyan ethnic minority in Myanmar faced *verified* persecution and violence from their country's military. Many Rohingya are also farmers, family-oriented, and likely hard-working (most farmers are). But they are non-White Muslims. Would Australia offer the Rohingya the same "non-discriminatory special attention" as the White South African farmers? After all, they are an industrious population that allegedly face race-based violence, just like the South Africans. If politicians designed Australia's migration policy to both rescue victims of extreme violence and bring in immigrants who could immediately contribute to the public welfare, then the Rohingya were excellent candidates for special attention too.[8]

The answer is no. Instead, Australia offered asylum to only two thousand of the estimated one million displaced Rohingya,[9] detained others indefinitely on Papua New Guinea's Manus Island, and offered AU$25,000 per person to return to Myanmar to face what the United Nations called "a textbook

5. R. Davis 2018.

6. BBC 2018a.

7. Dziedzic 2018.

8. Australian human rights groups have called Burmese treatment of Rohingya an "apartheid" (Mallinson 2017) or a "genocide" (Zarni and Cowley 2014). This label is ironic considering that the Australian government was willing to take in White refugees from South Africa—a formerly apartheid state—under dubious circumstances, while unwilling to take in non-White refugees experiencing an apartheid in another state.

9. Doherty 2018; Kohli, Markowitz, and Chavez 2018.

example of ethnic cleansing."[10] When asked whether Australia was offering such incentives for Rohingya to leave and whether it was safe for them to return to Myanmar, Mr. Dutton declined to answer. In the end, the Rohingya were not similar enough to the South Africans: they may have been hard-working farmers facing existential violence, but something was missing to persuade the Australian government to apply the same "non-discriminatory" policy to them.

Some argue that this something is race: Australia did not take in the Rohingya refugees because its leaders and citizens viewed them as a part of a larger "unregulated surge" that threatened their way of life.[11] These critics point to the resurgence of White supremacist opposition to immigration in Australia over the last thirty years,[12] and they highlight the first conversation between US president Donald Trump and Australian prime minister Malcolm Turnbull, in which the former praised the latter for being "worse than I am on asylum seekers."[13] Racism, these critics argue, continues to hide in plain sight because leaders like Turnbull boast of their country's nondiscriminatory migration policies with one side of their mouth and brag about excluding undesirable migrants with the other. These leaders simply dress up their desire to discriminate on the basis of race in "color-blind" clothing.

However, it is difficult to square this argument with the reality that migration policies throughout the world no longer discriminate on the basis of race. The issue is that leaders like Prime Minister Turnbull can always deny charges of racism on the grounds that their immigration laws are nondiscriminatory. They can respond that the goal of immigration policies is to use objective criteria to admit the best immigrants that will benefit the national interest, nothing more. It is not the head of state's fault, they will exclaim, that migrants from certain parts of the world are poorer, more prone to violence, or less educated than others. So, while the disparities in Australia's treatment of the South African farmers and the Rohingya suggest racial bias, the available evidence is not discerning because the lack of explicitly racist policies shrouds the intentions of policymakers in ambiguity.

As such, this book generalizes from individual cases and provides clear evidence that racial discrimination persists in international migration, regardless

10. Safi 2017.

11. Hogan and Haltinner 2015; Maguire and Elton 2017.

12. Flitton 2014; Dunn, Klocker, and Salabay 2007; Poynting and Mason 2007.

13. Bourke 2017.

of leaders' intentions. It explains why this *residual racism* remains in a "color-blind" international system that forbids racial discrimination, and it ties this inequality to the era of explicit racism, colonialism, and policies like White Australia. Abstracting from individual cases shows how structural racism operates in the international system, much like it operates in neighborhoods and cities.[14] Instead of arguing that the international system is full of racist leaders who covertly use race-neutral laws to produce a "global apartheid,"[15] the following story illustrates how discrimination persists even if all overt racism vanishes. Such *structural* racial inequality is ruinous because it hides in plain sight.

The Exclusionary Politics of International Migration

The Australian case evokes international migration's status as the most politicized area of world politics. No other issue so easily elicits fear from electorates, motivates states to collaborate, and spurs action from leaders. In the past decade, concerns over the movement of people swung the Brexit referendum, elected populist leaders, affected citizenship policies, and produced staggering levels of collaboration between the European Union and its neighbors.[16] Immigration engenders these responses because it taps into primordial questions of politics and the human experience: What is a political community? Who are the legitimate members of that community? How do we balance the interests of different groups within that community? What do we owe outsiders? The existential nature of these questions ensures that international migration will intervene in almost any political issue, international or domestic. Moreover, it is unlikely that conflicts over immigrants will abate because citizens in both the global North and global South have become increasingly reluctant to welcome outsiders into their communities.[17]

Two patterns stand out when one examines the politics of international migration in more detail. First, the pronounced public hand-wringing over immigration is an outlier when compared to the other tenets of the liberal

14. Bonilla-Silva 2006; Feagin 2006.

15. Alexander 1996.

16. Alarian 2017; Dennison and Geddes 2019; Goodwin and Milazzo 2017; Hansen and Randeria 2016; McAlexander 2020.

17. Buehler, Fabbe, and Han 2020; Semyonov, Raijman, and Gorodzeisky 2006; Cogley, Doces, and Whitaker 2018.

international order. In general, the weight of Western public opinion supports the freedom of movement of goods, services, and capital.[18] For example, although public opinion varies with the particularities of domestic politics, most educated citizens of the developed world support free trade and do not consider it to threaten the national interest.[19] This support provides further evidence that free market capitalism has become hegemonic in the post–Cold War era.[20] However, many of those who support the other tenets of the liberal world order are *against* immigration.[21] While states eliminated their explicitly discriminatory immigration policies during the postcolonial era in the spirit of these liberal principles, the public remains firmly suspicious of newcomers.

Second, although states eliminated racially discriminatory policies, their objective policies have become more prohibitive in recent decades.[22] Some scholars use the Western public's insatiable appetite for discriminating against undesirable immigrants to argue that migrants of color bear the brunt of these restrictions.[23] Leaders lend credence to these critics when they refer to migrants as "parasites and protozoa" (Jaroslaw Kaczynski),[24] "bank robbers" (Boris Johnson),[25] and a "swarm" (David Cameron)[26] that is "carrying diseases" (Andrzej Duda)[27] to "threaten Christian Europe" (Victor Orbán).[28] Yet, at the same time, many of those same leaders proclaim that their immigration policies are "non-discriminatory" (Australia) because they are based on "universal" (US), "clear" (Germany), or "objective" (UK) grounds.[29] This juxtaposition suggests that these objective laws may service nonobjective goals, and that evidence of inequality is not coincidental.[30] However, one

18. Murray 2019.

19. Hainmueller and Hiscox 2006.

20. Milanovic 2019.

21. Mayda 2008.

22. Peters 2017.

23. Ayers et al. 2009; Chatham House 2017; Douglas, Sáenz, and Murga 2015; Ellermann and Goenaga 2019; Ford 2011; K. R. Johnson 2000.

24. Cienski 2015.

25. BBC 2018b.

26. BBC 2015.

27. Al Jazeera 2015.

28. Karnitsching 2015.

29. Dernbach and Starzmann 2018; Dziedzic 2018; Secretary of State 2018; White House 2019.

30. The politics and ethics of race are difficult to navigate. Throughout this book, I use the term *Anglo-European* to refer to countries that laypeople may consider "White" or majority

cannot directly observe their discriminatory intent *because the laws are legally color-blind*. Ironically, racist laws like White Australia were inferentially useful to expose and combat prejudice because they clearly indicated where racism existed. Without these laws, that relationship, like many instances of racism in the modern world, hides in plain sight.

Some scholars downplay elite rhetoric and public opinion. After all, sovereign states have the right to control their borders,[31] and many leaders justify their restrictive policies on these grounds.[32] As long as the letter of the law is race-neutral, it does not make sense to conclude that states continue to restrict on the basis of race. Politicians changed explicitly racist laws, and now all potential migrants are welcome if they meet certain objective criteria. In this world, leaders, publics, and putative migrants are rational actors, and migration occurs when all the incentives line up for all the parties. Individuals decide to move if the expected benefits exceed the expected costs,[33] and states accept migrants if they will benefit society.[34] For scholars in this camp, there are many factors that produce different immigration policies, such as domestic business interests,[35] trade policy,[36] and war.[37] Immigration policies emerge out of this complex dance among firms, lobbyists, politicians, citizens, and the global economy, all of which vary over time to produce different levels of restrictiveness. But as long as the law forbids racist policies, any arguments linking race to immigration policy or the ability to migrate are ignored or rejected. Some even claim that nativism cannot explain changing levels of restrictiveness because it has remained more or less constant over time.[38]

For other scholars, the second observation explains the first: citizens of the West are against immigration because they are racist, and elites oblige

---

"White." I do so because this term alludes to the role the so-called Anglosphere has played in colonialism and explicitly racist policy throughout world history (Vucetic 2011). Unfortunately, this classification ignores the real diversity within these states and silences these populations. In the absence of a better term, however, I use *Anglo-European* because it connects to the important history that I unpack later in the book.

31. Martin 1989; Opeskin 2012.

32. Hathaway 1994; Shanks 2001.

33. Sjaastad 1962; Todaro 1969.

34. Adamson 2006; Rudolph 2003.

35. Freeman 1995.

36. Peters 2017.

37. Rudolph 2003.

38. Peters 2017, 7.

these desires for discrimination despite their distorting effect on the world economy. Immigration led to a racist backlash in the past, and it leads to a racist backlash today. This backlash occurs because leaders and citizens are explicitly racist against outsiders. In fact, immigration restrictions are inherently racist and are the product of racial capitalism. These policies have racist origins, have always been tied to colonial practices and raced notions of desirability, and continue to directly and indirectly perpetuate racist ends.[39] With this perspective, *any* immigration policy is suspect because "[immigration policies] legitimate racism, feed racism, and are explicable only by racism."[40] There is no puzzle for those in this group. Western states are more open to the freedom of movement for goods, services, and capital than people because, in such a world, elites and citizens would not have to share a society with racial undesirables, but would still reap the economic benefits of globalization.

This book is a response to both camps.[41] On the one hand, it would be intellectually dishonest to ignore the real progress toward racial equality in the postcolonial era. Decolonization led to the proliferation of new nation-states in the international system, which produced an international society of states that gives a voice to the former victims of Anglo-European colonialism and White supremacy.[42] This global transition coincided with Western states replacing immigration policies that discriminated on the basis of race with policies that admit immigrants who pass objective, inexplicitly racist criteria.[43] This real progress makes it difficult to completely vilify states and their leaders because it is impossible to argue that the problem of racism in the international system has not somewhat abated.

On the other hand, an overly optimistic or uncritical view leaves one blind to the remaining inequalities in the international system. Looking at the letter of the law is just one way that color blindness can blind one to persistent racial inequality. Human beings have a natural blind spot for racial inequality in contexts where such inequality is legally forbidden.[44] For example, during

39. Anderson 2013; Gutiérrez Rodríguez 2018; Hayter 2000; Sharma 2020.

40. Hayter 2001, 149.

41. To be sure, migration scholars do not fall into two neat camps. These are just ideal types, and I do not mean to perfectly represent the vast and diverse scholarship on international migration policymaking.

42. Bull and Watson 1984; Strang 1990.

43. Joppke 2005, 2.

44. Bonilla-Silva 2006; Sullivan and Tuana 2007.

the 2016 Brexit referendum, some leaders used racist caricatures of Muslims to argue that "open borders make us less safe,"[45] while others articulated a desire to protect social services from "objectively" poor and undesirable immigrants and to reassert "self-determination." These appeals resonated strongly with voters with heightened perceptions of Muslim immigration, even though they lacked a factual basis.[46] Yet, most policymakers and citizens fail to reckon with these examples, and they neither consider that modern immigration policies may still be racially biased nor interrogate how, in this example, British imperialism was complicit in *producing* that undesirability to begin with. Moreover, such examples run against the argument that nativism is constant and therefore cannot explain policy changes.[47] While nativism may be constant in rich countries, *exposure* to racial outsiders is not, and public support for the Brexit referendum emerged in response to increased emigration from the postcolonial world. This perspective allows for a nuanced view of how race and racism operate in the international system, does not depend on all politicians and citizens being "old-fashioned" racists, and helps explain how racial inequality in international migration can persist *and worsen* in the absence of legal discrimination.

How Race "Hides" in International Migration

Systemic racial inequality in international migration is a product of three interrelated processes: the need of sovereign states to restrict undesirable immigrants, the legacy of colonialism, and the expansion of sovereignty. These three processes are interdependent, but the story begins with the assumption that "proper" sovereign states control their borders and have an inherent right to exclude foreigners. Modern racial inequality in international migration begins with this assumption, which supposedly goes back to the 1648 Treaty of Westphalia and motivates leaders to restrict immigration and control their borders. However, I argue that the right to control one's borders is *not* an inherent feature of state sovereignty. Contrary to the rhetoric of most leaders and publics, international legal jurisprudence was ambivalent about border control during the seventeenth and eighteenth centuries. In fact, this "right" only emerged with the rise of the modern, "rational" nation-state during the

45. Virdee and McGeever 2017.

46. Carl 2018.

47. Peters 2015, 114.

nineteenth century.[48] Modern nation-states were intoxicated with ideologies of progress, which led them to embrace scientific racism as a tool to perfect their societies. In many Anglo-European states, such as the United States and Australia, this transformation coincided with an influx of immigration of racial outsiders due to industrialization, colonialism, and the expansion of global capitalism. Racist migration policies emerged from these historical processes as a means to limit immigration of racial undesirables and protect the sanctity of the native population.[49] Therefore, the right to border control is not an inherent feature of sovereign states; *it is a modern consequence of racism*. Racism and White supremacy merely ensconced this "right" into the conventional wisdom of how modern states ought to behave.

As a result, racial inequality in migration persists because the desire to limit undesirable immigration never went away, and the norms of sovereignty validate those desires as a legitimate and necessary exercise of state authority. Prior to decolonization, the standard of immigrant desirability was race. In the modern day, elites and citizens continue to clamor for policies that restrict undesirable immigrants, but race is no longer a legally allowable criterion for desirability. Instead, policymakers use supposedly objective criteria to determine desirability, such as education and language. The issue is that these formally "color-blind" criteria are still correlated with race. For example, a US president recently implored Congress to restrict immigration from "shithole countries" in Africa because they threaten the national interest.[50] However, there is little reflection on what makes some countries dangerous "shitholes" in the first place, or whether citizens deterministically embody their homeland's characteristics. Appearing undesirable often has nothing to do with an individual migrant and instead depends on how explicit racial inequality and colonial exploitation in international politics affects their home country.

This description of how Western states construct non-White migrants as undesirable finds common cause with W.E.B. Du Bois's "The African Roots of War."[51] More specifically, it highlights how long histories of explicit

48. Buzan and Lawson 2015, ch. 4.

49. As Adam McKeown notes in related work, migration control did not emerge as a logical necessity of the international system, but "out of the attempts to exclude people from that system" (McKean 2020, 3). However, McKeown does not discuss race in his exploration of this history; he focuses on "civilizations" instead.

50. Davis, Stolberg, and Kaplan 2018.

51. Du Bois 1915.

racism, chattel slavery, and colonialism produced "dangerous" modern subjects that Western states—often former colonizers—now routinely restrict. During decolonization, Anglo-European states assumed that recognizing former colonies as sovereign equals would settle the issue of racial inequality. These powerful states ignored the fact that former colonies gained independence after experiencing debilitating periods of domination at the hands of the great powers. Sovereign equality did not erase the long histories of exploitation that led to citizens from postcolonial states appearing inferior, undesirable, or even dangerous when compared to citizens of the Anglo-European states. Although the international system is now legally color-blind, we still observe inequality in migration because racism now hides in this uncritical view of why some migrants appear threatening. And the states that created those "dangerous" migrants are the same states that now categorize them as inherently unfit to immigrate. In this way, the decline of explicit racism and the rise of color blindness allow race to appear as a settled issue in the politics of migration, while obscuring that simply recognizing postcolonial states as equals does not create equality.

An unfortunate implication of this relationship between colonial exploitation and the ignorance of "color blindness" is that racial inequality in international migration is unlikely to abate *due* to the expansion of sovereignty in the postcolonial world. The conventional account of decolonization in international relations (IR) is that the European-dominated international society expanded to include former colonies, thereby becoming a global society.[52] Now that postcolonial states were recognized as equal members of the sovereign state system and its institutions, racial inequality was supposedly resolved. Instead, the globalization of the international society led to further closure and inequality because of the persistent hierarchy that lurks in contemporary global politics. Anglo-Europeans only conditionally accepted postcolonial states as members of the international society after years of exploitation, imposing arbitrary boundaries and, in many cases, disrupting centuries-long norms of freedom of movement.[53] This conditionality creates the perpetual need for postcolonial states to perform their legitimate statehood because, otherwise, Western states are free to intervene in their affairs.[54] Strict border controls are one important way of demonstrating authority and

52. Bull and Watson 1984, 432.

53. Herbst 2000, 228.

54. ICISS 2001.

legitimacy, as the closing and policing of international borders has become an important symbol of sovereignty. As a result, postcolonial states have built border fences and expelled foreigners at an alarming rate, which has increased racial inequality in migration by inhibiting migration within the global South. This shows that one cannot understand the postcolonial rise of restrictiveness in international migration without appreciating the history of Western colonialism.

This argument reveals how putatively good faith efforts to eliminate racial inequality can create conditions that perpetuate it. However, immigration policymaking takes place on a state-by-state basis, and Anglo-Europeans do not collude to intentionally discriminate against the postcolonial world. Accordingly, it is difficult to provide evidence of systemic racial inequality in this allegedly "color-blind" process. This inferential problem crops up whenever laws and behavior pull in opposite directions, and this book's task is to unmask the bias against non-White migrants that lurks beneath these face-neutral policies.

Why We Need a Measure of Racial Bias

At its core, my argument suggests that removing discriminatory laws is insufficient to dismantle racial hierarchies in the postcolonial international system. A significant proportion of the migrants the West now restricts on "objective" grounds come from countries that bore the brunt of colonial exploitation. This connection between past ills and present perceptions ensures that states and international politics cannot outrun their colonial histories. This assertion parallels other accounts of inequality in the postcolonial international system. For example, Antony Anghie argues that the West deliberately entrenched neoimperial economic relations into international law in response to decolonization.[55] Others like Siba Grovogui highlight how Anglo-European states continue to control institutions of global governance and function to disadvantage postcolonial states.[56] In these cases, identifying hierarchies is straightforward. One can point to exact moments and cases in international legal jurisprudence when Anglo-Europeans revealed their inclination to curtail the postcolonial world's sovereign equality.

55. Anghie 2007.
56. Grovogui 1996.

The case of international migration is more complicated. The absence of racist language in modern immigration laws makes it difficult to provide evidence of global patterns of racial discrimination. Modern laws *forbid* such discrimination; one can no longer point to a racist policy to warrant the existence of discrimination in the opportunity to migrate. Without these laws, it is no wonder why scholars presume that international migration is a race-neutral process. The West scrubbed racist language from laws and institutions during the transition to color blindness, so racial inequality is out of sight and out of mind. This problem resembles past difficulties in measuring racial discrimination in American cities after the civil rights era. Without scholarly intervention, those inequalities would have remained invisible as well.

Likewise, we need a measure of racial inequality in international migration because, without such a measure, this inequality is *invisible*. In other words, without a measure, one is left to use various cases and anecdotal evidence to argue that such inequalities persist. While there are many cases that suggest certain countries discriminate against some types of migrants,[57] these studies remain vulnerable to the critique that racial inequality in migration is fleeting, case-specific, or unintentional, and therefore not a real structural concern in international politics.

This issue relates to a broader debate in the global governance literature regarding how problems emerge as necessary targets of state and international intervention. This discussion is vital because issues of global governance are often collective action problems: all relevant states must act to solve them. However, this collective action requires a shared perception of the state of the world and its facts, and that those facts constitute a legitimate problem to solve.[58] As Bentley Allan argues, an epistemic community or organization must first observe and classify an entity appropriately before the international community will see it as a legitimate issue.[59] Without this step, it is difficult for leaders to recognize an issue because, if they cannot see it, they cannot fear it.

What is more, *how* something is classified also impacts how states respond. In the case of the global climate crisis, Allan argues that the US government and its scientists classified the climate as a deterministic object that states could control. This choice produced policies such as carbon pricing schemes that presume humans can control a slowly changing climate. However, the

57. Alexander 1996; Köhler 1995.

58. Wendt 2001, 1023.

59. Allan 2017, 137.

climate is not deterministic and likely will change too fast for such deliberate policies to help.[60] Had scientists and policymakers constituted the climate as a different sort of problem—a complex, nonlinear system—this emphasis on control may have given way to a different governance model that would have facilitated more experimentation and ultimate success. In short, how scientists and elites defined and measured the climate problem affected how states addressed it.

I argue that elites and scholars ignore or downplay racial inequality in international migration because it lacks such a clear designation. Without racist laws, one cannot denote this inequality as a legitimate problem because the social undesirability of racism in international politics has rendered it invisible. There is no way to indicate whether inequality exists, so it is impossible for one to observe and classify this inequality. As such, it is unlikely that racial inequality in migration will emerge as a problem in global governance, beyond a corner of the IR academy, if it is not measured and unmasked.

This issue is analogous to the difficulties in studying racial inequality and segregation within cities, and in countries that do not collect statistics on race, such as France. For example, the US Fair Housing Act of 1968 prohibits discrimination on the basis of race, sex, color, national origin, religion, familial status, or disability. One effect of the act was the end of *legal* segregation in the United States. However, despite the dawn of putative legal equality, it was clear that segregation continued, and scholars were forced to use other techniques to study the residential inequality that remained in the absence of explicit laws. These techniques compare observed racial distributions in housing to those we would expect in a truly desegregated world to infer the continued existence of spatial inequality, segregation, and redlining.[61] Without this scholarly effort, skeptics would still be able to dismiss continued residential segregation.

However, many scholars and policymakers oppose collecting statistics on race or ethnicity to inform policy. This resistance takes two forms. First, some resist racial classification for obvious historical reasons. The measurement of race—including the Human Genome Project—hearkens back to the age of scientific racism and raises important ethical questions.[62] This rationale against collecting racial statistics or measuring racial inequality finds

60. Allan 2017, 154.

61. Duncan and Duncan 1955; White 1983.

62. Phelan, Link, and Feldman 2013.

common cause with a similar debate among international relations scholars. Some argue that measurement and the use of indices hold disproportionate power in global governance. Measures constitute, rather than represent, the reality they claim to depict. There is no such thing as an objective measure; the creator's preconceptions always influence the index. As such, numerical indices in international politics reproduce relations of power, rather than simply measure objective facts about the social world.[63] When states, elites, and academics recognize the legitimacy of indices such as the World Bank's governance indicators, it gives credence to notions of good governance that Western states have used to warrant interventions in postcolonial states.[64]

Second, some states do not collect racial statistics because their model of comprehensive immigrant integration precludes it. France is the most extreme example of this policy. The French model of integration presumes that immigrants will lose their cultural distinctiveness on the path to citizenship. In fact, the definition of republican "Frenchness" explicitly forbids any mention of race or ancestry, and "the idea of a hyphenated Frenchman acquired no political or social legitimacy" in society.[65] As a result, there is no need to distinguish among French citizens on the basis of their national origin or race. Although the ideals of a color-blind society are admirable, this color-blind approach renders authorities effectively ignorant to still-existing racial inequalities. Rather than eliminate racial prejudice and other issues, the statistical invisibility of race conceals the extent of discrimination in French society and calls into question whether the government promotes civic nationalism and prioritizes assimilation to remain deliberately ignorant.[66]

This perspective implicitly subscribes to the philosophical position of *racial eliminativism*. Adherents to racial eliminativism argue that the concept of race must be eliminated from public discourse because it is scientifically inaccurate and rests on neither neutral nor factual grounds. In short, the concept of race refers only to a discrete group of people that share the same genetic features. Such genetic similarity can only emerge in a group of people that are genetically isolated, such as the Amish in the United States. However, by this standard, the concept of race only refers to groups that are not

63. Hansen and Porter 2012.

64. Gruffydd Jones 2013.

65. Simon 2015, 65–66.

66. N'Diaye 2006, 2008.

typically considered races (e.g., the Amish) and cannot apply to conventional racial groups (e.g., Black Americans) because the latter are not genetically isolated or distinct by any standard.[67] Eliminativists argue that this incoherence proves that scholars and laypersons should cease referring to races even when they do so in good faith.[68]

The issue with racial eliminativism is that it ignores the role of race as it currently exists in modern society. Critics of racial eliminativism argue that races are socially constructed, and despite their lack of scientific grounding, racial categories remain determined "by various historical, cultural, and social facts."[69] In other words, simply noting that there is nothing biologically real about races denies that many in the wider world continue to treat some people differently on this basis. These *racial constructivists* believe that race is "both real and unreal":[70] society groups humans on the basis of ancestry, phenotypic properties such as skin tone and hair texture, and other cultural markers. So, even though race is a scientific falsehood, society treats these groups as real and membership in racial groups affects one's experience in the world.

In this book, I take such a constructivist approach to the study of race in international migration. While I acknowledge that race has no biological reality, people throughout the world still categorize others on the basis of these imagined categories. Race is a powerful concept *because* it is a social fact, not in spite of it. This rationale justifies the need for a measure of racial bias in international migration. The color blindness of international politics presumes that the removal of racist immigration policies is sufficient to end discrimination in immigration policies. However, anecdotal evidence suggests that states continue to close their borders to "undesirable" immigrants. Without a measure of racial bias to investigate these practices, we are unable to address inequalities in the international system, even if the basis of those inequalities is pseudoscientific. Creating this measure and revealing that stark inequalities exist despite their legal prohibition will illuminate racial inequality, particularly in migration, as a legitimate problem in international politics. While measurement is not an unqualified good, I use the power of measurement and classification in the service of uncovering otherwise invisible structural inequality.

67. Appiah 1996, 73.
68. Mallon 2006, 526.
69. Mallon 2007, 103.
70. Mills 1998, 47.

Race, Racism, Racial Inequality

Even with this basic argument and empirical justification in view, however, we still need to define race and racism, as well as what they mean in an international context. Race is a multidimensional, hierarchical, and socially constructed label.[71] As such, the study of race raises ethical and conceptual issues that do not afflict other concepts in the social sciences. For one, the history of race is one of domination, genocide, enslavement, and pseudoscientific manipulation. The Anglo-European world constructed the concept of race to justify White supremacy, and its agents have used it to warrant countless incursions throughout the world.

François Bernier first used the term in 1684 to comment on the perceived distinctiveness of humans in different geographical areas,[72] and this classification quickly acquired its negative connotation and purpose in the eighteenth century. In fact, Immanuel Kant argued that "Negroes and whites are clearly not different species of human beings (since they presumably belong to one line of descent), but they do comprise two different races,"[73] and Europeans colonized the world on the basis of this newfound, objective (rather than theological) justification for their superiority. Given this history, many scholars, activists, and laypersons consider any "scientific" study of race to reproduce the historical injustices delivered in the name of human progress.

In addition, one of the perpetual methodological difficulties in cross-national research is *construct equivalence*, or "the instance where the instrument measures the same latent trait across all groups, or nations, or cultures."[74] Construct equivalence is important because it is impossible to make general explanations about a given concept if it lacks a consistent definition. These difficulties pervade the study of race in international politics. Different countries have different histories and cultures, which lead them to hold different racial classifications. Therefore, reluctance toward studying race and racism in the international system is warranted because races often are not stable categories *within* states,[75] much less between them.

However, these issues do not preclude the study of racial inequality in the international system. Following Stephen Cornell and Douglas Hartmann,

71. Omi and Winant 1994.

72. McPherson 2015, 677.

73. Kant 1777, 9.

74. Mills, Van de Bunt, and De Bruijn 2006, 623.

75. McPherson 2015.

I define a *race* as "a human group defined by itself or others as distinct by virtue of perceived common physical characteristics that are held to be inherent," but that have no actual biological basis.[76] As such, racial groups become racial groups when others act as if that group is inherently distinct. This categorization is often made on the basis of appearance, culture, or behavior, and it has profound implications for that group's power, its position in the social hierarchy, and the societal resources accessible to its members. In this way, race is "a relationship between persons mediated through things,"[77] and this broad definition is important because it avoids biological determinism; highlights the contingent, socially constructed nature of race; and emphasizes that this social construction occurs "relationally via the distribution of social, psychological, and material resources." Under this definition, White Australia was a "racial" restriction because it was "imbued with the negative thrust of excluding some immigrants as members of other-(rather than self-) defined groups that were deemed intrinsically inferior."[78] These policies reproduced racial groups because they withheld the ability to immigrate (a material resource) on the basis of putatively immutable characteristics that *others* defined (a racial classification).

Defining race this way clearly delineates it from the concept of ethnicity. The difference between a race and an ethnic group is that ethnic groups are self-defining and races are other-defining: ethnic groups *define themselves* on the basis of shared culture, language, religion, and history.[79] Ethnic groups only require members of a community to share a common origin and culture.[80] Races can, and often do, cross ethnic lines because the outsiders that use racial labels often are ignorant of ethnic divisions. As such, in this book, the distinction between race and ethnicity revolves around who defines the group, whether that group has an inherently negative connotation, and the effects of being placed in that group. Ethnicity is a horizontal label, while race is a vertical label: race implies hierarchy based on the implication of membership.

Be that as it may, the concepts of race and ethnicity further relate because the former has no biological basis and depends on the latter's cultural traits. This interdependence can complicate matters because scholars make sharp

76. Cornell and Hartmann 2006, 22.

77. Ray 2019, 29.

78. Joppke 2005, 32.

79. Cornell and Hartmann 2006, 19.

80. Joppke 2005, 3.

distinctions between their concepts. But adopting the racial ontology of Alain Locke provides guidance for navigating the murky waters between race and ethnicity, strengthens the utility of the modern concept of race, and is faithful to a racial constructivism that acknowledges the lack of a biological basis for race, as well as its social effects.

Locke (PhD, Harvard, 1918) was the first black recipient of the Rhodes scholarship,[81] lectured widely on race and international relations,[82] and was the most prominent philosopher of the Harlem Renaissance.[83] Locke responded to the conventional wisdom of the time that race was a scientific or biological reality; he was a racial constructivist who saw these distinctions as *social categories*. For Locke, racial divisions boil down to the socially inherited cultural traits that outsiders attribute to groups from particular geographic areas. To explain the "so-called permanency" of races that scientific racists sought to account for, Locke pointed to the "determinism" of "social heredity, and its distinctions due to the selective psychological set of established cultural reactions."[84] In short, ethnic groups are associated with certain cultural traits and geographic areas, which have "social and historical causes."[85] Race "operates as tradition" and as a "selective preference for certain culture-traits and resistance to certain others."[86] To summarize, an ethnicity becomes a race when its historically determined cultural practices are constructed as inherent. Races have no biological basis: they are "ethnic fictions" imposed on groups from the same geographic area on the basis of the favorability or unfavorability of their traits. This definition means that races are socially constructed, not Platonically real, but the construct still has devastating effects even in an era of putative color blindness. Locke's constructivist connection between social practices, geography, and perceptions inform my empirical strategy for unearthing racial inequality in international migration.

As a result, I define *racism* as both an ideology that characterizes and ranks human groups (races), with some being inferior to others, and "the unequal treatment" or "exploitation" of those groups.[87] Racism is complex because it is both an action and a belief, and the absence of one type of racism does

81. Vitalis 2015, 11–12.
82. Henderson 2017.
83. Locke 1925.
84. Locke 1924a, 191.
85. Locke 1924a, 192.
86. Locke 1924a, 195.
87. Williams, Lavizzo-Mourey, and Warren 1994, 29.

not falsify the existence of the other. The consequence is that we can label a practice, institution, or structure racist if it treats members of different racial groups unequally, even if the perpetrator does not hold explicitly racist beliefs. For example, a bank's loan officers commit a racist act if they deny a loan to a Black family because they live in a redlined neighborhood. Regardless of the loan officers' beliefs, they still treat members of a racial minority differently on the basis of a group-based attribute. This treatment is pernicious because, in this example, the racial and geographical disparity in mortgage lending is a racist *structure* that produces harmful environments, such as violent neighborhoods and vacant homes, which lead to racial isolation and fuel racist beliefs. Each of these aspects reinforces the others in a feedback loop that reproduces racial classifications. Black Americans living precariously in the same poor and violent neighborhoods appears natural and given, which further affirms the racial classification and the racist beliefs of Whites. This process is what Abigail Sewell calls the "racism-race reification process."[88]

This cycle of race and racism resonates beyond American society because it involves the relationship between economic inequality and racial subjugation. Postcolonial theorists have long considered how race and racism sustain unequal political and economic relationships, and they apply this logic to the international system. For instance, Aimé Césaire describes how European colonizers used racist practices to dehumanize indigenous populations, label them barbarians, and establish colonies on the basis of White supremacy. These overtly racist tactics were individual (theft, rape, and various forms of psychological abuse) and institutional (forced labor, conscription, taxation, and appropriation).[89] In Césaire's account, colonialism thrived on racism and the production of racial groups because this dehumanization created a self-fulfilling prophecy that justified colonial exploitation.

Likewise, Frantz Fanon claims that "European opulence . . . owes its very existence to the soil and subsoil of the underdeveloped world" because its "well-being and progress were built with the sweat and corpses of blacks, Arabs, Indians, and Asians."[90] However, decolonization did not end this cycle of exploitation, and Fanon describes how former colonist countries exchanged independence for a "return to the Dark Ages" and withdrew "capital and technicians and encircl[ed] the young nation with an apparatus

88. Sewell 2016.

89. Césaire 2000.

90. Fanon 1963, 53.

of economic pressure."[91] Anglo-European states may have acquiesced to independence, but they ensured that their former colonies would remain disadvantaged. This less visible dimension of decolonization crystallized postcolonial subjects as "undesirable," and it shows the antecedents of this book's main argument. With the benefit of hindsight, it expands beyond the immediate effects of colonialism to describe how this dehumanization and abuse affects contemporary politics.

Although these definitions do not subsume the myriad politics surrounding race and ethnicity, they highlight how I think of race operating in the international system. States and societies may have their own racial categories, but race and racism become international concepts when states (politicians, elites, publics) make or support policies on the basis of perceived difference. In many cases, scholars see race as a cause of various social phenomena: segregation, health inequality, police violence, and so on. However, race is better seen as an *effect* of social practices. In other words, states do not need to have the same racial ontology; they just need to act in similar ways in the face of groups that they consider racially different. This conception is similar to how Du Bois defines race when he remarks that "a black man is a person who must ride Jim Crow in Georgia."[92] Being a victim of Jim Crow—an effect of racism—defined one as "Black." Biological facts do not make race a coherent concept; rather, the inequalities and social conditions experienced by those labeled as racially distinct do.

Who Are the "Racists"?

At first blush, this argument seems quite sinister. Racial inequality in international migration continues to exist because elites enact laws that are race-neutral in name only. These leaders and their constituents still want to restrict on the basis of race, but since racism has become socially undesirable, they must act through race-neutral policies. Advocates must then appeal to sovereignty, "objective" criteria, and the need to protect national security to justify these restrictive policies. After all, what citizen of a respectable country would not want to be extra safe when admitting outsiders? The story becomes fully international when newly independent states of the non-White world adopt Anglo-European models of sovereignty and implement their own

91. Fanon, 53–54.
92. Du Bois 2007 [1940], 77.

restrictive immigration regimes in an effort to act like a legitimate state. In this account, the behavior of hidden racists catalyzes this circuitous mechanism, leading from the end of racist quotas through decolonization to the present day.

The "sinister" interpretation of this argument reveals an important dimension of this book: the role of intentionality. Am I arguing that citizens and politicians *intend* to produce racial inequality? In its broadest definition, actors are intentional when they use their mental states—beliefs, desires, and preferences—to act purposively.[93] I have intentionality because I have beliefs (that I should write a book) and then act deliberately on the basis of those beliefs (I wrote a book). Intentionality is a philosophical concept, but it has important implications for politics because it helps us answer questions of intent and responsibility. Why did two states go to war? Why does recidivism occur? Why did someone default on a loan? In these cases, the philosophical debates surrounding intentionality matter a lot.[94] Consider the case of a loan default. An "internalist" would answer that what matters in explaining this default is that person's own thoughts, beliefs, and preferences. To explain why the individual defaulted, we need to get inside the head of the defaultee and figure out why the person's mental state led to this bad behavior. In contrast, the "externalist" would answer that human society is not merely the sum of billions of individuals with their own internal mental states. Instead, one's environment also affects one's intentionality. Humans "think through culture,"[95] and the externalist would respond that we need to understand how *society* affects the defaultee's mental state that led to the bad behavior.

Intentionality plays a huge role in the study of modern racism, and this study is no different. For instance, many cities throughout the world are still racially segregated, even though explicit segregating practices—such as redlining—are now illegal. Competing explanations of this segregation fall along similar internalist/externalist lines. On the one hand, some argue that segregation is a product of structural racism, whereby non-Whites who would otherwise wish to move to a particular neighborhood are unable to do so because of factors that are out of their control, such as the history of income inequality between Whites and non-Whites. On the other hand, others argue

93. Wendt 1999, 172.

94. See, Wendt 1999, ch. 4, for an overview of the internalist/externalist debate over intentionality.

95. Shweder 1991.

that segregation is less a product of structure and more a product of preferential attachment or other deliberate behaviors. Cities remain segregated simply because people have a preference to live near those who are like themselves, or because lenders deliberately make it difficult for non-Whites to get loans. In these examples, intentionality matters. If non-Whites simply do not wish to live near Whites, or individual bankers deliberately hold non-Whites to higher minimum lending standards, then the solution is different than if society's structural or historical features perpetuate segregation.

Both of these cases reveal why we need to embrace "externalism" and appreciate the role of *collective* intentionality, particularly when we study racism. Collective intentions occur in supraindividual entities like societies, cities, and countries. For example, if you turn on a television news station, the commentators will discuss what countries and corporations intend all the time. The key point is that individual members of a supranational entity do not need to share its intentions. In the case of discriminatory bank lending, American society may collectively intend to restrict the frequency or size of the loans it gives to minorities because it intends to safeguard the loan market. This collective intention produces structural racial inequality regardless of the individual intentions of loan officers. The behavior of each officer matters—collective intentions do not come to fruition if individuals do not act—but collective intentions are not reducible to individual intentions, beliefs, or preferences.[96] Yet, the inequality that those collective intentions produce affects individual beliefs that can affect a loan officer's *future* intentions and behavior.

An account of collective intentions is vital for this book for two reasons. First, an important consequence of my argument is that racial discrimination in international politics persists irrespective of the distribution of individual racism. Put differently, racism in an international process does not require collective intentions to reduce perfectly to individual intentions, *just like in the domestic case*.[97] Leaders and citizens can have various intentions, but these intentions serve the collective intention of producing restrictions that lead to racial inequality. This makes locating responsibility a difficult task. Second, this logic scales up to the international level. All states implement immigration and border policies, and each may have a different intention. However, these state policies serve the collective intention of maintaining the sovereign state

96. Searle 1995, 23.
97. Gibbs 2001.

system. Individual states might not care about preserving the system and its ordering principles. But the structure, culture, and incentives of international politics makes it likely that the actions of individual states will serve the collective intention of preserving the status quo. In turn, when the international system expands after decolonization, this collective intention strengthens out of sheer numbers.

These points reveal the nature of modern racism in the international system and the problem of pinning down racist intentions. As I note above, racism is an ideology that ranks human groups and treats those groups differently on the basis of that ordering. Crucially, this definition means that individual leaders and citizens can be guilty of supporting racist policies without holding overtly racist views. All that matters is that their perceptions lead them to order groups on the basis of desirability and treat the migrants within each of those groups differently. As a result, racist immigration policies can emerge in several different ways. First, overt racists still walk among us, and they use explicit racism to justify restrictive policies. This case is the easiest to identify because the policymakers *state* that they want to restrict immigration by those they consider undesirable, and their definition of undesirability uses racist tropes.[98] However, because such racism is socially undesirable, all but the most overt racists will use "objective" facts to warrant policies: their state must restrict certain immigrants because not doing so will be dangerous. Second, some people are misled about the relative danger posed by certain migrants. Ideological news sources and motivated politicians have the incentive to propagate false information for their own gain.[99] Finally, others may selectively consume accurate information about certain migrant populations, but miss how the West benefits from an international system that caused the perceived danger in the first place. Those in this camp are prone to thinking that, for example, migrants from certain countries will bring their unproductivity with them and drag down the economy.[100]

The intentions with respect to race are different in each case, and we cannot know for certain whether behavior is "really" racist without the ability to read minds because all but the most prejudiced will use nonracial language. Overtly racist leaders are the exception, not the rule. Trying to parse the intentions of individual leaders only leads one to miss the bigger picture. As such,

98. Davis, Stolberg, and Kaplan 2018.

99. Bierbrauer and Klinger 2002; Martin and McCrain 2019.

100. Collier 2013.

this book is about unmasking structural racial inequalities that reveal *collectively racist intentions*. The sinister explanation for racial inequality need not hold for there to be sinister systemic outcomes in an ostensibly "color-blind" world. International politics is yet another arena in which "racism without racists" powerfully dictates the distribution of benefits.[101]

In short, states collectively intend to restrict on the basis of race irrespective of the individual intentions of its members. In fact, the importance of collective intent reveals why, in most cases, uncovering explicitly discriminatory intent of states' laws is so difficult. For example, take the argument that the language requirement in Germany's immigration policy is racist. Who would the "racist" need to be to substantiate this claim? For an internalist, one would need to observe a legislator (or group of legislators) using an explicitly racist justification for introducing or supporting the policy. For the externalist, one would need to consider how society as a whole constructs migrants that do not speak German as racially undesirable. My view is that the latter is representative of how White supremacy operates in the modern international system, though there are a few high-profile examples of the former in contemporary Western politics. We can be agnostic about whether leaders deliberately mask their discriminatory intent and focus on the structures that produce inequality.

As such, I explore how colonialism has led the West to construct migrants from the non-White world as undesirable. This bridge from colonial history to the present explains how color-blind laws that emerge from this construction nevertheless continue to have disparate racial impacts. This structural racial inequality is powerful and ruinous because it hides in plain sight, just like domestic White supremacy. However, *my* intention is not to absolve individuals of responsibility for behavior that perpetuates racism and racial inequality. Structures do not act; people do. This approach merely reveals why structural racial inequality continues to pervade the world without requiring thousands of internalist "smoking guns."

The Study of Race and Racism in International Politics

Unmasking this collective racism and racial inequality is vital because "race has been a fundamental force in the very *making* of the modern world system and in the representations and explanations of how that system emerged

101. Bonilla-Silva 2006.

and how it works."[102] In other words, race and racism lie at the heart of how international politics has unfolded for centuries, so exposing how these forces operate is part and parcel of studying international politics.

Be that as it may, recent international relations scholarship laments that the mainstream discipline has ignored issues of race and racism during the post-War era.[103] But this ignorance belies the discipline's dark racial history. Infamously, the field of international relations began its life as a science of race management during a time when policymakers reckoned with how to manage a world in which global capitalism's expansion and colonialism led to increased interactions between the West and the global South.[104] As Errol Henderson notes, the IR of the day had two axes. On the one hand, the dominant strand of White Anglo-European scholars pushed racist, pseudo-scientific accounts of a global racial hierarchy. Popular textbooks of the time argued vehemently about how this racial hierarchy was one of the fundamental facts of the social world, and this conventional wisdom informed debates in the United States and Great Britain over how to administer far-flung territories filled with racial undesirables.[105] On the other hand was the Howard School, which was composed of scholars like Locke, Ralph Bunche, E. Franklin Frazier, Rayford Logan, Eric Williams, and Merze Tate, who both combated the White supremacist foundations of the contemporary IR academy and developed their own theoretical approaches to international politics that preempted later theories, such as complex interdependence.[106]

Henderson, Robert Vitalis, and others have spearheaded efforts to highlight the early disciplinary history of IR and how the Howard School contributed to our total knowledge of international politics, but they also emphasize that scholars whitewashed this disciplinary history from the record after 1945. Indeed, Vitalis aptly notes that "scholars reliably produce unreliable accounts of the past of their own fields" and "International Relations is no exception."[107] This erasure of IR's foundational history has two consequences. First, it prevents contemporary scholars and graduate students from understanding the White supremacist foundations of the field and its theories, a task

102. Persaud and Walker 2001, 374.

103. See, e.g., Anievas, Manchanda, and Shilliam 2015.

104. Vitalis 2010, 911.

105. Henderson 2017, 493–495.

106. Henderson 2017, 497.

107. Vitalis 2015, 5.

to which several scholars have recently devoted their attention.[108] IR lies in a strange position within the social sciences because it only recently undertook this confrontation with its history, and this work will force scholars and practitioners to consider how the modern discipline descends from techniques of colonial administration that preserved (and expanded) international racial hierarchy.

Second, erasing the racial history of IR legitimizes the relative contemporary paucity of scholarship on race and racism in international politics. Although IR began its disciplinary life explicitly as a science of racial issues (and racist assumptions), modern IR largely ignores race, racism, and racial inequality. Like most examples of disciplinary ignorance, IR's blindness to these issues should disturb readers because prominent scholars have raised this issue since the early 1990s. Scholars such as Roxanne Doty, Siba Grovogui, Sankaran Krishna, L.H.M. Ling, Randolph Persaud, Robbie Shilliam, and R.B.J. Walker—to name a selection—have joined Henderson and Vitalis in highlighting both the absence of mainstream (and critical) IR scholarship on race and the aforementioned disciplinary history.[109]

What explains this absence in the face of such vehement claims? The first explanation derives from the racist history of the discipline. When scholars found a discipline on racist foundations, they build White supremacy into its assumptions and conventional wisdom. Vitalis describes this historical phenomenon as a "norm against noticing" race, which comes about because scholars privileged the Anglo-European core during the era of explicit racism. Despite the advent of color blindness in the contemporary discipline, the Anglo-European core composes the field's historical framework for thinking about the world.[110] Beyond ignoring non-White scholarship and contributions to the field, this framework perpetuates a norm of ignoring or obscuring White supremacy and the persistence of race and racism in the contemporary international system.[111] As a result, mainstream scholars come to view IR as the study of great power politics, war, and trade that this pre-WWII history shaped without considering how race and racism continue to play a role. This norm resembles the erasure of prejudice from the study of international migration after decolonization. Once the world

108. See, e.g., Henderson 2013; Hobson 2012; Rutazibwa 2020; and Sabaratnam 2020.

109. Doty 1993, 1999; Grovogui 2001; Krishna 2001; Persaud and Walker 2001; Shilliam 2013.

110. See also Henderson 2015, 90.

111. Vitalis 2000, 333.

becomes legally color-blind, the importance of race fades from scholarly memory.

The second explanation involves method and methodology. Doty and Krishna attribute the absence of race to the discipline's privileging of "theory building rather than . . . descriptive or historical analysis."[112] Mentors encourage their graduate students to take a positivist approach to social science, which prioritizes "abstraction" and the construction of "clear and ambiguous definitions of concepts." According to Doty, race and racism are complex, not "self-evidently neutral" facts, and therefore they are not well suited to the dominant way of studying IR in the mainstream academy. Although positivists certainly appreciate problems of moving from theory to concept to measurement, this critique maintains that using "methodological measurement" to solve these problems blinds scholars to issues of race.[113] This reliance on positivism contributes to making the study of race "taboo" in mainstream IR because it is "too historical or descriptive" and lacks "intellectual rigor."[114] These debates over method lead Persaud and Walker to suggest that race has "been given the epistemological status of silence."[115]

Despite these critiques, recent work demonstrates that the study of race and racism in international politics is well suited to positivist and quantitative approaches. For example, Henderson uses statistical analyses to reveal how White supremacy and Western imperialism intervened in African domestic institutions to produce particular patterns of conflict since decolonization.[116] While Henderson responds to the conventional wisdom in international relations theory, others like Thandika Mkandawire and Sonal S. Pandya reveal how racism, ethnocentrism, and colonialism intervene in the modern international political economy through domestic policies, such as taxation and foreign direct investment.[117] This work goes beyond merely highlighting the racist history of the field of IR and lamenting the absence of mainstream scholarship on race and racism to reveal how modern White supremacy works in practice. Moreover, these examples show how taking a concern for how race and racism continue to operate in the modern international system does not preclude one from using positivist methods.

112. Krishna 2001, 401.
113. Doty 1993, 448.
114. Krishna 2001, 402.
115. Persaud and Walker 2001, 374.
116. Henderson 2009, 2015.
117. Andrews, Leblang, and Pandya 2018; Mkandawire 2010, 2015.

This book builds on this existing scholarship, and it exposes a further aspect of modern international relations rife with racial inequality: international migration. The book recognizes Doty and Krishna's critiques of positivist scholarship. But rather than acquiesce, I develop a measurement strategy that imperfectly attends to the complexity of race and racism in the service of a historical argument. In so doing, I further demonstrate the inferential gains that positivist methods can bring to bear on unmasking the persistence of race and racism in the color-blind international system.

The Plan of the Book

Each of these themes emerges throughout the rest of the book. In the next two chapters, I situate immigration policymaking within the history of the rise of the modern nation-state. I overview the rise and fall of racist immigration policies and show that, contrary to conventional wisdom, the right to restrict foreigners was not an inherent principle of state sovereignty. This "right" arose only after settler colonial states began encountering racially undesirable immigrants, and I lay out how racist immigration policies emerged with the modern nation-state and its obsession with "rational" administration.

I then describe the transition from explicit discrimination to color blindness. There is a debate over whether this shift in policy orientation arose as a result of World War II and Nazi atrocities, or whether peripheral states successfully lobbied for the end of racist restrictions. I provide my historical synthesis of these perspectives to set the stage for the remainder of the book. The upshot is that by the end of decolonization, explicitly racist and discriminatory policies were gone. This sweeping sea change has led many leaders, policymakers, and academics to consider racial inequality in migration to be a settled issue. As I preview above, this assumption has prevented an inquisition into what makes some immigrants seem more desirable than others, and I reflect on the history of colonialism to describe how racial inequality persists in the color-blind international system. In chapter 4, I outline the inferential strategy for investigating these arguments and address some potential criticisms.

In chapter 5, I provide evidence that racial bias in the opportunity to migrate does remain, despite the end of racist quotas. The evidence in this chapter is the empirical centerpiece of my analysis, warrants the arguments, and sets the stage for the remainder of the book. To reveal the persistence of racial bias, I use an inductive strategy: I rule out all other possible explanations of the patterns of movement between states that are not discrimination. In so doing, I explain as much of the movement between states as possible and then determine whether the remaining, unexplained component exhibits patterns of racial inequality. In short, I estimate the ideal-typical amount of migration we should expect to see between every pair of states in the world from 1960 to 2015. I then reveal that deviations from these estimates fall along racial lines to substantiate my argument that migrants from the non-White world migrate less than expected, while migrants from the global North migrate in numbers far closer to expectations.

In the remainder of the analysis, I interrogate my explanation for why this inequality persists. I argue that colonialism and legal racism in the international system produced the conditions that states now use as objective justifications for restrictive immigration policies. These policies, therefore, disproportionately affect non-White migrants from the postcolonial world. In the rest of chapter 5 and in chapter 6, I test this hypothesis directly. The final section of chapter 5 digs deeper into the racial argument. Specifically, I expand the analysis to determine whether latent, symbolic racism in Western states leads to more restrictive policies. It is difficult to test this proposition directly. To get at this question, I test whether the racial composition of immigrant flows is associated with greater policy restrictiveness. Chapter 6 broadens this analysis to consider the colonial history mechanism. In this chapter, I analyze whether states that receive greater immigration flows from former colonies enact more restrictive policies. In chapter 7, I test the final piece of the theory. In so doing, I infer whether the expansion of sovereignty into the postcolonial world is also responsible for the persistence of racial bias in international migration. I explore the rise of border fences in the global South to show that postcolonial states have internalized the exclusionary logic of the rest of the world. Finally, the concluding chapter considers the implications of my argument, explanations, and evidence for the future of the international system, global prosperity, and the well-being of all individuals.

2

The State, Sovereignty, and Migration Policy

IN THIS CHAPTER, I provide a historical account of the rise of the institution of state sovereignty and the modern nation-state. This account dispels the commonly held belief among most citizens and leaders of Western states that countries have an inalienable right and duty to restrict their borders. The commonsense ideology of what it means to be a "proper" state motivates increasingly restrictive immigration policies throughout the world and has spurred the construction of massive and expensive border security apparatuses.[1] Most leaders who enact such policies and programs presume they are acting as good stewards of the nation-state. Under this conventional wisdom, the idea that border controls could somehow be racist or discriminatory is out of the question: it is merely the leader's duty to protect the state's borders.

This assumption is wrong; the earliest international legal jurisprudence defining state sovereignty began with the presumption that states do not have the unqualified authority to exclude foreigners and control their borders. This jurisprudence evolved over several centuries, and even Emer de Vattel—the totem of modern state sovereignty—admitted that states must prioritize the needs of human beings at the expense of their own interests. This even included foreigners that many would deride as mere "economic" migrants today. Instead, modern nation-states began arguing for this inherent sovereign right to exclude only after they began receiving racially undesirable immigrants. In this way, the explicitly racist immigration controls of the nineteenth and early twentieth centuries emerged out of the rise of the modern nation-state and its ideologies of nationalism, "scientific" racism, and

1. Benedicto and Brunet 2018; Rosière and Jones 2012.

high modernism. States and their leaders—inebriated on these ideologies of progress—wanted to restrict undesirable immigration because citizens are the lifeblood of modern states, and they appealed to supposedly timeless principles of sovereignty to justify their racist restrictions.

This chapter sets up the remainder of this book because it describes how restrictive immigration policies emerged out of Anglo-European encounters with so-called inferior races. While the social desirability of such explicit racism faded during the second half of the twentieth century, the imperative to restrict undesirables remained, as did the ideology that true, sovereign nation-states and their noble leaders ought to protect their borders from unwanted outsiders at any cost.

The Sovereign Right to Restrict

The United States' 1882 Chinese Exclusion Act is infamous because its passage marked the first time a Western state explicitly forbade immigration from a specific racial group. Although the United States had limited naturalization to "free white persons" since 1790, the Chinese Exclusion Act was the first policy that truly reflected the beliefs of many within American society that immigration from racial outsiders would risk the country's health and security. Senator John Franklin Miller of California echoed these sentiments during debate over the law. He argued that Chinese immigrants were not only a drain on the public's finances, they were also incapable of integrating into American society. Chinese immigrants were racially and culturally different from Americans, *it was in their nature* to resist integrating into society, and this inability was *dangerous*.[2]

Senator Miller's defense of the Chinese Exclusion Act signified the successful convergence of three historical processes that led to the modern nation-state: rationalism, nationalism, and scientific racism. By the end of the nineteenth century, scientific progress helped foster the belief that human beings were capable of rationally engineering all aspects of society.[3] The ideology of scientific progress was intoxicating, and citizens of all social strata rushed to use newfound objective principles to perfect their societies. Unsurprisingly, White supremacy was one such principle, and the "scientific" application of these long-standing ideas codified the conventional wisdom that there was

2. J. F. Miller 1882.

3. Allan 2018; Scott 1998.

an objective hierarchy of races and that superior races should only intermix with inferior ones at their own peril. Given the pervasiveness of these sentiments, it is no wonder that the United States would feel empowered to restrict immigration on the basis of race.

Although the American public broadly supported these views, the Chinese Exclusion Act faced legal opposition, and the result of this litigation would have far-reaching impacts beyond the United States. In 1875, Chae Chan Ping immigrated to the United States to work as a laborer in San Francisco. Prior to 1882, the Burlingame Treaty guaranteed Chinese citizens a "natural right" to immigrate to the United States, even if they would not be allowed to become naturalized citizens. Moreover, the original version of the Chinese Exclusion Act allowed Chinese nationals who were already in the United States to remain, even if they returned to China for the occasional visit, as long as they obtained a certificate of return. Ping obtained such a certificate prior to visiting China in 1885, assuming that he would be allowed reentry under the terms of this agreement. However, during his return journey, Congress voided all outstanding certificates of return, and customs officials denied his appeals. The ensuing court case quickly made its way to the United States Supreme Court, and Ping's team of lawyers argued that his certificate granted him a right to reenter the country. They argued that revoking this right ex post was akin to taking property without due process, that Congress had no right to expel lawful resident aliens, and that he only returned to China because the US government guaranteed his right to return.[4]

The Supreme Court rejected Ping's appeals under far broader terms than many expected. The court appealed to the United States' authority as a sovereign state to exclude those it deemed dangerous or undesirable:

> If, therefore, the government of the United States, through its legislative department, considers the presence of foreigners of a different race in this country, who will not assimilate with us, to be dangerous to its peace and security, their exclusion is not to be stayed because at the time there are no actual hostilities with the nation of which the foreigners are subjects.[5]

The court used this argument in two other Chinese exclusion cases to found the plenary power doctrine, the basic idea of which is that the

4. Cleveland 2002, 124–126.

5. *Chae Chan Ping v. United States*, 130 U.S. 581 (1889).

power to exclude foreigners is a fundamental aspect of sovereign statehood.[6] Accordingly, Congress has an inherent, extra-Constitutional right to regulate immigration because foreign immigrants pose an existential threat over which the state has total control. This doctrine applies to immigrants who are legally admitted, could be used to exclude foreigners of a specific race, and is not subject to judicial review.[7] In short, the government has the authority to enact any ban, even a total ban, and this authority supersedes the Constitution and judicial review.

The plenary power doctrine has had far-reaching influence in subsequent US history,[8] but it is most important to consider as an artifact of the *conventional wisdom* surrounding the nature of sovereign statehood worldwide. The right to control one's borders lies at the heart of what it means to be a sovereign state, and courts and politicians throughout the world have expressed similar sentiments over the past 150 years. For instance, during the 2016 debate over whether the United Kingdom should leave the European Union, respondents cited sovereignty and immigration as the primary justifications for leaving.[9] Desires to reassert "control," "self-determination," and "autonomy" presume that states in the international system have an almost divine right to be free of any external influences, and the predominance of the sovereign right to control one's borders has become common sense in both the academic and policymaking communities.[10]

I destabilize this common sense below. Specifically, I refute the claim that the right to control one's borders has always been an inherent feature of state sovereignty. To do so, I explore the history of the complex politics of immigration controls and how they relate to the evolution of the modern state. Curiously, managing a state's population in this manner has only recently become an unassailable component of what it means to be a sovereign state, and I begin this chapter with an overview of how international legal jurisprudence conceptualized migration within the doctrine of sovereignty in traditional immigrant-receiving societies. Although most believe that each state has the right to control its own borders today, this history shows that the right

6. *Chew Heong v. United States* 112 U.S. 536 (1884); *Fong Yue Ting v. United States* 149 U.S. 698 (1893); *Lem Moon Sing v. United States* 158 U.S. 538 (1895); *United States v. Ju Toy* 198 U.S. 253 (1905).

7. *Chae Chan Ping v. United States*, 130 U.S. 581, at 606 (1889).

8. The internment of Japanese Americans during WWII is one such instance.

9. Carl 2018.

10. Martin and Ferris 2017; Nisancioglu 2019.

to exclude foreigners was not a foundational principle of the sovereign state system during the seventeenth and eighteenth centuries. In other words, if the right to exclude foreigners was a fundamental aspect of sovereign statehood, then this norm would have emerged with the other primary nation-state institutions during the first 200 years of the modern state system. Instead, the original doctrine of international legal jurisprudence did not hold migration and sovereignty to be mutually exclusive. It is a modern invention and not at all inherent to sovereign statehood.

In fact, the right to exclude foreigners only became synonymous with state sovereignty after two developments during the nineteenth century. First, nation-states began to monopolize the legitimate means of movement.[11] Modern states need to identify who belongs in the state to effectively govern, tax, and protect their subjects. The creation of the modern passport and visa systems signified the evolution from the early- to late-modern state form, in which sovereign states monopolize the movement of people across their territories. Second, Western (mostly settler-colonial) states began encountering non-White migrants during the same period in the nineteenth century. This point is key because states started codifying desirability as a principle desideratum for admission only after the threat of racially undesirable immigration began to loom large. Our commonsense understandings of the modern sovereign state cannot be divorced from the White supremacy and racism of this period.

Thus, the need to identify populations and the fear of undesirable outsiders were powerful forces, and they were profoundly related. The late-modern state became integrated in the capitalist world economic system, which spurred massive labor migration throughout the world. A consequence of this migration was the injection of racial outsiders into societies that needed them for labor, such as the aforementioned case of Chinese immigration to the western United States in the nineteenth century. However, as modern states replaced nonterritorial (or smaller) political entities, they needed to construct and sustain their "social base,"[12] which required registering citizens and foreigners, and promoting a sense of solidarity among the former. Fostering a sense of community and identity led to a rejection of outsiders, particularly racial outsiders. So an influx of racially undesirable immigrants led states to consider the expulsion of foreigners to be a guiding principle of

11. Torpey 1998.

12. Torpey 1998, 244.

sovereign statehood, at the same moment they coalesced into late modernity. As such, these developments are deeply related to the aforementioned rise of rationalism, nationalism, and scientific racism. Below, I trace how the right to exclude emerged from this era as an obvious principle of sovereign statehood only in the recent past to set up a discussion of how this principle fosters color-blind racial discrimination in the modern day.

Sovereignty, Migration, and the Law of Nations

The conventional wisdom in the international system and in Anglo-European courts is that states have an unqualified right to refuse admission to foreigners. This assumption has played out in many high-profile circumstances over the past 150 years as states continue to use international legal theory to warrant their right to exclude. The United States Supreme Court case of *Nishimura Ekiu v. United States* in 1892 provides the best illustration of this strategy when the court held as follows:

> It is an accepted maxim of international law, that every sovereign nation has the power, as inherent in sovereignty, and essential to its self-preservation, to forbid the entrance of foreigners within its dominions, or to admit them only in such cases and upon such conditions as it may see fit to prescribe.[13]

As the story goes, the institution of sovereignty has imbued states with the immutable authority to control their borders and restrict who enters for as long as there have been nation-states. States are not states without this right, and therefore, it is ludicrous for one to contend otherwise.

In fact, this reading of international legal theory—specifically the work of Emer de Vattel—is based on a partial account of his views on the admission of foreigners and has contributed to a misapplication of foundational international legal principles since the nineteenth century.[14] This partial reading has led states, their leaders, jurists, and citizens to assume that immigration

13. *Nishimura Ekiu v. United States*, 142 U.S. 651, at 659 (1892), opinion of Justice Gray. Cited in Chetail 2016, 916.

14. McKeown 2008, ch. 1, also presents the history of migration within the law of nations. McKeown traces how original concerns over honor, obligation, and exile gave way to modern concerns over sovereignty and self-preservation. This shift begot modern policies of selection, assimilation, and border control that emphasize the state, rather than migration, as the fundamental property of the modern world.

control is the exclusive right of the state without any further inquiry into its rationale.[15] This maxim has influenced high-court decisions in the United States, United Kingdom, Australia, New Zealand, and elsewhere.[16] Such justifications typically take the form of US Supreme Court justice Antonin Scalia's claim that "as a sovereign, Arizona has the inherent power to exclude persons from its territory. . . . That power to exclude has long been recognized as inherent in sovereignty. Emer de Vattel's seminal 1758 treatise on the Law of Nations stated: 'The sovereign may forbid the entrance of his territory either to foreigners in general, or in particular cases, or to certain persons, or for certain particular purposes, according as he may think it advantageous to the state.'"[17]

The actual international legal jurisprudence on the admission of foreigners is much less decisive. Indeed, the freedom of movement has long coexisted with the institution of state sovereignty, and the foundational interpretations of international law reflect this fact. Francisco de Vitoria and Hugo Grotius derived the freedom of movement of persons across borders as a foundational principle of international law from the law of hospitality. Vitoria is infamous for his 1539 lecture "De Indis" at the University of Salamanca. This lecture on the legitimacy of Spanish colonial expansion in the New World affirmed Vitoria as the founder of international law and discourses on European colonialism. In "De Indis," Vitoria rebuts the ubiquitous justifications for Spanish conquest and reasons that "the Spaniards, when they first sailed to the land of the barbarians, carried with them no right at all to occupy their countries."[18] Ironically for this book, Vitoria's analysis of the legitimate grounds for the Spanish conquest is vital to the history of state sovereignty because it established free movement as a key principle of the international system.

The predominant ground was "the right of natural partnership and communication" (*naturalis societas et communicationis*),[19] which Vitoria

15. Chetail 2016, 902.

16. Cited in Chetail 2016, 902. In the US: *Kleindiest v. Mandel*, 408 U.S. 753 (1972); in New Zealand: *Ye v. Minister of Immigration* [2009] 2 NZLR 596, para. 116; in the United Kingdom: *R. v. Secretary of State for the Home Department Ex Parte Saadi and Others* [2002] UKHL 41 (Lord Slynn); and in Australia: *Ruddock v. Vadarlis* (2001) 110 FCR 491 at 543, para. 193 (French J); and *Chu Kheng Lim v. Minister for Immigration, Local Government and Ethnic Affairs* (1992) 176 CLR 1, para. 27.

17. *Arizona v. United States*, 567 U.S. (2012).

18. Vitoria, Pagden, and Lawrence 1991, 264.

19. Chetail 2016, 903.

considered a universal property of the international system (both European and non-European). Vitoria saw the right to natural partnership and communication in humans' inherent sociability and the long-standing tradition of *hospitality*. According to Vitoria, all polities have customarily recognized the right to freedom of movement and considered it "humane and dutiful to behave hospitably to strangers."[20] He used these principles to enshrine the freedom of movement as a universal principle of international law, and argued that "the Spaniards have the right to travel and dwell in those countries, so long as they do no harm to the barbarians,"[21] and he claimed that the parceling of the world into independent sovereign states did not vitiate this rule.[22] Importantly, the right to free movement was not unqualified. Vitoria makes it clear that states are able to reject foreigners, but only if they committed a crime. Although he does not specify which bases of refusal are legitimate, it is clear that "it is not lawful to banish visitors who are innocent of any crime."[23] For Vitoria, international relations is impossible without the freedom of communications among peoples, and he uses this principle to enshrine free movement and hospitality as foundational maxims of international law among sovereign states.[24]

Hugo Grotius not only maintained Vitoria's notion of the right to communicate, he expanded it to include the right to leave one's own country—which was controversial at the time—and to *remain* in a foreign country. In this way, Grotius firmly establishes the freedoms of movement and immigration as international legal principles concomitant with others he discusses in *Mare Liberum* and *The Rights of War and Peace*. Grotius writes:

20. Vitoria, et al. 1991, 278.

21. Vitoria et al., 278.

22. "Second, in the beginning of the world, when all things were held in common, everyone was allowed to visit and travel through any land he wished. This right was clearly not taken away by the division of property (*diuisio rerum*); it was never the intention of nations to prevent men's free mutual intercourse with one another by this division" (Vitoria et al., 278).

23. Vitoria et al., 278.

24. It is important to address the concern of the paradox of Vitoria's jurisprudence: he used *ius communicationis* both to conceptualize a universal society of equal nations on the basis of free exchange and hospitality and as the main legal justification for the European colonization of the non-White world (Chetail 2016, 905). This paradox makes it obvious why Vitoria is both lauded for his establishment of international politics as a cosmopolitan community of equal states (Cavallar 2008, 191) and critiqued as the father of colonial international law (Anghie 2007, 9).

> Persons also that pass either by land or water, may, on account of their health, or for any other just cause, make some stay in the country; this being likewise an innocent utility. . . . So likewise, a fixed abode ought not to be refused to strangers, who being expelled their own country, seek a retreat elsewhere: provided they submit to the laws of the State, and refrain from every thing that might give occasion to sedition.[25]

While some only focus on the implications of Grotius's thought for refugees and asylum seekers, it is clear that his jurisprudence extends beyond oppressed migrants. Grotius greatly extends Vitoria's position on free movement. He affirms the principle of communication as a universal principle of international politics, but he also strengthens the relationship between sovereignty and movement. In modern parlance, even "economic" migrants—those who seek to move not out of violence but out of economic just cause—must be accepted unless they refuse to submit to the laws of the state. As such, the historical foundations of international law clearly position state sovereignty and free movement not as opponents but as allies.

While Vitoria and Grotius proclaim the right of free movement, their immediate successors in international legal jurisprudence muddied the waters. Specifically, Samuel Pufendorf and Christian von Wolff inverted the "freedom of movement first, state sovereignty second" principle. Pufendorf *split* the right to leave one's country from the right to enter another. He writes in *The Law of Nature and Nations* that "every man reserved to himself the liberty to remove at discretion"; however, "it is left in the power of all states, to take such measures about the admission of strangers, as they think convenient; those being ever excepted."[26] Scholars associate Pufendorf with this statement about the rights of states and sovereignty because the work of Hobbes had such a profound impact on his thought.[27] That being said, although he was not as vehement in his criticism of the right of communication and hospitality as this quote implies,[28] Pufendorf prioritizes the

25. Grotius and Tuck 2005, book II, ch. II, 446.

26. Pufendorf 1703 [1672], para. IX.

27. Palladini 2008.

28. "To give a natural right to these favours [the right to hospitality], it is requisite that the stranger be absent from his own house on an honest, or on a necessary account; as, also, that we have no objection against his integrity, or character, which might render our admission of him, either dangerous or disgraceful" (Pufendorf 1703 [1672], book III, ch. III, para. ix).

interest of the state over the right to hospitality. In a preview of arguments about immigration to come, Pufendorf writes:

> Every State may be more free or more cautious in granting these indulgences, as it shall judge proper for its interest and safety. In order to which judgment, it will be prudent to consider, whether a great increase in the number of inhabitants will turn to advantage; whether the country be fertile enough to feed so many mouths; whether upon admission of this new body, we shall be strained for room; whether the men are industrious, or idle; whether they may be so conveniently placed and disposed, as to rend them incapable of giving any jealousy to the government. If on the whole, it appears that the persons deserve our favour and pity, and that no restraint lies on us from good Reasons of State, it will be an act of humanity to confer such a benefit on them.[29]

For Pufendorf, the main criterion for admitting immigrants is their *desirability* ("industrious" vs. "idle") and whether the state has sufficient resources to feed them. This shift from Vitoria and Grotius to Pufendorf is staggering because it signals a shift in the conception of the state's role in providing for its citizens. We saw above that the notion of state sovereignty began with a legal grounding that precluded states from restricting their borders. Over the next century, this status quo changed and a conventional wisdom resembling modern conceptions of state sovereignty began to emerge.

Wolff's jurisprudence consolidates this shift, as he advocated for a *stronger*, more modern-looking, assertion of state sovereignty: "No nation nor any private person who is a foreigner can claim any right for himself in the territory of another."[30] For Wolff, the right to enter is entirely at the discretion of the state, and the right of hospitality is nowhere to be found. In this view, states are territorial sovereigns: he equates ownership of territory with sovereignty, and "since an owner can dispose of the use of his property according to his liking, the conditions under which the ruler of a territory desires to permit approach to foreigners, depend altogether upon his will."[31] Instead of being a universal principle of the international system, admission into another state resembles charity. States have the moral duty to admit foreigners under duress, but this

29. Pufendorf 1703 [1672].

30. Wolff and Drake 1934, vol. 2, ch. III, 149, para. 293.

31. Wolff and Drake, vol. 2, ch. III, 150–151, para. 298.

duty is unenforceable, depends on the desirability of the foreigner, and is entirely at the discretion of the sovereign.

Vincent Chetail attributes these differences between the views of Vitoria and Grotius and those of Pufendorf and Wolff to the signing of the Treaty of Westphalia in 1648.[32] In this account, Westphalia enshrined state sovereignty as an immutable legal principle, and Pufendorf and Wolff proclaimed the state's discretion to reject foreigners accordingly. However, scholars question the significance of 1648 and the putative role Westphalia had in promoting the norm of state sovereignty.[33] The Peace of Augsburg in 1555 truly ushered in the modern conception of state sovereignty with the establishment of the principle of *Cuius regio eius religio* (whose realm, his religion). As such, Grotius staked out his position on free movement and its relationship with sovereignty *after* states enshrined the modern conception of that principle. Sovereignty's ambiguous relationship with international migration is reflected in its evolution throughout the nineteenth century and in the work of Vattel.

Vattel's synthesis of these two positions is noteworthy because it is the most oft-cited international legal justification for a state's right to expel or restrict the entry of foreigners. However, Vattel's true ambition was to reconcile state sovereignty and free movement. It is true that Vattel's legal thought is rife with apparent contradictions, which has made his writings potent fodder for later legal justification. On the one hand, Vattel is a true believer in state sovereignty. On the other hand, Vattel synthesizes natural law and legal positivism in such a way that protects the integrity of both positions. To do so, Vattel describes the distinction between necessary and voluntary law. The former is the internal law of nations that requires a right to free passage. The latter refers to the external law of nations that allows states to control their own territory. Both laws are binding upon states, and this "double law" allows Vattel to have the best of both worlds. Ex ante, when it comes to judging whether a foreigner must be admitted, states must carry out the internal duty of free passage. However, if that admission ends up being dangerous to the host state, the external right to control one's borders impinges on the internal duty.[34]

32. Chetail 2016, 910.

33. Buzan and Lawson 2014.

34. "He cannot then settle by a full right, and as he pleases, in the place he has chosen, but must ask permission of the chief of the place; and if it is refused, it is his duty to submit. However, as property could not be introduced to the prejudice of the right acquired by every human creature, of not being absolutely deprived of such things as are necessary,—no nation

To reconcile the internal and external laws, Vattel relies on the principle of necessity, an oft-neglected dimension of his jurisprudence because it disturbs the misperception that he represented "an early triumph of state sovereignty."[35] He defines this principle as "the right which necessity alone gives to the performance of certain actions that are otherwise unlawful, when, without these actions, it is impossible to fulfill an indispensable obligation."[36] The principle is a major restriction on state sovereignty, it overrules any predominance that the external right has over the internal right, and *"allows foreigners to force passage denied by the state."*[37] Vattel explains as follows:

> When a real necessity obliges you to enter into the territory of others,—for instance, if you cannot otherwise escape from imminent danger, or if you have no other passage for procuring the means of subsistence, or those of satisfying some other indispensable obligation,—you may force a passage when it is unjustly refused.[38]

Vattel endorses a conception of free movement that allows foreigners access to other states when they are in physical danger *or cannot provide for their own means of subsistence*. In this way, he prioritizes the needs of humanity over the right to control one's borders. Moreover, even if foreigners are not desirable, states cannot refuse them. This requirement holds even if they are mere economic migrants, to use the contemporary term. In other words, the clear implication of Vattel's legal jurisprudence, upon which reams of legal precedent lies, is that judgment about whether necessity can be invoked lies solely with the person seeking to immigrate, and not the state. Although Anglo-American jurists, scholars, and politicians have used Vattel to justify immigration restrictions and make claims about the state's right to restrict immigrants on the broad basis of desirability, they are doing so using an incomplete reading of the underlying legal principles. The sovereign right to control one's borders is hardly a settled claim or unworthy of interrogation.

---

can, without good reasons, refuse even a perpetual residence to a man driven from his country. But if particular and substantial reasons prevent her from affording him an asylum, this man has no longer any right to demand it,—because, in such a case, the country inhabited by the nation cannot, at the same time, serve for her own use, and that of this foreigner" (Vattel 2009, book I, ch. XIX, paras. 230–231).

35. Cavallar 2009, 9.

36. Vattel 2009, book II, ch. IX, paras. 119.

37. Chetail 2016, 920 (emphasis mine).

38. Vattel 2009, book II, ch. IX, 322, para. 123.

Instead, the international legal jurisprudence reflects a deep concern for both the security of states *and* the ability for individuals to seek out new homelands that would best provide for their subsistence and protection.

Sovereignty, White Supremacy, and the Late-Modern State

States have long sought to control the movement of people within and between their borders. Their leaders justify this desire on the grounds that all sovereign states have the inherent right to do so. Indeed, the rhetoric of leaders and the language of court opinions suggest that international norms and legal jurisprudence support an unequivocal right for states to exclude foreigners. However, as seen in the previous section, the foundations of international law provide a mixed perspective on the relationship between sovereignty and free movement. On the one hand, Pufendorf and Wolff proclaim the right of states to control their borders and populations. On the other hand, Vitoria, Grotius, and Vattel support varying degrees of free movement, particularly for those who experience violence, insecurity, or the inability to provide for their own subsistence. A skeptic may read this history and assert that the later theorists—Pufendorf, Wolff, and Vattel—each supported a strong conception of state sovereignty that allowed states the (near-) universal right to exclude. Even though Vattel wavered in his commitment, his writings suggest his acceptance of the sovereign prerogative. Despite minor differences and exceptions, as the institution of sovereignty coalesced during the sixteenth through eighteenth centuries, the international theorists that provided counsel and intellectual fodder for leaders were united in their views about the rights of states.

Yet, Vattel himself—the great symbol and defender of state sovereignty and its principles—was clear that the institution of sovereignty prioritized the needs of humanity over individual rights to exclude outsiders. Even economic migrants were allowed. Moreover, although the skeptical position reflects a misunderstood reading of Vattel, it is less important to reflect on the *words* of international legal theorists than on the *actions* of states. For if border control and the right to exclude foreigners became a foundational principle of the institution of sovereignty, we should expect to see states and their leaders begin to *behave* in a manner consistent with this putative conventional wisdom. In other words, if sovereign states possess the right and duty to control their borders and populations lest they give up their right to be called sovereign, then we should see proper states act in a manner consistent with this definition. However, the empirical record is unequivocal: the history of immigration policy shows that the rise of the conception of state sovereignty did not correspond to a rise in border controls or other restrictions. Although states were much more precarious and likely to "die" during the sixteenth through eighteenth centuries, this period saw no increase in border controls or restrictions on free movement. While one may dispute the interpretation of international legal theory above, one cannot dispute that the emerging and consolidating nation-states and their leaders did not see border control as foundational to their sovereignty. Instead, states in the early-modern state system were *ambivalent* about the right and need to restrict foreigners. If the right to exclude foreigners is not a fundamental aspect of state sovereignty, then where did it come from?

At the onset of the modern state system, much of the Western world was oriented locally rather than nationally. A variety of empires, principalities, city-states, duchies, and other political entities ruled over most populations. At the same time, private entities—individuals or their local masters—regulated the right to authorize movement. For example, masters controlled whether and where their indentured servants were allowed to move. The same can be said of serfs and their landlords, as well as slaves and their owners. Most Europeans (and others throughout the world) spent most of their lives within a small radius of their birthplace, and this small scale dominated the political, social, and economic nature of early-modern society. This local orientation persisted because agriculture fueled the society's economic engine. Those in the aristocratic classes ruled their estates, and those in the peasant classes worked the land. As a result, almost all administration and governance—even within empires—was done on the local level. This scale of life and governance led to a strong sense of local community during this period, and even towns and the aristocracy shared this localism and provincialism. What we describe as "international" migration today referred to *any* movement outside of one's immediate area up through most of the early nineteenth century. Citizens regarded those from the next town or province as equally "foreign" as those from another state.[39] This strong local character of early-modern Europe was strongest in Spain, France, Germany, and England, but the concept of neighborliness and the importance of local social bonds was present throughout the continent.[40]

39. Torpey 2000, 12.
40. R. B. Manning 1986, 354.

However, as modern states advanced with the Industrial Revolution and systems of forced labor declined, "states and the international state system stripped private entities of the power to authorize and forbid movement and gathered that power unto themselves."[41] In other words, as the early-modern state gave way to the late-modern state, the regulation of movement moved from the private to the public sphere. The transition from local to national control spurred this change. National states are amalgamations of smaller political entities. As such, the requirements of governing a much larger territorial space led states to centralize authority. John Torpey draws parallels between the nationalization of poor relief and the regulation of movement. In the early-modern state and prior, the administration of poor relief was entirely in the hands of private entities and religious organizations such as the Catholic Church. As the number of states declined in Europe, the size of markets for wage labor expanded out of the reach of local villages and landowners, breaking apart the extant localism of society. This expansion of labor markets led many to move to cities, which required poor relief to expand from the local to the national level as well. If labor markets expand beyond local areas, then the protection of the laborers must also expand out of necessity. This process helped expand the national borders of states. As the area in which citizens can expect to move freely without authorization grows, the principal boundaries that matter grow as well. By the nineteenth century, the boundaries that mattered most in society were no longer towns or municipalities, but nation-states.[42]

This expansion codified the nation-state as the primary unit of analysis in international politics during the nineteenth century.[43] The transition from the early- to late-modern state occurred at different rates in different places, and as citizens—rich and poor—throughout societies were able to move freely within states, controls over the movement of people concerned the external borders of states rather than internal ones. Each of these processes took place within the same context: the period of "rational state-building" during the nineteenth century when late-modern states accumulated "administrative and bureaucratic competencies" to assert their domestic and international preeminence.[44] As James Scott notes, the desire to control society and nature

41. Torpey 2000, 10.

42. Torpey 2000, 10–11.

43. Reus-Smit 2013.

44. Buzan and Lawson 2015, 6.

was ubiquitous in Europe and North America from the early nineteenth century through World War I, and such programs require immense administrative capacities and the expansion of state abilities to observe and document their populations.[45] Scott calls this ideology "high modernism," and it refers to the post-Enlightenment philosophy of Anglo-European states that they could and must rationally engineer all aspects of social, political, and economic life to improve the human condition.[46] High modernism sprang forth from beliefs in scientific and technological progress, as well as the unwavering confidence in the continued linear progress of humankind, the expansion of economic production, the ability to rationally design societies, and "an increasing control over nature (including human nature) commensurate with scientific understanding of natural laws."[47] Importantly, support for high modernism did not fall along political cleavages: citizens and administrators of all persuasions adhered to the idea that the state's role was to use its power as an instrument for achieving these goals.

However, the pursuit of high-modernist goals was not cheap. Scientific progress, social engineering, and ever-expanding economic production required states to extract and control resources from their populations. The easiest way for states to get their citizens to pay these costs was to foster a sense of collective identity. These collective identities were (and are) most often expressed through nationalism, or the idea that states should represent nations—self-identifying groups of people that share a sense of common history, experience, culture, language, or anything sufficient to generate a sense of "we-feeling."[48] Nationalism is a curious force because it combines the modern notion of the sovereign state with early-modern feelings of community.[49] The sense of common identity and destiny binds together nation-states and warrants the high-modernist ambitions of their elites. Nationalism bound together nation-states by overcoming societal cleavages that other aspects of the transition to the late-modern state created, such as class. A shared

45. Scott 1998, 88.

46. See Buzan and Lawson 2015, ch. 4, for an overview of several different "ideologies of progress" that were present during the nineteenth century, including scientific racism and liberalism. See also Mann 1988 for a description of how states "caged" these capacities within national boundaries during the state formation process.

47. Scott 1998, 89–90.

48. See Rejai and Enloe 1969; Benedict Anderson 1983; Bhabha 1990; and Buzan 2008 for further debate over the origins/nature of nationalism.

49. Buzan and Lawson 2015, 114.

sense of common national identity and shared fate connected members of the proletariat, bourgeoisie, and ruling class, created the conditions necessary for social mobility, and thwarted many attempts at social revolution during this period.[50] Nationalism, although rooted in local ideas of community and shared fate, overcame localism, joined together previously disparate communities within states, and constrained "the cosmopolitan impulses of revolutionary nationalism," such as appeals to class solidarity in Europe during the tumult of 1914.[51]

Nation-states appealed to nationalism because the creation of national, collective identities allowed states to pursue their goals. When citizens feel they are part of the larger community, they are more willing to acquiesce to various state incursions into their daily lives. This shift was a radical change in the relationship between states and their subjects. Specifically, those living within states transformed from being mere subjects of absolutist rulers to *citizens* of *nation*-states. This transformation relocated sovereignty from the absolutist ruler to the people. Not only did the idea of popular sovereignty arise from this historical shift, but territory also became associated with specific nations rather than with dynastic families and absolutist regimes. The physical spaces that make up states became entwined with specific people, histories, and customs. This conflation dramatically reshaped politics throughout the world, as common citizens were bound together within territories that all associated with a shared nationality. Now a specific territory could be "ours" and not "yours," based on whether one was a member of the nation.

The emergence of the late-modern state had two important consequences for the purposes of this book. These consequences emerged because states fostered a common identity to justify extracting resources and mass conscription, both of which were necessary for the modern state to function.

The first consequence was the rise of scientific racism and White supremacy in Anglo-European states. The emergence of nationalism and popular sovereignty demonstrated a change from elite-driven to mass-driven politics that supported prejudiced, xenophobic, and racist understandings of who should belong in a political community.[52] When states belong to specific people from specific national backgrounds, it is easy to draw the conclusion that those from other backgrounds do not belong, particularly in an era of pervasive racism like the nineteenth century.

50. Gellner 2008, 137–143.

51. Buzan and Lawson 2015, 117, citing Halliday 1999, 146.

52. Mann 2004; Buzan and Lawson 2015.

This combustible mix of the post-Enlightenment belief in the human capacity to control and improve their societies *and* White supremacy produced the ideology of *scientific racism*—the idea that humans can codify White supremacy and use it to rationally engineer society. It is a natural consequence of high modernism that suggests that it is possible to separate humankind into discrete races based on ancestry or observable markers, such as skin color; that some races are objectively superior or inferior to others; and that society should be organized hierarchically based on this ordering, naturally with the White race on top. Accordingly, scientific racism lent credibility to the idea that states needed to ensure their populations were of appropriate racial stock. In a world with growing nationalism and racism, this idea produced the mass belief in White supremacy and the idea that inferior races needed to be restricted from society for the good of the nation's health.[53]

Humans have long compared and ordered cultures throughout the world based on their ability to sustain economic growth, establish certain political systems, or produce the markers of "high" culture, such as art and music. For example, in *Spirit of the Laws*, Montesquieu famously proposed that races of people were defined by their *geography*, that climates affected temperament, and that these differences produced inherently different political systems and societies. However, Enlightenment thinkers like Montesquieu and Kant used the term *race* without much precision. They used the term to provide a schema for distinguishing among the world's populations based on supposedly immutable differences and to justify the differential allocation of rights and liberties. When this cultural racism was pervasive, there were clear guidelines for how inferior races could improve. These lesser races could simply assimilate the practices of civilized cultures. By way of illustration, Barry Buzan and George Lawson reveal how, in ancient China, an inferior non-Han could adopt practices and actually become Han, while a Han who ceased behaving appropriately could lose their status.[54] This fluid conception of race is foreign today, but it reveals how simply behaving properly was sufficient to transform one from racially undesirable to desirable almost immediately. The natural conclusion of this cultural definition of race was that superior races should use education, investment, and other initiatives to "civilize" inferior races.

The rise of high modernism and the modern nation-state, with its emphasis on science and rationality, gave racism a more insidious character. Modern

53. Hannaford 1996, 272–276.

54. Buzan and Lawson 2015, 120.

biology catalyzed the development of scientific racism and its subsequent effect on society. Scientific racism emerged out of the Darwinist belief that the extinction of inferior races would benefit society because it would remove "less-fit" subjects from the human population. The basic idea is that nature selects members of a population for survival based on their reproductive fitness. This process is known as *natural selection*. It was not long before nineteenth-century thinkers applied this idea to human populations: if natural selection is the biological mechanism that increases fitness in animal species, then why should it not apply to humans? Soon enough, Herbert Spencer applied Darwin's theory of natural selection to human beings and coined the phrase "survival of the fittest" in the process. While most readers will be familiar with the phrase, fewer realize that Spencer created the term to differentiate among human races. Indeed, Spencer emphasizes that "this survival of the fittest, which I have here sought to express in mechanical terms, is that which Mr. Darwin has called 'natural selection', or the preservation of favored races in the struggle for life."[55] Scientific racism fell out of this seemingly objective application of biological science to White supremacist ideology.[56]

The consequences of viewing racial differences in biological terms were immense. If races are differentiated according to inherent aspects of their biology, then civilizing missions are a fool's errand. If subordinate races are damned to perpetual inferiority, then superior races have a duty to protect the greater good from the damaging influences of undesirable populations. The proposed remedies for a world with biologically differentiated races are familiar and violent: restrictions and displacement (through direct colonial administration), selective breeding (through antimiscegenation laws and other eugenicist principles), and extermination (through genocide and

55. Spencer 1896, 144.

56. This connection between sovereignty, modernity, and biology also finds common cause in Agamben's philosophy of the modern nation-state (Agamben 1998). Biology gives democratic states the ability to define the "abnormal" within and place it outside the law. This "state of exception" occurs when the sovereign acts outside the law to remove the abnormal from society, such as in the case of concentration camps in Germany, the United States, and Great Britain. Agamben argues that all liberal democratic states are totalitarian because the state of exception is a normal thing that modern states do. One's citizenship and right to live in a state is temporary, and it is only given with the understanding that it can be removed. Although democratic states are lauded for their putative protection of individual rights and freedoms, they are totalitarian because they have totalitarian logics built into their foundation.

race war).[57] Therefore, scientific racism combined the logic of high modernism, the ideologies of White supremacy and nationalism, and the needs of the modern state. Scientific racism gave credence to arguments that certain nation-states were superior to others due to the inherent nature of their race, and that it was the duty of states to rationally perfect their societies. These arguments bolstered ethnonationalistic fervor, furthered White supremacy, and provided the social glue to hold together the modern nation-state by giving states leave to record, tax, and conscript their populations that were intoxicated with racism, nationalism, and rationalism.

Along these same lines, the emergence of the modern nation-state and ubiquity of scientific racism led to the second consequence: racist immigration controls and other restrictions. In many ways, racist immigration policies are a natural extension of this transition, rather than a concurrent effect. As I describe above, modern nation-states required immense powers to tax, administer, monitor, and conscript its citizens. The easiest way to coerce acquiescence from populations that had previously identified exclusively with their local environments was to promote nationalism. If citizens were convinced that they were a part of a larger nation, rather than a mere pawn of a "stationary bandit,"[58] they would be less likely to balk at the incursions of the modern state. In this way, nationalism and the rise of the nation-state went hand in hand, and they spurred the rise of scientific racism as a natural lodestar of public policy. As a result, the aforementioned ethnonationalist fervor entrenched White supremacy, and belief in the ability of states to engineer their societies catalyzed the idea that it was the duty of states to restrict racially undesirable immigrants.

To be sure, this mechanism is not the only plausible explanation for the rise of nationalism. Elites did not merely dictate the rise of nationalism and ethnonationalism within their states; populations played an important role. The key point to keep in mind is that the rise of nationalism was functional for the era, given the existence of racism, high modernism, and expanded labor markets, even if nationalism itself is not functional. In other words, I am not arguing that this explanation is the only explanation for how and why nationalism emerged. Instead, I argue that *racist immigration policies* were an obvious extension of several sociopolitical transformations that took place at the same time.

57. Barder 2019; Hobson 2012.

58. Olson 1993, 568.

Although the national state displaced the local and overlapping polity forms that had ruled for centuries, the strict administration of populations was not a new phenomenon. States (monarchs, lords, chieftains, etc.) had long considered their populations to be their greatest source of power and raw material. Leaders could not wage war without their subjects, and the more subjects they had, the greater their chance of survival. However, upon the dawn of the nineteenth century, common ideas of how and why populations mattered to polities changed. Citizens were no longer mere sources of raw military power or production. These commoners, long forsaken by monarchs and autocrats, were now the greatest source of *social* power at a state's disposal. In a national state, the population not only affects its military might and economic production. The population also affects the character and society of the state. Because sovereignty—the justification for rule—transferred from absolutist monarchs to the people, the composition and "quality" of the people now determined the state's future. It now did not matter if states took in thousands of new citizens to bolster their military might. If those new citizens were deficient in any way, then the state would be worse off because its underlying nation would be corrupted. In short, nation-states depended on narratives of national superiority to justify their actions and reassure their public of their superiority. If racially undesirable "invaders" corrupted the existing population, then rulers were to expect mass chaos, social degradation, and a return to the Dark Ages. This sentiment persists to this day,[59] and in the next section, I unpack how racist immigration quotas emerged as a natural response to this social fact in more detail.

Scientific Racism and High Modernism Fulfilled: The Rise of Discriminatory Immigration Policies

In the previous section, I outline how the transition to the modern nation-state created the conditions that produced scientific racism and immigration restrictions. Before this transition, rulers cared little about the composition of a state's population. Instead, states saw human capital as the essence of sovereign power. States in the seventeenth and eighteenth centuries sought to retain their human capital to fuel their economic production and war-fighting capabilities. Immigrants were welcome, but emigrants were treasonous: unauthorized emigration was punishable by death. During this

59. D. Miller 2016.

period, population growth was slow, so states tried to acquire neighboring populations. States welcomed the refugees of their neighbors, not out of humanitarianism but out of self-interest. As a result, there was very little emigration during this period, so immigration posed little problem.

States only began to enact border controls, restrict foreigners, and litigate their legal rights when they became concerned with the undesirability of their immigrant populations. Above, I note that this change occurred with the rise of the modern nation-state. When sovereignty passed from the absolutist leader to the people, the composition of the public began to matter. If states were now only as strong as their populations, it became imperative to ensure that undesirables did not enter society. At a time when White supremacy was socially desirable and high modernism empowered states to rationally engineer their societies, it is unsurprising that the nineteenth century became the century of scientific racism and the racist administration of populations.

The formation of the United States and the conditions in North American colonies were the first symptoms of this important shift toward rational restrictiveness throughout the world. In many ways, the immigration policy of the United States was an important bellwether that foreshadowed modern policies. Prior to the American Revolution, the colonists petitioned King George III to allow them to restrict undesirable immigrants—Catholics, felons, and paupers—and to naturalize those they considered desirable.[60] Concerns over immigration policy were also fundamental to the instigation of American independence. After independence, the United States actively encouraged White Anglo-Saxon immigration during its early years, and sought to limit the immigration of undesirables who were likely to become public charges or otherwise upset the composition of society. Thus, the fear of undesirable immigration encouraged policy to limit the inflow of foreigners, and this fear catalyzed what was to become the state's "police power" to take all necessary steps to protect the health, safety, and welfare of its citizens.

This precedent was confirmed throughout the early- to mid-nineteenth century. During the antebellum period, the United States used a variety of laws to regulate its immigration flows. In each case, states and the federal government continued to fear admitting too many foreigners that would become public charges. This example is illustrative that the United States led the general trend away from seeking to attract as many immigrants as possible and

60. Zolberg 2008, ch. 2.

toward using the institution of sovereignty to justify the restriction of undesirables. While this summary glosses over the intricacies of the history of US immigration policy,[61] it demonstrates the trends that would eventually sweep the rest of the world.

For instance, in the landmark Supreme Court case *City of New York v. Miln* (1834), a shipping company challenged a New York law that required the head of every vessel arriving in New York from any foreign port to provide a complete passenger list that included their last legal settlement. The purpose of the law was to prevent the state from being inundated with foreigners who were likely to become paupers. The court held that states are able "to provide precautionary measures against the moral pestilence of paupers, vagabonds, and possible convicts, as it is to guard against the physical pestilence, which may arise from unsound and infectious articles imported."[62] Importantly, the author of the opinion, Justice Philip Barbour, cited Vattel and asserted that states have the unqualified right to regulate entry into their territory.[63] This example is indicative of how leaders began to lean on their rights as the heads of sovereign states to justify their duty to restrict the inflow of foreigners. These so-assumed rights were not immutable features of the institution of sovereignty. If they were, we would have seen this reflected in state behavior as the institution of sovereignty crystallized during the seventeenth and eighteenth centuries. Instead, states' leaders and jurists only used references to their sovereignty and Vattel et al.'s treatises once it became expedient to justify actions that accorded with their worldview.

The major shift in policy disposition occurred in the 1870s and 1880s. By this time, the principles of high modernism and scientific racism were firmly entrenched in how states made policy. As such, the immigration policies in the United States and other immigrant-receiving states would dramatically change and converge on a strikingly similar set of principles. Economic interests had always driven immigration policy, but tension between opponents of immigration (native workers and others) and proponents (business owners in need of labor) came to a head in the late nineteenth century in response to the perceived excesses of the first wave of globalization. The first wave was a period of unrivaled free movement of goods, services, capital, and people during the nineteenth century, coupled with expanding transportation

61. See Zolberg 2008 for a complete history.

62. *New York v. Miln*, 36 U.S. 134 (1837).

63. *New York v. Miln*, 36 U.S. 132 (1837).

and communication technologies. While many constituencies within Anglo-European states embraced the force-multiplying gains of globalization, there were opponents as well. This first period of globalization, coupled with a lack of domestic regulations on working hours and conditions and the lack of a social safety net, produced immense anxiety.[64] Indeed, one of the main initiatives of states during the late nineteenth century was to protect their native labor markets in the face of the unfettered immigration of cheap labor.

In the case of the United States, prior to the 1870s the general policy orientation was primarily concerned with the immigration and naturalization of free White people with good moral character who would provide a large, stable workforce for its growing industries. Yet, economic concerns were not the only impetus for policy. It was the *composition* of that cheap labor that mattered most. Native worker constituencies and their representatives sought to protect domestic labor throughout the Anglo-European world, but the rationales for these policies extended to concerns over the racial desirability of immigrant workers. Opponents presumed that it was the inherent disposition of certain immigrant groups that made them willing to work for lower pay and under worse conditions, and these features were what was dangerous about immigrant groups. Prussia's expulsion of Polish seasonal migrants in 1885 is an illustrative example. Christian Joppke highlights Max Weber's pointed concern that Polish workers would harm society because of their "different propensities to consume" and that "capitalistically disorganized economies" needed to fear losing "the existential fight with lower cultures."[65] It is important to keep in mind that Weber was concerned about the putative effects of racially suspect immigrants whom many Americans would consider White today.

It is clear that states throughout the Anglo-European world were obsessed with preserving their higher culture from the effects of lower cultures. While there were certainly cases in which states took action in the face of immigration flows from neighboring people in Europe (in the case of Prussia, Great Britain, and other Western European states) or from Ireland, Germany, and Italy (in the case of the United States), these concerns did not spur a dramatic change in policy. States were concerned about the composition of immigrant flows and that admitting too many workers from inferior cultures would have detrimental effects, but claims about the sovereign right to exclude, and the

64. H. James 2001, 13.
65. Joppke 2005, 35.

desire to exclude, did not become rapacious until they encountered immigrants from an entirely different civilization. Although Europeans (in the literal and racialized sense) certainly constructed those from other European cultures (Irish, Italians, Poles, etc.) as racially distinct and inferior, the perceived supremacy of White Europeans over the perceptively non-White peoples of the world produced a sea change.[66] The desire to exclude racially undesirable migrants, coupled with *encountering* large populations of such migrants, led states to assert a right to exclude on the presumed, inherent principles of sovereignty.

This desire to exclude non-White migrants accelerated in the United States after 123,000 Chinese immigrated during the 1870s, joining the 105,000 that arrived between 1850 and 1870. The United States has long been complicit in the "global politics of empire and subject peoples, complemented by a generalized hierarchical view of the world's people."[67] Because Chinese laborers often came to the United States as "coolies"—a form of indentured servitude—Americans regarded them as inferior and assumed (like African slaves) that there must be something inherent to people from Asia that made them willing to submit to bondage (despite the long-standing history of indentured servitude in Europe and North America), which led to the further belief that the Chinese could not and would not assimilate into American society.[68] Moreover, it is important to keep in mind that the sort of regular, non-White immigration that we imagine today was not possible in the nineteenth-century United States. And even though immigration from Asia, the Ottoman Empire, and other regions of the global South to Europe was possible, Westerners responded to these incursions with animus.[69] During this period, Asians were the most racially different population in the world that could plausibly immigrate to settler colonial societies.

As such, it is no wonder that the encounter with Asian immigration in the nineteenth century would interact with this racist, hierarchical view of White supremacy to "support racially restrictive immigration policies."[70] There was a generalized fear that the United States would be inundated with a massive foreign population of racially inferior migrants who would upset the balance of society. During this period, Europeans and North Americans,

66. Hunt 2009, 78.

67. Cairns 1999, 34.

68. Zolberg 2008, 177.

69. Goutor 2007; MacMaster 2001.

70. Cairns 1999, 34.

facing declining birth rates, saw declining mortality rates in inferior Asian societies as an imminent threat. Geoffrey Barraclough cites "an almost neurotic awareness of the precariousness of (the European) position in the face of an expansive Asia,"[71] which led the United States and Australia to fear that their encounters with racially inferior immigrants were a preview of their ultimate demise.

Fears of being overrun by racial undesirables were based in the scientific racism that marked this period of high modernism. Specifically, prior to the 1920s, eugenics—the science of racial improvement—was seen by publics, policymakers, and scientists as a "morally acceptable and scientifically viable way of improving human heredity.[72] It was a mainstream ideology; eugenics appealed to the idea that the duty of states was to improve and perfect their societies, and immigration policies were the "single most internationally significant and consistent policy and legal application" of these ideas.[73] David Fitzgerald and David Cook-Martin use the case of US president Theodore Roosevelt to emphasize the pervasiveness of this ideology: "He praised the democratic wisdom of the United States and other Anglophone settler societies for selecting immigrants on racial grounds."[74] The basis of this argument was that the non-White peoples of the earth were inferior and incapable of governing themselves in a democracy, by virtue of their intrinsic, inherited traits.

In response to the fear of racially undesirable immigrants, a booming urban Chinese population at a time when a lack of cleanliness was linked with disease, and the early advent of scientific racism, the United States enacted three types of national immigration policies. The first policy was an individual-level screening process that still exists today. This process was/is putatively race-neutral and screens potential immigrants for health, character, and other features that would make them otherwise problematic for society.

The second and third policies were group-level selections. The second policy, the Chinese Exclusion Act of 1882, was the first US law that explicitly prohibited a nationality from immigrating to the United States.[75] Coupled with related legislation during the 1880s, the Chinese Exclusion Act mirrored

71. Barraclough 1964, 80, cited in Joppke 2005, 36.

72. Dikötter 1998, 467.

73. Bashford 2010, 158.

74. FitzGerald and Cook-Martin 2014, 1.

75. The Chinese Exclusion Act revised the 1875 Page Act, which prohibited the immigration of Chinese women to the United States. As such, the CEA came from a clear lineage of racial

attempts in the earlier part of the century to minimize the size of the Black population by returning freed slaves to Africa, and it was the most successful "instance of ethnic cleansing in the history of American immigration."[76] Between 1900 and 1920, the US population of Chinese origin shrank by 30 percent. This pronounced reaction to the fear of racially undesirable immigrants spurred the United States to shut its doors to Asian immigrants—the most racially different and undesirable population of potential immigrants in the world—in a manner similar to White Australia and the 1905 Aliens Act in Great Britain.

The third policy also followed the principles of group-level selection and maximizing desirability. However, rather than categorically *restricting* Asian immigrants, this policy was meant to filter out the undesirable "European races." At this time, all Europeans were not considered White or desirable, and there was a profound shift in the origin of European immigrants at the end of the nineteenth century. In 1882, about 67 percent of European immigrants arrived from northwest Europe; however, this number would drop to 19 percent by 1907. Instead, most new European immigrants were arriving from south and eastern Europe, mostly "degraded, ignorant, brutal Italians and Hungarians" who "are not freemen, and have no conception of freedom" and were not a "desirable acquisition to our population."[77] These immigrants were the original "economic" migrants, and many complained that "they show no disposition to become citizens of this country, but, on the contrary . . . and are brought into competition with skilled as well as unskilled labor, and it is fast as bad as the Chinese in the West."[78] Just like the case of Asian immigrants, Americans were concerned about the mixing of higher and lower races because such intermixing would always lead to a lower type. The United States was obsessed with these concerns from the late nineteenth century through the passage of the 1924 National Origins Act. As Joppke describes, this racist ideology drove American restrictionists during this period, as Americans sought to use the scientific principles of physics and biology to perfect and protect society.[79]

revulsion to undesirable immigrants that was based in stereotypes and misguided scientific racism regarding the link between "filth" and disease (see, e.g., Trauner 1978).

76. Zolberg 2008, 192.

77. US House of Representatives, *Congressional Record*, 48th Congress, 1st sess., vol. 15, 5349, June 19, 1884.

78. US House of Representatives, 48th Congress, 1st sess., report no. 144, 8.

79. Joppke 2005.

Specifically, this ideology separated Europeans into three races based on the same eugenicist principles: "Nordic," "Mediterranean," and "Alpine." Each race had its own unique skull shape, disposition, stature, and so on, but "Nordics" were the only "pure" Europeans. All others were instead "western extensions of Asiatic subspecies."[80] A desire to prioritize Nordic Europeans and restrict others drove the national origin quota system from the 1920s to 1965.

While proponents of the quota system certainly responded to these racist incentives, politicians did not couch these laws in terms of negative discrimination. Instead, the stated goal was to preserve the "racial status quo of the United States," for the greater good of societal stability. So when the quotas for each state were calculated, the government used the national origins of the *entire* American population, not just the immigrant population. In this way, the justifications for pre-decolonization American immigration policy resembled contemporary justifications: "This was a policy whose discrimination was hidden under a cloak of nondiscrimination."[81] Politicians framed racial quotas as serving the American people and principles of equality. The sponsor of the original bill, David Reed, claimed that the quota law was *nondiscriminatory* because it was an "equal" way of allocating the right to immigrate rather than the "unequal," haphazard method of the nineteenth century.

These quotas were only available to White Europeans. Despite separating Europeans into distinct races, the American population used to compute the quotas excluded "aliens ineligible for citizenship," descendants of slaves, Native Americans, and immigrants from the Western Hemisphere. Excluding these groups from the population calculation removed them from the quotas and effectively ended immigration from all non-White European sources.

Moreover, the national origin quotas were not based on an immigrant's race, even though the purpose of the quotas was to restrict undesirable races. Instead, the quotas were based on the immigrant's country of birth, and this definition informs the strategy of inferring racial bias later in this book. It did not matter whether an immigrant was truly racially undesirable or appeared racially distinct. Instead, this law imposed a racial classification on all citizens of particular countries; the quotas *created* race.[82] In many ways, this method

80. Grant 1924, 167.

81. Joppke 2005, 40.

82. See, e.g., Gratton 2018; Ngai 2003; and Stumpf 2006 for examples from the United States.

of constructing race still occurs when countries categorically restrict immigration from specific states: regardless of the actual characteristics of individual immigrants, merely being from a certain state imparts that racial identity.

Conclusion

In this chapter, I dispel the idea that the right to exclude foreigners was a fundamental principle of the institution of state sovereignty. Had this "right" existed, then rulers would have acted accordingly during the first two centuries of the sovereign state system. Instead, I use the history of international jurisprudence to show that the right to exclude was hardly a settled issue, as states and theorists grappled with the often contradictory implications of the sovereign state system. Immigration and border restrictions did not emerge for two hundred years after the dawn of the post-Westphalia international system. The implication of this discussion is that the desire to exclude foreigners and secure borders was a *consequence* of the emergence of the modern nation-state, rather than a primordial feature. States did not inherently receive the right to exclude from the god of sovereignty; they developed the thirst for exclusion during the post-Enlightenment transition to the modern nation-state form.

Modern states have many more requirements than premodern states. They need vast administrative capacities to tax and conscript their populations. This taxation and conscription fuels the finances and protects the security of the state and its citizens. This post-Enlightenment expansion of state capacity coincides with the ideology of "high modernism"—the idea that humans can rationally engineer their societies for the greater good. A consequence of this shift was that the state transformed from being diffuse to being centralized. The relevant borders of a citizen's imagination expanded from their local town or village to the state's external borders. As a result, the sovereign state seized the legitimate means of movement away from private, local entities, created national labor markets, and set up the administrative capabilities to record and control its population. This historical process decreased the number of effective polities in the system and established the nation-state as the dominant unit of analysis in international politics.

To stimulate acquiescence among their newly centralized populations, states (and citizens) fomented national myths that spurred the creation of modern *nation*-states. This transition to the modern nation-state emphasized that all territories were tied to a specific national population with a common founding myth, language, ethnicity, or other cornerstone. Unsurprisingly, this emphasis on common ancestry and founding myths interacted with the high modernism of the day to produce immense racism and White supremacy. This was no ordinary White supremacy, however. This racism was "scientific" in that it attributed all differences among races to biology. Superior races could no longer civilize inferior races, which suggested the former do what they could to ensure that these undesirables not corrupt the sanctity of the national population. In an era of high modernism in which states and citizens presumed that humans could rationally engineer their societies for good, and nations were the lifeblood of the state's future, many began clamoring for policies that restricted immigration on the basis of racial desirability. To do otherwise would endanger the health, safety, and future of the nation-state. Anglo-European exposure to racially different immigrant populations only catalyzed these fears.

This method of racial restriction marked immigration policy in the United States and the rest of the immigrant-receiving world until the mid-twentieth century. States were concerned about their exposure to racially undesirable immigrants, so they enacted laws that either explicitly restricted them or restricted them in an indirect way. As we will see below, this desire to restrict undesirable immigrants did not dissipate, and states continued to use similar nondiscriminatory (now called "color-blind") methods to protect the putative health of their societies. Immigrant-receiving states throughout the world relied on supposedly immutable principles of state sovereignty to justify these sets of laws. This principle is found nowhere in the founding myth of state sovereignty. It only took exposure to racially undesirable populations to activate the obvious sovereign responsibility to restrict and expel foreigners. Even though the right to exclude was not a fundamental principle of sovereignty in practice, racial threat created it as one. This trend would continue into the modern era.

3

Colonialism, Immigrant Desirability, and the Persistence of Inequality

IN THE PREVIOUS CHAPTER, I destabilize the conventional idea that the right to restrict foreigners is an inherent right of sovereign states. Instead, I argue that this right only emerged after states began receiving more immigrants from racially undesirable populations during the rise of the modern nation-state. Leaders invented this sovereign duty to justify racist immigration restrictions that emerged from high-modernist desires to use "objective" race "science" to cultivate an ideal national population and protect the state from ruin.

As I note above, the nineteenth-century Anglo-European transition to late modernity was marked by an expansion and centralization of state function. To stabilize society and smooth this transition, the modern state fostered a common national identity, which catalyzed the rise of nationalism. This rise combined with the post-Enlightenment belief that humans can and should engineer their societies to mark this transition toward the modern system of nation-states. An important consequence of this change was that state sovereignty transferred from absolutist rulers to common citizens. But this change meant that the composition of the national population now directly affected the health of the state. Leaders assumed that the best way for this new type of state to protect its interests and guarantee its future prosperity was to ensure that its population was industrious, moral, and desirable. "To govern is to populate well,"[1] and a society filled with vagabonds, paupers, and otherwise undesirable sorts would cripple the state.

High modernism resonated strongly with the day's scientific racism. So it is not surprising that the clearest marker of undesirability quickly became

1. Alberdi 1899, 266.

racial undesirability, and the only rational policy was for states to admit immigrants of acceptable racial stock. States that acted against their sovereign duty to keep out undesirables would risk "race suicide."[2] As such, explicit racism and racial discrimination formed the bedrock of migration policy throughout the immigrant-receiving world. Although the United States' history of racial selectivity receives the most attention, this racist ideology was also prevalent in other immigrant-receiving states in the Western Hemisphere. Many Latin American states[3] enacted race-, ethnicity-, and national origin–based restrictions to ensure that undesirable influences would not corrupt their societies and that suitable, European immigrants would be the only new arrivals.[4]

The status quo quickly changed during the twentieth century as states rewrote or removed most of their explicitly discriminatory laws. Although Latin American countries began to accept a new norm against discrimination in 1928 and removed their discriminatory laws in turn, other settler colonial states took much longer to change their policies. However, beginning in the 1960s, the United States (1965), Canada (1970), Australia (1973), the United Kingdom (1981), and New Zealand (1986) each dismantled their racially discriminatory immigration policies and ushered in a new era in which one's "objective" characteristics determined their ability to move. Regardless of whether the horrors of the Nazi genocide or pressure from newer, postcolonial states spurred this change,[5] politicians and academics laud the post-1965 world as free of racial discrimination in immigration.[6]

While the letter of immigration law no longer uses race as an explicit standard for desirability, politicians and scholars have been too quick to declare victory. This global change in policy orientation did not end inequality in international migration, and existing work shows that colorblind immigration and citizenship policies disproportionately affect non-White migrants.[7] Yet, few studies interrogate the mechanism generating this

2. Emerick 1910; W. S. Thompson 1917.

3. Argentina (1916), Bolivia (1899), Brazil (1899), Chile (1915), Colombia (1847), Costa Rica (1862), Cuba (1902), Dominican Republic (1905), Ecuador (1899), El Salvador (1886), Guatemala (1896), Haiti (1805), Honduras (1902), Mexico (1921), Nicaragua (1897), Panama (1904), Paraguay (1903), Peru (1856), Uruguay (1890), and Venezuela (1891).

4. FitzGerald and Cook-Martin 2014, 353.

5. Joppke 2005; FitzGerald and Cook-Martin 2014.

6. Hawkins 1991; Garcia y Griego 1994; Borjas 1999; Joppke 2005.

7. Boucher 2007, 2016; Bonjour and Block 2016; Dauvergne 2019; Ellermann and Goenaga 2019; Elrick and Winter 2018; Mau et al. 2015; Orgad and Ruthizer 2009; Rajaram 2018; Tannock 2011.

inequality. Scholars assume that politicians who enact these laws either are explicitly racist or are simply acting in the objective national interest. And each ignores one piece of the status quo. The first group ignores that policies are color-blind; none have the *stated* goal of restricting on the basis of race. The second group ignores that these face-neutral laws disproportionately affect non-White migrants; regardless of intent, states find ways to write laws that seem to reproduce racial inequalities.[8] Moreover, it is unlikely that all of the institutionalized, socially acceptable, and desirable racism from the fifteenth through the mid-twentieth centuries would vanish overnight. So where is this racism hiding? Why do we see the persistence of racial inequality in the opportunity to migrate when laws that explicitly forbid racial discrimination no longer exist?

In this chapter, I apply the insights of W.E.B. Du Bois and Frantz Fanon on colonialism and racial imperialism to theorize how color-blind immigration policies reproduce structural racial inequalities.[9] In short, the idea that states were obliged to restrict immigration to only those they considered desirable remains a commonsense assumption in the present day. States that do not control their borders and prevent undesirable immigration are not *real* states, but the postcolonial era is different because states no longer define desirability in explicitly racist terms. However, states now use "objective" criteria to restrict that correlate with race because the history of colonialism and legal racism in the international system produced modern subjects in the non-White world that now appear undesirable. In short, *Western states created the conditions that produced the undesirable migrants that they now restrict today.* Crucially, this undesirability need not be rooted in fact—perceptions and constructions of inferiority produce the impetus to restrict regardless of reality. At the same time, the restrictive ideology of sovereignty has spread to the postcolonial world. As states gained independence in the postwar era, they inherited the modern institutions and logic of sovereignty—the logic that encodes border control into the definition of what it means to be a state. It is imperative for modern states to protect their populations; so, while postcolonial states are not "racist" per se, the notion of what it means to be a legitimate state leads them to reproduce the exclusionary, Western status quo. In this

8. To be sure, a third group falls between these poles that recognizes the persistence of inequality in migration policy-making. However, this work typically focuses on exploring specific laws and regimes, not the international structure and its antecedents.

9. Du Bois 1915, 1943, 1947; Fanon 1963.

way, the histories of colonialism, state sovereignty, and racial inequality coalesce to produce a color-blind international system that exhibits more rather than fewer restrictions on movement.

Theoretical Framework

States have sought to restrict undesirable immigration since the nineteenth century, and prior to the 1960s and 1970s, they equated desirability with racial desirability. Although explicit racism is no longer socially acceptable, the goal of restricting undesirables remains. This theory describes how states continue to restrict undesirable migrants, justify their practice of doing so, and reproduce the same racial inequalities as the colonial era.

First, fear of racial undesirables continues to affect immigration policy throughout the world; leaders simply no longer explicitly address the issue of race. In a color-blind world without explicitly racist immigration policies, race hides in the widely accepted notions of the national interest and national security. Politicians and publics want immigration policies that restrict undesirable immigrants, and many assume that color-blind policies are appropriate ways of doing so. Moreover, all assume that the national interest and national security are neutral political objectives. So long as states do not explicitly discriminate on the basis of race, or state an intention to do so, politicians have wide latitude in the means they can employ in service of these obvious and neutral policy goals. The public and its leaders rarely interrogate the implications of assuming that what we consider to be in the national interest is always appropriate and always outside the bounds of scrutiny. Any evidence that color-blind immigration policies have disparate effects on, for example, immigrants from Central America (in the case of the United States) is merely incidental, or irrelevant, because they are in the service of national security.[10]

This presumption of innocence produces objective laws that are in the national interest. However, we should expect color-blind immigration restrictions to correlate with race: replacing racist laws with face-neutral ones does not erase the history of colonialism and explicit racism in the international system. This history produced modern postcolonial subjects that citizens and politicians in the global North consider dangerous or undesirable. In other words, Anglo-European states *made* undesirable migrants, and I lean on the work of W.E.B. Du Bois and Frantz Fanon to argue that the actions

10. Kohli, Markowitz, and Chavez 2011.

of states during colonialism and in the immediate aftermath of decolonization produced non-White migrants that the West can so uncritically restrict as objectively undesirable without resorting to explicit racial quotas. In the color-blind era, states restrict undesirable immigrants *that they helped create*, but these laws are considered neutral and objective because they are not explicitly discriminatory and serve the neutral national interest.

Importantly, this ideology has spread to the postcolonial world. Decolonization led to a proliferation of new sovereign states in the international system, each of which has internalized the ideology of sovereignty that I outline above. Since the nineteenth century, the norm of the sovereign right to exclude has proliferated, despite the notable absence of this "right" from the rise of the modern state during the seventeenth and eighteenth centuries. This expansion is a form of Western hegemony, and it contributes to the increased closure of the international system. There are now more states passing more policies to restrict migrants on the basis of objective criteria. I do not argue that these states are "racist" or are complicit in their own subjugation; rather, Anglo-European hegemony shapes their behavior. The closing of this vicious circle suggests that movement in the international system has become *more* restrictive since the 1960s and 1970s.

The Neutrality of the "National Interest"

In 1951, Hans Morgenthau argued that the United States should pursue a foreign policy that follows only one principle: the national interest.[11] Ever since, the idea that states ought to pursue their national interest above all else has been a staple of realist international relations theory, public pronouncements by policymakers, and conventional wisdom among citizens. States have a duty to their citizens to provide for their security and interests, and politicians have a duty to make policy that protects the national interest at the expense of other goals, such as the economic prosperity and security of other states. The national interest and its companion, national security, are so widely accepted and referenced throughout society and the academy that it is almost a truism to note their importance.

Despite the centrality of the national interest and national security to foreign policymaking goals, politicians and citizens rarely interrogate the politics of defining these terms. To put it differently, politicians make policy that they

11. Morgenthau 1951.

justify as being in the state's national interest or in the service of national security. The public then assumes that such goals are legitimate. This allowance presumes that the national interest is a neutral objective, and citizens give politicians wide latitude to pass laws that may infringe upon other rights. In this way, the national interest gives politicians license to pass laws that they would otherwise be unable to pass because the institutions that constrain them presume that the national interest supersedes other concerns.

The neutrality of the national interest is the background for how race hides in modern, color-blind immigration policy. Concerns over the national interest drive immigration policymaking and have done so since the nineteenth century. As I describe above, once states started to encounter immigration from undesirable migrants, they began restricting access and arguing for their inherent sovereign right to expel foreigners. Politicians justified these restrictions on the grounds that admitting racially undesirable migrants would harm the national interest: these immigrants would depress native workers' wages, and their regressive morals and unwillingness to assimilate would tear at the fabric of society. Immigration policy remains a function of these fears. Although states no longer use eugenics or White supremacy to warrant policies, they still rely on arguments that presume that immigrants with specific attributes threaten the national interest. Now, instead of arguing that certain migrants should be expelled or restricted on explicitly racist grounds, politicians make similar arguments about the propensity of immigrants to commit crimes and terrorism, depress wages, and undermine democratic institutions through their lack of assimilation. Each of these purported qualities of modern undesirable immigrants is similar to the qualities of *racially* undesirable immigrants prior to the color-blind period. The only difference now is that the justification for their restriction is no longer explicitly racist and instead relies on the ambiguous concept of the national interest, broadly defined as national security, economic prosperity, and cultural cohesion.[12]

This acceptance of the national interest as a neutral and apolitical goal of states effectively isolates immigration policy beyond the realm of critique. If it is routine and obvious that states should do whatever it takes to protect their national interest, then it is difficult to interrogate the policies that politicians enact in service of that interest. After all, who is not concerned about national security or the economic prosperity of native workers? To ignore these goals would be to abrogate one's sovereign responsibility, and

12. Collier 2013; D. Miller 2016.

this assumption shields these policies from criticism. Simply put, the near-universal acceptance of these values as goals to be maximized by the state ensures that politicians have nearly unlimited power to restrict immigration so long as they can tie it to any of the myriad subcomponents of the national interest. Since it is the sovereign duty of states to protect this interest, the burden of proof falls entirely on opponents to show that a given policy outstrips this mandate. In practice, politicians, judges, and publics have been more than willing to give restrictionists the benefit of the doubt and sacrifice other (often constitutionally provided) rights and obligations on the alter of border protection.

The litigation of the Trump administration's "Muslim ban" is the clearest example of this ideology in practice. While the district and appellate courts ruled that the ban exceeded the president's powers under the Immigration and Nationality Act and violated the First Amendment of the Constitution, the Supreme Court reversed these rulings on the grounds that the president has wide authority to make policy when it is deemed to be in the national interest. The court presumes that the national interest is an objective goal to which the president has access and that this objective goal transcends politics and human motivations. Chief Justice Roberts emphasizes "whether the President's chosen method" of addressing perceived risks is justified from a policy perspective is "irrelevant to the scope of his authority." And when the president adopts "a preventative measure . . . in the context of international affairs and national security," he is "not required to conclusively link all the pieces in the puzzle before [courts] grant weight to [his] empirical conclusions."[13] In other words, the president has unchecked authority to act when that action is deemed to be in the national interest because the national interest is always an objective, neutral goal. The president does not even have to have evidence that the target of restrictions is a real threat; at least, evidence does not have to be provided to the court, Congress, or the public. This case further ensconces the precedent that the president has the *plenary power* to use immigration policy to protect the national interest.[14]

13. *Trump v. Hawaii*, 585 U.S. 13 (2018), citing *Holder v. Humanitarian Law Project*, 561 U.S. 1, 35 (2010).

14. For example, in *Kleindiest v. Mandel* (1972), the US Supreme Court ruled that the attorney general may decide that it is in the national interest to refuse someone's entry into the country, and the court will not weigh this right against the First Amendment interests of those who would communicate with the alien. In this case, the alien was a Marxist academic whom the plaintiff wanted to bring to the United States to participate in academic conferences

The neutrality or objectivity of the national interest goes beyond the particular politics of the United States. Similar debates over the relationship between executive power, the right to exclude, and the presumed neutrality of the national interest have taken place in Australia, the United Kingdom, New Zealand, Germany, and elsewhere.[15] When states and their judiciaries are presented with the opportunity assert the neutrality of the national interest and a sovereign right to exclude, they rarely fail to impose restrictions on movement.

These examples reveal one way that the presumably objective and democratic institutions of modern states permit race to hide in color-blind immigration policies. When politicians and citizens presume that the national interest is a neutral standard, they make it difficult to strike down discriminatory laws. This neutrality raises the bar for the evidence required to call a law discriminatory. Since the 1960s and 1970s, elites and citizens have presumed that immigration policies are no longer discriminatory. Instead, these policies restrict objectively undesirable immigrants to protect the national interest—an obviously neutral and apolitical policy goal—on color-blind grounds. This piece of the story sets up how states continue to discriminate on the basis of race. Their institutions are not equipped to interrogate the nuance of color-blind discrimination because the ideology of the national interest is so pervasive. Below, I explain why they do so.

How Colonization Created Undesirables

The national interest is a widely accepted justification for policies throughout the world. When, for example, Victor Orbán warns that migrants are invading Hungary, he implies that these migrants threaten society's security and prosperity. He is not making a racial argument, or so he claims. Orbán just wants to protect his country from threats, and he would make the same argument about any dangerous group. This desire to restrict immigration is a result of

---

and other discussions. The justification of this ruling lies in the idea that if the executive (or Congress) decides something is in the national interest, all other considerations are suspended.

15. New Zealand: *Ye v. Minister of Immigration* (2009) 2 NZLR 596, para. 116; United Kingdom: *R. v. Secretary of State for the Home Department Ex Parte Saadi and Others* (2002) UKHL 41 (Lord Slynn); and *European Roma Rights Centre and Others v. Immigration Officer at Prague Airport,* (2004) UKHL 55, para. 11, (Lord Bingham); Australia: *Chu Kheng Lim v. Minister for Immigration, Local Government and Ethnic Affairs* (1992) 176 CLR 1, para. 27, and *Ruddock v. Vadarlis* (2001) 110 FCR 491 at 543, para. 193 (French J).

observing obvious, face-neutral features of migrants, and he makes the natural decision to forbid them. Politicians throughout the world make similar claims all the time, and they have done so with increasing frequency over the past decade.

The crux of the politician's argument is that the desire to restrict is not racist. Some migrants are simply more dangerous than others. They come from dangerous places. These places are poor, violent, and teeming with militant organizations and terrorists that want to harm our homeland. Why would we risk admitting migrants who may commit violent crimes, diffuse low productivity to our society, drain the public purse, or transmit other traits responsible for our home country's relative destitution?[16] Yes, these laws may be discerning, but there is nothing discriminatory about restricting immigration from those that we *objectively* see as threatening or otherwise harmful. These policies are rational. As such, the second piece of this theoretical core connects the objectivity of protecting the national interest to the history that produces migrants that states naturally want to exclude. In short, I expect to find the persistence of racial inequality in migration—despite the end of explicit racial restrictions—because non-White migrants come from places that we see as obviously dangerous, poor, and otherwise undesirable. This allows politicians to pass restrictions that appear face-neutral but have the effect of reproducing the same racial restrictions. In this section, I outline how Anglo-European colonialism helped produce the conditions that warrant this objectivity.

This piece of the argument will attract detractors. Some will dispute its validity because some states like China rival the economic might of the Anglo-European world. To be clear, this part of the story includes perceptions rather than just material reality. Although some postcolonial states have experienced immense economic growth, the West still perceives them as obviously different or inferior, just as they did during the nineteenth century.[17] This insight connects color-blind inequality in international migration to extant theories of racial constructivism. Recall that race has no biological reality; these categories arise when people classify groups on the basis of supposedly inherent desirable or undesirable features. My account of colonial history uses the same logic; the West uses imperial histories to *construct* the inferiority of the global South. In chapter 6, I provide an extensive discussion

16. Putterman and Weil 2010; Algan and Cahuc 2013.

17. Kim 1999; Junn and Masuoka 2008; Tessler, Choi, and Kao 2020.

of my constructivist ontology and how I apply it to this account of international racial inequality to warrant this argument for how material conditions color perceptions about migrants from the global South. But for now, I introduce three related processes that produce the "obviousness" of non-White migrants' undesirability.

CHATTEL SLAVERY AND EARLY RACIAL IMPERIALISM

First, the early history of explicit racism in the international system—in the form of chattel slavery—catalyzed the creation of the migrants we fear today. W.E.B. Du Bois provides the clearest description of this in "The African Roots of War." In this essay, Du Bois argues that slavery and European colonization—in the service of transnational capitalism—created the vision of a dangerous and "helpless" Africa that invites and justifies exploitation. Du Bois writes:

> That sinister traffic [slavery], on which the British Empire and the American Republic were largely built, cost black Africa no less than 100,000,000 souls, the wreckage of its political and social life, and left the continent in precisely that state of helplessness which invites aggression and exploitation. 'Color' became in the world's thought synonymous with inferiority, 'Negro' lost its capitalization, and Africa was another name for bestiality and barbarism.[18]

This observation is vital because it shows the historical antecedents of constructions of non-White inferiority. The actions of Europeans, through the enslavement of millions, crippled the African continent, and constructed the non-White migrant as dangerous, infantile, and undeveloped. Importantly, slavery affected the global South beyond Africa through the triangular trade and the development of slave societies that pervaded in the West Indies, the Indian Ocean, Brazil, and Central and South America.[19]

Be that as it may, the direct effects of slavery are starkest in Africa. Europeans "cost" Africa countless lives, and the persistence of the slave trade can help explain current economic underdevelopment and perceptions of those who live on the continent.[20] Europeans trafficked roughly twelve million slaves during the trans-Atlantic slave trade alone, and they trafficked a further

18. Du Bois 1915, 708.
19. Piketty 2020, 253.
20. Nunn 2008.

six million over the Red Sea, trans-Saharan, and Indian Ocean slave trades. Slavery's effect was so pronounced that Patrick Manning estimates Africa's population was only 50 percent of what it would have been in its absence.[21] The slave trade decimated Africa, its many societies, and ultimately, the broader perception of its fitness for modern institutions.

The abuses of the slave trade created a political economy of fear and violence. The Europeans brought a demand for slaves and a bundle of technological innovations that had perverse knock-on effects for African societies. For example, Europeans traded many different goods in exchange for slaves, but the impact of firearms was the most pronounced. African leaders exchanged slaves for guns beginning in the eighteenth century, and firearms became decisive in conflicts on the continent. Only states with guns were able to resist outside attacks, and the demand for both slaves and guns encouraged violence. One could trade slaves to the Europeans for these weapons, which led to more kidnappings. This incentive led to a spiral of uncertainty that led to more enslavement and violence, all in the name of self-defense.[22] This spiral is what scholars call the "gun-slave cycle."[23]

Moreover, slavery had effects beyond incentives for violence and loss of life. Some argue that slavery also catalyzed the pronounced ethnic fractionalization seen in Africa today. And this ethnic fractionalization contributes to conditions that Anglo-Europeans continue to perceive as undesirable and evidence of underdevelopment. Prior to the slave trade, groups of villages used to coalesce into larger federations; however, relations between villages became hostile during the seventeenth century due to the role of firearms and the incentives to kidnap people from nearby villages and sell them to the Europeans.[24] These hostilities and incentives to commit violence weakened ties among villages, inhibited the development of larger communities, and impeded the construction of broader identities. There is strong evidence that ethnic fractionalization is associated with long-term economic growth,[25] and this connection suggests a direct link between the slave trade and economic underdevelopment in the modern day.

The consequences of this internal strife and violence led to more political instability, the collapse of existing government structures, and ultimately,

21. P. Manning 1990.

22. Mahadi 1992.

23. Lovejoy 2000.

24. Hubbell 2001.

25. Easterly and Levine 1997.

colonization.[26] Indeed, there are many examples of robust trading routes, modern state systems, and burgeoning societies prior to slavery throughout the global South, but in each case, we see stagnation and collapse after the arrival of Europeans. Most notably, this history of violence and the collapse of political order, running back to the beginning of the slave trade, would plague Africa for centuries and has helped entrench the West's view of Africa as violent, destitute, and politically backward. As Du Bois describes, these perceptions fueled later justifications for colonialism, beyond the obvious economic incentives. Slavery produced conditions in the global South that Anglo-Europeans later identify as undesirable and unfitting for incorporation into their societies.

The transition from slavery to colonialism and direct administration reveals the tight relationship between racial imperialism, White supremacy, and modern capitalism.[27] The story begins with slavery and the exploitation of non-White labor for profit, but it extends to the modern day because slavery's impetus and effects justified colonial expansion *far beyond the African continent*. As such, White supremacy fed and was fed by capitalism, and chattel slavery composed one piece of a global structure.[28]

The conventional wisdom asserts that abolitionist movements are responsible for Western powers ending chattel slavery "at great cost." However, Du Bois argues that global economic and political processes were responsible: "the diminishing returns of the African slave trade itself, the bankruptcy of the West Indian sugar economy through the Haitian revolution, the interference of Napoleon and the competition of Spain," and that "investment and colonial profit" in fact *benefited* from the end of the slave trade.[29] In other words, the new imperialism of the late nineteenth century was merely a new, preferred

26. Lovejoy 2000, 68–70.

27. There is an extensive history of racial capitalism and its connection with slavery and White supremacy that is beyond the scope of this book. See, e.g., C. James 2001 and E. Williams 2021 for further foundational expositions.

28. "This degree of inferiority is not based in scientific study—indeed the careful anthropological and social study of Africa has only just begun. Again, we must come back to dollars, pounds, marks, and francs. The judgement on Africa was rendered on economic grounds (although, of course, pseudo-scientific dogma was added to bolster it). Liberal thought and violent revolution in the eighteenth and early nineteenth centuries shook the foundations of a social hierarchy in Europe based on unchanging class distinctions. But in the nineteenth and early twentieth centuries the Color Line was drawn as at least a partial substitute for this stratification" (Du Bois 1943, 725).

29. Du Bois, 722.

way for Europeans to exploit non-White labor and increase capitalist profits beyond Africa. While the power of the European working class modestly increased during this period, imperial powers could establish colonies and exploit so-called inferior races to "insure a virtual monopoly of material and labor."[30] And White supremacy in the Anglo-European world produced an alliance between capitalists and workers:

> The white workingman has been asked to share the spoil of exploiting "chinks" and "niggers." It is no longer simply the merchant prince, or the aristocratic monopoly, or even the employing class, that is exploiting the world: it is the nation; a new democratic nation composed of united capital and labor.[31]

In sum, not only did slavery provide economic benefits to the Anglo-European world, but its effects also justified the necessary shift toward a new type of exploitation: colonialism. White supremacy supported capitalism's eternal striving for profits, and the latter reinforced the former by creating the self-fulfilling prophecy of an inferior and destitute non-White world. This justification for colonialism would become its effects, and these effects remain at the heart of Western perceptions about non-White migrants in the modern day. Racial imperialism persists in the color-blind international system because its initial catalyst, global capitalism, continues to reinforce the self-fulfilling prophecy of White supremacy. Past became prologue.

COLONIAL EXPLOITATION

The effect of the slave trade was limited to the areas of the world that the Europeans enslaved. However, there was a tight relationship between the impetus for the global slave trade and the further colonization of the rest of the non-White world. Slavery created the conditions that proved fertile for the European colonization of Africa, but slavery was just one part of the larger global process of colonialism and racial capitalism. Colonialism and extractive forms of capitalism harmed the colonized world economically, socially, and politically. Colonialism created postcolonial spaces that became dependent on former colonial powers for manufactured goods, finance, aid, and integration into the world economy. And colonialism created the *perception*

30. Du Bois, 723.
31. Du Bois 1915, 709.

held by many in the Anglo-European world that countries in the global South are inherently poor, dangerous, unstable, and autocratic *regardless of reality*.

On the eve of European colonialism, there was little difference in economic development between the richest and poorest places on earth. The world's richest countries were only four times as rich as the poorest countries, and there was relative parity in the sophistication of economic, social, and political institutions. Today the gap between rich and poor is a factor of more than forty, and there is substantial evidence that colonialism helped produce these inequalities.[32] Although statistics on the true effects of colonialism are incomplete, it is clear that Europeans contributed to the widespread decimation of human life in the Americas—where nine-tenths of the population was destroyed through war, famine, enslavement, and diseases[33]—and beyond.

Scholars have developed a variety of economic, sociological, and political theories to explain how colonialism affected the colonized. As one may expect, these efforts are wide-ranging, occasionally antagonistic, and contradictory. Different scholars use different lenses to paint broad pictures of centuries of human history. Here, I outline the evidence for how Anglo-European colonialism affected the non-White world and produced citizens that Anglo-Europeans would later perceive as undesirable. I focus on colonization's effect on the institutions of the colonized, the economic relations among states, and how histories of colonial violence created perceptions of the violent non-White subject. I unpack these effects, and the associated debate surrounding theories of dependence, further in chapter 6.

First, colonialism affected the institutions of colonized societies. The European colonization of the non-White world, beyond those colonies that would eventually become White settler colonies, created the institutional conditions that the global North would later critique as dangerous or undesirable. This included fostering corruption, election rigging, and promoting fragile authoritarianism.[34] This point may seem obvious, but it is important to note how both indirect and direct colonial rule benefited the colonizer at the expense of the colonized. When Europeans arrived, they set up their own means of administration, and these new forms of administration superseded existing forms of government. However, European colonial tactics differed depending on location, and these differences impacted how the

32. Acemoglu, Johnson, and Robinson 2005.

33. McNeill 2010, 16.

34. Angeles and Neanidis 2015.

colonized developed in the long term. While there are debates over what makes some countries prosper and other countries fail, Daron Acemoglu and James Robinson provide one theory that links colonialism to economic development *via* the institutions Europeans set up when they arrived. In short, a colony's "initial conditions" affected how colonization influenced later economic development. This variance in outcomes occurred despite colonizers having similar intentions for their colonial possessions. In areas of the world with large indigenous populations, such as Latin America, Europeans established colonial institutions to exploit these people, their labor, and capital. Europeans found similar conditions in places like Zimbabwe and South Africa, and when they did, they established similar extractive institutions to extort rents and labor from indigenous peoples. Moreover, when European settler mortality was high, they were unable to set up "modern" governance structures, which led them to establish more extractive institutions. Acemoglu and Robinson argue that these institutions are associated with modern poverty in Africa and Latin America.[35] In places where Europeans did not find large indigenous populations, Acemoglu and Robinson suggest that they had to encourage more colonizers to settle and invest in the colonial project. This mechanism worked in conjunction with low settler mortality rates. As a result, Europeans encouraged the development of political and property rights that eventually produced a society with more democratic institutions.

The unspoken subtext of this story is that the historical mechanism is confounded by race. The places where Europeans faced the highest settler mortality rates, and therefore established extractive institutions, were the places with the most ascriptively non-European populations. In the so-called "neo-European" colonies,[36] there were lower rates of settler mortality, which is associated with less extractive institutions. Yet, it was in these colonies that the Europeans systematically exterminated the indigenous population and established White settler colonies. In the other—mostly African and Asian—colonies, Europeans faced high mortality rates, large non-White populations, and natural resources that incentivized exploitative institutions. So, while one can criticize Acemoglu and Robinson for their theory of development, there is a clear relationship between colonial rule and the quality of postcolonial political institutions. Whether these institutions *cause* modern-day economic development or not is not of concern here. Rather, the fact that

35. Acemoglu and Robinson 2012.

36. Acemoglu, Johnson, and Robinson 2001.

TABLE 3.1. Shares of world GDP, 1700–1952

	1700	1820	1890	1952
China	23.1	32.4	13.2	5.2
India	22.6	15.7	11.0	3.8
Europe	23.3	26.6	40.3	29.7

Source: Maddison 1998.

colonizers established extractive institutions that exploited native workers in the non-White world is most instructive.

Second, the exploitative relations of colonialism turned the global balance of economic power on its head. In 1492, on the eve of its contact with the rest of the world, Europe's economy was sluggishly moving out of feudalism and its economic growth was slow compared to other regions of the world. All areas of the world were at relative economic parity, and the idea that European civilization was somehow more advanced or predisposed to civilize the rest of the world is at odds with the historical record. In fact, "it is very likely that, in the middle of the eighteenth century, the average standard of living in Europe was a little bit lower than that of the rest of the world."[37] Indeed, when the French Revolution began in 1789, the world's largest manufacturing regions were not in London, Manchester, or Berlin; they were in the Yangtze Delta and Bengal.[38]

European colonialism disrupted this relative parity, as table 3.1 shows. Between 1700 and 1890, India's share of the world economy shrank from 22 percent to 11 percent and China's share shrank from 23 percent to 13 percent. At the same time, Europe's share increased from 23 percent to 40 percent.[39] Although China, India, and the Arab world experienced dramatic economic growth and intellectual development during the precolonial period, the fortuitous confluence of factors that promoted European colonialism would soon produce a divergence. How did this happen? In one typical story, colonial powers prevented industrialization in their colonies, and they instead exploited them for their low-wage labor and raw materials. This occurred beyond the well-cited case of India: European colonialism led to the deindustrialization of much of Asia, the Middle East, and Latin America, and

37. Bairoch 1982, 107.

38. Bairoch 1982, 107.

39. Maddison 1998, 40. See also Maddison 1995.

produced a violent decline in Africa.[40] This deindustrialization and economic exploitation produced narratives of the underdeveloped "Third World" that continued to justify European dominance until decolonization and helped produce the image of the poor and undesirable non-White migrant.[41]

Finally, the violence of Anglo-European colonial expansion created the perception of the non-White world as brutal, wild, and dangerous. When colonizers expanded their territorial holdings, they often used force. The racist ideology of the time ensured that Anglo-Europeans considered their military operations as "civilized" and the resistance and practices of the colonized to be "barbaric." So when colonizers faced violence from their colonial subjects, they constructed these actions as uncivilized and justifying further violence. These actions and reactions were a vicious cycle of violence that perpetuated the perception of the non-White world as violent and inhospitable. Anglo-Europeans colonized the non-White world, and when faced with violent opposition to their incursion, colonizers deemed their colonial subjects inherently violent. This justification is key to the production of modern races and racism that I describe in chapter 1.

This construction allowed the colonizer to justify any sort of colonial administration and use of violence. If the colonized were inherently violent and insensible to ethics, it would be imprudent for the colonizer to moderate its behavior in the face of insurrections. For example, when the United States defeated the Spanish in the Spanish-American War, it "inherited" the Philippines, a Spanish colonial holding. Tensions emerged between the Americans and the Filipinos, as the latter had struggled for several years against Spanish rule by the time the Americans declared war in 1898. Racism marked the ensuing colonial war between the United States and the Philippines, as American leaders justified their brutal military tactics on racial grounds. The Filipinos used guerrilla tactics that the Americans perceived as barbaric. President Roosevelt admitted that the Americans engaged in unsavory tactics to suppress the Filipinos, but at every opportunity, he rationalized this behavior out of fear of "a very cruel and very treacherous enemy" that had committed "a hundred acts of far greater atrocity."[42]

This example is just one in which colonizers constructed the colonized as barbaric to justify their actions and continued expansion into the non-White world. However, this construction extended throughout colonial history and

40. Bairoch 1995, 88–92.

41. M. Davis 2000.

42. Kramer 2006, 169.

into the period of decolonization. Fanon describes how colonizers set up the native as the inherent embodiment of evil and backwardness and carried this perception through to his modern day:

> As if to show the totalitarian character of colonial exploitation the settler paints the native as a sort of quintessence of evil. Native society is not simply described as a society lacking in values. It is not enough for the colonist to affirm that those values have disappeared from, or still better never existed in, the colonial world. The native is declared insensible to ethics; he represents not only the absence of values but also the negation of values. He is, let us dare to admit, the enemy of values, and in this sense he is the absolute evil. He is the corrosive element, destroying all that comes near him; he is the deforming element, disfiguring all that has to do with beauty or morality.[43]

Indeed, Anglo-European construction of the colonized world as violent, "absolute evil" remains in the present day. When the colonizers experienced violent resistance to their incursions, they reasoned that such barbarism must be an inherent property of this inferior racial subspecies. This argument extends Du Bois's insights about Europe to the modern day. Famously, Du Bois critiqued European culture for downplaying the violence and inhumanity of slavery and colonialism. He argued that Western institutions—schools, newspapers, and other accounts—buried the truth about these effects in the service of deliberately fostering White supremacy. European institutions cultivated the conventional wisdom that these "dark" regions of the world were inherently backward because they had not been exposed to Western Reason.[44] This ignorance was deliberate because it accorded with and amplified extant racism and justification for colonial exploitation. Although explicit, old-fashioned racism of this sort is now out of fashion, the historical legacy and collective memory of these claims shape how we think of the non-White world and its inhabitants in the modern day. It is easy to see how the West continues to perceive migrants from this part of the world as dangerous and undesirable. This "global white ignorance" is a legacy of racial imperialism, and it continues to drive perceptions that animate the prejudice of color-blind racism.[45]

43. Fanon 1963, 40.
44. Du Bois 1947, 22, 37.
45. Bonilla-Silva 2006; Mills 2015.

To be sure, the precise, material effects of colonialism are not a panacea. Several countries in the global South—China, South Africa, Brazil, for example—forged a path to economic development in the postcolonial era. Others, like Ethiopia and Liberia, were not even colonized. Be that as it may, these examples do not call this account into question. This theory involves *perceptions*, rather than reality, and Western perceptions of the global South persist despite variation in postcolonial economic development. Even though colonialism (and present neocolonialism) did not have universal effects, representations of the global South from the past through the present crystallize Anglo-European presumptions about these places and their inhabitants. The result is that many in the global North consider many places in the South to be naturally dangerous, poor, or otherwise undesirable without considering reality or why their beliefs appear true.[46] The fact that these perceptions remain despite evidence to the contrary epitomizes the perniciousness of centuries of White supremacy and racial imperialism. The construction of inferiority presents a fact-resistant worldview that defines how the global North relates to the global South and highlights how modern, color-blind racial inequality operates. This prejudiced vision of the non-White world is similar to what John Hobson calls the "Peter Pan theory" of the East, which "conjured up a romantic vision of the Other as more helpless than cruel . . . who would never grow up of his/her own accord."[47] The colonized world is full of childlike subjects who, depending on one's perspective, were either untamable or irredeemable without the intervention of the West. The rhetoric of the contemporary immigration debate demonstrates the salience of this perspective on the undesirability of non-White migrants from the postcolonial world.[48] Recalling the discussion in chapter 1, this construction of seemingly inherent inferiority is how race and racism are reified throughout the world in general.

In sum, colonialism created the perception that people from certain parts of the world are inherently dangerous, poor, and undesirable. Colonialism reorganized global economic relations and made the colonized states satellites of the colonizing states; it turned the balance of economic power on its head. This dependence facilitated the large-scale transfer of resources from the colonized to the colonizer. Rather than merely stunting the independent development of the non-White world, colonialism led to underdevelopment and

46. Junn and Masuoka 2008; Kim 1999; Tessler, Choi, and Kao 2020.

47. Hobson 2004, 228.

48. Narkowicz 2018, 357–358.

perceptions of inferiority. The magnitude of resource extraction transformed the global South into being dependent on the global North for exports, imports, capital, and technical expertise.[49] Frantz Fanon—linking chattel slavery and colonialism—argues that Europeans built their advancement and modernity "on the backs of slaves" and that the West "owes its very existence to the soil and subsoil of the underdeveloped world."[50] Finally, colonial violence, *in response to the actions of the West,* led Anglo-Europeans to construct the non-White world as inherently violent and barbaric. These constructions would persist, and each element accounts for how Western actions throughout history "created" the undesirable, modern non-White migrant that these states later so naturally restrict. In chapter 6, I move from these broad contours to discuss specific evidence for how Western colonialism affected realities in and perceptions of the global South.

Decolonization and the Expansion of Closure

The first two components of the theory explore why racial inequality persists in international migration despite the end of formal racial quotas. States still want to restrict undesirable migrants, only now they do so in "objective" rather than racist terms. The gist of the argument is that the history of chattel slavery and colonial exploitation created non-White migrants as those the West now deems obviously undesirable. The nearly unlimited prerogative of state leaders to propose policies in the national interest and the correlation between race and undesirability allows color-blind racial discrimination to persist. The reality of this objectivity matters little.

In this section, I explore how the logic of exclusion expanded to the postcolonial world after decolonization. The final piece of the explanatory puzzle develops an account of why we should see more inequality and restriction in migration in the postcolonial era, rather than less. The culmination of decolonization was that former colonies adopted the nation-state form. These newly independent polities, rather than adopt a different form of political organization, became nation-states. This trend was important because it codified the future trajectories of the postcolonial states: they would look to the Anglo-European world as models for how to be members of the international society.[51]

49. Thomas 1999.
50. Fanon 1963, 53.
51. Bull and Watson 1984, 1–2.

It was also not a free choice; since the seventeenth century, the nation-state has become the only legitimate model for actorhood in the international system. The nation-state remains the only such model because the benefits of membership in the international society are only afforded to nation-states. So after decolonization, newly independent states internalized what it means to be a sovereign state from former colonial powers because they had no alternative. This indirect coercion is a form of *hegemony*;[52] leaders of newly independent states thus took great care to highlight the myriad ways they now behaved and appeared as typical states, such as participating in the United Nations General Assembly.[53] All in all, postcolonial states adopted both Western day-to-day modes of governing (such as parliaments and ministries) and the general cultural models of sovereignty (such as referring to themselves as nation-states). These adoptions provide strong evidence of "the transmission of the legitimizing institutions that sustain sovereignty" worldwide.[54]

As I discuss above, the duties to control one's borders and to exclude foreigners have been defining features of proper states since the nineteenth century. Naturally, these norms transferred to newly independent states after decolonization. The key is explaining why this transfer occurred. Realist accounts of foreign policy may argue that restrictive immigration policies are rational for newly independent states pursuing their national interest. New states need to assert their territorial control to ward off any challenges to their sovereignty. To do so, it is rational to impose modern borders and stringent border policies. However, the evidence suggests doing so is not in these states' true national interest. States enact immigration policies to satisfy many dimensions of the national interest,[55] but for newly independent states from which colonial powers withdrew their capital and technical expertise, economic development is the most vital consideration. Economic development and stability is paramount in new states because there is strong evidence that political violence and unrest is associated with economic underdevelopment and inequality.[56] Therefore, postcolonial states act against their national

52. Gramsci 1971; Rupert 1995.

53. President of Ghana, Kwame Nkrumah, September 23, 1960, at the UN General Assembly in New York: "This is a new day in Africa and as I speak now, thirteen new African nations have taken their seats this year in this august Assembly as independent sovereign states. . . . There are now twenty-two of us in this Assembly and there are yet more to come."

54. Reus-Smit 2013, 22.

55. Rudolph 2003; Adamson 2006.

56. Muller 1985.

interest when they enact strict border controls, running against strong economic incentives to liberalize their immigration policies. For example, there are an estimated 470,000 vacancies in the labor market of southern African states.[57] Yet, South Africa, Namibia, Zimbabwe, Botswana, and Mozambique remain committed to restricting high-skilled foreigners even though their labor markets would benefit from an infusion of labor. In general, restrictive border policies are not functional for postcolonial states, and more open borders would lead to dramatic increases in the quality of life for their citizens. Realist models of state behavior cannot explain why a state like Namibia would enact immigration policies that are economically harmful, just to pursue less tangible goals, such as societal stability. Moreover, these restrictions on movement contradict the freedom of movement that was pervasive throughout much of the postcolonial world during the precolonial and colonial periods.[58]

To explain the diffusion of these policies (and their logic), I partially rely on *world polity* or *world society* theory. This approach, pioneered by John W. Meyer, explains why we see a world "in which national states, subject to only modest coercion or control, adopt standard identities and structural forms,"[59] such as a constitution, a Western-style educational system, *and restrictive immigration policies*. World polity theory rests on two key pillars. The first is that nation-states (and other constructed actors in world politics) use world models, like citizenship, economic development, and human rights, to legitimate themselves and their behavior. Second, there is relative consensus about the content of these models, and they are universal. For instance, the neoliberal model of economic development is a world model that states adopt to legitimate themselves as members of the international society of states. This world cultural model is powerful because the epistemic community of experts, international organizations, and leaders presumes it is applicable *everywhere*, not just in certain areas of the world. Two propositions connect this world culture to the proliferation of postcolonial states. First, Western states explicitly transmitted these cultural models and the nation-state form to their colonial dependencies; and second, postcolonial states and movements imitated these Western models.[60]

57. Kitimbo 2015.

58. Herbst 2000.

59. Meyer et al. 1997, 174.

60. Strang 1990, 847.

The world society perspective is fruitful because it allows one to theorize how certain models of statecraft, administration, and other behaviors become institutionalized worldwide and diffuse throughout the world. This perspective is *macrophenomenological*:[61] the modern state is the product of a culture that is organized at the level of the international system, "not simply built up from local circumstances and history."[62] State administrators, politicians, and citizens may either push for policies that they believe are rational to protect their national interest (à la realists[63]) or be shaped entirely by global systems of economic or political hegemony (à la world systems theorists[64]), but the historical record suggests that modern post-WWII states coalesce around a set of structures, behaviors, and modes of governance that are remarkably homogeneous and organized at the level of the international system. In other words, theorizing the existence of a macrophenomenological world society allows one to explain how certain features of Western states become rampant within new postcolonial states even though these features are not functional for the latter.

Consider the example of public education. The conventional wisdom is that formal education is necessary and beneficial for economic growth, the development of human capital, technological innovation, citizen loyalty, and so on.[65] These arguments are rarely contested, except in rare circumstances, even though many studies of the relationship between mass formal education and economic growth suggest any causal relationship is likely weak and conditional. However, the murky association between education and economic growth did not prevent postcolonial states from implementing Western models of education. Global models of this sort are constitutive of world culture, and "as they are implemented in the furthest corners of the globe, they operate

61. *Macrophenomenological* is not a user-friendly term. It is an example of the worst kind of social scientific jargon. The easiest way to understand a phenomenological theory is to describe what it *is not*, a realist theory. Realist theories make strong assumptions about the rationality, boundedness, and autonomy of actors. These theories assume that actors have preferences and beliefs and that they act in accordance with basic rules, like utility maximization, with little influence from institutions or diffuse systems of meaning, like culture. In contrast, pheonomenological theories do not assume that actors are prior or fixed entities that behave according to narrow rules. Rather, cultural models and meanings construct actors and their preferences, beliefs, and interests.

62. Meyer et al. 1997, 147, citing Thomas et al. 1987; Powell and DiMaggio 1991.

63. Waltz 1979.

64. Wallerstein 2011.

65. Langton and Jennings 1968; Barro 2001.

as framing assumptions producing consequences that in no reasonable way can be seen as 'functional' for the societies that implemented them."[66] States enact certain policies and modes of governing without regard for their own unique circumstances and context *because doing so is a marker of being a modern state.*

This approach is distinctive because it does not rely on direct coercion (i.e., sanctions or military interventions) for explanatory power. Contrary to world systems theory, for instance, postcolonial states are embedded in a world culture that diffuses what it means to be a sovereign state to them. New states and their leaders pick up from world culture, often with minimal coercion, the "right" institutions and policies to adopt, which accounts for the convergence I describe above. To be sure, the world society approach *can* account for more direct control. It can be the case that Francophone West Africa enacts certain democratizing initiatives due to both political conditionalities from the European Union and internalizing world cultural norms.[67] However, the need for external actors to impose themselves on the postcolonial world is not required, and therefore it is capable of accounting for decolonization and the diffusion of Western forms of governance. It can still be the case that non-Western forms of governance flourished outside the European cultural sphere and that colonial subjects contested global norms through a transnational struggle, and this approach is attractive because it allows Western social scientists to remain ignorant of persistent White supremacy. Yet, world polity is a useful social theory because it helps explain how we see tremendous similarity among states, *despite* these facts. This approach is flexible enough to do so because it is an institutionalism that denies the ultimate primacy of the rational actor, yet allows for humans to make boundedly rational decisions within an overarching world culture of both norms and hegemony.

There is an important consequence of this mismatch between a state's needs and the policies it implements to fit in to the world society. Meyer calls this consequence "decoupling," and it refers to the gaps that emerge between the policies states adopt and their actual organizational practices. Within global diffusion processes, it is easier for states to adopt some elements than others, which often leads to incoherence in the application of certain cultural models. Consider the difference between richer states with a lot of resources

66. Meyer et al. 1997, 149.

67. Manners 2002; Koch 2015.

and poorer states with few. On the one hand, when the former are faced with world cultural imperatives, they are able to marshal significant resources to make policy changes that have meaningful effects at the local level. On the other hand, the latter are only able to enact symbolic reforms when they face the same world cultural pressures. Poorer countries typically codify general principles into statements about their identities and values when they lack the resources to effect real change in a given area. Decoupling is beyond what realist theories would predict. Realist theories view policy as a deliberate tool of the national interest: states act to pursue a given goal, not to conform to world cultural models. Such perspectives cannot account for how and why postcolonial states write constitutions and enact laws with grand principles that are similar to those in Western states, yet are unable to implement them. Recognizing the importance of world culture allows one to explain why postcolonial states commit to unrealistic policies that are often not functional for their interests and context, such as border fences.

Decoupling reveals the *hegemony* hiding in world culture and explains why the nation-state form did not passively spread. Yes, Western states did not use military force to coerce newly independent states into adopting the norms and institutions of world society. But the absence of direct coercion does not mean there was no coercion. The nation-state form and the norms of international society were hegemonic—often unstated requirements of membership based on Anglo-European principles—and if polities wanted to be recognized, they needed to become nation-states and demonstrate their sovereignty. Moreover, evidence shows that colonial powers transferred their domestic governance structures to their colonies.[68] So neocolonial institutions carried over domestically while Western powers imposed the norms of the sovereign nation-state internationally. This degree of coercion is missing from world polity and traditional realist accounts, but it is vital to explain why postcolonial states implemented policies that were not functional and reproduced global inequalities. I unpack these mechanisms further in chapter 7.

Hegemony and decoupling have important empirical implications for inequality in international migration. By the end of the Cold War, most of the 130 colonial dependencies of the Anglo-European states became sovereign states.[69] I argue above that these postcolonial states adopted the legitimizing institutions and practices that sustain sovereignty out of necessity. Many

68. Henderson 2009, 2015; Mkandawire 2015.

69. Strang 1990, 846.

postcolonial states remain under close scrutiny and various forms of neocolonial administration, so they need to constantly demonstrate their legitimacy to the West. This performance includes modern border controls, visa restrictions, and other aspects of immigration policies. The consequence of this process is that the postcolonial world has many more sovereign states that all seek to control their borders just like Western states. A clear implication is that the postcolonial international system, while nominally more equal in political terms, contains more states that each internalize the importance of immigration policy restrictiveness, and therefore we should expect *more* immigration restrictiveness in the contemporary international system. Increased racial inequality in international migration will follow because the majority of global movement is within the global South. Non-White migrants now face increased migration restrictiveness on average because they now attempt to move between states that each enact their own version of restrictive immigration policies. While racism and White supremacy may explain the increase in immigration policy restrictiveness in the global North, the increase in policy restrictiveness within the global South—associated with the expansion of national sovereignty—solidifies the persistent barriers to movement for those in the non-White world. These restrictions reflect how persistent Western hegemony ties the hands of postcolonial states and produces an increasingly closed international system.

However, these newly independent states lack the resources of Western states, particularly in the area of immigration policy. In immigration policymaking, it is difficult to ensure that a law will actually fulfill a desired goal, and many migration scholars have argued over the past twenty years that the best efforts of states to regulate and restrict their immigration flows have failed.[70] The argument holds that structural factors drive international migration patterns more than the policies of states, so conditions such as income inequality across countries, economic shocks, and violence are far more important than the variables that migration policies can influence. Rather than affect whether migration occurs, these policies only affect *how* people migrate, such as moving from legal to illegal conduits. In other words, states try to make policy to curate or restrict immigration flows, but such tight control is beyond their capabilities. This fact does not mean states do not try to conduct immigration policy, nor does it mean that they no longer view it as being in their sovereign prerogative to do so. Enter the importance of hegemony and decoupling.

70. Castles 2004; Cornelius and Tsuda 2004.

In a world in which the world culture dictates that sovereign states ought to control their borders and enact restrictive immigration policies but also that doing so is difficult at best and impossible at worst, we should expect to see newly independent states enact more *symbolic* policies to signal their commitment to the general principle of sovereignty.

The construction of border fences is such a symbolic policy. Although there is significant debate over the effect of border walls on interstate conflict, smuggling, terrorism, and trade,[71] it is clear that such barriers have symbolic value, even if they do not always "work."[72] As such, the construction of border walls is an obvious way to signal that a state internalizes the norms of the modern state system because strong borders are an important symbol of sovereignty and legitimacy. Figure 3.1 shows the total number of constructed border fences worldwide since 1965. I separate former colonies from former colonizers to demonstrate that the former enact this largely symbolic strategy in far greater numbers than the latter, and that this gap has widened over time. This figure is descriptive evidence of how the institution of sovereignty has diffused to postcolonial states, and I expect this diffusion is associated with a persistent *increase* in racial inequality in migration since decolonization. In this way, contrary to expectations, the globalization of international society has led to more racial inequality rather than less.

Hypotheses

In this section, I present the hypotheses that fall out of the preceding discussion. Each hypothesis corresponds to a dimension of the theory, and I test each in the remaining chapters of the book. The first hypothesis deals with the overall racial inequality in international migration processes; the final three concern the empirical implications of the historical discussions linking colonialism and sovereignty to this inequality.

The Racial Bias Hypothesis

I have argued so far that we see persistent racial inequality in international migration despite the end of explicitly racist policies. I base this argument on the observed instances of explicit and symbolic racism within many Western

71. Avdan and Gelpi 2017; Carter and Poast 2017, 2020; Getmanski, Grossman, and Wright 2019; Huth, Croco, and Appel 2011.

72. Benedicto and Brunet 2018; Pallister-Wilkins 2011; Rosière and Jones 2012.

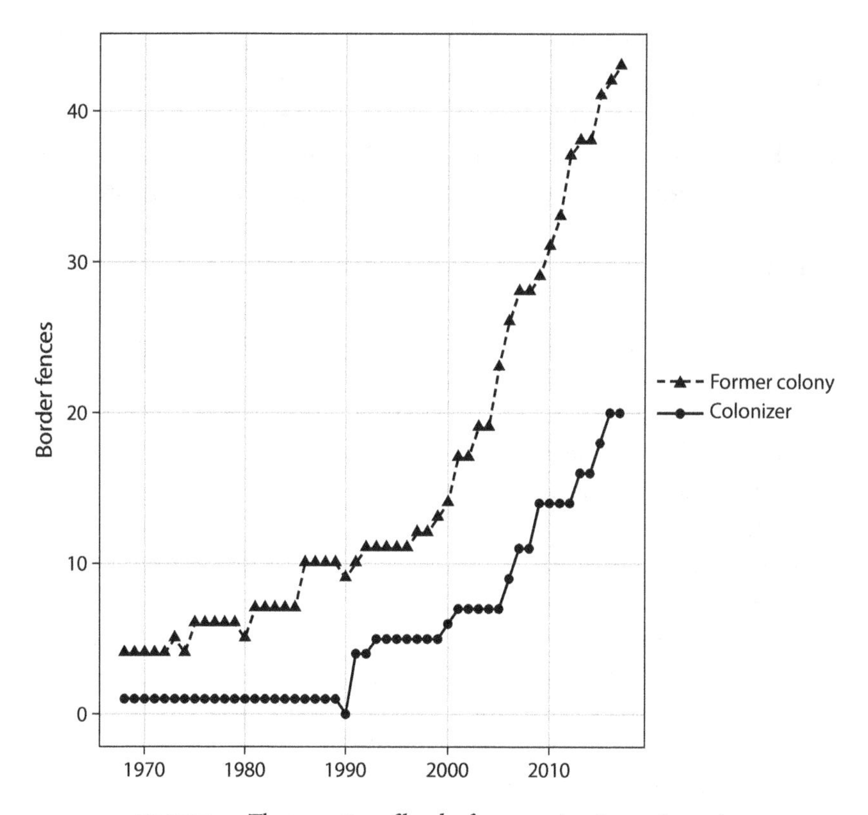

FIGURE 3.1. The expansion of border fence construction, 1965–2016.

countries, as well as on well-known accounts of how face-neutral policies still predominantly affect migrants of color. However, these propositions are difficult to test because immigration policies are now color-blind. In other words, racist immigration policies clearly delineated which countries were discriminatory and to what degree. In a world without such overt racism, these inequalities are less visible because the letter of the law calls any claims of bias into question.

In chapter 5, I develop a method for inferring racial inequality in international migration. The method leans on the existing literature on the political economy of migration to develop a model of how global migration patterns would appear in a world without racial inequality or discrimination. Income disparities, violence, geography, and other related variables still drive the migration between states throughout the world. I call this ideal type the *baseline model* of migration. I use this model to generate predictions for the amount of migration we ought to see between every pair of states in the world *if there were no racial discrimination in migration.* I estimate this baseline value for each pair of states in the international system from 1960 to 2015. The key is to compare this amount of migration to the migration flows we actually observed between these pairs of states. One can think of this comparison as a simple model residual: the difference between predicted and observed migration.

Imagine what we will have calculated at this point: every country in the world will have an estimate for how many more or fewer migrants it both sent and received from every other country in the world. I use these various estimates to generate one estimate for the overall difference between observed and predicted emigration and immigration for each country in the world from 1960 to 2015. For example, in 2010, Uganda will have a predicted overflow or underflow in emigration *and* immigration. This is how I measure racial bias in international migration.

The core proposition of this book is that we continue to observe racial inequality in migration in the postcolonial world. Proponents of neoliberal theories of migration argue that racial quotas are a market distortion that hurt economic exchange and inject bias into the number and composition of worldwide migration flows.[73] Therefore, once Anglo-European states removed their discriminatory policies, we should observe no difference (on average) between observed and predicted migration. Yet, the extant evidence on the persistence of discrimination in color-blind policies suggests that this trend toward equality has not occurred.[74] This standoff produces the *Racial Bias hypothesis*:

> *States from the non-White and/or postcolonial world will have systematically fewer emigrants than the baseline model predicts. This pattern should increase over time.*

If the global data support this hypothesis, it will further strengthen the case made in the existing literature on the persistence of discrimination in color-blind policies.

The Racial Reaction Hypothesis

In the first two parts of the theory, I make the case that the history of colonial exploitation created undesirable migrants and that the supposed neutrality of

73. Karemera, Oguledo, and Davis 2000; Grogger and Hanson 2011.

74. Ellermann and Goenaga 2019.

the national interest ensures that leaders face little pushback when they use that national interest as justification for laws. When leaders use the national interest and national security to justify their policy prescriptions, it is nearly impossible for others to critique those policies. After all, it is better to be safe than sorry when dealing with the existential security of the state. So leaders no longer speak explicitly about restricting racially undesirable migrants, yet they still implore their governments to restrict objectively undesirable migrants because the national interest demands it. This gives states and leaders the power to let race and racism hide in color-blind policies.

To see why, consider how two leaders—one explicitly racist and one not—would behave in a similar situation. The racist leader may want to restrict migration on the basis of race but is unable to say this aloud. The leader therefore will use the language of the objective national interest to warrant policies of exclusion. The nonracist leader will still be motivated to do right by the citizens and therefore will respond to perceived threats to the national interest with restrictive policies. Because we cannot pinpoint a leader's true intentions, we are in an inferential stalemate. However, the idea that the national interest allows cover for racism to hide in seemingly objective policies suggests a further hypothesis that I test in the second part of chapter 5:

> *When Anglo-European states receive increased immigration flows from racially different migrants, they should respond with an increase in immigration policy restrictiveness.*

This *Racial Reaction hypothesis* refers to a state's reaction to undesirable immigrants. Yet, this hypothesis tests the idea that states and their leaders are reacting to racial *difference*. Instead of just investigating whether states enact restrictive policies in response to any immigration, this analysis tests what happens when states receive immigrants from racially different populations. To conduct this test, I employ several different measures of racial difference.

The Colonial Legacy Hypothesis

In the second part of the theory, I argue that the history of colonialism, slavery, and explicit racism in the international system created the migrants that Anglo-European states dismiss as objectively undesirable today. Colonialism and slavery exploited the non-White regions of the world, created economic dependence, depleted populations, and provoked instability and violence. These effects of colonialism feed the narratives of instability, violence, and poverty that Western politicians and citizens cite as evidence that their government should restrict migrants with a certain profile. Since discourses of race and racial inequality have been scrubbed from international politics, there is little engagement with this history. As a result, the undesirability of non-White migrants appears natural and objective. The obviousness that some migrants are unfit for membership in one's political community ensures that states are able to enact policies that are putatively color-blind, yet still target non-White migrants. This component of the theory suggests the following hypothesis that I test in chapter 6:

> *When states receive increased immigration flows from former colonies, they should respond with an increase in immigration policy restrictiveness. This association should be stronger for the former colonizers.*

Put another way, the *Colonial Legacy hypothesis* posits that Anglo-European states should be sensitive to receiving immigration flows from countries that are former colonial subjects and enact more restrictive immigration policies in response. This reaction is rooted in the perception of undesirability; therefore, this relationship should emerge even when one accounts for the actual economic development, human capital, and violence of a given postcolonial state.

The Expansion of Closure Hypothesis

The final part of the theory discusses how modern principles of sovereignty diffuse to the postcolonial world to produce increased closure and racial inequality in the modern day. Although I show in chapter 2 that the sovereign right and duty to exclude foreigners is an invention of the modern state, these responsibilities have still become a part of what it means to be a state in the contemporary international society. I use principles from world polity theory to argue that postcolonial states internalized these world cultural forms of state sovereignty—including the duty to restrict one's borders—when they established themselves after independence. However, due to persistent Western hegemony and a lack of resources, postcolonial states implement more symbolic policies to gesture toward their commitment to adhere to the principles of sovereignty. One such policy is the construction of border fences, which produces the *Expansion of Closure hypothesis*:

Postcolonial states will be more likely to build border fences. Postcolonial states that participate in more international institutions should also build more border fences.

Why does this final hypothesis include an auxiliary proposition about participation in international institutions? The answer is that postcolonial states that are poorer face greater pressures to build fences because of their symbolic power. Poorer states lack the resources to overhaul their immigration enforcement systems, so they will resort to building symbolic walls. In addition, postcolonial states that participate more in international forums will internalize the norms of sovereign statehood more than those that do not.[75] As a result, these states should have a greater impetus to build walls to demonstrate their commitment to international norms of sovereign statehood. The modern institution of sovereignty, created and propagated by the Anglo-European world, creates a modern international society that incentivizes non-White states to perpetuate further racial inequality.

Conclusion

In this chapter, I argue that racial inequality persists in international migration despite the end of explicitly racist policies. To warrant this claim, I adopt insights from Du Bois and Fanon to explain how this inequality can persist despite its legal prohibition. In short, racial discrimination occurs because the history of legal racism, White supremacy, and colonialism produced non-White subjects that appear objectively undesirable. Because state leaders often appeal to the national interest to justify their migration policies, the public rarely interrogates policies that restrict immigration on the basis of objective desirability, or why some migrants might appear more desirable in general. After decolonization, this inequality has gotten worse because postcolonial states, attempting to perform proper sovereign statehood, enact restrictive policies that reproduce the same restrictions in the global South. The consequence of this process is that international migration is more unequal in the postcolonial era, and the Anglo-European world remains blind to this modern racial imperialism.

The roots of this theory lie in recent observations that color-blind immigration policies established by the Organisation for Economic Co-operation

75. Jakobi 2009; Greenhill 2016; Sommerer and Tallberg 2019.

and Development, or OECD, continue to disparately affect migrants of color.[76] However, recent work on discrimination in the immigration policies of liberal states stops at acknowledging the specific features of policies that produce discrimination, such as profiling and positive selection,[77] or uses this evidence to put forth a radical cosmopolitan argument in favor of open borders.[78] In this chapter, I acknowledge the importance of unmasking and investigating policies that seem benign, such as visa waivers and medical restrictions, yet continue to produce discrimination outside public discourse. That being said, I go further to theorize why these color-blind sources of discrimination emerge in the first place. To do so, I draw on broad theoretical work on the national interest, the political economy of colonialism, sociological institutionalism, and hegemony.

Unlike prior approaches that consider immigration policymaking and discrimination in country-specific cases, I generalize racial inequality to the level of the international system. In so doing, I theorize how the logic of the institution of sovereignty—what it means to be a modern state—stymied transnational political movements and ensured the nation-state form became hegemonic in the postcolonial world. This step is key because it reveals how the ostensibly positive developments that came with decolonization created the conditions that have led to further inequality, in spite of strong transnational political movements in the global South.[79] Indeed, this account reveals the true might of Western hegemony and structural power in the international system to impose their existing cultural models of sovereignty on the rest of the world. As I outline in the next several chapters, these theoretical expectations bear out and reveal where and how racial inequality persists in international migration.

76. Law 1996; K. R. Johnson 2000, Ellermann and Goenaga 2019.

77. Ellermann and Goenaga 2019.

78. Hayter 2000, 2001.

79. Cf. Getachew 2019; Shilliam 2006; Valdez 2019; Wilder 2015.

4

A Forensic Approach to Racial Inequality

THE PREVIOUS TWO CHAPTERS destabilized the common assumption that the power to exclude immigrants is inherent to sovereign states and theorized how racial bias can continue to exist in international migration despite the end of racist policies. In short, sovereignty provides a convenient justification for protecting one's population from undesirables. Leaders only began to assert this natural right after they faced increased immigration from racial undesirables during the era of rational state building, scientific racism, and nationalism. These leaders used the "science" of eugenics to guide their cultivation of the ideal society, and racist immigration laws were an obvious application of this plan. Accordingly, the modern theology of the sovereign's duty to control its borders is a *consequence* of the rise of nation-states (and their racism), rather than a basic feature. However, modern immigration laws reveal that the desire to protect one's population from undesirable outsiders persists even though scientific racism became socially undesirable. These color-blind laws perpetuate racial inequality because they restrict immigration on the basis of face-neutral features that are highly correlated with race.

The previous chapter connects these two threads: the history of Anglo-European colonialism and the effects of explicit White supremacy in the international system produced the migrants that states "objectively" restrict today. The chapters also engaged with two other important mechanisms for perpetuating continued racial inequality in international migration. The first is the presumed objectivity of the national interest. Specifically, racial bias in migration hides in the widely accepted notion that leaders have a duty to protect the national interest of their states, that this interest always rises above all other concerns, and that no one has the right to challenge that interest. The consequence is that leaders—regardless of their own views on migration—have the incentive to restrict objectively undesirable migrants because not doing so would present a needless risk to the state. In this way, all states enact similar policies, ones that limit immigration to only those migrants who pass muster on various criteria, such as language, income, and education. The most pernicious implication of this process is that the postcolonial international system will have more racial inequality in movement because postcolonial states also enact restrictive policies. When postcolonial states gained independence, they forcibly adopted the nation-state form and internalized the world cultural norms of sovereignty from the Anglo-European international system. Even though the right and duty to protect one's borders is a convenient fiction of the nineteenth century, it is still a norm that expanded throughout the postcolonial international society. In this way, these norms ensure that a structure of racial inequality in international migration remains long after decolonization and the end of explicitly discriminatory laws.

The remainder of this book adds empirical flesh to each dimension of this theory. In the next two chapters, I reveal the presumptive, persistent racial inequality in international migration. There are several important theoretical and technical concerns with unmasking this inequality. I present the theoretical issues as a conversation with three different groups of skeptics. These theoretical skeptics address both the ethical and practical considerations associated with studying race and racial inequality in international politics. The first group cites supposedly mass immigration from the global South to the global North and the lack of explicitly racist laws to invalidate the argument that racial bias persists. These skeptics care a great deal about intentionality. They argue that if one claims that racial bias or racism exists, then they need to provide evidence of an explicitly racist intention. The second group are racial "eliminativists," and they lie on the opposite end of the spectrum from the first group. Eliminativists protest the use of the concept of race for completely different reasons. They claim that race and racism are social constructions that have immense power. As a result, we should refrain from referring to them or measuring them because doing so breathes life into a damaging, violent fiction. The final group lies orthogonal to the other two. These folks claim that the concept of race is contextual and does not travel across national borders. While Black/White racism may present the most salient cleavage in the United States, this is not the case elsewhere. As a result, it does not make sense to consider racial inequality in migration at the level of the international system. Instead, scholars should focus on specific cases. To respond to these theoretical skeptics, I adopt and discuss the racial ontology of Alain Locke, which I allude to in chapter 1.

The technical issues associated with uncovering racism, racial bias, or racial inequality in international politics are similar to those in domestic political contexts. The first technical issue relates to the familiar problem of color blindness: laws are no longer explicitly racist, so how can we make credible arguments in favor of or against the existence of racism, racial inequality, or racial bias in international politics? Examples of obvious racism are rare in the modern international system, which complicates the task of making claims about racial inequality rather than mere circumstantial inequality. The second concern relates to a broader issue with studying ideologies. Racism is an ideology, and this ideology props up persistent racial inequality in migration. But there are serious technical concerns associated with studying such subconscious, background features of social life. Is the presence of ideologies or ideological thinking falsifiable? What are the barriers to evidence? How can one be sure that this project does not succumb to its own ideological thinking? The final technical concern is easier to describe, but it may be the least permissive obstacle. In short, data on international migration flows are notoriously poor and incomplete. This fact has prevented substantial growth in large-N studies of international migration that are commensurate with its importance to contemporary domestic and global politics.

The goal of this chapter is to be transparent and judicious toward those skeptics who may have either theoretical or technical concerns. To be sure, this list of concerns is not exhaustive. However, it provides a well-rounded overview of the various issues associated with uncovering racial bias in international migration in the present world.

Theoretical Concerns

In chapter 1, I outline the claim that modern immigration policies continue to disproportionately affect migrants of color. For many critical theorists, sociologists, and other analysts of immigration policy in specific cases, this is a familiar argument.[1] Laws that restrict immigration to only those migrants who make a certain amount of money, speak a given language, or employ certain skills are racially biased because these criteria are highly correlated with race. Color-blind schemes value certain technical skills and devalue

1. Boucher and Gest 2018; Ellermann and Goenaga 2019; K. R. Johnson 2000.

"nontechnical" skills, such as care-giving and hospitality, which biases immigration toward natives of Anglo-European countries. Although these systems do not explicitly refer to race, ethnicity, or nationality, they are discriminatory because they produce the *effect* of discrimination: they disproportionately restrict non-White migrants. This argument's warrant is simple: discrimination occurs when one group is privileged over another. Therefore, this argument implies that truly color-blind policies would not reproduce the same inequities that racist policies intended, and this idea has surfaced in the popular discourse over immigration policy.[2]

Some readers will take exception to this argument and its underlying logic. Identifying racial discrimination is difficult, particularly in an era when being called a racist is often seen as being more damning than actual racist behavior.[3] Skeptics often exclaim that one needs a "smoking gun" to call someone or some institution racist or discriminatory. In this view, claims in the absence of such evidence are a problem because they risk harming an innocent person's life without proper evidence. The interests of the discriminated rarely show up on this side of the debate. However, these concerns are important because they raise issues associated with inferring racial bias and discrimination in a color-blind world. Although I spent the bulk of two chapters outlining a story for how and why racial inequality can persist in the international system in spite of a lack of explicitly racist laws, I have yet to engage directly with these inferential concerns. I address this lacuna in the subsequent sections on the theoretical and practical issues associated with inferring racial bias in the modern, "color-blind" international system.

Racial Skepticism: Don't Play the "Race Card"

In this book, I wage a three-front war against different theoretical skeptics. The first front is against those who are skeptical of any racial inequality or discrimination in the absence of formally racist laws or "smoking gun" rationales for certain policies. I dub this category the *racial skeptics.* Racial skeptics argue that the absence of racist laws and the presence of migration flows from the global South invalidate the claim that racial inequality exists in the modern international system. How could one argue that such discrimination exists if I observe migration from East Africa to the United States? If immigration policies in Anglo-European countries were "racist" (as this skeptic would

2. Gest 2018.

3. López 2015.

characterize this book's argument), then we should observe the same international migration patterns as we saw during the era of explicit racial quotas. At the very least, we would not see the "vast" amounts of non-White migration that we see today.

Instead of racism, these skeptics lean on a different explanation for real and desired immigration policy restrictiveness. Citizens simply prefer hard-working immigrants in "high-status jobs," so they are more likely to prefer that their governments accept migrants who fit this profile. Opposition to other immigrants is not racist in this perspective; rather, opposition to immigrants from certain countries is just a reaction to "objective" facts.[4] Note how this argument slips into the historical precedent of preferring racially desirable migrants I describe in previous chapters. For centuries, Anglo-Europeans have used arguments about certain migrant groups' "values" and economic fitness to warrant exclusion. The United States restricted Chinese immigrants on their moral and social incompatibility with American society. These worries are similar to modern claims that migrants from certain places have inherent characteristics that make them unsuitable. The only difference between these arguments and previous warrants for restrictive policies is that the latter explicitly use the language of race while the former do not.[5]

Racial Eliminativism: "Races" Do Not Exist; Studying Them Gives Racism Credibility

The second group of skeptics is on the opposite end of the spectrum. This group, the *racial eliminativists*, is composed of those who believe that the study of race brings to life a discredited label. Eliminativists deny that race exists in any sense, which warrants its removal from public and academic discourse. Rather than not believing that racial inequality exists in the international system—like the racial skeptics—because they do not observe explicit racism, the second group believes that no one should use racial labels because doing so makes racism more likely. There is no biological basis to racial labels, so studying racial inequality in international migration gives race

4. Salam 2016.

5. However, some claims still rely on explicit racism. They describe non-White migrants as "lazy and aggressive" and worse: "Along those lines, the 'refugees' aren't really trying to prove themselves in combat or anything. It's just simple cosmic justice to them. You are silly and confused, and too pretty for your own good, western fool, so taste my boot. It will be good for you. You deserve this. Learn how to man up, for Allah's sake" (Deace 2017).

legitimacy that could be used for nefarious purposes. In other words, studying a pseudoscientific concept gives it scientific credibility even if it is not biologically true. Anthony Appiah has been a notable defender of this argument, though his position has changed somewhat over time.[6]

Racial eliminativists take one side of an important philosophical and ethical debate that takes place in the social sciences and humanities. This debate rages between eliminativists and constructivists, and it has deep implications for how scholars and policymakers engage with inequality throughout the world. On the one hand, eliminativists are correct that race has no biological foundation and that racial classification has been responsible for hundreds of millions of deaths throughout world history. I take this position seriously because one cannot dispute its premises and the consequences of abused pseudoracial science are severe. On the other hand, the fact that race is a social construct also *justifies* its study. Dominant groups impose racial categories to justify their own ambition, and therefore race has real effects even if it is not based in biological reality. This is an important distinction. Human culture and behavior create the effects of race, so even though it has no biological foundation, the term is meaningful. Humans still group other humans together on the basis of race, and there are important differences in opportunities, resources, and treatment on the basis of which grouping one belongs to.

Eliminativism has an important consequence that runs counter to its initial aims. Eliminativists argue that race does not exist, so it should not be studied; however, this logic can perpetuate racism. To be more specific, racism is an ideology: a set of ideas that justify a system of domination. Regardless of whether races are real, the ideology of racism is real because many employ its constituent ideas to justify why some people are more desirable than others. Many White Americans, for instance, believe that racism is a thing of the past because the law now prohibits racial discrimination. A corollary of this belief is that since racism no longer exists, then any remaining hardships that non-Whites face must be the result of some inherent failing.[7] Since one's life chances are no longer affected by racial prejudice or its historical legacy, then "some people" in society must simply be doing something wrong. This language is code for describing certain groups of people as inferior to others. Those in this camp lament when people "play the race card," and

6. Compare Appiah 1992 with Appiah 1996.

7. Bonilla-Silva 2012.

they argue that antiracist measures are unnecessary appeals to "White guilt" that extract undeserved, special treatment for non-Whites.[8] Many people throughout Western societies also find structural explanations unpersuasive, which amplifies these voices and attracts broad support. So eliminativism not only obscures our ability to reveal persistent racial inequalities; it also gives life to these forms of "dog-whistle" or "symbolic" racism.[9]

Racial Contextualism: "Race" Does Not Travel across National Borders

The final group of theoretical skeptics might be agnostic about the first two debates. Members of this group can be open to the idea that racial discrimination occurs in the modern international system, despite color-blind laws, but also can agree that race is important to study to uncover its persistent effects in modern society. However, members of this group, which I call *racial contextualists,* argue that it does not make sense to study racial bias in *international* migration because racial categories do not travel across national borders. For example, slavery and White supremacy have inculcated American society with a specific racial hierarchy, one that emphasizes a Black/White distinction and anti-Black racism. Although other races may exist, the most meaningful racial categories for citizens of the United States are White and Black. Yet, the White/Black distinction does not represent the most important racial contrasts in American immigration policy. In the United States, Mexican and Muslim immigrants are the immigrant groups that face the most othering and opposition. These groups are constructed as racial outsiders in the context of the politics of immigration despite not being racial categories that travel to different dimensions of American life, much less those of other countries. To put it differently, is it possible to study or uncover racial discrimination in international migration when the relevant racial categories are not stable within countries, much less between them?

This critique raises important concerns about the type of inference that I conduct below. How can I argue that racial inequality in the opportunity to migrate is truly "racial" for all people, in all countries, in all years? For instance, if I find that migrants from Central America migrate far less to Europe than they should given economic conditions, then is this inequality racial? This question relates back to issues of intentionality that I raise in chapter 1. Who

8. Bobo 2011; Shelby 2014.

9. Kinder and Sears 1981; López 2015.

are the racists in this story, and do those who make policy have to explicitly state their intentions to not let certain migrants in on the basis of their race? In the previous two chapters, I went to great lengths to claim that racial inequality exists *despite* such explicit intentions. The point is that non-White migrants from the global South can still face inequality even though laws are color-blind because the long history of Anglo-European exploitation constructed those from beyond the West as dangerous, poor, and otherwise undesirable. Those from the non-White world are inherently undesirable much in the same way the United States and other settler colonial societies viewed certain races as inherently undesirable. It does not need to be the case that racial categories cross national borders and contexts for the process of racial othering to take place. This argument resonates with how Charles Mills conceptualizes White supremacy as a global system. All societies do not need to hold the same racial categories for global White supremacy to exist. It just must be the case that individuals constructed as "White" are presumed to be desirable and those constructed as "non-White" are presumed to be undesirable. Although other racial categories may differ across time and space, the modern international system was born out of a racialized social system where, throughout history, those constructed as White were at the top of the desirability hierarchy and other racial groups fell below.[10] Therefore, racial inequality can persist in international migration if non-Whites migrate less than expected, regardless of whether cultures define race in the same way. All societies are participants—willing or not—of the same history that constructed the same system of global White supremacy.[11]

These three groups of skeptics come from different perspectives, but the underlying message of each is that identifying racial inequality in international migration is either irrelevant or impossible. These are important theoretical and ethical concerns. However, each falls back on a concept of racism that prioritizes the identification of individual acts of discrimination. In these accounts, racism is an action against *identifiable, well-defined,* and *universal*

10. Mills 2015.

11. This logic relates to the complement operation in probability theory. Global White supremacy ensconces those constructed as White (W) at the top of the hierarchy. This hierarchy, by construction, implies that everyone constructed as not White ($1-W$) is inferior. We do not need a consistent conception or social ordering of this pseudoscientific concept as long as we can identify the dominant group. Everyone not in the dominant group is inferior by definition, even if subcategories of inferiority are not consistent across space and time.

racial groups that reveals an *individual's* prejudice. The racial skeptics reject the existence of racism in migration because policies are color-blind and we see non-White migration in the Anglo-European world. Racial contextualists claim that racism in international migration is an empty concept because racial ontologies change from country to country. And eliminativists are concerned that studying a concept with no true foundations will bring it to life and encourage bad actors to weaponize it for nefarious purposes, like modern race science.[12] Each skeptic considers racism to be an individual act that racists deliberately perpetuate in the service of a racial belief.

Race and Racism in the International System

These theoretical concerns are important because each raises questions that possess the potential to damn a study of race and racism in the international system. If the target of an analysis is too muddled or too contested to allow study that is relatively undisturbed by existential issues, then the project is futile. Being required on every page to defend one's ontology—the stuff that is "out there" in the world—defeats even the cleanest analyses. As a consequence, I propose conceptions of race and racism that are faithful to extant scholarship and provide meaningful inroads into the study of the inequality that I theorize in the previous chapters. To do so, I rely on the work of Alain Locke, the first African American Rhodes scholar,[13] whose racial constructivism provides a clean base from which I can ground my theory of how racial inequality persists in international migration as the effect of the ideology of racism.

Alain Locke and Racial Constructivism

For most scientists and laypersons, the idea that race is a "social construction" has become a truism. The American Sociological Association epitomizes this common sense when it describes race as "a social invention that changes as political, economic, and historical contexts change."[14] The notion that race is a social construction is important to emphasize because it reinforces the scientific truth that races have no biological basis. Even studies that seem uncomfortably close to reifying a biological foundation for race find no evidence:

12. Schaffer 2007.

13. Henderson 2017, 111.

14. American Sociological Association 2003, 7.

studies of the complete genomes from all the world's regions find that, for example, there are *zero* genes for which sub-Saharan Africans have one genetic variant and Europeans have another.[15] Races are not scientific and have no basis in biology. They are invented.

But if race is a social construction, does that mean the eliminativists are correct? Does this mean that race is an empty concept both within and between states? In short, no, and a bit of perspective on the debate over racial ontology during the early twentieth century reveals more about what races "are" and how they operate in the modern international system. On the one hand, the majority opinion emanating out of the eugenics and scientific racism movement was that races were biologically real and that perceived differences between races boiled down to inherent, genetic differences.[16] According to this group, races are distinct, genetic, and scientific, and this perspective motivates the history of racial immigration restrictions I cover in chapter 2.[17] On the other hand, some anthropologists and social scientists argued that race is a cultural and historical construction with little grounding in biology. Many associate Franz Boas with this latter position, as he was the first to challenge contemporary "evidence" of the relationship between racialized physical attributes and intelligence.[18] Boas saw race as a social, rather than biological, invention, and he argued that most assumptions about inherent differences were a product of racism and political inclinations.[19] So when we say races are "constructed," we mean that human beings create them when they talk and act as if they are real.

However, Boas continued to presume that human groups had some hereditary differences, and this conception of race does not accord with modern scientific evidence: such biological differences do not exist.[20] To account for this evidence while remaining within a constructivist ontology, I adopt Alain Locke's conception of race. Locke's notion of race is powerful because it is completely devoid of biological or anthropological essentialism: he argues that race does not determine culture but that culture determines race. Cultural groups have features that the majority views either positively or negatively,

15. Yudell et al. 2016.

16. Locke 1924b, 164–165.

17. Kevles 1995.

18. Boas 1911.

19. Baker 1998, 94–95.

20. See Henderson 2015, ch. 3, for a complete discussion of how this debate and history fits into the epistemic silencing of the study of race and racism in international relations.

and if it is the latter, then that group is considered racially inferior. In other words, race is an "ethnic fiction" because it lies "in that peculiar selective preference for certain culture-traits and resistance to certain others."[21] Races have no basis in reality; they are social constructions because they exist only as perceptions of "favorable or unfavorable social inheritance."[22] Society constructs certain cultural traits as desirable and undesirable, and social groups that share those traits and a "common history or culture and occup[y] a geographic region" are defined as distinct races.[23]

Locke's conception of race fits nicely within the social constructivism that I adopt in previous chapters, and I elaborate further on this connection when I discuss the long-term effects of colonialism in chapter 6. In short, racial classifications depend on cultural practices because they have no scientific basis. As a result, their ontological reality in society depends on perceptions of the superiority and inferiority of certain groups and their social practices. Adopting this insight from Locke provides a key for theorizing how race and racism exist in the international system. Because races have no scientific reality, or true essence, we can rely on a purely constructivist definition devoid of pseudoscience. But such a constructivist definition does not preclude the importance of material realities. In fact, perceptions of the favorability of cultural traits are related to material conditions because they are often highly correlated with exogeneous interventions, like colonial exploitation *and the ideological motivations thereof*. Anglo-European states construct various non-Western practices as foreign or inferior to their own, many of which result from the actions of the Anglo-European states themselves. This knowledge about the construction of race produces insights into how we can study racism in the international system. It motivates a study of racism that goes beyond focusing on individual acts of prejudice and instead highlights the historical and institutional antecedents of perceptions of inferiority. I explore the implications of this conception of race for my argument in chapter 6, and I discuss it in conversation with recent antiracist scholarship.

Racism as an Ideology

Adopting Locke's racial ontology suggests a conception of racism that obviates the concerns of racial contextualists. In the rest of this book, I rely

21. Locke 1924a, 195.
22. Locke 1916, 12.
23. Stewart 1992, xiv.

on this conception of racism—one that focuses less on identifying individual racist actions and instead focuses on understanding the subtle dynamics of institutional racism. This book unmasks how the governing dynamics of international migration produce inequality for all non-White migrants, regardless of how they are racialized in specific contexts. This move is faithful to how Kwame Ture and Charles V. Hamilton wrote about modern forms of racism in *Black Power*.[24] In *Black Power*, the authors note that old-fashioned forms of racism were less common (even in the United States in the mid-1960s), yet racial minorities were still oppressed. In response, Ture and Hamilton developed a conception of racism that focused on the unfair burdens that racial minorities were forced to carry and how color-blind institutions continued to oppress non-Whites. They argued that antiracists should spend less time identifying individual racist practices and more time identifying whether major social institutions treat everyone the same, regardless of their race. Personal morality is less important than showing that the seemingly benign institutions of social life continue to produce unequal outcomes despite their putative color blindness.[25] To return to an example from chapter 1, it does not do society much good if all loan officers do not have racist beliefs, but the collective intentions of the mortgage market continue to disadvantage Black Americans.

I use similar logic here. The goal is not to tie individual actions to various laws nor is it to verify the racist intentions of various leaders. Instead, I intend to expose how the violent history of colonialism and its legal White supremacy created the conditions under which the "color-blind" institution of sovereignty permits states to pass face-neutral laws that allow racial inequality to persist. To this end, I define racism as an ideology.[26] However, I use the term *ideology* in a way that differs from everyday usage. Here, an ideology does not refer to one's preferences, for example, for a particular political doctrine. Instead, an ideology is a set of loosely connected attitudes, beliefs, and assumptions that appear universal or connected with universal interests, but instead mask specific power relations. And these distortions bring about or perpetuate unjust social relations.[27] For example, citizens may think that

24. Ture was born Stokely Carmichael, and he changed his name in 1978 to honor Guinean president Ahmed Sékou Touré and Ghanaian president Kwame Nkrumah (Kaufman 1998).

25. Ture and Hamilton 1967.

26. Bobo, Klugel, and Smith 1997; Fields 1990; Fredrickson 2002; Holt 2000; R Miles 1989; Shelby 2014; W. J. Wilson 1973.

27. Shelby 2003.

the free market is natural and beyond scrutiny if they live a society in which powerful actors have an interest in commercializing as many aspects of human life as possible and have been quite successful at doing so. This belief is not false; it reflects how things appear to work best in their society. However, "free" markets require powerful actors to constantly intervene to maintain their existence. Yet, people come to view the market as natural in societies in which that intervention has been successful over a long period of time. As a consequence, actors that gain from the market, such as private health care companies, are able to present their particular interests as universal interests. This ability to represent the free market as a universal feature of successful societies allows those with vested interests to maintain their power and ensure that the public supports them.[28]

In this case, racism is an ideology because it is "a set of misleading beliefs and implicit attitudes about 'races' or race relations whose wide currency serves a hegemonic function."[29] Although many people do not have stable or sophisticated views about race, the ideology of racism guarantees that their core background assumptions—their common sense—about those from different racial backgrounds affect how they engage with the social world. This is a form of bias; it can be conscious or unconscious, and its existence helps perpetuate White supremacy. These biases ensure that, when many think about their position on immigration, they react viscerally to the idea that people from certain countries will immigrate to their country because "those people" are violent, poor, or otherwise undesirable. For example, some postcolonial states appear objectively worse off than the Anglo-European world when one looks at measures of GDP, political violence, and human capital. And others that are economically developed, like China, appear objectively inferior on the basis of cultural differences. Applying Locke's reasoning, we can see how races and racial undesirability are constructed via this racism. These citizens will worry that these supposedly undesirable environments corrupt immigrants that grow up in them, which makes such migrants a danger to their new homeland. This reasoning leads the skeptic to use country-level information to infer that all immigrants from that state take on those same features, which is a form of ideological thinking. Using indicators that may be correlated with race to protect the state from dangerous immigrants does not appear to rely on racist illusions about the "natural" inferiority of non-Whites. Objective

28. Geuss 2008, 52.
29. Shelby 2014, 66.

statistical inference leads to these conclusions; there is no racism. However, this behavior is a form of racism because it uses aggregate data to make an argument about the inherent desirability of all individuals from that state.[30] It perpetuates a set of misleading beliefs about a group of people based solely on where they are from. These beliefs become seen as universal interests even though they only help support specific interests.

As a result, the drive to restrict undesirable immigrants reinforces ideological beliefs about the inherent dispositions of people from certain parts of the world. Those who defend practices of exclusion rely on these prejudices to justify them. So, although explicit racism is no longer socially desirable, racist assumptions about the desirability of certain parts of the world continue to be a part of the "background knowledge of everyday life."[31] When we see data and news images about violence in the Middle East, for example, we confirm that these people are just as we suspected and unfit to enter our society. A racist ideology thus legitimizes immigration policies that restrict objectively undesirable migrants. It "makes racial domination and exclusion appear legitimate by, for example, representing blacks [or any non-White group] as morally and intellectually inferior,"[32] and therefore not worthy of immigration. Put another way, racist ideology *reifies* oppressive social relations by making it appear that the "inferiority" of certain parts of the world is natural or universal, rather than the product of histories of human action (colonialism, slavery, etc.) and in the service of particular interests.[33]

This ideology does not require all countries to have the same racial categories, or even for a state's categories to be stable over time. Racism exists in the international system as long as ideological beliefs about the inherent undesirability of non-Whites pervade. An important implication of this construction of race and racism is that non-Whites themselves become a cog in the ideological machine that perpetuates racism. Postcolonial subjects experienced the brunt of Anglo-European colonialism, which led them to view other postcolonial subjects through the colonizer's lens. One can see this as a form

30. This reasoning is an example of the *ecological fallacy*, which occurs when one uses group-level data to make inferences about individuals.

31. Shelby 2003, 176.

32. Shelby 2003, 177.

33. Hunt 2009 applies similar insights to an analysis of the history of United States foreign policy. He argues that US foreign policy is informed by myths of national greatness, racism and racial hierarchy, and a hostility to social movements and change. These core ideas provide leaders with a clear and uncontroversial view of the world and a guide for action that reinforces those same ideological beliefs.

of propaganda; when colonial masters reinforce the superiority of "White culture," the natural inferiority of non-Whites carries through. This diffusion of ideology has deep implications for the contemporary international system. Indeed, a vital component of the theory of persistent racial inequality in migration is that postcolonial states internalize the logic of sovereignty, the duty to exclude foreigners, *and the ideology of restricting undesirables*. This process ensures that racial inequality persists and worsens in the contemporary international system as postcolonial states seek to restrict their undesirable postcolonial counterparts. To be clear, I am not arguing that postcolonial states and their leaders are "racist"; Anglo-European hegemony forced these states to adopt the nation-state form, which prioritizes border controls and the restriction of undesirable outsiders. This common sense is a product of Anglo-European colonialism and has catalyzed anti-immigrant movements throughout all regions of the global South.[34]

If racism is an ideology, then evidence that non-White migrants have fewer opportunities to migrate than their White counterparts is evidence of racial discrimination. Such inequality is a key implication of the common sense that migrants from certain parts of the world are inherently less desirable. It leads to formal and informal measures that perpetuate this inequality throughout the world. It need not be the case that leaders intentionally desire to restrict non-White migrants; rather, as long as states limit the immigration of those they consider undesirable, racial discrimination can persist. The objectivity of undesirability and its correlation with originating from the postcolonial world is sufficient to produce racial bias. Although race has no biological foundation, the social construction of difference through perceived physical differences, amplified through cultural and historical particularities, allows race to have important effects without being true.

Technical Concerns

These theoretical concerns are not the only issues associated with studying racial bias in international migration. While the previous section highlights several arguments against unmasking racial inequality in contemporary international migration, this section addresses technical concerns. Specifically, I deal with several obstacles that may prevent us from inferring racial bias in international migration in a world without racial quotas. Just as above,

34. Buehler, Fabbe, and Han 2020; Cogley, Doces, and Whitaker 2018; Meseguer and Kemmerling 2018; Peidong Yang 2018.

I address three separate points of contention: the lack of explicitly racist laws, the general difficulties associated with studying ideologies such as racism, and the issue of data availability.

The "Problem" of Color-Blind Laws

The first technical concern is not new; I have discussed the problem of written laws in previous chapters. Namely, it is difficult to identify racial inequality in migration because laws no longer restrict immigration on the basis of race, ethnicity, or even national origin. Explicitly racist laws were inferentially useful because they clearly delineated where racial discrimination occurred, who was perpetuating that discrimination, and its extent. Although the historical epoch of explicit racism and explicit racial quotas was undoubtedly a violent and inhospitable one for non-Whites, it was much easier to diagnose and, in theory, address putative concerns of racial bias. For example, the United States' Immigration Act of 1924 used a quota system to limit the number of immigrants allowed entry into the country. The act stipulated that countries would be allocated a number of visas equivalent to 2 percent of its population living in the United States according to the 1890 census. According to this system, it is straightforward to argue that the United States discriminated against migrants from country A more than those from country B if the latter had a higher quota. Moreover, since Asian immigrants were entirely forbidden and there were no restrictions on immigrants from Western Europe, one could unambiguously claim that the United States racially discriminated against Asians and preferred White Europeans.

Examples of such clear-cut discrimination are rare in the postcolonial international system. In a world in which the immigration laws of states no longer refer to race, ethnicity, or even national origin, it is impossible to make similar arguments about racial discrimination. For instance, one can argue that a given law that requires an immigrant to have a certain level of income is racially discriminatory because non-White migrants are less likely to meet that income threshold. Yet, this argument is *correlational*: a skeptic could always claim that there was no intention to discriminate against non-White racial groups. The government simply wanted to guarantee that immigrants would not become dependent on the state; it is not discriminatory to safeguard the public purse.[35] This argument has a familiar form. It reflects the

35. And even if the government did discriminate explicitly, it only did so to protect its national interest and the interests of its citizens.

same difficulties in inferring racial bias in the "color-blind" international system that I have discussed previously, and it is another key illustration of the theory for how race can continue to hide in face-neutral laws.

This technical concern restates the inherent problems associated with studying race and racial inequality in the international system, as well as within states. If one cannot look to laws or institutions that specifically discriminate, one will always be at the mercy of skeptics who dispute the mere association between race and opportunity. However, the inability to parse "real" racist intentions from "good" intentions that have racist effects does not mean that inequality is beyond the scope of study. Indeed, this issue does not preclude scholars in other disciplines from studying color-blind racial inequality. For example, although Thomas Schelling demonstrates that racial segregation can occur without explicitly racist intentions and laws,[36] sociologists, geographers, economists, and political scientists continue to study its pernicious effects.[37] These fields use a variety of methods to unmask segregation, study its effects, and consider mitigation strategies. The fact of the matter is that racial inequality remains, regardless of whether those who make laws and govern institutions intend to perpetuate it.

This project is a model for similar research in international relations. I posit a historical and structural account for how racial inequality persists in the modern international system, and I provide a variety of evidence to buttress each component of that theory. This argument does not preclude the difficulties in studying racial inequality in the color-blind international system. It remains the case that laws do not explicitly discriminate on the basis of race, and we still need a way of providing evidence on the basis of observed behavior. On the one hand, it would be irresponsible to abandon the study of racial inequality in international migration just because skeptics question its correlational or case-specific evidence. On the other hand, it is important to consider the most sound way of conceptualizing racial inequality in a color-blind world.

Can We Study an Ideology?

This latter issue raises a second, and related, technical concern. In the previous section, I make the case for studying racism as an ideology rather than

36. Schelling 1971.

37. Clark, Chein, and Cook 2004; Massey, Condran, and Denton 1987; Musterd and Van Kempen 2009; Williams and Collins 2001.

as an individual lapse in morality.[38] The logic is that individual acts of prejudice are less common in the postcolonial international system; however, racism continues to function in society and its institutions, so it cannot be the case that racism is reducible to individual racist actions. Instead, racism is an ideology—a set of commonly held beliefs or background implicit judgments that legitimize inequalities—that is attributed to social groups rather than individuals. This shift dampens the critique that racism does not exist in an international system where acts of explicitly racist sentiments and policies are on the decline. However, it does introduce an additional threat to inference: how to study an ideology and its effects.

Ideology is a Marxist concept, and a major critique of Marxian analyses is that they tend to be less than rigorous in their analysis of putative ideologies.[39] Indeed, even sympathetic opponents of Marxist approaches argue that they are arbitrary, reckless, flippant, and unscientific when unmasking ideologies in capitalist society.[40] As a consequence, when analysts proclaim something is ideological, they are using the term as a mere epithet with no deeper theoretical significance, because there is no scientific demarcation between the ideological and the nonideological. In other words, a limitation of many ideological critiques is that they are unfalsifiable: it would be impossible to contradict such a claim, even with the best available evidence. For example, I can argue that the free market is an ideology in the United States, but there is no way for me to prove this is the case. My argument's warrant rests solely on persuasion, insinuation, and anecdote. How would American society appear if the free market was not a dominant ideology?

The idea of racism as a global ideology, and the argument that racial inequality in international migration emerges from it, raises similar concerns. How can I unmask racial inequality in international migration, claim it arises from a racial ideology, and not fall prey to concerns that this argument itself is ideological or simply reflects my own beliefs rather than evidence? The answer lies in considering the nature of racist ideologies. It does not make sense to look for evidence in the minds of individual subjects because people are often surprised to find that they harbor racist beliefs, or are unlikely to report such beliefs,[41] and that the important effects of racial ideology are often

38. Shelby 2014.

39. Popper 1962.

40. Elster 1985, 460.

41. Corstange 2009; Kuklinski, Cobb, and Gilens 1997.

at the societal or institutional level.[42] Instead, one should study ideologies—specifically, racist ideologies—by looking at the effects that those ideologies produce. In other words, one should first form hypotheses about an ideology's observable implications, then look for those putative effects to judge whether an ideology obtains in a given context. This approach is falsifiable.

In the present example, I propose that we should observe racial inequality in international migration because such inequality is the result of a global racist ideology. To be sure, such inequality may be the result of a complex process, and racism is not the only possible explanation. However, if a global racist ideology exists, then we must observe the inequality. Put another way, racial inequality in international migration implies the existence of racism, but it is not sufficient to produce it. The inequality is necessary but not sufficient. Accordingly, not finding such inequality would falsify that hypothesis and call the theory into question. This simple move shows the advantage of using falsifiability as a benchmark when studying amorphous concepts, like ideologies and belief systems, particularly if they are socially undesirable. While falsification is not the only legitimate goal of science, it orients one's thinking toward skeptics and promotes intellectual empathy. Setting up a falsifiable hypothesis presents a high inferential bar, and finding evidence in favor of the theory under this framework is stronger as a consequence.

Data Availability: The Fundamental Problem of Migration Scholarship

The first two technical concerns associated with testing this theory of racial inequality in migration lead to a natural conclusion. Namely, we should look to the observed behavior of states and migrants to study this aspect of international politics. Racial inequality in international migration has natural implications, and if we do not find evidence for these implications, then we need to rethink our theory. Specifically, we should look to see whether non-White migrants are able to move to different countries as easily as their White counterparts and whether states enact more restrictive laws if they foresee an increase in racially undesirable migration. If we do not observe these patterns, then we must question the theory. It may be the case that racial bias

42. This point is one reason why Shelby argues (with others) that analyses of racism in society need to refrain from identifying individual acts of racism. These acts, while despicable, are less important than identifying how racism acts *institutionally*, and how such societial institutions reproduce racial inequalities. See Shelby 2014, 61–62.

and discrimination occur in individual instances but not at the level of the international system.

This strategy raises a final technical hurdle for this project: the availability of data. Data issues have plagued the study of global migration patterns, and Gary Freeman admits that while it is "time for scholars to turn their attention to [large-N] modes of analysis, the main obstacle to such research designs is the absence of sufficient cross-national data." For Freeman, this technical issue is the best explanation for why international relations scholars have paid so little attention to immigration over the years.[43] Likewise, this issue rears its head in this study. The ideal quantitative test for racial bias would be to see whether changes in immigration policy affected the volume of migrants from the non-White global South. Yet, this test requires three variables that are hard to measure. The first is a measure of bilateral migration flows. Until recently, the United Nations produced the only available data on global net migration estimates. However, net measures are notoriously misleading because they disguise underlying patterns.[44] Country-to-country measures of migration are superior because they are much more detailed and are able to unmask and explain global migration patterns. Unfortunately, only a small minority of countries collect annual flow data. Moreover, different national statistics agencies use different definitions and measures, and their data series rarely cover the same time period. As such, it is difficult to compare the available measures of bilateral flows.[45] In the next chapter, I take advantage of Guy Abel's new dataset on bilateral migration flows from 1960 to 2015.[46] These data overcome previous data availability issues because they cover every pair of countries in the world. The full data provide dyadic migration flow estimates for 196 countries and account for changes in populations due to births and deaths.

Second, immigration policies are difficult to measure, and most existing datasets are geographically limited to the OECD and a select group of other states.[47] It is not surprising that existing datasets on immigration policy are limited. It is not obvious what policies should qualify as immigration policies in a world without strict quotas. For example, it makes sense to include a reduction in the number of available visas as a tightening of immigration

43. Freeman 2011, 1548.

44. Rogers 2010.

45. Abel 2018; Kupiszewska and Nowok 2008.

46. This dataset expands on Abel's previous work with Nokola Sander that only provides estimates from 1990 to 2010 (Abel and Sander 2014).

47. Bjerre et al. 2014; Freeman 2011; Peters 2017; Shin 2017.

policy; however, is a change in the tax code that provides incentives to hire workers who do not need visas also an immigration policy? Such a change would lower incentives to immigrate to that country, but it is impossible (without an explicit policymaker statement) to infer its true intention. The global scope of immigration regimes makes reconciling these issues across states a daunting task, which is why most data on immigration policies are quite limited. As such, my initial unmasking of racial bias does not involve these policies. Instead, I take advantage of the panel nature of the migration flow dataset to account for destination-specific changes in policy restrictiveness. Later, I investigate the relationship between migration flows and immigration policies to build on this exposure of systemic inequality and test other components of the theory.

Finally, the cross-national measurement of race is difficult, and it is unclear how to infer whether inequalities in movement are associated with such racial perceptions. The measurement of race will always be a sensitive issue because of its obvious and violent historical legacy. White supremacists often use racial classifications to justify their presumptions about the inferiority of non-Whites, and I take these ethical concerns seriously. Yet, this eliminitavist position is a double-edged sword. On the one hand, refusing to measure race drains the concept of its legitimacy and prevents White supremacists from marshaling it for their own goals. On the other hand, this logic has produced examples like the French Republic, where a lack of racial measurement has obscured the real racial inequality that persists in a putatively colorblind society.[48] Moreover, simply refusing to study race and racial inequality in a quantitative sense does not ensure that race will not be reified. For instance, international relations scholars have increasingly turned to studying race and its role in constituting international politics and their discipline.[49] Each of these studies uses race as an object of study, and one can argue that this focus on studying race in the international system—albeit historically and qualitatively—reproduces the pseudoscientific concept as well. However, allowing for the ethical study of race in international migration does not solve the technical problem of how to actually measure it. In the next chapter, I go into more detail on how I operationalize race in international migration, paying particular attention to the issues of cross-national comparability that I raise above.

48. Ware 2015, 186.

49. Anievas, Manchanda, and Shilliam 2015; Henderson 2013; Gruffydd Jones 2008; Shilliam 2013.

Conclusion

This discussion has been a necessary prelude to the remaining chapters of this book. While previous chapters have theorized how racial inequality persists in international migration in a color-blind world, this chapter acts as a segue to testing the implications of that theory. Namely, I have taken the opportunity to address several theoretical and technical concerns associated with the analysis to follow. These debates are necessary because of the unique issues associated with studying race and racial inequality in international migration. Each step layers on additional complications in this analysis.

These complications are unavoidable. Studying the politics of race in the modern world will always address skeptics of the sort I describe above; some critics will always consider a focus on persistent racial inequality to be pandering or ideological when those affected simply need to pull themselves up by their bootstraps. On the other side of the debate, any measurement or quantitative study of race will concern others because of the ghastly history of race, genocide, and eugenics that have plagued the not-so-recent past. These discussions are unavoidable and reveal one reason why scholars have, perhaps subconsciously, given the study of race in international relations the epistemological status of silence.[50] Race and racism are not like war or trade. The latter have clear empirical implications. We can quibble about the best way to study war, be it using quantitative, qualitative, or interpretive approaches. We can debate thresholds for classifying something as a war, or how IR scholars should incorporate civil war into their theoretical frameworks. But war is war; it is a social fact of international politics that scholars agree exists. Race is a different matter altogether. No concept in international politics suffers from this extensive mix of theoretical, ethical, and technical concerns. One must address each sort regardless of audience: an IR scholar of any persuasion would ask such questions of any analysis of race. Such unanimity is rare in the social sciences.

As such, I have been as transparent as possible, and the purpose of this chapter is to lay all the cards on the table. In lieu of a magic bullet, the analysis that follows provides several types of evidence that international migration is not a color-blind process, despite what some policymakers and academics may believe. Migrants from poor, non-White, and postcolonial states migrate less than we would expect in a world in which only geography, economics,

50. Persaud and Walker 2001.

and other "rational" incentives affect migration patterns. I then show that OECD states have enacted increasingly restrictive migration policies after receiving inflows of racially different migrants. This is just one possible mechanism for perpetuating racial inequality, and it shows how the desire to restrict undesirable immigrants persists to this day. To complete the analysis of Anglo-European states, I dig deeper into how colonialism produced postcolonial states and migrants that the West claims are undesirable. I lay bare how the construction of racial undesirability and "obvious" reasons to restrict certain migrants today emerged out of the history of explicit racism during colonialism. To conclude the book's empirics, I provide evidence that the sovereign impetus to restrict one's borders and to prevent undesirable immigration has spread to the postcolonial world, producing more restrictions in the putatively color-blind international system.

5

Unmasking Racial Bias in a "Color-Blind" World

UNMASKING RACIAL INEQUALITY in international migration is difficult because systematic evidence of how racism affects larger migration patterns remains absent. States no longer restrict immigrants on the basis of race, nor do they use overtly racist justifications to warrant their immigration policies. Even leaders who have expressed racist opinions in the past continue to use race-neutral language to argue that their politics are objective and nondiscriminatory.[1] In this way, the end of explicitly racist policies, ironically, provides the most pressing obstacle to inference, and I outline several technical and theoretical consequences of this barrier in the previous chapter. In the end, I define racism as an ideology that has empirical implications. Doing so makes it possible to study color-blind racism in international migration. I argue that states still want to restrict undesirable immigrants, that these criteria for desirability are correlated with race, and this combination produces increasingly restrictive policies that lead to racial inequality.

Unfortunately, this move does not solve the problem of how to study this racism. There are two outstanding issues. The first concerns demonstrating that racial inequality in migration exists. This is the first step because, without this evidence, the rest of the theory falls apart. The second issue involves tying this inequality to the behavior of states. I presume that states pass restrictive laws when they are faced with increased immigration from non-White migrants. Leaders may not intend to respond to these inflows in a racist manner, but they do because of the aforementioned relationship between perceived undesirability and race.

1. Doherty 2018; White House 2019.

Accordingly, I address each of these issues in two separate steps. In the first part of the chapter, I use a forensic approach to infer racial inequality in international migration flows. This approach is forensic because it uses observed patterns in migration data to make inferences about underlying structural inequalities. Scholars use similar inductive approaches to study racial segregation in American cities: they compare observed residential patterns to those we would expect in a nonsegregated city to infer inequality in the absence of legal segregation.[2]

In short, I rule out all other possible explanations of international migration that are not explicit discrimination. The goal is to use standard economic, geographic, and political variables to explain as much of the movement between states as possible and then determine whether the remaining unexplained component exhibits patterns of racial inequality. These variables compose the "baseline model" of international migration that predicts how much migration we should expect to see between states in a world in which race, racism, or racial difference plays no role and all actors are rational profit-maximizers. Importantly, the baseline model is just a regression model, and the variables are just standard control variables.

After specifying the baseline model, I regress the observed migration flows between all states from 1960 to 2010 on these variables. Then I use the model results to predict how much migration we should have seen between every pair of states during this period. Finally, I subtract these predictions from the flows we observed to create a measure of how far the migration between two states deviates from the baseline world. I use these deviations as a first-cut measure of racial bias in international migration flows. If the model is correct, there would be no racism or prejudice, and the deviations would look like random noise. However, if racial bias exists, then we should see large deviations between observed and expected migration from non-White parts of the world.[3]

We cannot discern whether deviations are indicative of true racial bias or error. In fact, the motivating assumption in this measurement strategy is that deviations are composed of both factors, but it's hard to separate them. To remedy this issue, my goal is to show that non-White states suffer from larger

2. Duncan and Duncan 1955; Massey and Denton 1988; White 1983.

3. The analysis in this chapter builds on my previous work, which uncovered racial bias in international migration from 1990 to 2010 (A. Rosenberg 2019). In addition, Savage and Deutsch 1960 use an analogous strategy to measure deviations in trade flows.

deviations, which requires a measure of a state's race. However, the cross-national measurement of race is fraught because race is a social construction. It has no objective or biological basis.[4] Given this difficulty, I use several imperfect measures of racial difference to see if migration deviations are associated with racial bias. Keep in mind that this measure *does not* presume that all migrants from all states should migrate in equal numbers. Instead, I show that migrants from non-White states migrate less than we would expect *given their economic, political, and geographic circumstances*. This association provides a systematic measure of racial bias in the international system and shows evidence of its validity.

This approach sounds complicated, and in a technical sense, it is. I use a Bayesian approach to estimate the counterfactual model, which requires significant computational power, time, and technical expertise. However, anyone who has taken a basic statistics course can understand the interpretation of the underlying model, and any layperson should be able to understand the basic rationale for the approach. As such, I present as much detail of the model as possible without getting too bogged down in the mathematics and relegate the rest to appendix A.

In the second part of the chapter, I build on these patterns of racial inequality to explore why they persist. To do so, I consider the relationship between racially different immigration flows and restrictive immigration policies. In chapter 3, I argue that modern initiatives to restrict undesirable immigrants remain correlated with race. This proposal contains two empirical implications: (1) immigration policies have become increasingly restrictive over time, and (2) states enact these increasingly restrictive policies in response to receiving racially undesirable immigrants. Such relationships highlight how undesirability and racial difference remain bound together even though leaders no longer use racist language to justify their policies. I test both implications below.

The results are conclusive. I show clear evidence that immigration policies have become unambiguously more restrictive since 1960.[5] Although there are many reasons why states may be more reticent to admit outsiders, this analysis shows that race plays a role. Not only have Western states increased the restrictiveness of their immigration policies, they have done so after they

4. Morning 2008, 243.

5. Peters 2017 uses her own measurement model to show this increase in restrictiveness, while De Haas, Natter, and Vezzoli 2018 show that some types of policies are more restrictive.

experienced increased immigration from racially different immigrants. These results are important because they connect the forensic patterns in the first part to the larger story of that inequality's origins. Regardless of individual intentions, racial bias continues to course through patterns of international migration.

Such bias is precisely the sort of institutional racism that Ture and Hamilton warned about in the 1960s, and it has important, self-fulfilling consequences for how people view race and racial differences.[6] As such, measuring racial bias and its constituents presents a difficult, yet important, problem. This chapter fills an epistemic need because it reveals a dimension of the international system that the mainstream discipline ignores, provides the first batch of evidence for the claims of the previous chapters, and sets up the remaining empirical work below. In chapter 6, I explore the colonial origins of this racial inequality before showing the spread of closure throughout the postcolonial world in chapter 7.

Measuring Racial Bias in International Migration

To begin, the first part of this chapter uncovers color-blind racial inequality in international migration. This analysis does not presume that all migrants from all countries should have the same ability to migrate to every other country. Pointing to the fact that fewer Haitians than Australians migrate to New Zealand as evidence of racial bias is nonsensical. Instead, when considering racial inequality in international migration, I think in terms of *racial bias*. Racial bias exists when non-White migrants migrate less than their circumstances suggest.

The key word in this definition is *bias*. Something is biased if it is unfair, if it favors one group over another, or if it does not match reality. Everyone walks around with a folk definition of bias in their head, and we often find ourselves applying it to television personalities, articles, and news reports. Importantly, bias is a relative concept, not an absolute one; something is biased if it leaves out relevant information or seems wrong relative to our expectations. Without those expectations, it is impossible to talk about bias. Bias has a confrontational connotation, which leads most people to use the term as a pejorative, rather than as an actual critique. This conventional usage has rendered the term devoid of all but the most partisan meaning in most

6. Ture and Hamilton 1967.

day-to-day life. Indeed, many political science undergraduate and graduate students are surprised to learn the technical definition of bias in their statistics courses because of the conventional usage.

So why use the term *racial bias*, and how should we measure it? I use the word *bias* because of both the statistical and commonsense definitions. A statistical technique is unbiased if it gives you the correct answer on average.[7] Unbiasedness does not guarantee that any individual use of a technique will give you the right answer, just that the average of all your uses of a technique will be centered on the right answer. In other words, unbiasedness does not mean perfection; it only means that you could get the right answer in the long run. Racial bias in migration is a similar concept. Migration flows are not racially biased if any given non-White migrant is denied entry into the UK; migration bias is not an individual-level phenomenon. It could be the case that individual acts of prejudice or discrimination can help sustain racially biased practices, but racial bias in migration is the result of an *aggregate* process. Instead of considering the case of each individual migrant, the idea is that migration flows are biased if, on average, we see fewer people than we would expect migrating from country A to country B or from the global South to the global North.

The commonsense definition of bias is less technical. In common parlance, something is biased if it distorts the truth, if it is not fair, or if one side receives a disproportionate amount of favor. Typical examples of commonsense bias come from the news media. For example, one calls a television network biased if it misrepresents news stories that do not fit its perceived political agenda. In other words, our TV network is biased because it is not covering the stories as it should be covering them; the coverage is distorted or deficient compared to some baseline. In this same vein, scholars and urban planners who study inequality within cities proclaim a housing market to be segregated (their term for bias) if racial groups are not distributed across the neighborhoods relative to their proportion in the population.[8] This bias does not imply that all races should live in equal proportions in each neighborhood, only that they should live roughly proportionate to their numbers in the larger population. The concept of the relevant baseline is important when considering commonsense bias.

Let us unpack the idea of bias a bit further and relate it to international migration. The racial skeptics I describe above are the most hostile to the

7. Let $\hat{\theta}$ be an estimator of a population parameter θ. If $E[\hat{\theta}] = \theta$, then it is unbiased.

8. Massey, Rothwell, and Domina 2009.

idea that there is racial inequality in international migration. They do not dispute that races exist or that race is a meaningful concept, only that non-White migrants do not experience any inequality. The absolute number of immigrants guides this thinking, but our notion of bias reveals the flaws in this reasoning. To be more specific, these skeptics might argue that the United States is not "racist toward" (read: biased against) non-White migrants because it experiences "a lot of immigration from Mexico."[9] However, significant Mexican migration to the United States does not foreclose the possibility of racial inequality because racial bias is a relative concept, not an absolute concept. To determine whether there is bias in a given migration flow, it is not enough to show that some flow exists. The United States and Mexico are not autarkic; they both allow for immigration and emigration and are integrated into the world economy. Deeming that inequality does not exist because more than zero migrants from Mexico immigrate to the United States is an unrealistic standard. This position is akin to arguing that a neighborhood is not segregated if one non-White family moves in. Instead, one needs to look at whether there is more or less migration from Mexico to the United States *relative to a principled baseline.*

What determines this baseline? The modern international system is complicated because each state has a different relationship with every other state, and those relationships shape and are shaped by the contours of the global economy. Every bilateral relationship is unique and depends on the context of each state, their relationship, and the system in general. The United States and Mexico are contiguous, they have an intertwined history of conflict and cooperation, their economies are interdependent, and they have a long history of circular migration.[10] Compare this relationship to the United States and Fiji, which are far apart, have no shared history, and are less interdependent. No reasonable person would argue that the migration flow from Mexico to the United States should resemble the flow from Fiji to the United States. We have different baseline expectations because the contexts are so different.

The Measurement Strategy

This insight informs my strategy for studying racial bias in international migration. The first thing to do is set up baseline expectations for how much migration we should see between every pair of countries in the world and then determine whether our expectations match reality. Migration bias occurs

9. Salam 2016.

10. Balderrama and Rodríguez 2006.

TABLE 5.1. Example of dyadic migration deviations

Origin	Destination	Year	Flow	Baseline	Deviation
Italy	Argentina	2000	800	900	−100
Italy	Canada	2000	600	300	300
Italy	Nepal	2000	0	25	−25
Argentina	Italy	2000	600	350	250
Canada	Italy	2000	275	800	−525
Nepal	Italy	2000	5	0	5

when those expectations do not match reality, and racial bias occurs when that bias is larger for non-White states.

A key point, though, is that the baseline model reflects a fantasy world in which international migration is devoid of distortions like racism, and migration occurs when rational costs and benefits align. The baseline estimate simply takes into account the context of each sending and receiving state, as well as the relationship between them. Because the estimate only includes factors that should rationally affect different baseline levels of migration, such as distance, relative wage rates, previous colonial histories, and population, it provides a good benchmark against which we can compare reality.

I use this estimate to compare how much migration we see to how much we should have seen if we lived in an idealized world. This comparison is powerful because it allows me to say, for example, that we should see more migration from Ghana to the United States even though some migration exists between the two states. Some scholars will recognize this measure as a type of model residual. It is the simple difference between the data we observe and what the model predicts. In table 5.1, I provide an idealized example to illustrate this model in action. This table records how many migrants moved from Italy to three different countries and to Italy from those same countries in 2000. The fifth column lists how many migrants the baseline model predicts should have migrated during this period, and the final column subtracts the baseline estimate from the observed flow to indicate whether there was a migration overflow or underflow for each dyad during this period. This difference is what I call migration *bias* or the migration *deviation*.

This unit of analysis, the directed dyad-year, is ideal for examining individual cases: Did more or fewer people actually migrate from the United States to Mexico? However, it is not ideal for looking at global patterns of inequality in movement because it says nothing about the general ability to migrate from

TABLE 5.2. Example of sending-state migration deviations

Origin	Year	Outflow	Baseline	Deviation
Italy	2000	1400	1225	175
Botswana	2000	600	900	−300
Chile	2000	850	650	200

a given country. To investigate this question, we need to summarize these individual partnerships to see whether states are sending or receiving more migrants than we would expect. One way of summarizing these data is to add up all the pairs of migration deviations for every sending and receiving country in the world in each time period. In the case of table 5.1, we would estimate that Italy sent 175 more emigrants and received 270 fewer immigrants than the baseline model predicts. Table 5.2 reflects this calculation for Italy, as well as for two other countries. In the analysis below, I create these estimates for each country in the world in five-year increments from 1960 to 2015.

The final step is to use estimates of migration overflows and underflows to infer racial inequality in international migration. So far, I have argued that racial inequality in migration persists despite the end of explicitly discriminatory quotas. The implication of this argument is that we should observe migrants from the non-White world being less mobile than their counterparts in the global North. However, I do not suggest that, if we lived in a world without racial inequality, we would see more migration from the global South than the global North. Rather, a world without racial bias would exhibit *no pattern* in migration overflows and underflows. Migrants would move to and from all countries in amounts that more or less match our expectations given economic, political, and geographic context, and the bias that did exist would not correlate with race. Alternatively, if we see persistent underflows in emigration from non-White states, then we will have evidence for racial bias. This result means that fewer people are able to leave these states than we expect want to leave. We will see that global migration bias has increased since 1960 even as absolute migration has increased as well.

Accordingly, the empirical strategy in the rest of this part is simple. I provide more detail of the baseline model and the data therein. After creating the measure of the sending-state migration deviation, I investigate patterns in underflows. In a world without racial bias, we should not see any patterns in the deviation between baseline and observed levels of migration throughout the world; the deviations should look like random noise. In a world with racial bias, we should see emigration underflows from non-White states in the global South. This tests the *Racial Bias hypothesis*:

> *States from the non-White and/or postcolonial world will have systematically fewer emigrants than the baseline model predicts. This pattern should increase over time.*

Migration Flow Data

Recall that the lack of reliable data presents a substantial technical hurdle for studying cross-national patterns in international migration. Existing data on international flows are limited or inaccurate because these data are expensive to collect. States that do collect migration data often use different criteria for defining migrants based on their stated reason for migrating and their length of stay. The implication of these data issues is that cross-national comparisons have been difficult to conduct and detailed studies of international flows have been scarce. Moreover, this incongruence has forced large-N studies of international migration to focus on the determinants of inflows to the OECD and other states for which these data issues are less severe.[11] However, if one wishes to investigate trends in international migration to unmask inequality, data on the full population of migration flows are necessary. Ignoring all but the OECD and a few other states obscures the full patterns of the international system.

Recent innovations in measuring international migration flows have centered on indirect methods that use changes in bilateral stocks to infer movement. In previous work, I use data from Guy Abel and Nikola Sander, who estimate bilateral flows from 1990 to 2010 in five-year periods.[12] These data overcome previous availability issues because they cover every pair of countries in the world. The full data provide dyadic migration flow estimates for 196 countries and account for changes in populations due to births and deaths. Recently, Abel has updated this technique to "account for contradictions between demographic and stock data."[13] This new technique is an improvement because it uses a variety of migration stock and demographic data to estimate flows. The outcome is a vastly extended dataset that estimates bilateral migration flows by gender from 1960 to 2015.[14]

11. Ortega and Peri 2013.
12. Abel and Sander 2014; A. Rosenberg 2019.
13. Abel 2018, 811.
14. Abel 2018; Abel and Cohen 2019.

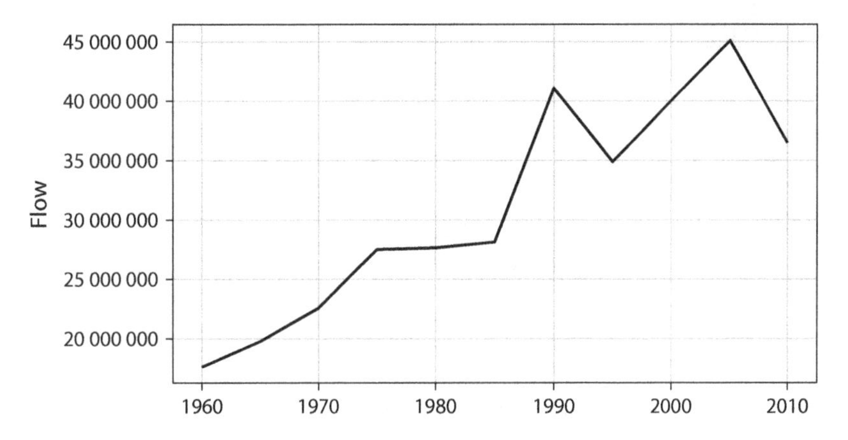

FIGURE 5.1. Estimated total global migration flow from 1960 to 2015 from the United Nations World Population Prospects (WPP) 2015 demographic data. Each point corresponds to the first year of the five-year interval. From 1960 to 1995, I use the 2011 World Bank migration stocks. From 2000 to 2015 I use the 2015 UN migration stocks.

In this book, I use these updated data as the dependent variable in the baseline model of migration. To summarize, the data used here estimate the migration flow between 41,568 unique pairs of states (dyads) in each of eleven five-year periods from 1960 to 2015. Note that these are directed dyads. For example, the migration from Germany to France from 1960 to 1965 is recorded independently of migration from France to Germany from 1960 to 1965. This choice allows the baseline regression model to make predictions about migration for both Germany to France and France to Germany.

Following Abel, I use the estimates based on the 2011 World Bank bilateral migration stocks from 1960 to 1995 and those based on the 2015 UN migration stocks from 2000 to 2015 in this analysis.[15] Figure 5.1 shows how global migration flows have changed over time, and figure 5.2 plots the distribution of bilateral migration flows in each time period. There are two important features of these data to note. First, figure 5.1 demonstrates that global migration has increased in absolute terms from 1960 to 2015. Although there is some period-to-period variation after 1990, the postcolonial international system is a more mobile world than the previous system. Second, figure 5.2 highlights an important feature of global migration processes: there is no migration between most pairs of states. In fact, from 1960 to 2015, over 60 percent of all pairs of countries experienced no migration. This *zero inflation* requires

15. Abel 2018, 820.

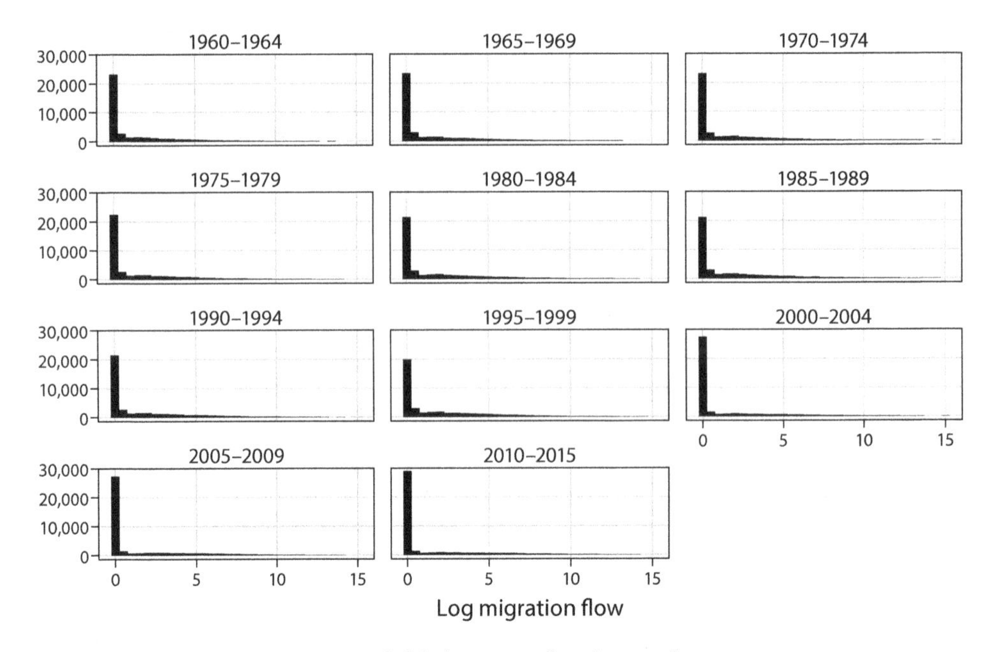

FIGURE 5.2. Logged global migration flows by period, 1960–2015.

a unique modeling strategy because the baseline model of migration will need to discriminate between dyads that we do not expect to have migration (because they are too far apart, etc.) and ones that otherwise could have had migration but did not.

The Baseline Model of Migration

The purpose of the baseline model is to construct the counterfactual world in which there are no racial or ethnic prejudices, and migration depends only on "rational" transaction costs. It is intended to be the closest possible approximation of a world in which only economic and political variables drive the migration between two states. In this world, flows between states occur if the economic and political fundamentals overcome other costs, such as distance and language barriers. To build the baseline model, I rely on the extensive literature on the determinants of migration flows. This literature investigates whether variation in migration flows is driven by destination state variables—mostly economic—"pulling" migrants, or origin state factors "pushing" them away.[16] CEPII, a French government research center

16. Data on existing migrant stock, population, bilateral distance, and contiguity are available at http://data.worldbank.org/.

on international economics, provides resources on most of these necessary data.[17] (These data are available at http://www.cepii.fr/CEPII/en/.) These variables would catalyze or inhibit migration between states regardless of processes such as self-segregation, preferential attachment, or specific policies in destination states. Accordingly, these variables represent the most comprehensive picture of what affects the migration between states in an ideal-typical world without racial bias. This choice keeps the baseline model within the well-established literature on the rationalist determinants of migration flows.

Geography. The baseline model of migration assumes that migration decisions boil down to the transaction costs and perceived benefits of migration for both states and individuals. Geographic barriers provide the first, and most obvious, barrier to migration between two states.[18] For even if we lived in a world in which only economic rationality drove the movement of people, geographic barriers to movement would still loom large. Accordingly, I include two variables that capture the geographic distance between origin and destination states: the logged bilateral distance between capital cities and an indicator for whether or not the origin and destination are contiguous. These variables control for the fact that migration is more likely between two states that are right next to each other and less likely between those that are far apart.

Social Networks. Existing social networks of migrants play a significant role in determining whether a particular country is attractive.[19] While scholars have long categorized these variables as "sociological"[20] or as a part of the "social process" of migration,[21] they fit comfortably within a rational, utility-maximizing model because they decrease expected risks and transaction costs.[22] Simply put, social networks in destination states make it easier for one to find work[23] and housing[24] and to integrate into host societies.[25] This support dramatically reduces the transaction costs of migrating to a given state and features prominently in the decision-making calculus. Therefore, any measure of migration deviations must take into account this rational self-selection in existing migration networks. To capture this important role,

17. Mayer and Zignago 2005.
18. Hatton and Williamson 2005; Ravenstein 1885, 1889.
19. Epstein 2008.
20. MacDonald and MacDonald 1964.
21. Massey and España 1987.
22. Faist 2000.
23. Joly 1987.
24. Sassen 1995.
25. Massey and España 1987.

I include the existing stock of migrants from the origin country that live in the destination. This variable accounts for the important history of migration from the origin to the destination, as well as prior influences on past flows. In addition, "the stock variable also captures prior institutional arrangements such as the history of guest worker agreements between countries."[26]

Economic and Political Conditions. In addition to geographic and social network variables, the economic and political conditions within states also play a large role in driving dyadic migration. The baseline model of migration includes several standard economic and political factors that spur or inhibit migration. In a world without racism, prospective migrants are more likely to move to states where the perceived economic benefits outweigh the costs of migrating.[27] First, I include a measure of the difference in logged GDP per capita for each dyad in the data. This measure captures both relative wage rates and the general economic health of each state. It represents purchasing power parity and is from the Penn World Table.[28] Second, to account for the effect of the poverty trap and other nonlinearities in income, I include the logged GDP per capita for sending and receiving countries, as well as their squares.[29] Third, I include the log population of the destination state because, all else equal, larger countries receive smaller migration flows and send more migrants to other states.[30] Fourth, I include the unemployment rate of the origin and destination state because migrants are less likely to travel to a state that has poor economic fundamentals, yet they are more likely to move if their home country has high unemployment. Fifth, I control for the education level of the origin state to account for the possibility that international migration is mostly composed of individuals with high levels of education.[31] If potential migrants are highly educated, it makes sense that they would be attractive to destination states for economic reasons. In addition, higher levels of education are related to higher levels of human capital.[32] Therefore, I use a variable that measures the average years of education among citizens who are older than fifteen.[33] Moreover, all states walk the line between potential economic gains and perceived security threats of

26. Fitzgerald, Leblang, and Teets 2014, 415.

27. Grogger and Hanson 2011; Kennan and Walker 2011; Ortega and Peri 2009.

28. Feenstra, Inklaar, and Timmer 2015.

29. Barro 2001, 13.

30. Fitzgerald, Leblang, and Teets 2014, 420.

31. Mountford 1997.

32. Barro 2001.

33. Coppedge et al. 2019, 375.

immigration.[34] As such, I include a measure of political conditions because different systems of government are more prone to accept immigration, even in a world without racism. This heterogeneity is due to the various incentives different governments—particularly liberal ones—face when trying to satisfy diverse interests.[35] Therefore, I include the regime type of both the origin and destination states. I use the continuous measure of liberal democracy from the Varieties of Democracy (V-Dem) dataset, as it better captures the variability of a state's regime type.

Colonial and Cultural Ties. Cultural linkages between origin and destination states also reduce transaction costs and make migration more likely. If we lived in the baseline world, then these cultural relationships would drive migration because moving to a place with a similar culture is more comfortable, all else equal. First, states that share a common colonial history likely have common cultural characteristics that would make migration less costly, such as common institutions. Second, and related, if two states share a common currency, then they most likely have common institutions that make transitioning easier. Finally, language is an additional factor that can reduce or increase the transaction costs of migration.[36] If two states do not share a language, then the costs of moving, getting a job, and settling in to a new life are dramatically higher. In addition, these factors are related to other social mores that affect one's day-to-day life. Migrating to a society that is similar in some important aspects makes the transition much easier and more available.[37] I include an indicator for whether a pair of countries shares each of these attributes.

Political Violence. Political violence also affects the propensity for migration between two states.[38] Civil wars and other man-made disasters have forced individuals out of their homes for centuries,[39] and any counterfactual model of migration without racism must take this "push" factor into account. Accordingly, I include an indicator for each sending country period that notes whether a state is experiencing a civil war, as defined in the UCDP/PRIO armed conflict dataset: "a contested incompatibility that concerns government and/or territory where the use of armed force between two parties, of

34. Adamson 2006; Rudolph 2003.
35. Bearce and Hart 2017; Breunig, Cao, and Luedtke 2012; Hollifield 2004; Money 1999.
36. Chiswick and Miller 1995.
37. Caragliu et al. 2013.
38. Schon 2019.
39. Breunig, Cao, and Luedtke 2012, 834–835.

which at least one is the government of a state, results in at least 25 battle-related deaths."[40] However, it is important to note that often migrants who flee civil war qualify under the refugee statute of international law because they have a "well-founded fear of persecution" in their homeland, and these migrants are captured in the migration flow data. Others do not qualify as refugees because they do not meet the strict standards of the statute. These migrants are not in the data, and therefore the parameter estimate from this variable is likely to be biased downward.

Statistical Model

These independent variables affect international migration in an ideal world without racism. In this section, I describe how I turn these variables into a machine that produces estimates for the migration we should see between states. In other words, how do these variables "become" the baseline model? Those without experience in quantitative methods can freely skip this section, but trust that there is no magic here. I just use the information provided by the variables in the previous section to arrive at sensible, fair estimates for migration between all states.

The baseline model of migration is just a regression model. It has a dependent variable (y)—the bilateral migration data—and several independent variables (X). When I fit this model, I estimate coefficients and use these coefficients to predict how much migration we should see between every pair of states.[41] Call these predictions $\hat{y}_{ij}$. This procedure is identical to generating fitted values from a simple regression model. After generating these predictions, we subtract observed migration from predicted migration $\hat{y}_{ij} - y_{ij}$ to estimate how much more or less migration we saw than expected. This number is our estimated migration deviation. We estimate the migration deviation in the exact same way one would estimate a residual from a standard regression model.

Although the baseline model is just a regression model, it is atypical in an important way. Previous studies of international migration use a version of the economic gravity model to estimate the determinants of flows.[42] The gravity model rests on an analogy between the migration flow between states and the

40. Gleditsch et al. 2002, 618–619.

41. Coefficients just tell us how much each variable is related to the migration between states and in which direction, i.e., *increasing* distance *decreases* flows.

42. Fitzgerald, Leblang, and Teets 2014.

gravitational pull between two bodies. This approach is ubiquitous in studies of trade and migration because of the strength of this analogy and because the strategy has produced consistent and reliable results for decades.[43] Scholars typically use ordinary least squares to estimate gravity models, which assumes that the dependent variable—migration from state A to state B—is Gaussian distributed, or shaped like a bell curve. However, this approach is not appropriate in this instance. Figure 5.2 shows that the international migration data are zero inflated. The high proportion of zero migration observations presents an econometric issue with linear gravity models because it severely biases inferences. The consequence is that such a model would not provide accurate predictions. If our baseline model does not provide valid predictions, then our estimates of migration deviations will also be invalid. Accordingly, I use a zero-inflated mixture model to estimate the baseline model. This model fits this analysis because it simultaneously models the zero and nonzero flows without inducing bias.

The baseline model is a mixture of two processes. The first process models the probability that no migration takes place between two states. The second component models the magnitude of the nonzero flows with a different probability distribution. To summarize, the baseline regression model gives predictions for the number of people that ought to have moved from one state to another. The use of the mixture model allows for an accurate prediction of the number of zeros, while allowing for the usual determinants to drive the magnitude of flows. Technical detail of the model can be found in appendix C. A frequentist version of this approach—the Poisson pseudomaximum likelihood model—has become standard in the literature for estimating gravity models of trade and migration in the presence of zero inflation.[44]

Scholars usually include destination-year and dyad fixed effects when they estimate models of migration.[45] The rationale is that a model with these fixed effects gives unbiased estimates of the casual effect of dyad-year–varying and origin-year–varying variables, such as border fences, on the migration flow between states.[46] However, I do not use the baseline model to estimate the effect of the independent variables. The goal here is to develop the best model

43. Carter and Poast 2020; Goldstein, Rivers, and Tomz 2007; Gowa and Hicks 2013; Tinbergen 1962.

44. Carter and Poast 2020; Beine, Bertoli, and Fernández-Huertas Moraga 2016; Silva and Tenreyro 2006.

45. Silva and Tenreyro 2006.

46. Carter and Poast 2020.

of the underlying data-generating process of international migration. The baseline model is a theoretical model; it is meant to include the important variables that should drive the migration between states. The actual coefficient estimates are not important. The predictions from this model, as long as it is theoretically sound, are the estimate of interest. This difference in target is what separates this analysis from most previous studies of bilateral migration flows.

As a consequence, I use *random effects* for origin, destination, dyad, and year. Using random effects in lieu of fixed effects allows the model to learn the variation between and within the groups in the data (countries, years, dyads, etc.). Models that use information in this way provide better predictions and estimates than fixed-effects models. Moreover, using a random-effects model allows me to retain the time-invariant variables in the model, like common language.[47]

Trends in Migration Bias

To begin unpacking the presence of racial bias in international migration, I first highlight the general pattern of migration deviations from 1960 to 2015. This trend shows the extent to which more or fewer migrants are moving than the baseline model expects, irrespective of region, race, and so on. To do so, I add up all the emigration underflows for every country in the world in each time period. For example, I add up all the country–time period emigration underflows in table 5.2 to get an estimate of the global migration underflow or overflow in each period. This procedure is a simple exercise in exploratory data analysis, but it is also a logically sound estimate: the baseline model estimates the underflow for each country, and adding up each of these country-level underflows is the definition of worldwide migration underflows.

Figure 5.3 presents this general trend in global migration underflows. The results are clear. Since 1960, there has been a steady increase in global migration underflows (i.e., fewer people have migrated than the baseline model

47. The fixed- vs. random-effects debate has raged for years, and it shows no sign of slowing down. In political science, most scholars are trained to use fixed effects because the conventional wisdom has been that this approach allows one to estimate causal effects from observational data. However, recent work calls this into question (Imai and Kim 2019). Regardless of one's position, applied Bayesian statisticians have long shown that random-effects models are ideal when one's goal is prediction (McElreath 2020).

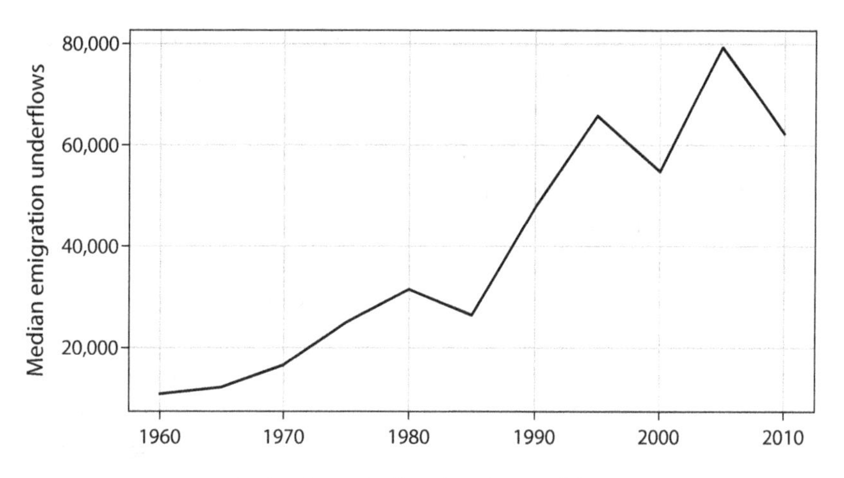

FIGURE 5.3. Emigration underflows have increased from 1960 to 2015.

predicts), and this underflow has gotten larger over time on average. Keep in mind that these estimates are based on legal migration flows: this measure of global migration deviations does not include irregular migration flows. This absence is important because it suggests that these estimates are conservative because irregular flows are not in the dataset. Although it is unfortunate to describe it in these economic terms, irregular flows represent a demand for emigration not captured in the baseline model. As such, I suspect that the true levels of emigration underflows in each period are larger than what we observe in the results.

REGION AND INCOME

Despite the aggregate increase in global migration from 1960 to 2010, the previous section shows that fewer people were able to migrate than the baseline model predicts and that this underflow has increased over time. This result may be surprising considering the recent angst in some political circles that the world is experiencing dangerous levels of unfettered migration.[48] In fact, only during early periods of decolonization did the world experience migration flows close to the magnitude the baseline model predicts, that is, if we lived in a world in which only rational variables affected the flows between states.

48. Kaplan 1994; D. Miller 2016.

However, this result says nothing about the topic of this book: Is there a *racial* bias in the opportunity to migrate worldwide? Naturally, this question is more conceptually and ethically difficult to investigate. To begin addressing this question, I uncover differences in migration underflows across several dimensions of international inequality that are often associated with racial difference. Race is a hierarchical concept, and the presence of W.E.B. Du Bois's "global color line" implies that non-Whites experience greater inhibitions on movement than their White counterparts. I have spent considerable effort discussing the difficulties associated with measuring race, but it is important to note that race is highly correlated with other variables, such as income and geography. In fact, this correlation is the point of studying race in an international context: certain countries are poorer than others, and those countries are often concentrated in certain regions of the world. There are historical antecedents for each of these correlations, and I unpack each of them in subsequent chapters.

One simple way of thinking about the global color line is along the global North–global South divide. Scholars have long used the global North/South distinction to refer to income disparities between the "developed" (i.e., the OECD) and the postcolonial world. In common usage, being in the North implies that a country has a high level of economic development; however, most usage of these labels is rhetorical, and there are few attempts at systematically categorizing countries on this basis. Be that as it may, the North/South divide is useful for thinking about the global color line because of its natural association with race. Most countries in the global South are predominantly non-White despite their large diversity of ethnic groups. As such, comparing Northern and Southern countries resembles a racial comparison, and many scholars refer to countries in the global South as being "racialized" or constructed as "racially distinct."[49]

The North/South divide represents a useful way to conceptualize racial differences in the international system because its clearest discriminating dimension is income. So, although there are few clear guidelines for separating the countries of the world into racial categories or into North/South bins, looking to differences between income groups can illuminate racial differences in the international system.

For now, I begin with investigating how different countries with different levels of income—as defined by the World Bank—compare. These results are

49. Mullings 2005.

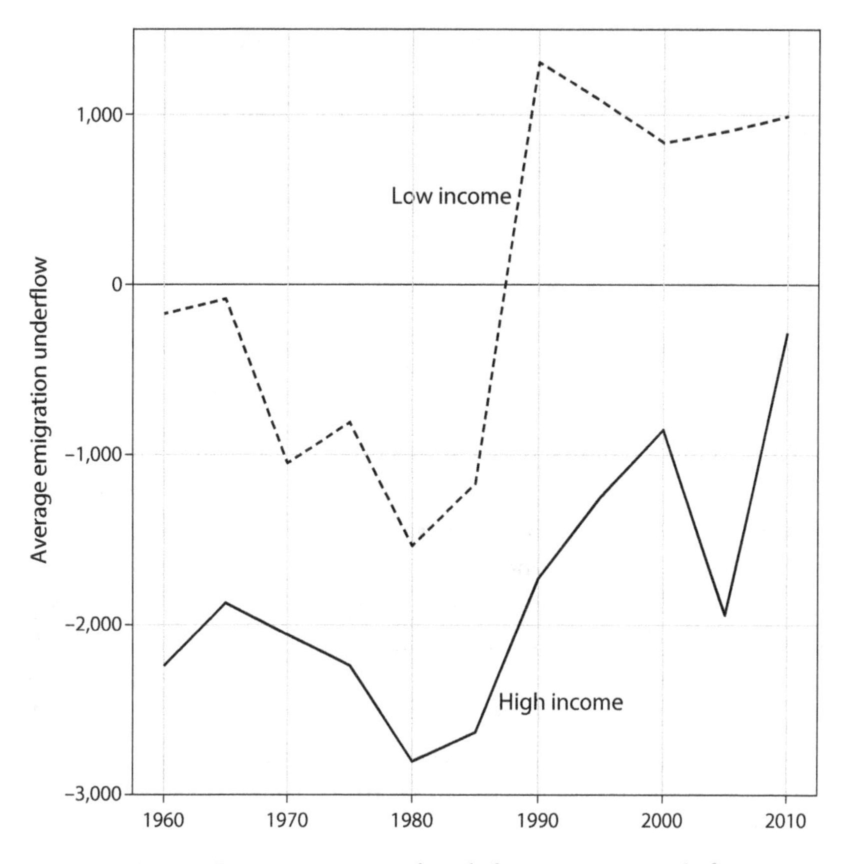

FIGURE 5.4. Low-income countries have the largest emigration underflows.

found in figure 5.4. Two results stand out. First, in every time period, there is a persistent gap between high- and low-income countries. In other words, citizens from high-income countries have a greater ability to migrate than those from low-income countries. Although I do not present the other income groups (low-middle- and high-middle-income), these states fall in the middle. The presence of a gap between high-income and low-income countries is not sufficient to show that there is a racial bias in the opportunity to migrate to other countries. However, it does show a correlation between income and the ability to migrate relative to baseline expectations, and if we think that race and income are correlated for historical reasons, this result corroborates the theoretical expectations I lay out in chapter 3.

Second, we notice that both income groups have emigration overflows during the first six periods of the analysis: on average both low- and high-income

TABLE 5.3. Average migration bias by world region

	Region	Migration Bias
1	Central Asia	3700
2	Sub-Saharan Africa	1518
3	Middle East & North Africa	1106
4	East Asia & Pacific	−8218
5	South Asia	−8376
6	Latin America & Caribbean	−9550
7	OECD	−19262

Note: This table shows the average emigration underflow in each of the world's regions.

countries had more emigrants than the baseline model predicted, indicating a glut in global migration from these two income groups relative to rational expectations. Between 1985 and 1995, this pattern changed for citizens of low-income countries. During this period, these countries experienced a sharp reversal in fortune: they went from experiencing emigration overflows to emigration underflows. This reversal is consistent with the overall trend toward increased immigration policy restrictiveness over the same period. All in all, this comparison shows that the world has been a less receptive place for immigrants from low-income countries since 1985. Economic theory suggests that citizens of low-income countries should be attractive to employers in richer countries due to their relatively low wage demands, as well as incentivized to move abroad to reap the higher return on their human capital. Yet, we see migrants from poorer countries being less able to migrate, even taking factors such as credit constraints, geography, and education into account.[50]

To home in on racial differences in international migration bias, I move from income groups to regions. It is true that racial differences in the international system often reduce to income differences; however, there are several states in other income groups that we would consider "non-White" or postcolonial, such as Congo-Brazzaville, Kenya, Nigeria, and Zambia. Although the World Bank does not classify these states as low income, we have reason to believe that Western countries would consider their citizens to be undesirable migrants due to their religion or perceived lack of education. Accordingly, I next look to see whether regions with non-White states have larger emigration underflows. These results are found in table 5.3.

50. Hatton and Williamson 2005.

Several features stand out in this table. First, central Asia and sub-Saharan Africa have the largest emigration underflows. With the Middle East and North Africa, they also are the only regions whose average value is positive, indicating that all the countries have emigration underflows rather than overflows. Central Asian countries include Kazakhstan, Kyrgyzstan, Russia, Tajikistan, Turkmenistan, and Uzbekistan, which suggests that post-Soviet countries that have not joined the European Union experience far less emigration than the baseline model expects. Their value of 3,700 means that each country in central Asia, on average, sends 3,700 fewer emigrants to the rest of the world than expected. To be sure, it is unclear whether this region's underflows are driven by the postcommunist distinction. However, being a postcommunist state brings with it a host of cultural differences that are bound up with the concept of racial undesirability, particularly given our adoption of Locke's notion of race as an ethnic fiction.

In addition, the fact that sub-Saharan African countries have the second-highest emigration underflows is also not surprising and corroborates the suggestion that there is a racial bias in the opportunity to migrate. The migrants from these regions are considered racially different or undesirable for similar reasons. Migrants from each of these regions are culturally different from those in the global North, and they possess the stigma of a lack of human capital.

A second feature that stands out in table 5.3 is that the OECD falls at the other end of the spectrum. Citizens of the OECD migrate far more than the baseline model predicts, which implies that other countries place a premium on migrants from these countries. This is not surprising considering the countries of the OECD are predominantly rich and racialized as White, both of which carry a natural association with desirability. The difference between the OECD and sub-Saharan Africa is stark and can be found in figure 5.5. Surprisingly, the region with the second-largest emigration overflow is Latin America and the Caribbean. This result indicates that those from this region migrate more than the baseline model expects, which may lead some to question the existence of racial bias. However, migration to the United States accounts for a majority of this overflow, and we will see that dramatic changes to immigration law accompanied these overflows in later years. In fact, the migration overflow becomes an underflow in later periods, as the United States responds to overflows from Latin America with greater restrictions. This cause and effect is not represented in these migration bias estimates, but the analysis below demonstrates that the effect of these overflows ensures that they will

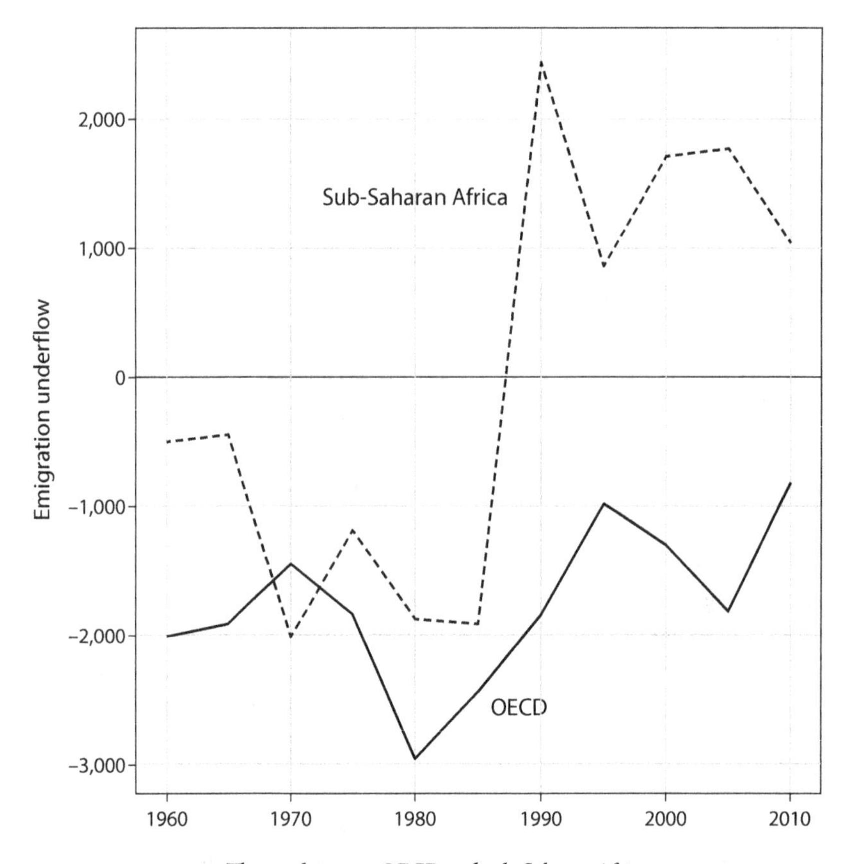

FIGURE 5.5. The gap between OECD and sub-Saharan African countries.

not be present in the future. US immigration policy during the Obama and Trump administrations is indicative of these trends.[51]

In general, looking at differences between the global North and global South reveals important patterns in the ability to migrate from 1960 to 2015. It is clear that citizens of low-income countries are far less mobile than their richer counterparts, and this pattern accords with the theory that desirability still runs through processes of international migration in the current day. But are these patterns racial? Above, I looked to see whether there are regional differences in the ability to migrate, and I found patterns that suggest that inequality in migration is a complex picture. This much we knew. In the next

51. Andreas 2012; Coleman 2005; King and Valdez 2011; Nevins 2002.

section, I explicitly look to racial differences to discern how much of a factor observed racial differences play in one's ability to migrate worldwide.

RACIAL BIAS

Given the conceptual ambiguity of using regional and income differences to proxy for race, I next use an explicit measure to study system-wide racial inequality in international migration. I use this measure of race to directly address the Racial Bias hypothesis: I expect that migrants from non-White states will have systematically larger migration deviations than migrants from White states and that this difference will increase over time. I find broad evidence for this hypothesis, but this analysis reveals added nuance.

As I mention above, the measurement of race is fraught with ethical and technical issues. Ascribing racial categories to an individual based on their country of origin has a dark history that requires mindfulness and attention to why such measurement may be problematic. Moreover, it is also technically difficult. States are diverse and their populations change over time. Is the United States a "White" state? Either response can have dangerous implications and may be more or less correct depending on the year in question. In this book, I do not measure the race of any individual, nor do I argue that racial categories are natural categories that remain stable throughout space and time. Instead, I use the language of race to consider how others may knowingly or unknowingly discriminate against others based on a scientifically unsound category that remains socially powerful.

To do so, I rely on one specific measure. Canadian public health scholars have created the only accessible measure of race that does not rely on old-fashioned racist pseudoscience. These scholars use Statistics Canada's official visible minority groups and *The CIA World Factbook* to estimate racial categories based on country of origin.[52] This measure corresponds well with the definition of race that I use above: descent-based classifications, imposed by others, that racists can wield with negative intent. Even though such a classification is overly coarse because most states are diverse, it picks up on the idea that race is a relationship between persons mediated through things. For instance, when the United States enacted the Chinese Exclusion Act, the Chinese were a racial category because they were a distinct, externally defined group with a common origin that were considered undesirable.

52. Rezai et al. 2013, e87.

While Chinese subjects may not have considered themselves a race, their social position constructed it into being. Rezai et al. did not create this measure with ill intent. They created the measure to reveal persistent racial inequalities in immigrant health outcomes. I adopt this measure for similar purposes.

To be clear, I use this variable for practical reasons: it is the only measure available that classifies states based on racial perceptions.[53] Public health experts and epidemiologists use this measure to study the etiology of diseases across populations, inequalities in health outcomes across immigrant populations, and different practices of health care delivery.[54] In many ways, this effort to measure racial differences in health outcomes is the polar opposite of the French case I highlight in chapter 1. France does not collect racial statistics because under the mystique of the French Republic there are no racial categories, only French citizens. However, this leaves the French government blind to the inequalities in health, education, violence, and so on within its population. The logic of using a racial measure is that, despite its ethical issues, measuring and revealing these inequalities is a vital first step to designing policies to combat them.

Beyond these practical concerns, this measure remains consistent with the ontology of race that I adapt from Alain Locke in previous chapters. Recall that Locke argues that race has no biological basis; it is merely a social construct. Biologically distinct categories of human beings neither exist nor represent anything real about our species. Instead, "race" is "simply another word for a social or national group that shared a common history or culture and occupied a geographical region."[55] This conception of race fits comfortably within both the existing policies of race and racial inequality within states and my argument about racial bias in international migration. It is not the case that each country throughout the world has an overlapping or consistent racial ontology. Instead, international and local history—in our case, colonialism and imperialism—inflicted real and perceived harm onto certain areas of the world that led to the construction of people from these regions as inferior, dangerous, or undesirable. As Locke notes, people from the same geographic location have similar cultures and histories that produce socially constructed

53. For example, an immigrant from Botswana is classified as being from a "Black" state. This is the only measure that classifies the race of immigrants based on country of origin.

54. Rezai et al. 2013, e86.

55. Stewart 1992, xxiv.

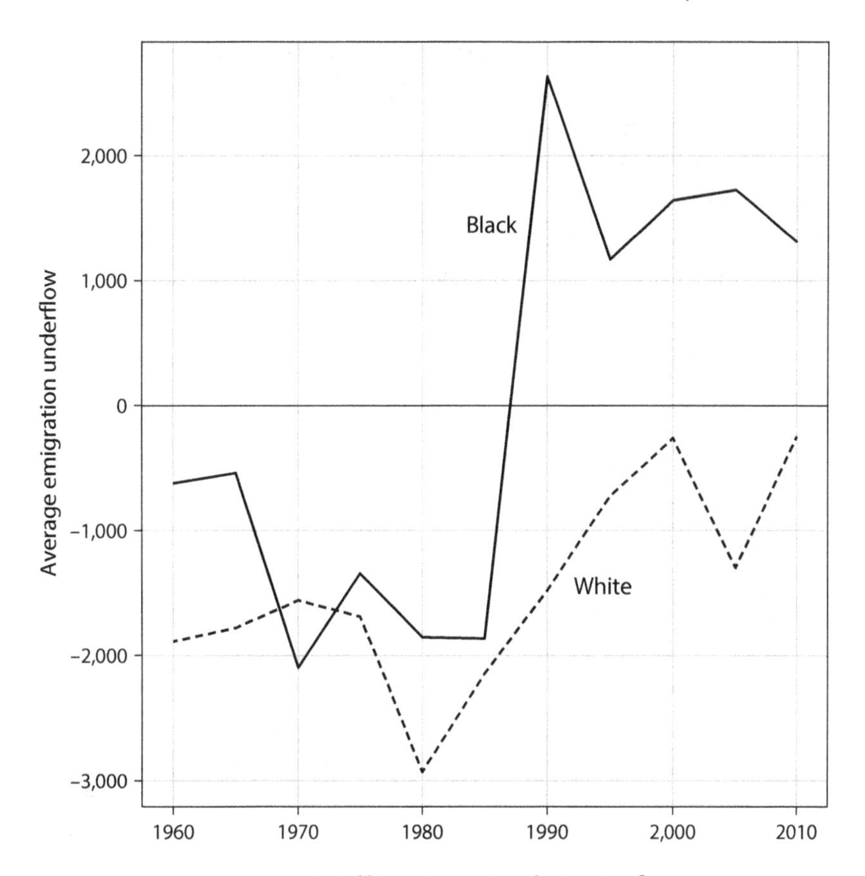

FIGURE 5.6. Racial bias in international migration flows.

racial categories, many of which fall along national or regional lines.[56] The Rezai et al. measure is a good, if imperfect, approximation of this conception of race applied to the international system because it explicitly adopts this idea that broad cultural characteristics are correlated both with pseudoscientific racial classifications and geography.

Figure 5.6 provides evidence of how racial bias in migration has emerged and evolved since 1960. In this figure, I look at those countries in the "Black" and "White" categories. I make this choice because it is the most salient difference for thinking about racial inequality in the international system. The results paint an interesting historical picture. During the early years of the

56. "[Race] must be explained in terms of social and historical causes such as have caused similar differentiations of culture-type as pertain in lesser degree between nations, tribes, classes, and even family strains" (Locke 1924a, 192).

time series—from roughly 1960 to 1980—there was little difference between the migration bias faced by Black and White migrants. Importantly, both of these racial groups had emigration overflows. This means they experienced more emigration than the baseline model predicts. This pattern is similar to the overall trends in the data and accords with labor patterns and policy in the post-WWII era. Figure 5.3 shows the general upward trend in migration bias during this period, and the other figures in this section paint a similar picture for the other comparisons of interest.

Once again, the mid-1980s were an inflection point. After this period, we see dramatic differences between White and Black states. While White states still experience emigration overflows for the remainder of the time series, Black states now experience underflows, and the observer will notice the precipitous difference that has opened up between the racial groups. This trend tracks with the evidence from elsewhere in this chapter and in other scholarship: although raw immigration flows have increased since decolonization, policies have gotten more restrictive and immigrants from the global South are now moving in numbers far less than we would expect.

Keep in mind that these are just the raw data. I simply added up the migration deviations by race for each year and made a line plot. That is why the lines in figure 5.6 are so volatile: one or two outliers in either direction can pull the lines up and down. To be more precise, I fit a multilevel regression model that only has random intercepts for year and race. This model estimates the mean migration deviation by race. Rather than just assuming that each racial category and year are independent groups and that one cannot learn anything about the migration deviation in one group by looking at another, this model updates its inferences about each year and group as it moves between them. Not estimating averages in this way would be akin to assuming that you cannot learn anything about the average migration deviation in 1990 from investigating the deviation in 1985. This approach provides much better inferences about the differences across years and racial groups.

The results of this exercise are in figure 5.7. In this analysis, I took the profile of the "average" White and Black state and used the fitted model to simulate the migration deviation for each from 1960 to 2015. In this way, I avoid the pitfalls of outliers, and we can better observe the substantive differences between the groups. As you can see, there are no differences in the slopes of the lines. This is by construction: I am making the assumption that each racial group will be affected by the unobserved variables within each year in the same way. The difference to note is *between* the lines. This figure makes it

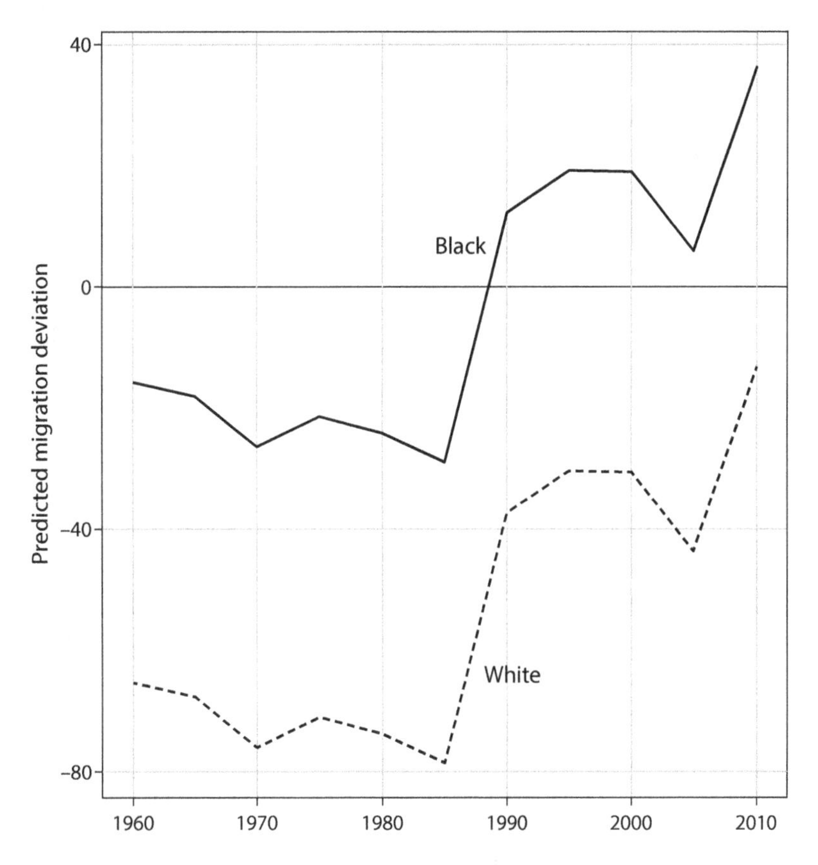

FIGURE 5.7. Simulated differences in migration bias between White and Black states, 1960–2015.

much clearer that there are pronounced differences between White and Black states. Although I estimate that both groups experienced overflows from 1960 to 1985, there is far less ambiguity in this model. It is clear that Black states still experienced larger deviations than White states, even though both experienced overflows during this period. Moreover, while this model estimates that White states still had more emigration than the baseline model predicts from 1990 to 2015, it reveals profound racial inequalities between White and Black states, particularly since the end of the Cold War.

To conclude, the descriptive evidence in this section presents racial inequality in international migration in several ways. Whether one considers race along regional, income, or explicit lines, this analysis provides evidence that the ability to migrate relative to expectations is not distributed evenly. We do see less inequality in the 1960–1985 period, but this relative parity immediately gives way to stark inequality that remains to this day. In the next part of the chapter, I explore one reason why this inequality emerged: Western states enacted restrictive laws after experiencing migration overflows in the immediate postcolonial period.

Racial Bias, Racial Difference, and Migration Policy

Observing racially biased migration flows reveals that migrants from the poorer, non-White states of the global South move less freely than those from the global North. This pattern emerges even in the nominally equal, postcolonial international system. Indeed, this analysis demonstrates both a lack of equality and equity in international migration. One may protest that these results simply reflect that prospective migrants from sub-Saharan Africa, for example, are less educated than those from Western Europe, and therefore it does not make sense for them to move in equal numbers. To be clear, these patterns are not mere artifacts of the differences among different regions of the world. The strategy I use above averts this concern: the unequal patterns explicitly account for these differences. The results above show that migrants from the global South move less freely *relative to baseline expectations* that account for these differences. Not only do migrants from the global South not move equally, they do not move in numbers that their position in the international system affords them. This inequity is color-blind racial bias.

From where does this bias arise? The theory in chapter 3 describes how the history of colonialism and chattel slavery produced conditions in the postcolonial world that leaders and citizens now routinely highlight as "undesirable" or threatening to the national interest. This is how race and racial inequality continue to hide in an international system without explicitly racist policies. When we assume that independence is sufficient to remove racial inequality, we miss how the history of White supremacy impacts a state once it is free. Racism fades away without the ability to highlight explicitly discriminatory policies. But those policies that replaced discriminatory quotas must be responsible for biased migration flows, at least in part. Immigration policies are the principal way states control who is allowed to enter and join their political community. Politicians still design immigration policy to encourage some types of immigration and discourage other types. Even if it is unclear whether these policies work,[57] it is the case that restrictive immigration policies can

57. Czaika and Haas 2013, 2014.

still produce inequality and bias even if they do not discriminate on the basis of race, ethnicity, nationality, or religion. As such, in the remainder of this chapter, I test the *Racial Reaction hypothesis*:

> *When Anglo-European states receive increased immigration flows from racially different migrants, they should respond with an increase in immigration policy restrictiveness.*

In contrast to the first part of this chapter, this analysis is monadic—it takes place at the country-year level. I investigate whether a destination state in a given year enacts more restrictive immigration policies after it encounters racially different immigrants in previous years. Although we cannot know for sure whether states and their leaders only respond to the perceived "threat" of racially undesirable immigration when making their policies, the goal of this analysis is to control for other possible explanations for policy changes to isolate this association. These results are not a causal (or explanatory) panacea; they are merely an important first step toward discerning how the allegedly nondiscriminatory policies of states in the modern international system can perpetuate tremendous inequalities.

Dependent Variable: Immigration Policies in the Developed World

I do not suggest that immigration policies have universally become more restrictive since decolonization. Indeed, De Haas et al. show that immigration policies on average have become less restrictive in the Western world.[58] However, there is considerable variance in restrictiveness across dimensions of immigration policymaking. Although some policies have become more lenient—those governing high-skilled workers, students, and refugees—others governing border control, exit, irregular migration, and family reunification have become more restrictive. This heterogeneity reveals the complex reality of immigration policymaking in which different dimensions become more lenient while others become more punitive.[59] This reality emerges because immigration policymaking often requires complicated bargaining among different stakeholders with different interests, particularly in liberal democracies. For example, Martin Ruhs and Philip Martin argue that one must distinguish policies that affect the number of migrants from those that

58. De Haas, Natter, and Vezzoli 2018.
59. De Haas et al. 2018, 325.

affect the rights the states afford to those migrants upon arrival.[60] They posit a trade-off between volume and rights; for instance, an initiative in liberal democracies to expand the rights of immigrants—such as family reunification—should accompany policies that restrict their absolute numbers.[61] This balance of permission and restriction tilts global patterns of international migration away from the non-White global South, even though migrants that do manage to move often receive more rights than they would have in the past.

Raw patterns in immigration policy data support this trade-off hypothesis. In this analysis, I use an immigration policy dataset from Oxford University and the Amsterdam Institute for Social Research to explore the determinants of immigration policymaking. Table 5.4 presents the DEMIG policy data, which tracks over 6,500 immigration policy changes from forty-five countries from the eighteenth century through 2013. As this table shows, there is considerable variation in the time series available for each country. Accordingly, this analysis focuses primarily on the period from 1945 to 2013.

To construct the database, coders classify whether each immigration policy represents a "more restrictive" change (labeled +1), a "less restrictive" change (labeled −1), or no change in restrictiveness (0) within the context of that country's system.[62] As such, the unit of analysis in the DEMIG policy dataset is a policy change occurring within a specific country in a given year. The DEMIG team chooses to measure immigration policy changes because the stated goal of their project is to generate new insights into how states and their policies affect migration processes, as well as how these policies evolve over time. To be sure, this coding scheme is quite simple, and one may worry that it fails to account for the full complexity and nuance of policy realities. The trade-off between nuance and parsimony is inherent in any coding scheme, and the DEMIG team chose to prioritize comparability, which requires a degree of simplicity.[63]

Immigration policy changes fall into four categories: border and land control, legal entry and stay, integration, and exit.[64] Border and land control policies regulate internal and external borders. These policies include surveillance, detention, and other acts of bordering and restriction to secure the

60. Ruhs and Martin 2008.

61. Freeman 1995; Hollifield 2004; Ruhs 2013.

62. De Haas, Natter, and Vezzoli 2015.

63. De Haas et al. 2015.

64. DEMIG 2015.

TABLE 5.4. Country-years included in the DEMIG policy database

Country	Years
Argentina	1812–2013
Australia	1901–2013
Austria	1863–2014
Belgium	1920–2014
Brazil	1822–2014
Canada	1867–2013
Chile	1824–2013
China	1850–2013
Czech Republic	1990–2012
Czechoslovakia	1918–1993
Denmark	1950–2013
Finland	1900–2012
France	1793–2014
German Democratic Republic	1949–1990
Germany	1913–2014
Greece	1856–2012
Hungary	1920–2014
Iceland	1898–2012
India	1874–2013
Indonesia	1945–2011
Ireland	1900–2013
Israel	1948–2012
Italy	1861–2013
Japan	1885–2014
Luxembourg	1940–2014
Mexico	1821-2013
Morocco	1912–2014
Netherlands	1892–2014
New Zealand	1840–2012
Norway	1888–2013
Poland	1919–2012
Portugal	1959–2012
Russia	1721–2014
Slovak Republic	1990–2012
Slovenia	1991–2012
South Africa	1900–2011
South Korea	1910–2013
Spain	1852–2014
Sweden	1894–2013
Switzerland	1848–2013
Turkey	1923–2014
Ukraine	1991–2013
United Kingdom	1905–2013
United States	1790–2013
Yugoslavia	1918–1992

TABLE 5.5. An excerpt from the DEMIG policy dataset

Country	Year	Policy Change	Policy Area	Restrictiveness
Italy	2009	Law 94 of the "Pachetto Sicurezza": made it easier for foreign grads of Italian universities to find jobs	Integration	Less restrictive (−1)
Italy	2009	Law 94 of the "Pachetto Sicurezza": can detain illegal immigrants in detention centers for 180 days	Border and land control	More restrictive (+1)
United States	2005	Real ID Act of 2005 that increased surveillance technologies used for border security	Border and land control	More restrictive (+1)
Sweden	1985	Foreigners given permanent residence permit if they were going to be in the country for >= 1 year	Legal entry and stay	Less restrictive (−1)

national territory. Legal entry and stay policies involve all areas related to entry and stay permits. Integration policies regulate the postentry rights of immigrants and other target groups, such as refugees. Finally, exit policies regulate forced or voluntary exit, such as deportation and other methods of return. Table 5.5 presents an excerpt from the DEMIG policy database to show how coders took individual policy changes, examined their content, and classified them by policy area and level of restrictiveness. In most cases, this coding is straightforward. For example, in 2005, the United States enacted the Real ID Act. DEMIG coders classified it as a more restrictive border and land control policy because it increased surveillance technologies used for border security.

While the policy change in a given year unit of analysis may be useful for certain applications, the goal of this analysis is to determine whether previous racially different immigration affects contemporaneous policy changes. As a first approximation, I use addition to aggregate a country's individual policy changes into one number for a given year. In other words, if a country passes two more restrictive policies and one less restrictive policy in a year, their overall policy restrictiveness change will be +1. In figure 5.8, I plot immigration policy changes in each of these four categories for Argentina, Canada, Denmark, France, Japan, South Africa, Sweden, the United States, and the United Kingdom. I choose these countries because they vary in geography,

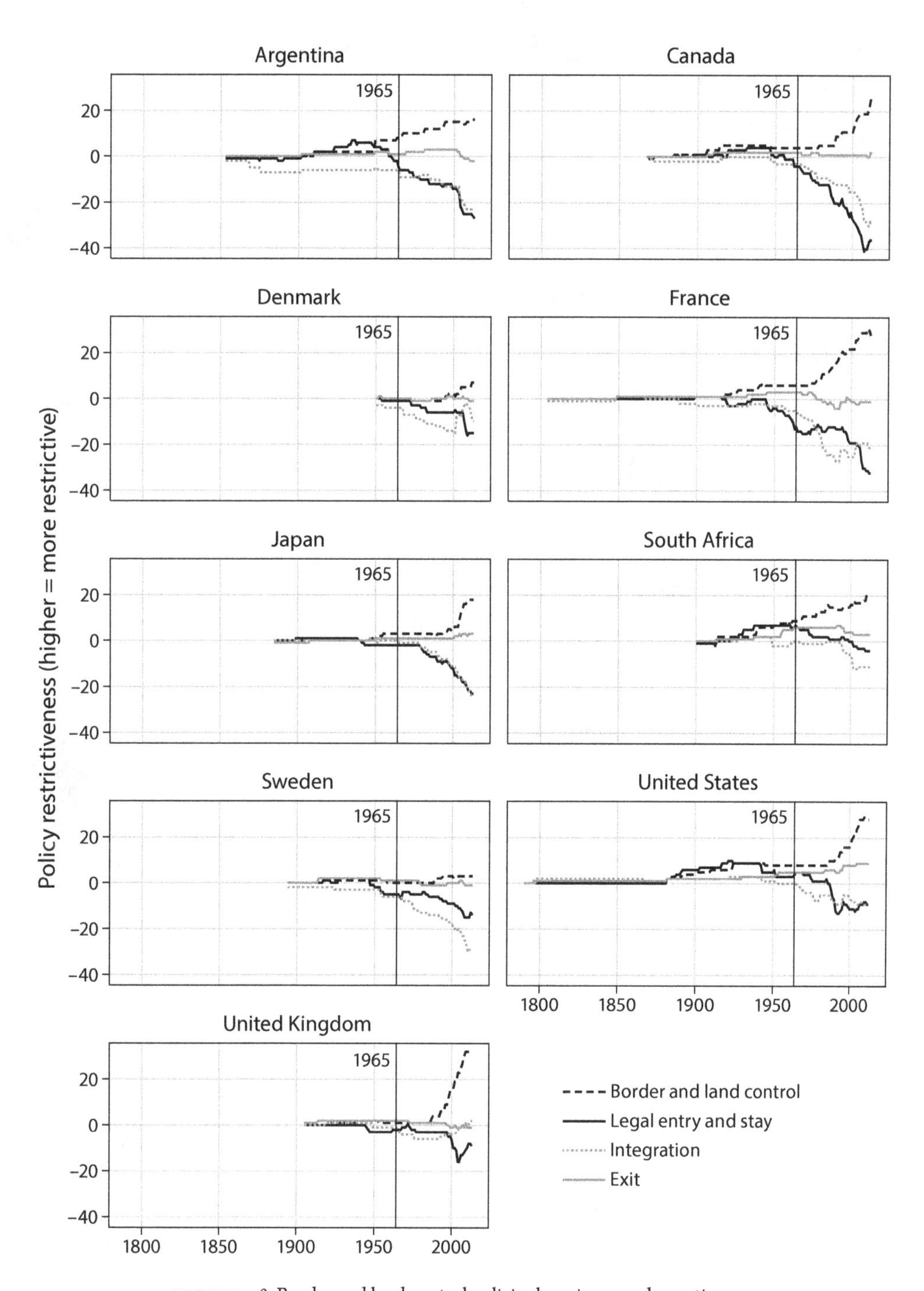

FIGURE 5.8. Border and land control policies have increased over time.

colonial history, and "demand" for immigration. One can see that border and land control and exit policies have become more restrictive since decolonization, while legal entry and integration policies have become more lenient. These patterns reflect the shifting priorities of rich states in the postcolonial era. When explicit racism lost its normative authority in the second half of the twentieth century, integration and entry policies became less restrictive and border and land control and exit policies became more restrictive. Although it is risky to read too much into these descriptive shifts, this changing pattern is consistent with Western countries pushing their desire to limit undesirable immigration from one policy dimension into another. States can no longer explicitly discriminate on the basis of race, but they can enact increasingly restrictive bordering and exit policies that covertly target those same undesirable migrants.

Immigration Policy Restrictiveness as a Latent Variable

Although the DEMIG data comprehensively cover all immigration policy changes in this sample of states, it is still not obvious how to measure a state's overall level of restrictiveness. For instance, should we just add up all the state's policy changes in a given year? Or should we limit ourselves to just one of the four policy dimensions? In the previous example, I chose a compromise between these choices: I used simple addition to approximate a country's change in immigration policy restrictiveness in a given year.

But while it is simple to infer whether an individual immigration policy represents a change toward more or less restrictiveness, it is not clear how this accounting translates to inferring how policy changes contribute to changes in the overall level of restrictiveness. Do policy changes contribute linearly to overall restrictiveness? Exponentially? Logarithmically? Moreover, adding up policy changes tells us something about how the explicit letter of the law changes, but it reveals nothing about a state's underlying restrictive intentions, which are vital to the story of racial bias. The theory suggests that states become more restrictive after they receive more racially different immigrants, not that they enact more restrictive border and land control policies. The DEMIG team even explicitly states that their coding scheme is based on "the *explicit text* of the policy measure, not our subjective interpretation of its *underlying, alleged implicit or 'hidden' political intentions*"[65] (emphasis mine).

65. De Haas et al. 2015, 13.

The aggregate, underlying, and "hidden" nature of restrictive policy intentions, coupled with the fact that observed immigration policymaking occurs along multiple dimensions, reveals that overall immigration policy restrictiveness is a latent, or unobserved, multidimensional quantity. Each state in a given year has an unobservable disposition toward immigration that manifests in various observed policy changes. In this way, immigration policy restrictiveness is similar to measures of a student's analytical and verbal skills,[66] the political ideology of legislators,[67] and a country's level of democracy.[68] In each case, scholars only have observed measures on various indicators (correct/incorrect answers to specific questions), which they must use to make inferences about their latent quantity of interest (underlying ability).

Measuring overall immigration policy restrictiveness poses a similar inferential problem. We cannot directly observe a country's overall level of immigration policy restrictiveness; we only observe policymaking behavior. We observe various policy changes in a given year, but each policy and policy area's contribution to latent restrictiveness may vary across both countries and years. Moreover, as with any other problem of inference, an unstated issue with measuring immigration policy restrictiveness is measurement error. Whether we use a simple or sophisticated method to aggregate different indicators into one measure of an underlying trait, we always do so with error. Simply using addition to summarize policy changes ignores that some policy changes may have a larger impact on overall restrictiveness, depending on the context. To remedy these issues, I use a statistical technique called the *graded response model* to measure the immigration policy restrictiveness for each country and each year.

The graded response model is agnostic about these questions, and it uses information across countries and years to estimate a state's underlying level of policy restrictiveness in a given year. For instance, it learns from the data whether increasingly restrictive border and land control policies contribute more to a state's overall level of restrictiveness in a given year compared to the other categories, countries, and years. This technique is a fully Bayesian version equivalent to Peters's approach to measuring overall immigration policy restrictiveness.[69]

66. Samejima 1997.

67. Clinton, Jackman, and Rivers 2004.

68. Treier and Jackman 2008.

69. Peters 2017, 44, 285–287.

TABLE 5.6. United States immigration policy changes, 2005

Country	Policy Area	Policy Change
United States	Border and land control	3
United States	Exit	1
United States	Legal entry and stay	1
United States	Integration	−1

Here is the basic idea: The graded response model treats a country's underlying level of restrictiveness as a latent variable that predicts whether a country enacts a more or less restrictive immigration policy in a given year.[70] We cannot directly see a country's overall level of immigration policy restrictiveness, but we can assume countries that are more restrictive enact more restrictive policies. Every year, countries either enact an immigration policy change or not in each of the four policy areas. The model assumes that a country's latent restrictiveness affects its change in observed policy. More restrictive countries are more likely to enact more restrictive border and land control policies, and so on. The model estimates how restrictive a country's immigration policy is in a given year from these observed changes. This approach is the same idea as that behind standardized tests. In a standardized test, the administrator uses a student's responses on various questions to model her underlying ability in a given area, such as mathematics. This model of immigration policy restrictiveness is the exact same process, except now I use a state's observed policymaking behavior in four categories as the dependent variable in a type of generalized linear model. The model produces a distribution of parameter estimates that correspond to a country's latent level of restrictiveness in a given year.

Table 5.6 provides an example for the United States in 2005 to show how the model behaves. One can see that the United States became more restrictive in border and land control (three more restrictive policies), exit (one more

70. The graded response model is a type of ordered logistic regression. I use a fully Bayesian approach to estimate this model. The advantage of this strategy is that I estimate the joint posterior distribution of all parameters in the model, which means I estimate the *uncertainty* in the immigration policy restrictiveness of each country in each year. I model the response to the observed indicators directly as a function of the latent variable for each country-year. The difference between this model and the factor analysis approach used by Peters 2015 and others is that factor approaches are models for the covariance structure among factors and not for the factors themselves (Treier and Jackman 2008, 205).

restrictive policy), and legal entry and stay (one more restrictive policy), but became more lenient in integration policy (one less restrictive policy). One can think of these yearly changes as a country answering four different test questions in each year of the dataset, one for each category. The model then assumes that the United States' underlying policy restrictiveness in 2005 drives these individual policy changes and uses this information to make a prediction about that level of restrictiveness. Importantly, I use Bayesian inference to estimate this model, so each estimate of policy restrictiveness has many possible values, each with an associated probability.

The graded response model is illuminating because it allows us to combine information from different policy areas to estimate each country's unobservable level of restrictiveness. Without a principled statistical method for making this inference, we would underestimate both levels and variance in overall immigration policy restrictiveness. To see why, consider figure 5.9. In this figure, I plot changes in border and land control policies and legal entry and stay policies. One can see that these patterns are mirror images of each other. As policies that control legal entry have gotten more lenient, those that control the border have gotten more restrictive. If we merely added these policies together, they would cancel each other out, and we would miss the important shift from one form of control to another. Specifically, we would obscure the fact that bordering policies became dramatically more restrictive after 1980, while policies that control legal entry became more lenient, but with far greater variance across countries. The graded response model parses the number and magnitude of immigration policy changes and estimates a country's underlying level of restrictiveness in a given year from these changes that often pull in different directions and in different magnitudes.

Figure 5.10 displays several important implications of the graded response model. First, figure 5.10(A) provides country-level estimates of immigration policy restrictiveness. One can see that restrictiveness varies substantially across countries, with some countries—such as France—displaying consistently high levels of restrictiveness and other countries—such as Iceland—displaying consistently low levels of restrictiveness. One should interpret this figure as a country's *average* level of immigration policy restrictiveness from 1945 to 2012 and appreciate that there is significant within-country variance in restrictiveness that accounts for the fact that countries can go through cycles of restrictiveness and leniency. Second, figure 5.10(B) shows convincing evidence that the countries in this sample have gotten unambiguously more restrictive since 1990. This result accords with the evidence in figure 5.3 that

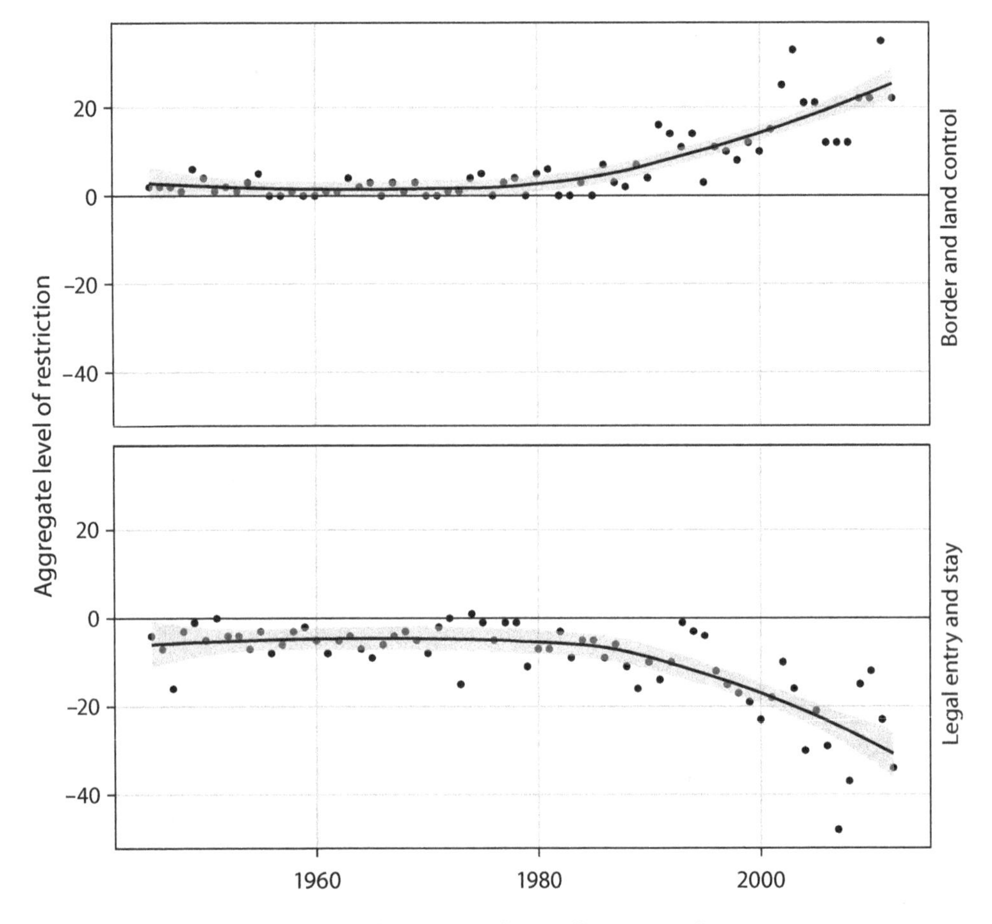

FIGURE 5.9. Bordering and legal entry policies pull in opposite directions across all countries in the DEMIG dataset.

shows worldwide emigration underflows increasing from 1960 to 2015. The countries sampled in figure 5.10(B) are mostly to the left of zero from 1945 to 1990, indicating a general pattern of openness in their immigration policies. However, since 1990, the yearly averages have shifted dramatically to the right, indicating a general pattern of restriction.

In the next section, I reveal the associations between the composition of immigration flows and subsequent policy restrictiveness. For simplicity, I return to the aggregate measure of restrictiveness, but the results are robust to various measures. While there may be several possible explanations for why states become more or less restrictive, an influx of racially different migrants moves states to become more restrictive. I do not dispel all possible alternative explanations; rather, the goal of the remainder of this chapter is to establish a plausible story for how racial bias can persist and hide in color-blind international politics. The desire to restrict racial undesirables never went away; only now, it hides in the increasingly restrictive, putatively race-neutral policies of the postcolonial era.

Three Measures of Difference

I argue that states enact restrictive immigration policies when they receive inflows from migrants whom they perceive to be racially different or undesirable. This argument raises the issue of how to measure racially different or distant immigration flows, which is a particularly thorny problem because race is not a scientific concept. As such, I cannot measure it and neither can anyone else. Does a solution exist? On the one hand, this book purports to unmask racial bias in international migration in a quantitative fashion. Such a goal seems to presume that I can use some measurement strategy. On the other hand, measuring race or racial distance directly is not scientifically defensible because it is a social construct that has no genetic basis. While human groups certainly possess a range of observable characteristics, and phenotypes are associated with genotypes, no such groupings are distinct enough to permit any racial classification by any scientific standard. Dominant groups have used a wide and inconsistent range of characteristics to impose racial classifications that are constituted arbitrarily across space and time. Even though they seem obvious, everything we "know" about different races depends on our own social, political, economic, and historical context because there is nothing inherent or objective about them. This is what it means for race to be "socially constructed" and why different countries have different racial categories. This point represents the culmination of over one hundred years of scholarship throughout the social and natural sciences that vitiates the concept of race as being a natural or scientific kind. As such, I do not wish to acknowledge these conceptual points, but then use a measurement strategy that walks back or disputes this progress.[71]

As an alternative, I use three different indicators that do not (and cannot) measure race but are useful for testing the argument above. The first way I measure the volume of "different" immigration flows is to calculate the *average ancestral distance* of a country's immigration flows. A destination country receives immigration flows from several origin countries, and each origin country is a different ancestral distance away from the destination, just as each

71. I thank Errol Henderson for pushing me on this point and for providing guidance on the social scientific study of race and where this project fits.

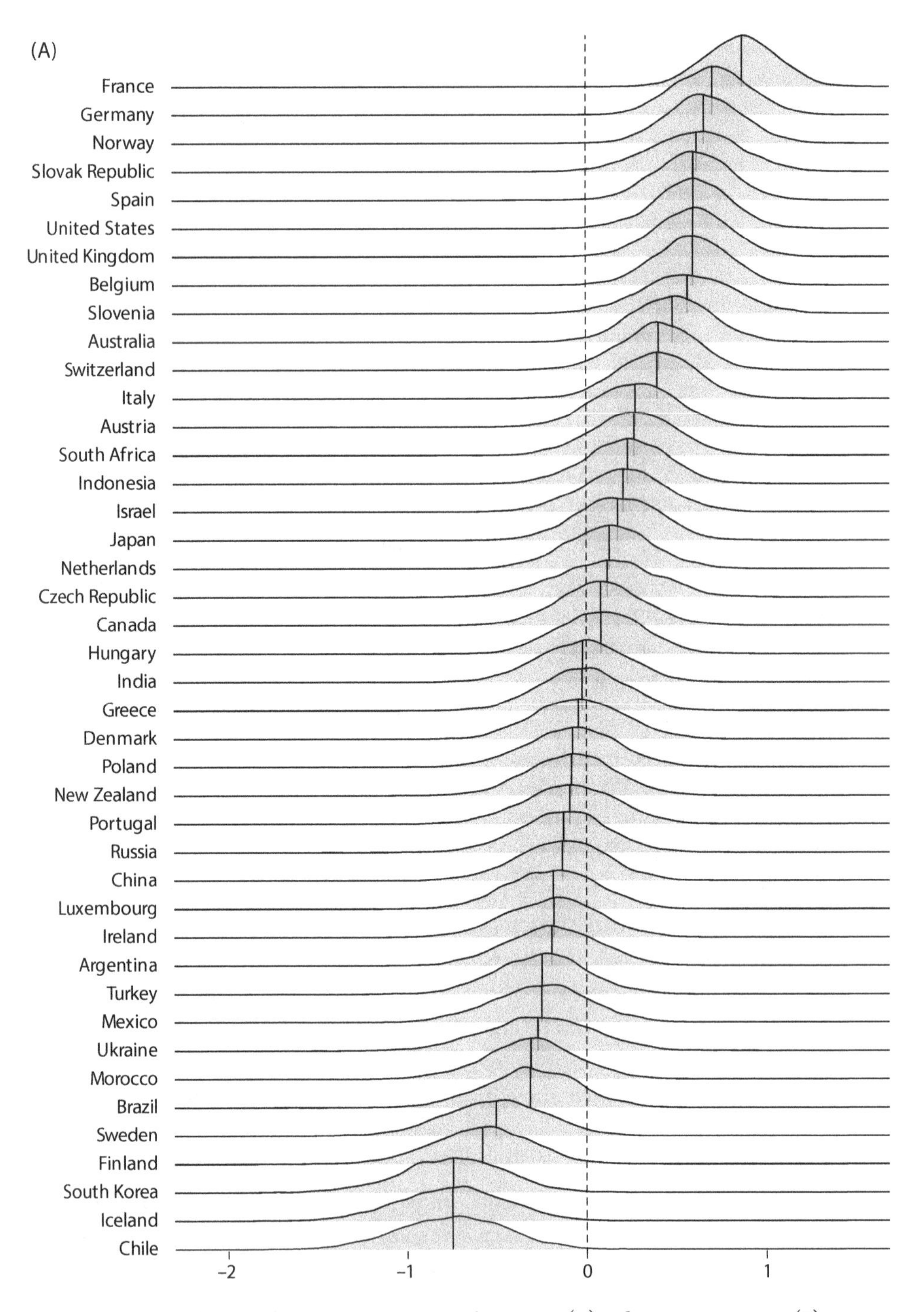

FIGURE 5.10. Latent policy restrictiveness varies by country (A) and increases over time (B).

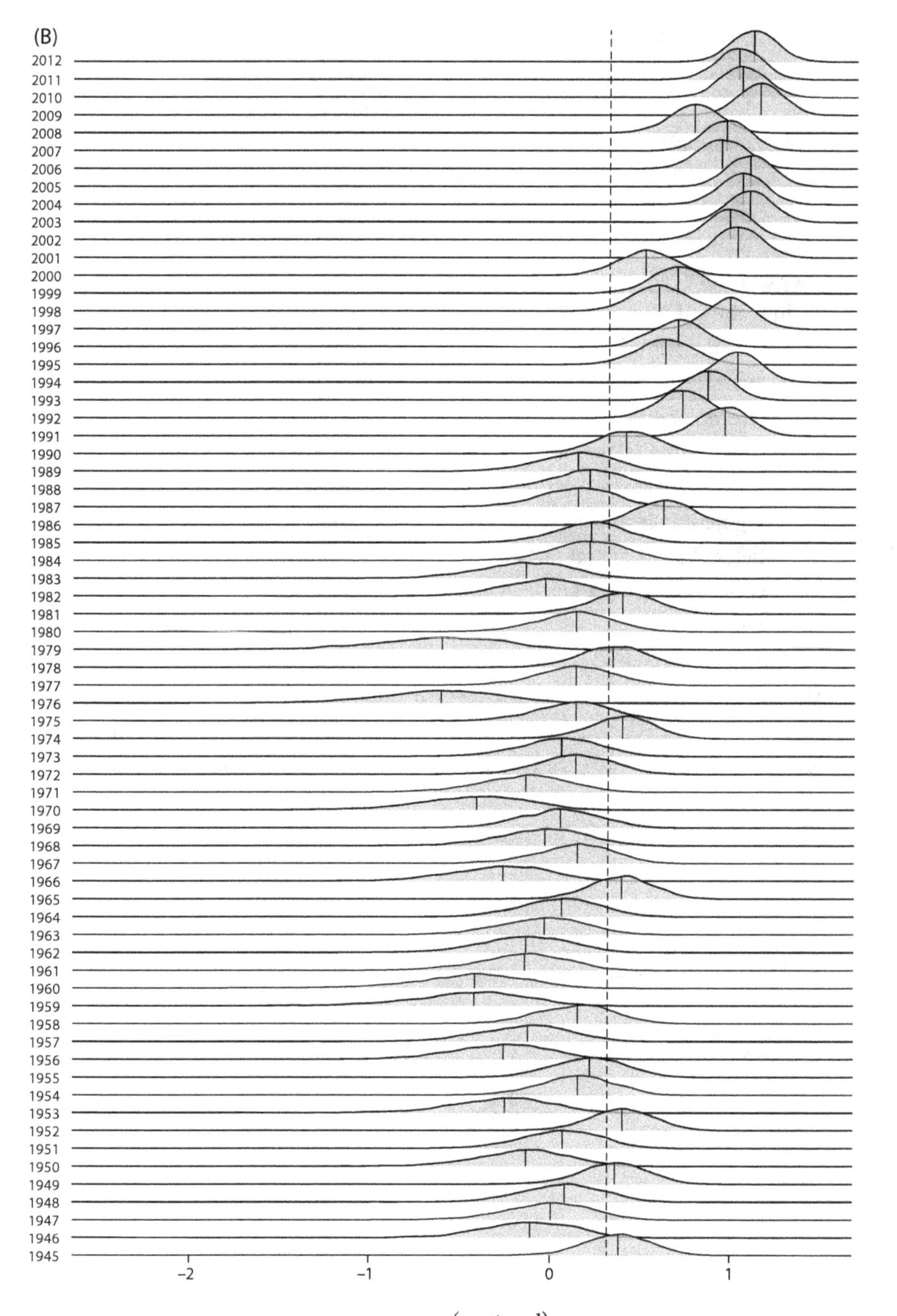

FIGURE 5.10. (continued)

is a different physical distance from the destination. This average ancestral distance measure accounts for how "different," on average, a country's immigrant flow is from its native population. According to the theory, the overall level of migration restrictiveness should decrease during decolonization, as states remove explicitly discriminatory quotas. However, after the composition of immigrant flows begins to change, I expect a concomitant increase in policy restrictiveness. Although states can no longer explicitly discriminate by race, they can still enact laws that disproportionately affect these same migrants.

In technical terms, ancestral distance measures the distance between two states based on how long it has been since their populations shared a common ancestor.[72] It is a "molecular clock", and the original authors used it as an aggregate measure of differences in beliefs, traits, habits, and cultures.[73] Geneticists use data on 120 alleles from dozens of world populations and calculate the frequency in alleles in each to construct this measure. Then they calculate the weighted ancestral distance between the populations for all the available alleles. The ancestral distance between two populations is zero if alleles are identically distributed, which implies that the two populations developed together.

Then scholars use the bilateral distances between populations to compute the bilateral distances between *states* (see equation 5.1).[74] To do so, they tabulate each of the ethnic populations in each country. Then they multiply the share of population i in country 1 by the share of population j in country 2 by the ancestral distance between them. Finally, they add up all these bilateral weighted distances to create one measure of the weighted distance between the two countries. The theoretical minimum of ancestral distance implies that the population distribution is identical across the two states, while the maximum implies that all individuals in each state have the same ethnic ancestry and that these ancestries are dramatically different. Economists use this measure to estimate how observable and unobservable prejudices affect economic exchange.[75]

$$\text{Ancestral distance}_{1,2} = \sum_{i=1}^{I} \sum_{j=1}^{J} (\text{share}_{i1} \times \text{share}_{j2} \times \text{allele distance}_{ij}) \quad (5.1)$$

72. Spolaore and Wacziarg 2009, 2016.

73. Spolaore and Wacziarg 2009.

74. Cavalli-Sforza et al. 1994.

75. See, e.g., Guiso, Sapienza, and Zingales 2009.

I use this bilateral measure of ancestral distance to estimate the average ancestral distance of a destination country's immigration flows. To create this measure, I begin with the same Abel data on global migration flows from 1960 to 2015.[76] Recall that these are directed dyad estimates of the size of the migration flow for nearly every pair of states in the world. For every destination state, I calculate the proportion of its immigration flows that come from every country in the world. Then I multiply this proportion by the ancestral distance between the origin state and the destination state. Finally, I add together all these weighted distances for each destination country (see equation 5.2). The result is the *average ancestral distance* of each country's immigration flows in a given time period. The larger the number, the more ancestrally different a country's immigration flows are in that year. Because states no longer explicitly discriminate, this measure captures how a given state responds to general increases in immigration flows that it constructs as racially different.

$$\text{Average ancestral distance of immigrants to country } j \text{ in time } t$$
$$= \sum^{i} \frac{\text{flow}_{ijt}}{\text{total flow}_{jt}} \times \text{ancestral distance}_{ij} \qquad (5.2)$$

Keep in mind that this measure presumes neither an essentialist nor a biological conception of ancestral (or racial) difference. It simply stipulates that populations at a greater ancestral distance from each other had more time to diverge in terms of intergenerationally transmitted traits, such as cultural norms, values, beliefs, habits, language, and religion.[77] This caveat is important because it emphasizes that *I am not measuring "race" or "racial distance" at all*, and I do not validate the pseudoscientific "measurement" of race. Ancestral distance may be associated with differences across groups that many presume are racial differences, but I do not refer to this genetic-based measure as "racial." Ancestral distance merely measures ancestral distance: race is not a scientific concept as a noun, and it does not become one as an adjective.[78]

Be that as it may, average ancestral distance remains an ideal measure for this analysis because it is rooted in perceptions of difference between two states and is consistent with Locke's racial ontology that I adopt throughout

76. Abel 2018.

77. Spolaore and Wacziarg 2018, 750.

78. I thank Errol Henderson for providing this phrasing.

this book. To repeat, "race" for Locke is an "ethnic fiction" that depends on the social construction of difference: "rather than particular races creating Culture, it was culture—social, political, and economic processes—that produced racial character."[79] There is nothing biologically inherent or scientific about racial categories; rather, races exist only insofar as different cultures produce differences that outsiders construct as racial. Therefore, this measure is consistent with racial constructivism because it picks up on the culture, characteristics, and geographic origins that do not define biologically "real" races, but do inform beliefs and perceptions that affect the construction of *socially real* racial groups.[80]

In this theory, when policymakers consider whether to enact a given immigration policy change, they consider the overall "cultural" or "ethnic"—to use Locke's phrasing—similarity and desirability of their country's *overall* immigration flows. This aggregate perception is important because states no longer explicitly target their policies against specific groups or individual migrants. In this theory, the more different a state's immigration flows are *on average*, the more likely that it will enact more restrictive policies. The ancestral distance measure provides a facsimile of these general perceptions because the distance between states is weighted by their respective ethnic groups. As such, the measure accounts for the diversity within states, such as the White minority in South Africa, and perceptions thereof. Finally, the ancestral distance between two states is a contextual measure. Rather than assuming that every country interprets difference in the same way, ancestral distance measures the relative distance between states. For instance, this measure allows for the possibility that Japan and Germany interpret immigration from Indonesia differently.

Ancestral distance is not the only measure of racial difference I use in this analysis. To provide validity, I use two other indicators that measure the magnitude of a country's immigration flows that it perceives to be racially different. These measures focus on more common references to anti-Black and anti-African racism. The second indicator is a measure of the percentage of a

79. Stewart 1992, xxv, cited in Henderson 2017, 87.

80. The constitutive theory of race in Obasogie 2014 highlights the simultaneous importance of perceptions to racial construction and the nonneutrality of those perceptions: "'Seeing race' is not a neutral or exogenous engagement with human engagement. Rather, race becomes visually significant only as a product of these social practices" (Obasogie, 43). The ancestral distance measure is a good compromise because it taps into the likelihood that one state would perceive the culture and social practices of another state as racially different.

country's immigrant flows that come from sub-Saharan Africa, North Africa, or the Middle East. For the countries in our sample—predominantly the OECD—the majority of citizens would view immigrants from these regions as being racially different. Of course, this perspective comes from those in the racial majority. However, given that most members of the ruling class in OECD states are not members of a racial minority, this perspective is warranted.[81] The third measure is the percentage of a country's immigrant flows that come from outside the OECD. While the second measure predominantly targets perceptions of physical and cultural otherness, this measure is slightly different. While citizens and leaders may perceive immigrant flows from outside the OECD as racially different in the "old-fashioned" sense, this measure taps explicitly into perceptions of economic difference and hierarchy. OECD states are the richest and the most powerful states in the formal and informal institutions of global governance. As such, I expect their leaders and citizens to perceive immigrants from outside this club to be undesirable, even if it is in the color-blind sense. Recall that some economists warn that immigrants from "low-productivity" states may transmit some of that low productivity to their new homes.[82] This measure captures this perception of inferiority that is likely correlated with overt perceptions of racial inferiority but not reducible to them.[83]

Unlike ancestral distance, the second and third measures are absolute rather than relative. Immigrants from sub-Saharan Africa are from the same region, regardless of destination country. So these measures assume that destination countries perceive immigrants from outside the OECD or from other regions in the same way, and they mask differences across states. This trade-off is inherent in measures of perceptions of racial difference that do not change with context. As one can see in table 5.7, there are slight differences among the three measures. This table reports three bivariate regression models. I estimate the association between each measure of, and a destination state's change in, immigration policy restrictiveness in a given time period. I log both the independent and dependent variables so one can interpret the coefficient as the percentage change in immigration policy restrictiveness that

81. Hughes 2013.

82. Algan and Cahuc 2013.

83. These two alternative measures are only correlated at 0.22, which implies that states with a large inflow of immigrants from sub-Saharan Africa, North Africa, and the Middle East do not necessarily have large immigrant inflows from other non-OECD regions, such as Latin America.

TABLE 5.7. Association between inflows and increased policy restrictiveness (1960–2013) by three measures

	Immigration Policy Restrictiveness		
	(1)	(2)	(3)
Average ancestral distance	0.160**		
	(0.049, 0.272)		
Percentage African/Middle Eastern		0.111*	
		(0.012, 0.210)	
Percentage non-OECD			0.226**
			(0.062, 0.391)
Fixed Effects	X	X	X
N	1,853	1,853	1,853
R^2	0.040	0.038	0.041
Adjusted R^2	0.018	0.015	0.019
Residual Standard Error (df = 1810)	0.974	0.975	0.973

Note: *p < .1; **p < .05; ***p < .01.

accompanies a 1 percent change in the independent variables. To simplify this analysis, I report estimates from linear regression models with fixed effects. Table 5.7 reports a positive association between difference and immigration policy restrictiveness: as the volume of racially different immigrants increases, so does the restrictiveness of a destination's policies. The estimated association ranges from 11 percent (for the sub-Saharan Africa/Middle East measure) to 22 percent (for the non-OECD measure). These models provide a first cut at corroborating my arguments about the continued importance of racial desirability in "color-blind" immigration policy.

Restrictive Laws Follow Undesirable Immigration

Table 5.8 examines the relationship between the composition of a state's immigration flows and its immigration policy restrictiveness in more detail. As such, the unit of analysis is the *destination country–year*. This section's main hypothesis suggests that states that receive larger proportions of racially different migrants will enact more immigration restrictions. Because of the monadic nature of this analysis, I pool a state's migration inflows to determine the aggregate proportion of racially different immigrants it received in a given period. As a result, I cannot include various dyadic variables that confound the association between racially different inflows and immigration policy restrictiveness, such as colonial relationships.

TABLE 5.8. Regression models of immigration policy restrictiveness, 1960–2013

	Immigration Policy Restrictiveness			
	(1)	(2)	(3)	(4)
IHS Average Ancestral Distance	0.071**			
	(0.009, 0.133)			
IHS Average Ancestral Distance (1500)		0.077**		
		(0.015, 0.140)		
IHS Percentage SSA Flow			0.058*	
			(−0.008, 0.124)	
IHS Percentage Non-OECD Flow				0.096**
				(0.022, 0.170)
Negative GDP Shock	0.079**	0.073**	0.079**	0.082**
	(0.009, 0.149)	(0.003, 0.143)	(0.009, 0.148)	(0.012, 0.152)
Liberal Democracy	−0.071*	−0.084**	−0.071*	−0.070*
	(−0.148, 0.005)	(−0.161, −0.008)	(−0.147, 0.006)	(−0.146, 0.007)
Inflation Rate	−0.048	−0.045	−0.049	−0.047
	(−0.112, 0.015)	(−0.108, 0.018)	(−0.112, 0.015)	(−0.111, 0.017)
Trade Openness	0.003	−0.008	−0.015	0.020
	(−0.065, 0.071)	(−0.075, 0.058)	(−0.082, 0.052)	(−0.051, 0.090)
Conflict	0.060	0.080	0.041	0.034
	(−0.131, 0.252)	(−0.113, 0.273)	(−0.150, 0.233)	(−0.157, 0.226)
(Intercept)	−0.128***	−0.126***	−0.128***	−0.132***
	(−0.169, −0.087)	(−0.167, −0.085)	(−0.169, −0.087)	(−0.175, −0.089)
Country RE	X	X	X	X
Year RE	X	X	X	X
N	1,686	1,686	1,686	1,686
Log Likelihood	−1,610.115	−1,609.732	−1,611.105	−1,609.200
AIC	3,238.229	3,237.465	3,240.209	3,236.400
BIC	3,287.100	3,286.336	3,289.080	3,285.271

Note: *p < .1; **p < .05; ***p < .01. SSA = sub-Saharan Africa. IHS = Inverse hyperbolic sine transformation. The racial distance variables are transformed by the IHS function.

In this analysis, I use ordinary least squares to regress immigration policy restrictiveness on our various measures of racial difference. This table has four regression models. In the first three models, I use the same measures of racial difference as above. The fourth model uses an index that measures the average racial distance of a state's immigration flows, using the ancestral distance between states in 1500. Spolaore and Wacziarg suggest scholars also use this measure to corroborate their findings because populations in 1500 are not affected by mass migration flows.[84] Ancestral distance in the twentieth century and immigration policy changes may both be correlated with confounding variables that will bias inferences. So, to assuage these concerns, I include this final measure. Just as in table 5.7, I log each of the race measures, along with the independent variable, to aid in interpretation.

I also use several other independent variables in this model. The first is an indicator for whether a state experiences a negative GDP shock in a time period. I expect that countries with negative GDP shocks will enact stricter immigration policies because citizens will call for restrictions to protect native workers. I measure GDP shocks in the same way Nielsen et al. measure foreign aid shocks.[85] I calculate the five-year change in aid for each country time period (UK GDP in 2010 − UK GDP in 2005). I then define the bottom 15 percent of those GDP changes as negative aid shocks. Second, and using a similar logic, I suppose that policymakers in countries with higher inflation rates will face pressure to enact greater restrictions. To account for this pressure, I include a measure of a state's inflation rate in a given year, calculated using the Penn World Table. Third, Peters shows evidence that countries with greater trade openness have stricter immigration policies.[86] In such countries, firms do not have the incentive to lobby for open immigration policies because labor-intensive firms will go out of business or lay off workers, thereby increasing the number of unemployed workers and reducing firms' needs for immigrant labor and less restrictive policies. Accordingly, I use the World Bank measure of trade openness that accounts for a country's imports and exports as a share of GDP.[87] Fourth, Rudolph argues that countries at war often opt for more lax immigration policies to increase their economic returns from liberal borders.[88] To control for the effect of conflict, I use data

84. Spolaore and Wacziarg 2009, 502.

85. Nielsen et al. 2011, 224.

86. Peters 2017.

87. World Bank 2019.

88. Rudolph 2003.

from PRIO to note whether a country is at war.[89] Finally, I include a measure of liberal democracy from the Varieties of Democracy (V-Dem) database.[90] Many scholars argue that liberal democracies are less likely to enact restrictive immigration policies,[91] so I include this variable in kind. I use the V-Dem measure because recent work shows that the liberal democracy index outperforms alternative indices, such as Freedom House and Polity, because it better captures the "multidimensional" nature of democracy.[92]

These are multilevel linear regression models. I use this modeling strategy because random-effects models constrain the variance of coefficient estimates to produce results that are closer to the truth in a particular sample.[93] This justification for random effects mirrors the one above for the baseline model. I choose to trade off bias and variance in this way because I am not using these regressions to warrant causal identification. Instead, my goal is to take advantage of partial pooling to specify the best model of the underlying data-generating process. In addition, multilevel modeling is a popular approach for modeling hierarchical data (observations clustered in countries and years) because it outperforms classical regression in predictive accuracy and description. Multilevel modeling is also capable of separately estimating predictive effects for individual groups (e.g., the effect of the racial composition of immigrants on policy for the United States).

The key result from this analysis is that the racial difference variables have a significant association with immigration policy restrictiveness in each of the models.[94] This implies that there is a strong relationship between the composition of a state's immigration flows and the number of restrictive policies it enacts in a given time period. For example, a 1 percent increase in the average ancestral distance of a state's immigration flows is associated with around a 7 percent increase in immigration policy restrictiveness. This association is large in the context of policymaking, where the modal number

89. Gleditsch et al. 2002.

90. Coppedge et al. 2019.

91. Hollifield 2004; Joppke 2005.

92. Lindberg et al. 2014, 159.

93. Clark and Linzer 2015, 401.

94. I conduct several robustness checks in appendix c. To be specific, I reestimate the models with several different methods of accounting for temporal and spatial dependence. I also reestimate the models with a variable that measures whether a destination state was a former colonial power. These results are consistent with the main thrust of this analysis. The sub-Saharan Africa association is insignificant in table C.3, but this is likely due to the correlation between former colonial status and inflows from sub-Saharan Africa.

of policy changes in a given year is zero. Put in more concrete terms, this increase in the independent variable is equivalent to a shift from the ancestral distance of Australia's immigrant population from 1961 to 1965 (~ 210) to the United States' immigrant population from 1971 to 1975 (~ 805). This shift in immigration flow composition is meaningful because Australia did not begin to dismantle the White Australia Policy until the Migration Act of 1966. So this coefficient estimates the association between going from an explicitly racist immigration regime to a "color-blind" one. This association provides strong evidence for the relationship between the composition of a state's immigrant population and its color-blind policy restrictiveness. We also see consistent results across the three models with relatively little variance: the effect ranges from roughly 6 percent (sub-Saharan Africa/Middle East) to roughly 10 percent (non-OECD).

Second, we see a positive and significant relationship between GDP shocks and immigration policy changes. This provides evidence that states that experience negative GDP shocks are more likely to enact restrictive immigration policies. This result may be surprising depending on how one interprets the interdependence between immigration policy and economic conditions. On the one hand, domestic-based firms that cannot outsource production have the incentive to push for more lenient immigration policies to get access to cheaper labor. For these firms, economic downturns should amplify this desire. On the other hand, economic downturns are fertile moments when leaders and citizens look to blame outsiders for their troubles. When times are tough, states use immigration policy to signal that they are protecting native workers to mollify public opinion. The subtext of many of these policy changes and proclamations often contains racism, nativism, and xenophobia. This result is evidence for the latter, although we cannot be sure of the exact mechanism from the analysis.

Third, the conventional wisdom is that liberal democracies are more likely to reduce their immigration policy restrictiveness. Liberal democracies tend to have more free and open societies that are more pluralistic and accepting of outsiders. I find evidence for this argument. In each of the models, I estimate a negative and significant relationship between a state's level of liberal democracy and whether it enacts restrictive immigration policy measures in a given time period. In model (2)—that with the ancestral distance in 1500 measure—this association is significant at the 95 percent level, while in the other models, these associations are significant at the 90 percent level.

Although I find evidence of a negative relationship between liberal democracy and immigration policy, it could also be the case that liberal democracy moderates the effect on immigration policy changes of receiving immigration flows that are racially distant. In other words, countries that receive racially different immigration flows may enact more restrictive policies, and this effect may be dampened (or heightened) in liberal democracies. I do not argue that liberal democracy has a nonlinear main effect on immigration policy restrictiveness; I do not expect an "inverted-U" association between these variables, for example. Instead, I argue that a state's relationship between its previous immigration flows and its future immigration policy *depends on its level of liberal democracy*. This hypothesis is interactive, and the the use of multiplicative interactions is the typical method for investigating these relationships in regression models.[95]

However, standard linear interaction models[96] make a strong linear-additive assumption. Technically speaking, these models assume that the interaction effect of some third variable, X_2, on the effect of X_1 on Y follows the function $\frac{\partial Y}{\partial X_1} = \beta_1 + \beta_3 X_2$. Substantively speaking, this assumption means that the effect of X_1 on Y can only change with X_2 at a *constant rate* β_3. Put a third way, the linear-additive assumption states that all the heterogeneity in the effect of X_1 on Y comes from changes in X_2 that moderate the effect by a constant β_3. However, Jens Hainmueller and coauthors replicate forty-six interaction effects in twenty-two prominent published papers between 2006 and 2015 and find that the linear-additive assumption holds in only 48 percent of cases.[97]

As a consequence, to test this hypothesis, I take the advice of Hainmueller et al., who suggest that scholars use a nonlinear, kernel-based interaction technique that does not make the stringent linear-additive assumptions of conventional regression models with interaction terms.[98] This approach may surprise some readers, but using a graphical test of this interaction will ensure that I do not make unwarranted claims based on unsubstantiated assumptions about the data. The results of the test in appendix C (figure C.3) definitively show the need for the kernel-based method in this case. This method is based on the following semiparametric model: $Y = f(X) + g(X)D + \gamma(X)Z + \epsilon$. The standard interaction model is a special case when $f(X) = \mu$, $g(X) = \alpha$, and $\gamma(X) = \gamma$. However, in the fully flexible kernel regression, the conditional effect of D on Y need not be linear, which allows one to control for

95. Braumoeller 2004; Brambor, Clark, and Golder 2006.

96. $Y = \beta_0 + \beta_1 X_1 + \beta_2 X_2 + \beta_3 X_1 X_2$.

97. Hainmueller, Mummolo, and Xu 2019, 164.

98. Hainmueller et al., 164.

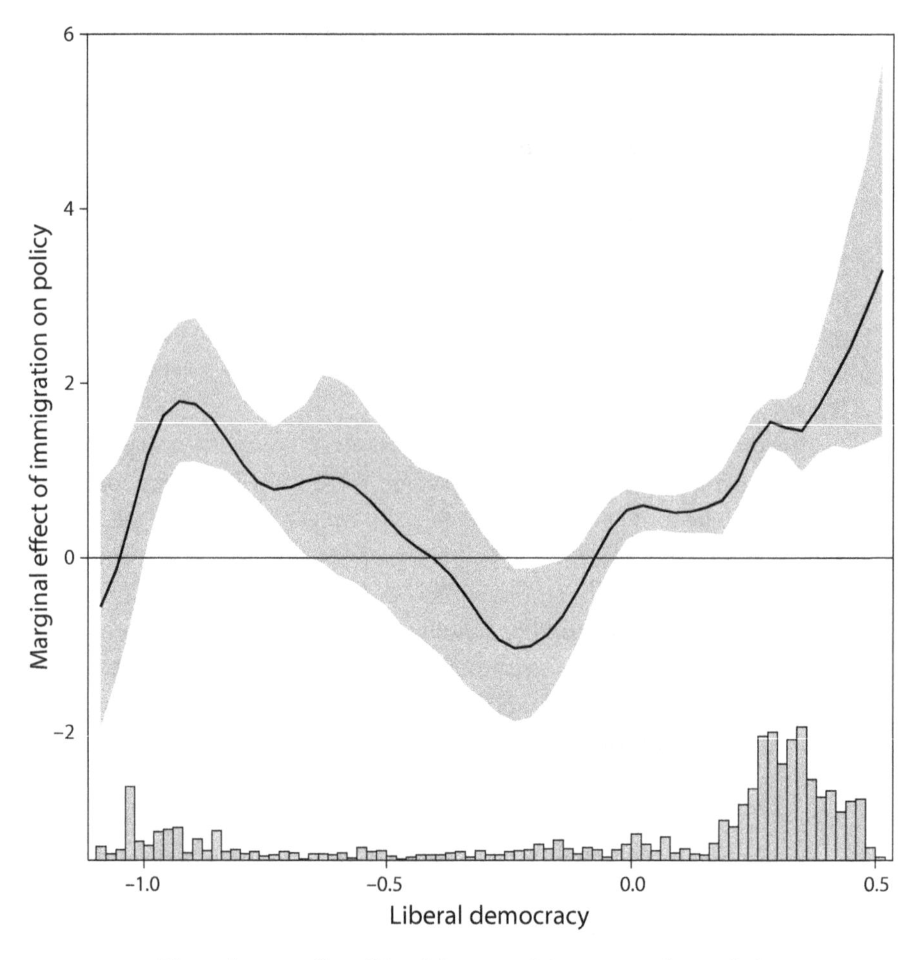

FIGURE 5.11. The moderating effect of liberal democracy? Autocratic and strongly democratic states respond to increased immigration from non-White states with restrictive policies.

nonlinear interaction effects.[99] As such, using this method costs little since the kernel-based model nests the standard interaction model as a special case.

The results of this test are in figure 5.11.[100] In this analysis, I plot a state's level of liberal democracy on the x-axis and the marginal effect of racially different immigration on the y-axis. This figure tests whether the main effect of interest—racially different immigration on policy—is different for states

99. Hainmueller et al., 173–174.

100. In this figure and in the remaining analysis, I use the ancestral distance measure from model (1). All the results are consistent when I use each of the other measures.

TABLE 5.9. Countries with the largest positive effect of average ancestral distance of immigration population

	Country	(Intercept)	Lag Avg. Ancestral Dist.
1	Argentina	−0.02	0.31
2	India	0.05	0.28
3	Luxembourg	0.06	0.28
4	Netherlands	0.13	0.25
5	Norway	0.13	0.23
6	France	0.05	0.19
7	Denmark	0.06	0.16
8	United Kingdom	0.11	0.16
9	United States	0.05	0.10
10	New Zealand	0.05	0.10

with different levels of liberal democracy. The results reveal a more complicated picture than previous studies presume. Namely, there is a nonlinear interactive relationship between liberal democracy and racially distant immigration flows. To be specific, states that have relatively low (China, Morocco, Indonesia, Russia) or high (Denmark, Norway, Sweden, US) levels of liberal democracy are more likely to enact restrictive immigration policies when they receive racially different immigration flows. However, states that fall in the middle (Iceland, Portugal, Spain) have a more ambiguous effect: there is some evidence that these countries have either no relationship or a negative relationship between racially different immigration flows and policy restrictions. All in all, this analysis does not disprove the theory that liberal democracies are less likely to enact restrictive immigration policies; it merely provides context and an additional layer of evidence suggesting that there may be a less straightforward relationship between regime type and restrictiveness.

Finally, one of the benefits of using multilevel regression models is that I can estimate a different effect for each country in the dataset. Rather than assume that all countries have the same association between the racial distance of the immigration flows and policy changes, this model allows this effect to vary across countries. The results are in table 5.9. In this table, I report the ten states with the strongest positive relationship between racially distant immigration flows and policy restrictiveness. This model picks up on contentious politics of race and immigration policy in high-profile countries like the United States and United Kingdom. However, it also reveals an even stronger relationship in Norway and Denmark, two Nordic states with strong social democracies. Rather than calling into question the validity of this analysis, the presence of Norway and Denmark accords with the recent rise of right-wing parties, xenophobia, and anti-immigrant racism in each country.[101] Although Norway and Denmark are bastions of social democracy, it is clear that each has a segment of society that reacts strongly to immigration from racial outsiders (i.e., Muslim immigrants) and government policy has responded in kind. Opponents to racially different immigration use their strong social democracies and liberal values as a justification to restrict outsiders.[102]

This analysis shows convincing evidence of an association between the racial composition of immigration flows and immigration policy restrictiveness. Although states no longer restrict immigration explicitly on the basis of race, it is clear that they are mindful of the "desirability" of their immigrant populations. Some dimensions of this relationship, such as that between liberal democracy and restrictiveness, are perhaps more complex than scholars previously assumed. However, this analysis shows that racial bias in international migration goes beyond the mere descriptive patterns of racial and geographic difference and remains closely tied to the policymaking behavior of states in the Anglo-European world.

Conclusion

This chapter has taken a long journey into two key empirical implications of my theory. First, I use data on the entire international system to provide evidence that migrants from non-White states migrate less than their counterparts in the global North, relative to our baseline expectations. Second, I use data on immigration policy changes for forty-five states to show that Anglo-European states often enact more immigration policy restrictions when they receive immigrants from non-White states. To put a finer point on it, these pieces of evidence together suggest that two equally qualified migrants, one from France and one from the Central African Republic, do not have equal opportunities to migrate, and that their difference in opportunity widened from 1960 to 2015. And even when migrants from the Central African Republic (or Afghanistan, or Algeria, etc.) immigrate to the West, their new homelands react by enacting increasingly restrictive immigration policies.

These results are important because they represent the first systematic evidence of racial inequality in the international system of any kind. Specifically,

101. Rydgren 2008.

102. Knudsen 1997; Wren 2001.

I show that migrants from sub-Saharan Africa and the rest of the global South emigrate significantly less than expected in every period from 1960 to 2015. These underflows have increased over time. This pattern is surprising because it suggests that, in the immediate aftermath of decolonization, international migration was at its most equal, even though the world had just emerged from centuries of legal White supremacy. The farther away we have gotten from decolonization, the more unequal international migration processes have become. This pattern is the exact opposite of what we would expect. In a world transitioning from colonialism and legal restrictions on race, we would expect less initial migration from non-White migrants, but that these flows would increase as colonialism retreated farther into history. In fact, we observe the exact opposite, and we would remain blind to this pattern without this measurement strategy. Previously, we could only look to estimates of the absolute numbers of global migrants in figure 5.1, see the increase in overall numbers, and reason whether this increase is characteristic of or in spite of any potential racial bias that we observe in individual countries.

Importantly, this measurement strategy guards against claims that citizens of the postcolonial world migrate less because they are poorer, farther away, less educated, and so on. I design this measurement strategy specifically with these sorts of critiques in mind. Yes, it is the case that states have different contexts that make it difficult to compare their absolute levels of emigration and immigration. This complexity is the point: we cannot use absolute levels to make inferences about differences between states because their ideal levels of migration are different. I use the baseline model to make predictions about that ideal level of immigration and emigration in every time period to see how the actual level of migration compares. This strategy fends off two tendencies. First, some may contend that the increase in immigration from the global South is sufficient to dispel the existence of racial inequality in migration. Second, others may argue that case-specific evidence of anti-immigrant elite and public rhetoric proves the existence of racial inequality. These groups are on opposite ends of the spectrum with respect to their belief in the existence of racial inequality, yet they each make the same mistake of looking at absolute levels of migration when warranting their claims. In contrast, the baseline model approach provides an easily interpretable and comparable measure of, for example, how many more or fewer emigrants a country sent to the rest of the world than expected. Although each country has a different baseline level, one can directly compare different deviations from this baseline.

Although this evidence shows the presence of racial bias in international migration worldwide, it does not overcome the aforementioned issues with intentionality. For instance, it could be the case that non-White migrants prefer to either stay in their home countries or migrate to a nearby (and theoretically similar) state. However, we do not have to provide a smoking gun of explicit racist intent to prove the existence of racial inequality. These issues relate to those regarding the persistence of residential segregation within cities. Ever since Schelling first demonstrated that racial segregation can occur in the absence of overt racism, it has been clear that racial inequality can persist and expand in the absence of individual racist intentions among policymakers.[103] People may simply want to live near people that look, live, and act like themselves. This possibility makes racial inequality in a world without racist laws so pernicious. Even in the absence of old-fashioned racist intentions, both residential segregation and underflows in migration have dire economic and social consequences.[104] Moreover, we should consider why some neighborhoods or countries are more or less amenable to new residents from different backgrounds. Racial inequality in movement has important economic and social consequences, and therefore is important to study in the absence of explicitly racist intentions. Outcomes matter; conscious intentions do not.

As such, this chapter exposes an important pattern of inequality in the international system despite there being several plausible explanations for why this pattern exists. This evidence says nothing about the views, intentions, or beliefs of individual politicians, policymakers, citizens, or migrants. I simply reveal the presence of structural inequality in this "color-blind" international process and show that restrictive immigration policies are correlated with increased immigration flows from the non-White world. This ambiguity is a feature, not a bug, because this inequality is the sort of modern racism that Ture and Hamilton discuss in *Black Power*.[105] It is true that explicitly racist laws no longer govern international migration, and world leaders rarely express racist views, despite several high-profile counterexamples. But pinning down individual examples of moral failings is not the goal. Instead, as Ture and Hamilton argue, antiracists should expose instances of institutional or structural inequality because these examples play a larger role in

103. Schelling 1971.

104. Clemens, Montenegro, and Pritchett 2019; Williams and Collins 2001.

105. Ture and Hamilton 1967.

maintaining systematic racial oppression. The most consequential form of racism or White supremacy does not lie in individual moral failings, but in the inequality lurking beneath the veneer of equality. In accordance with this view, this chapter reveals that the seemingly benign—or economically rational—institutions underpinning international migration continue to produce unequal outcomes despite their putative color blindness. We can change the rules of international institutions and immigration policies; changing people is much more difficult.

Now that I have unmasked these patterns of inequality, I can examine whether the further implications of the theory in chapter 3 hold. In the next chapter, I investigate whether we can pin this racial bias and increasingly restrictive policies on colonialism. In other words, I consider whether European colonialism created the conditions that leaders now use to justify these restrictive policies. Then I investigate whether postcolonial states engage in the same performative border policies—fence construction—as their counterparts in the global North. This evidence suggests that postcolonial states took to heart the necessity to "perform" border security, and this diffusion corroborates my explanation for why we see an increase in immigration underflows from 1960 to 2015.

6

Colonialism and the Construction of Undesirability

IN THE PREVIOUS CHAPTER, I provide descriptive evidence of racial bias in international migration. I outline an inferential strategy whereby I rule out all other explanations that are not discrimination for the migration between two states and predict how much movement we should see if the world were truly color-blind. Then I measure whether there was more or less emigration from every state in the world from 1960 to 2015. The balance of the evidence shows that emigration underflows increased over time and that poorer, non-White states from the global South bore the brunt of these underflows. Why do these patterns persist even though laws are now color-blind and nondiscriminatory? Why were emigration underflows at their smallest during the 1960s? Why was international migration at its most equitable during the earliest periods of legal racial equality in international migration policy? These answers lie in our misplaced faith in the letter of the law and the true power of the norms of the sovereign state system. In the remaining chapters of this book, I unpack this explanation in more detail.

The answer inheres in perceptions of undesirability, and in this chapter I interrogate one historical mechanism that makes some migrants seem more desirable than others. Although most colonies gained some form of political independence, the scars of Anglo-European incursions—and the perceptions that justified those incursions—remain. In short, the history of colonialism and explicit racism in international politics created the migrants that today are often viewed as dangerous, poor, and otherwise undesirable. This mechanism explains in part why we see continued racial inequality in international migration despite the end of formal racial quotas.

This argument concerns both material conditions and Western perceptions. To be sure, evidence shows that Anglo-European imperialism stifled economic growth, created neopatrimonial and unstable states, and catalyzed conditions of violence. In these cases, Western countries produced the conditions in the global South that they use today to warrant restrictive immigration policies. However, the social science of attributing cause remains fraught, and the direct evidence regarding the material effects of colonialism varies throughout the world, as I discuss below. In some cases, many of which are in the Middle East and Asia, the postcolonial state achieved a degree of economic growth, prosperity, and political stability, but the West still perceives them as unequal or undesirable. Viewing the non-White world through colonialism-colored glasses is a political condition that stretches back decades to prominent Western concerns that poor migrants from postcolonial states' new "urban underclasses" would threaten the existing order.[1] Racial bias persists in international migration because states make policies that restrict immigration on the basis of these supposedly objective criteria that come either from colonialism's material effects or from misguided perceptions. We cannot empirically distinguish between these two explanations, but both mechanisms suggest that states restrict immigration when faced with the prospect of increased immigration from places they construct as undesirable. The veracity and historical antecedents of those perceptions matter little.

For instance, although China has achieved tremendous economic growth in recent decades, "Yellow Peril" racism rooted in long-standing perceptions of cultural inferiority and "savagery" continue to structure Western public opinion toward its citizens.[2] These perceptions have roots in colonial-era encounters between Europe and Asia, gunboat diplomacy, and the former's coercive impositions on the latter that have structured anti-Asian racism ever since.[3] The fact that some non-Western states do not accord with outsiders' perceptions does not preclude the social construction of inferiority from persisting—often through "distortions" in the conventional historical narratives of international politics[4]—and the argument in this chapter acknowledges both aspects of the postcolonial experience. In short, the mechanisms that reinforce prejudice within states also reinforce prejudice between them.

1. Bayat 2000; Huntington 1968.
2. Del Visco 2019; Heale 2009.
3. Suzuki 2009.
4. Koyama and Buzan 2019, 188.

Put differently, this argument examines how the West *constructs* the undesirablility of the non-White global South. And in the next section, I review the social construction of race as it relates to previous discussions in chapters 1 and 3. However, in this chapter, I go further to connect Du Bois's description of the "global color line" to the racial constructivism that I adopt from Locke and others. Doing so reveals a further synergy between the study of race, racism, and antiracism and the study of international politics via the benefits of adopting a shared positivist constructivism. After describing how material conditions contribute to the social construction of racial undesirability, I present various explanations for how colonialism led postcolonial states to be seen as economically, politically, and socially undesirable. I also discuss the debate over theories of dependency and underdevelopment. Finally, I provide a quantitative assessment of this part of the argument before discussing its implications.

Constructivism, Colonialism, and Antiracism

In 1900, W.E.B. Du Bois spoke at the third annual meeting of the American Negro Academy. In this lecture, Du Bois laid out his vision to consider "the problem of the color line, not simply as a national and personal question but rather in its larger world aspect in time and space," and inquire how that color line would affect politics in the twentieth century.[5] To do so, he looked back to the nineteenth century. Du Bois identified several instances of Anglo-European colonial incursion into the African continent, and he remarked how this influence transformed life for non-White peoples throughout the world. In the remaining pages of the lecture, Du Bois delved deeper into the consequences of colonialism, and he concluded that his enumeration of these consequences "confirms the proposition with which I started—the world problem of the 20th century is the problem of the color line—the question of the relation of the advanced races of men who happened to be white to the great majority of the undeveloped or half-developed nations of mankind who happen to be yellow, brown or black."[6] To put it simply, Du Bois considered the relative underdevelopment of the non-White world to be a direct consequence of colonialism and that this underdevelopment would play a massive role in the world politics of the twentieth century. For Du Bois,

5. Du Bois 1996, 47.

6. Du Bois, 54.

the modern color line operates when Anglo-Europeans ignore this history, take the "underdevelopment" of the world's non-White peoples as given, and devalue their existence. As I have discussed above, Anglo-Europeans constructed the concept of race to categorize the colonial world as inferior or destitute, and Du Bois notes how " 'color' became in the world's thought synonymous with inferiority."[7] Being designated as non-White was being damned to devaluation, degradation, and domination, and the historical process that follows this labeling is a self-fulfilling prophecy.

What does it mean for colonialism to create race and the global color line? Race lacks any biological, essential, or otherwise scientific foundation. However, race still affects contemporary society because it is a means of categorizing people and assigning status based on how close one fits into the paradigm of Whiteness. The social system that operates according to this paradigm is called racism. Racism is not synonymous with racial prejudice. *Racial prejudice* is the act or feeling of hostility toward a person or group based on negative assumptions about their race, while *racism* is the social system that arises as a result of racial categorization. While racial prejudice is always direct, racism can be either direct or indirect. When the Europeans colonized the non-White world, their frame of reference for appropriate behavior was their own. As a result, they deemed those they encountered inferior because they behaved differently than Europeans.

As Alain Locke argues, races are ethnic fictions that center on the favorability or unfavorability of groups' cultural traits. Naturally, Europeans lionized their own culture, which led them to categorize other cultures as savage, primitive, or defective. This categorization generated a spurious correlation between race and putative inferiority, which justified further European incursion into the non-White world. Du Bois clarifies this idea later in "The African Roots of War." In this essay, Du Bois exclaims how the history of chattel slavery and colonialism crippled the African continent and its inhabitants. These centuries of exploitation not only made Africa more vulnerable to further colonial advances but also codified non-White peoples as inferior in the minds of Europeans. In other words, the actions of Anglo-Europeans over the course of four centuries constructed the inferior non-White subject, constructed the concept of race, and constructed the global color line, a component of which I reveal in chapter 5.

7. Du Bois 1915, 362.

The legitimacy of colonialism was a significant topic of debate among European philosophers from the first colonial encounters of the fifteenth century. This debate intensified as it became clearer that colonialism, which often involved brutal violence, quasi slavery or indentured labor, and exploitation, contradicted the principles of Enlightenment philosophy. Although European philosophers developed principles of natural law that applied to all peoples, when Europeans encountered non-Europeans, they interpreted cultural and physical differences as violations of that natural law and therefore deviant. These deviations from natural law and acceptable behavior evolved into justifications for colonial exploitation. This is the paradox of liberalism: it is assumed that all humans have the capacity to reason and therefore should be afforded equal dignity. Yet, when one observes practices that are different from how Europeans behave, the Anglo-European observer interprets them as inappropriate or deviant, which justifies a denial of respect.[8]

As you recall from chapter 2, these colonial-period perceptions about the inherent difference of non-White peoples play a pivotal role in this book's story. Initial colonial encounters created a cycle of subjugation, and the effects of the colonial period carry through to the present day. Colonial powers reached out to the rest of the world, deemed the people they found different or inferior, and used this "evidence" to justify further colonization. This imperialism produced significant effects on the economic, political, and social conditions in colonial states, which led to further "evidence" that colonial subjects were inferior and that European influence was a positive or necessary step in the civilizing process of the non-White world. However, there was little reflection that the initial colonial encounter created the conditions that Europeans later used to justify their further action. Colonization is a memory-less process; the amnesia of the Anglo-Europeans ensures a steady stream of rationales for further encroachment or subjugation. This amnesia resembles what Charles Mills calls "global white ignorance."[9]

The social construction of race lies at the heart of this argument. Europeans, faced with incentives to conquer and expand their empires, encountered the rest of the world and deemed non-Anglo-European appearances and practices inferior. This motivated perception of inferiority became ideology throughout the Anglo-European world and forms the basis of modern racism. These racial differences are socially constructed because they are not

8. Mantena 2010; Muthu 2003.

9. Mills 2015.

biologically real; there is no inherent basis to the racial differences that hold such currency in society. But this discussion belies the debate over what *constructivism* means. In this section, I lay out my modernist social constructivism and distinguish it from competing constructivisms in the social sciences. I then describe how my constructivist ontology relates to the racial constructivism I adopt in previous chapters. Finally, I connect this discussion to the growing interest in international hierarchy and note how the construction of undesirable non-White migrants contributes to inequality in the postcolonial order.

Positivist and Postmodern Constructivism

The construction of undesirability happens because people act on the basis of beliefs they have about the world, as well as the material conditions in that world, which reproduces those beliefs and makes them seem obvious or natural. This argument is *constructivist* because "constructivism is about human consciousness" and how some facts—social facts, like Christmas, money, and states—"depend on human agreement that they exist," while other brute facts, like mountains and broken bones, exist irrespective of whether people agree that they do.[10] In political science, constructivism plays its most significant role in international relations, but the approach matters in any circumstance in which institutions, norms, and social interaction rear their heads.

Most IR scholars consider constructivism to compete with structural realist and rationalist accounts of international politics. While scholars in the latter group use the distribution of material capabilities to explain international politics, the former contend that the distribution of *ideas* plays an equal, if not greater role. Constructivists do not neglect the importance of material factors: the number of nuclear warheads, tanks, and guns that a state owns still matters. However, constructivism contends that the intersubjective meanings of the material context hold considerable explanatory power. After all, Canada does not assume the worst about American intentions even though the distribution of material capabilities is not in its favor, because the two states interact in a friendly, collaborative culture.[11] Shared meanings of material conditions produce social constructions.

Unlike realism, however, constructivism is not a substantive theory about world politics; it merely makes statements about the nature of social life. In

10. Ruggie 1998, 856.
11. Wendt 1999, 109.

this vein, constructivists question how identities, interests, and norms emerge in the international system, rather than make predictions about who will fight whom. For example, Nina Tannenwald investigates why states build up their nuclear arsenals but do not use them when they are strategically rational. She contends that states have constructed a nuclear *taboo* that prevents their use,[12] but she does not provide any predictions about the construction of future taboos. Research like Tannenwald's exemplifies Alexander Wendt's claim that constructivism adds to substantive theories about international politics because it "call[s] attention to perhaps tacit presuppositions that may create problems, and identifying questions that have not been asked."[13] Race, racism, and racial inequality in international politics certainly apply here.

Yet, this depiction of constructivism belies the influential divisions among scholars who use the label. For our purposes, the main division to note is between positivist and postmodernist constructivists because the two sides differ in their view of intellectual purpose, what can be truly known about the world, and the independent existence of material factors. As David Campbell notes, postmodern constructivists "see their works as interpretive interventions that have political effects," while positivist constructivists see themselves as participating in a cumulative and objective social *science*.[14] By this time, the reader will recognize my position on the first two points of contention: this book is a work of positivist social science. While I recognize the power of the researcher and the inherent difficulties in coming to one's research from a purely neutral standpoint, my argument and analyses proceed from the presumption that scholars can know something about the world. I bracket questions of epistemology.

The question of ontology remains important, particularly as it relates to the colonialism argument. On the one hand, postmodernist (or "radical") constructivists argue that "brute material forces have no independent effects on international politics."[15] These scholars argue that the material of the international system—like guns, tanks, and ships—has no objective or universal quality beyond the meanings that humans give them. As such, postmodern constructivists focus on uncovering "the social construction of objects (chemical weapons), subjects (state identity), events (Cold War), institutions

12. Tannenwald 1999.

13. Wendt 2000, 180.

14. Campbell 1992, 221–222.

15. Wendt 1999, 110.

(sovereignty) and so on."[16] These scholars would take issue with my argument that colonialism affected the economic, social, and political conditions in the non-White world. Instead, they would implore me to consider the social construction of "poverty," state "failure," and political "instability," rather than fetishize these concepts as real or objective.

On the other hand, positivist constructivists believe that an independently existing physical reality governs our ideas about the world.[17] This constructivism adopts Wendt's "rump materialism" argument "that material conditions do have . . . constitutive effects on their own, independent of ideas."[18] For instance, technological capabilities affect how a state responds to threats. To illustrate this point, Wendt distinguishes between the Roman Empire and the United States: the former lacked the latter's technological ability to bomb its adversaries from a distance. Neither this difference nor the latter's ability depends on ideas or the social construction of threat. The material context independently constrained the Romans' ability to act.[19] Positivist constructivism treats ideas and material conditions as separate but linked phenomena, which allows scholars to consider material conditions as both *explanans* and *explanandum*. In some contexts, it makes sense to investigate the causes of material factors (What explains the persistence of global inequality?) or how actors give those material factors meaning (How do discourses of state "failure" reinforce international hierarchy?). In other contexts, material conditions are an important independent variable; they constrain actors' room for maneuver or affect costs and benefits (How does child poverty constrain a state's ability to maintain a robust liberal democracy?).

My argument in this book adopts this positivist constructivism. The Anglo-European world constructs migrants from the rest of the world as undesirable; the ideas that these countries' citizens and leaders have about people from the rest of the world govern their policies and dispositions toward them, *irrespective of material reality* (i.e., whether these countries are actually poor or whether immigrants are actually violent, etc.). However, the world's brute material facts still have independent effects that come before the social content individuals impose on them.[20] Much of the postcolonial world is

16. Price and Reus-Smit 1998, 270.
17. Wendt 1999, ch. 3.
18. Wendt 2000, 166.
19. Wendt, 166.
20. Searle 1995, 55–56.

poorer and experiences more domestic instability than the Anglo-European core, and scholars have spent great effort investigating colonialism's role in these conditions.[21] I take material conditions, like poverty and the infant mortality rate, as given and real examples of suffering, and I make a historical argument about how Western colonialism created these bases for labeling migrants from the non-White world as undesirable. This approach is consistent with antiracist scholarship that considers, for example, how racism (a social construction of inferiority and undesirability) made Black Americans more vulnerable to the COVID-19 pandemic (a material reality).[22]

Positivist Racial Constructivism

However, IR constructivism has a tenuous relationship with the scholarship on White supremacy and structural racism. To take one example, Henderson critiques Wendt's social constructivism because it "implies that only the Western states could be entrusted to transfer to the third world the requisites for a higher level of social evolution to lift them out of their lower condition."[23] This critique arises out of Wendt's distinction among Hobbesian, Lockean, and Kantian "cultures" of anarchy,[24] and Henderson highlights that Wendt's depiction of these cultures and how they emerge ignores colonialism, White supremacy, and imperialism. These critiques of constructivism center both on Wendt's (and others') epistemic silencing of the non-White world in theorizing changes in the distribution of ideas and how his social theory's "high level of theoretical abstraction" obscures the "meanings of specific episodes," like European imperialism.[25]

While critics point out several legitimate failings of IR constructivism, John Hobson reveals that nearly all international theory leans on a Eurocentric foundation.[26] "Eurocentrism" means that IR theory—as discussed in chapter 1—privileges Western stories, dates, and political forms and marginalizes non-White voices, stories, and contexts. And the discipline privileges these perspectives too. These critiques are welcome because reckoning with them will lead scholars to broaden the field's theoretical, substantive, and

21. See, e.g., Henderson 2015.

22. Kendi 2020.

23. Henderson 2015, 101–102.

24. Wendt 1999, ch. 6.

25. Sabaratnam 2020, 21.

26. Hobson 2012.

social tent. This consequence is both normatively and intellectually desirable because it will mean that more scholars, voices, and histories will add to our knowledge of international politics. To be sure, this book and any work written by a Western scholar at a Western institution will likely fail to some extent in this regard, and it is incumbent upon all scholars to acknowledge that IR is a global discipline with a global history and study it accordingly.[27]

Be that as it may, these critiques center on specific applications of constructivism's social theory to the study of world politics and *not the social theory itself*. Critics remain concerned that, for instance, Wendt's characterization of the cultures of anarchy presupposes that Western states possess a "White man's burden" to lift up the rest of the world into a Kantian culture. But there is nothing inherently White supremacist about theorizing how intersubjective meanings and the distribution of ideas affect world politics. This distinction matters because it reveals the power of constructivism's social-theoretic base to theorize how race and racism continue to operate in the international system. We can use the social ontology for good, and this is the goal of this book. I contend that the histories of Western imperialism led the Anglo-European core to construct the non-White world as undesirable. This construction began with the explicit racism of the fifteenth century that justified imperialism and slavery, carries through to the "scientific" racism of the nineteenth century, and persists in the color-blind racism of the present day.[28]

Positivist IR constructivism and racial constructivism share a social ontology, which allows me to use both to theorize how race and racism operate in the international system. Both constructivisms are *objectivist*; they refer to objects in the social world that exist, but are not natural kinds. Positivist constructivists in IR hold that material factors like nuclear weapons exist and have independent effects, and racial constructivists believe that race "is a contingently deep reality that structures our particular social universe, having a social objectivity and causal significance that arise out of our particular history."[29] However, there is nothing epistemically true or natural about what states believe either about the distribution of ideas in the international system (Are we in a system of friends or enemies?) or about racial

27. Acharya 2014; Dunne and Reus-Smit 2017.

28. This color-blind racism and embrace of colonialism persists in academia too. For example, Bruce Gilley has recently written a book lauding colonialism that relies on nineteenth-century justifications.

29. Mills 2018, 48.

groups (the same person is often raced differently in different social systems). Races have no biological or eternal basis, but they have a "social objectivity" that causes different people to experience the world in different ways that arise out of particular histories and social contexts.[30] In the case of the international system and international migration, the shared global context of Anglo-European imperialism and White supremacy structures how race and racism operate. Western imperialism fostered the global beliefs in the inferiority of the global South and created material conditions that the global North later considers undesirable.

This racial constructivism also relates to recent scholarship on antiracism. For instance, Ibram Kendi's work explores the history of racist ideas since 1500 and how they have affected politics and society in the United States.[31] Kendi traces the emergence and stature of segregationist, assimilationist, and antiracist ideas, and he claims that there is little distance between the first two groups. On the one hand, segregationist ideas center on beliefs about the natural, inherent inferiority of Black people, which justifies racial disparities in society that serve White self-interest. In this account, because Black people suffer from a defective ancestry, they should be excluded from White spaces and deserve unequal treatment. On the other hand, assimilationists believe that racial discrimination produces societal racial inequalities *and* that Black culture is also to blame.[32] Assimilationists argue that "ugly" Black behavior can adopt White "cultural traits and ideals" and improve their cultural standing.[33] This capability for cultural improvement sets them apart from segregationists. Kendi forcefully argues that members of the latter group—including prominent figures like Abraham Lincoln—are as racist as segregationists because they privilege White culture over Black culture. Even Barack Obama succumbed to assimilationist ideas when he appealed to the "erosion of black families" and other disproved social theories to explain racial inequality in the United States.[34]

Antiracists stand apart from segregationists and assimilationists and hold that all cultures "are on the same level," and that "Black Americans' history of oppression has made Black opportunities—not Black people—inferior."[35]

30. Mills, 48.

31. Kendi 2016.

32. Kendi, 2.

33. Kendi, 3.

34. Kendi, 492.

35. Kendi, 11.

Kendi's antiracist political project destabilizes common assimilationist tropes that reify the supposed pathologies of Black culture. The core of antiracism is the belief that "the only thing wrong with Black people is that [White Americans] think something is wrong with Black people,"[36] and once one truly believes that racial groups and their cultures are equal, then one must accept that racial discrimination produces racial inequalities. In his work, Kendi forgoes a discussion of racial ontology in favor of a presumption that racial groups are both real and unreal: there are no true differences between groups that society classifies as races, but one's racial category has fundamental consequences for their lives and prospects.

This position reveals an implicit racial constructivism that accords with my conception of race and racism in international migration. But this constructivism differs from most contemporary or empirical constructivists because it highlights how norm diffusion can lead to injurious outcomes. While the former implicitly assume that norm diffusion is a benign or positive process,[37] I argue that Anglo-European imperialism created the conditions that the global North uses to justify restricting migrants from the global South. This is a form of racial discrimination; the effects of past colonial exploitation and present presumptions and hierarchies are not inherent. Rather, these material consequences structure global beliefs about the global South that affect citizens' abilities to move throughout the world and reap the same benefits as those from the global North. There are no inherent differences among the regions of the world, only differences in the histories they experienced and Western beliefs about these places. This argument is akin to Kendi's assertion that "racist policies have benefited White people in general at the expense of Black people (and others) in general."[38] The story of racism is a story of unequal opportunity, unequal history, and unequal material consequences that reinforce ideologies of undesirability and inferiority. The fact that these presumptions have no natural, inherent, or biological bases makes race and racism powerful and pernicious.

Postcolonial Racial Hierarchy

This memory-less construction of inferiority is the chief way racism operates in the international system today. Historical beliefs motivated the West

36. Kendi, 511.

37. Finnemore and Sikkink 1998; Keck and Sikkink 1999; Tannenwald 1999.

38. Kendi 2016, 503–504.

to erect an international hierarchy based on racial difference, and the residue of this period affects how modern international institutions operate. The result is a contemporary international system, rife with racial hierarchy, that appears objective because Western states and their citizens neither recognize its historical antecedents nor have the incentive to do so. The material and ideological consequences of the past support present beliefs and behaviors.

The postcolonial international system is a direct descendant of the colonial international system in which the Anglo-Europeans codified a "natural" ordering of races based on their level of "civilization."[39] The pernicious thing about this "standard of civilization"—the requirements that Anglo-European states imposed on others for membership in their club—was that it was a moving target and that an outsider's level of civilization required recognition from members. Member states claimed that the standard was objective, but its pliability revealed its true nature: "like Sisyphus the less 'civilized' were doomed to work toward an equality which an elastic standard of 'civilization' put forever beyond their reach."[40] However, there were few requirements for retaining one's membership in the colonial international society once a state was a member. In other words, as long as a state was "civilized" and possessed European-like institutions,[41] they had few requirements to remain in the club. Notoriously, the standard of civilization applied only to outsiders, and this permanence codified international racial inequality. Even states that were formerly powerful members of the non-Western world, such as the Ottoman Empire, Siam, Mexico, and the Brazilian Republic, were subject to predation from Anglo-European states, no matter how hard these former powers tried to modernize.[42]

Students of international relations will immediately recognize this as a form of legal hierarchy. *Hierarchies* are "deep structures of organized inequality that are neither designed nor particularly open to negotiation."[43] This organized inequality establishes that some actors in world politics are inferior to others, that some past action or general history is responsible for this inferiority, and that things are unlikely to change. Hierarchies are deep structures, but they can arise out of explicit or implicit intentions. Colonial racial hierarchy

39. Gong 1984.

40. Gong 1984, 63.

41. Anghie 2007; Grovogui 1996.

42. Buzan and Lawson 2015; Chibber 2013; E. Rosenberg 2012.

43. Zarakol 2017, 7.

is an example of the former: it was explicit and obvious. White states placed themselves at the top of the pile, and they used their own civilized status to justify their right to recognize others as civilized or uncivilized. The story is the same as above: Anglo-European states had achieved a higher form of civilization, based explicitly on race, and this superiority required them to colonize, civilize, or dominate the non-White world. This perspective permeated international politics for generations.

In the postcolonial world, things are a bit more complicated. Race is no longer the (stated, explicit) basis for domination in the modern world. Leaders rarely use old-fashioned racism to justify a given policy, and the states of the postcolonial world are nominally equal members of the international system. In the conventional story of the international system's expansion, decolonization in the mid-twentieth century diffused liberal norms to the non-Anglo-European world and ushered in the modern period of legal equality.[44]

However, the end of colonialism was not sufficient to end inequality in the international system. Although scholars suppose that all states are now equal, like units, this assumption is not borne out in reality. Instead, the postcolonial international system remains deeply hierarchical, and these hierarchies are interconnected with previous empires that were drawn along racial lines.[45] I reveal that hierarchy in international migration in the previous chapter. What is the mechanism that perpetuates these hierarchies and how do they appear?

Simply put, as the number of sovereign states has increased, so too have the obligations required for membership in the international community. In the modern international system, legal sovereignty no longer requires recognition: states become sovereign when they become states. According to the 1970 UN General Assembly Resolution 2625, states are equal in the eyes of international law irrespective of their institutions or social and political differences.[46] States no longer need to demonstrate that they are prepared to take on the mantle of sovereign statehood; they become members of the club upon achieving statehood. Although the requirements for *initial* membership have vanished, the requirements for *maintaining* membership have skyrocketed.

44. Bull and Watson 1984; Dunne and Reus-Smit 2017; Philpott 2001.

45. Anghie 2007; Keene 2002, 2014; Reus-Smit 2013.

46. Declaration on Principles of International Law Concerning Friendly Relations and Cooperation among States in Accordance with the Charter of the United Nations, GA Resolution 2625 (XXV), October 24, 1970.

The most significant form of hierarchy in the postcolonial international system involves the number of international legal obligations that sovereign states need to fulfill. Although existing sovereign states grant membership in the United Nations to all "peace-loving states," the international society still needs to judge whether a state satisfies this standard. In other words, the principle of sovereign equality provides for the "disciplining of those that do not adhere to the rules and norms of contemporary international society."[47] As Aalberts notes, the key attribute of sovereignty in the modern international system is that sovereignty "entails a task to fulfill, rather than a freedom to indulge," and that "crucially, the scope of sovereign obligations has multiplied" as non-White states have been admitted as members.[48] So while the international system of the colonial period allowed states great freedom to act as they pleased, the postcolonial globalization of membership comes with far more strings attached. These new rules have been imposed during an era of increased attention to minority rights, the Washington Consensus, and the democratic peace; however, one would be remiss to ignore that these developments arrived precisely at the time of admission for non-White states.

For example, scholars and activists from the global South have critiqued the World Trade Organization on the grounds that it imposes undue standards on postcolonial states and these standards reinforce international inequality. The ideology of free trade was prominent during the colonial international system, but these strict standards are a modern phenomenon. From the perspective of postcolonial states, developed states require postcolonial states to achieve standards of free trade that the United Kingdom—the paragon of free trade ideology in the nineteenth century—did not practice during their own formative periods of economic development.[49] Free trade is just one example of the dramatic increase in obligations of sovereign states in the modern era. Those states that subscribe to these principles hold a higher place in the economic hierarchy than those that do not. Although I caution one to conflate correlation and causation—the association between postcolonial membership and new obligations is strong—it is instructive to highlight the shifting nature of sovereign statehood in the modern day. Justifications for these new duties often refer to the conditions within new states that require special attention. These conditions arose from long histories of

47. Aalberts 2014, 283–284.
48. Aalberts, 284.
49. Chimni 2006, 11.

colonialism, but they remain a burden on postcolonial states that will follow them indefinitely into the future.

One such burden concerns the construction of "failed" states. For Western policymakers, failed states earn this moniker when their government no longer is in control of its territory.[50] This definition seems straightforward, but discourses around failed states often include colonial concerns about the capacity for non-White states to govern themselves. After decolonization, Anglo-European states shifted from the colonial ideology of racial civilization to ideologies of development and modernization. Anglo-European states recognized that postcolonial states lacked certain markers of modern progress, which justified Western state interventions to provide policy advice and technical guidance to these new states.[51] This new ideology created new categories of least-developed, developing, and developed states that bears a striking resemblance to older categories of civilization. However, these sanitized categories, devoid of explicitly racist language, obscure the role that colonial histories had in creating inequality and the conditions that place non-White states in certain developmental categories.

The implications of categorizing postcolonial states without appreciating their history are severe. Calling a state "failed" not only has justified Anglo-European states providing advice and counsel but also has led to a more exclusionary and interventionist world order. This interventionist world order imposes further requirements on its members lest they want to risk external intervention in their affairs. A key example of this transformation has been the evolution of the Responsibility-to-Protect Doctrine (R2P). The United Nations International Commission on Intervention and State Sovereignty (ICISS) established the principles of R2P, and its founding report claimed the following:

> In an interdependent world, in which security depends on a framework of stable sovereign entities, the existence of fragile states, failing states, states who through weakness or ill-will harbour those dangerous to others, or states that can only maintain internal order by means of gross human rights violations, can constitute a risk to people everywhere . . . in security terms, a cohesive and peaceful international system is far more likely to be achieved through the cooperation of effective states, confident of

50. See, e.g., *Financial Times* Editorial Board 2020.

51. Gruffydd Jones 2013, 62.

their place in the world, than in an environment of fragile, collapsed, fragmenting or generally chaotic state entities.[52]

"Failed" or "failing" states may be members of the international system, but this modern interpretation of sovereignty *justifies* intervention in their affairs. This discourse inverts the institution of sovereignty in the modern international system. Prior to decolonization, being a member of the international society meant that a state was sovereign and had the right to resist intervention. If a state was not sovereign, then it was *terra nullus*—nobody's land—and sovereign states had the right to intervene, impose, and colonize. Now that non-White, postcolonial states are sovereign, existing members of the international order use sovereignty to justify policies and interventions into their affairs.[53] As such, the expansion of international society has led to a less absolute institution of sovereignty, particularly for new states, and this implicit tiering of the modern international system helps explain why some see this institution as "organized hypocrisy."[54] Using the effects of Anglo-European colonialism to justify the inversion of the rights/duties/features of sovereignty exemplifies how the ideology of race perpetually constructs designations of "Europeanness" and "non-Europeanness."[55] This construction evolves to fit the historical context.

In sum, the histories of colonialism and legal racism have led to the modern policies that intervene or restrict postcolonial states. These interventions reflect how the institution of sovereignty has changed as the international system has globalized to include the postcolonial world. Importantly, colonial exploitation created the conditions in postcolonial states that former colonial masters now use to justify interventions and policies like the Washington Consensus. International migration is an obvious example of this process. The racial bias in migration that I uncover in the previous chapter suggests that migrants from poorer, postcolonial, and non-White states migrate less than conditions suggest. This evidence, coupled with the argument from this chapter, suggests that one way this inequality persists is through more restrictive immigration policies throughout the world. States enact more restrictive policies when they are faced with more immigration from undesirable migrants from the supposedly dangerous or poor states that they helped create. This is how racism and racial inequality persist and

52. ICISS 2001, 5–8.

53. Grovogui 1996, 2002; Gruffydd Jones 2013.

54. Krasner 1999.

55. Hesse 2007, 646.

hide in the modern international system. In the sections that follow, I outline the evidence for the economic, political, and social consequences of colonialism. These consequences, coupled with the discussion above, provide the impetus for investigating whether exposure to undesirable migrants from former colonies has led Anglo-European states to further restrict their borders.

The Broad Consequences of Colonialism

The effects of colonialism hold together postcolonial racial hierarchies. Although Western states emancipated many of their colonies, the damage had already been done: the years of colonial exploitation created nation-states that the West would always perceive to be flawed.[56] The key word here is "perceive" because these constructions of inferiority persist despite variance in the postcolonial fortunes of states in the global South. And the reader should keep in mind that individual cases remain under detailed study by regional experts. However, perceptions are often more influential than nuanced reality, which is why prejudice is so pernicious. Yet, in this section, I explore the evidence that unmasks some of the damaging effects of colonialism and legal White supremacy.

Many of these effects were material: colonialism was coercive and brutal, and "empires were killing machines."[57] Colonial powers whose imperial forms and ambitions varied wildly—such as the United States, Britain, Germany, and Belgium—all left devastating effects through war, famine, disease, and exploitation. In regions as varied as "Tasmania, Tahiti, and Southwest Africa, the result was the extermination or massive reduction of the indigenous population,"[58] and the "loss rate" in some colonies was as high as 95 percent.[59]

However, as I describe below, colonialism affected different parts of the world in different ways depending on their geography, natural resource endowments, preexisting political forms, and so on. On the one hand,

56. The literature on Anglo-European colonialism and imperialism is vast. I address several of its axes in this section, but I focus on elaborating how colonialism and colonial policies affected living standards, wages, and political forms that those in Western countries later use to warrant a classification of undesirability (see, e.g., Berinzon and Briggs 2016; Cooper 1996; Frankema and Van Waijenburg 2012; W. F. Miles 2014; Moradi 2008; and C. Young 1994).

57. Buzan and Lawson 2015, 133.

58. Busan and Lawson, 133.

59. Mann 2012, 38–39, cited in Buzan and Lawson 2015.

in colonies that had existing centralized polities—such as Botswana or Burundi—colonization held further political development in check, and European exploitation destroyed the fruits of this previous development. One can make the same argument about White settler colonies. In these colonies—such as Mozambique or Zimbabwe—European rule was extractive, and the appropriation of land from Africans led to a massive increase in inequality. On the other hand, it is plausible that the effects of Anglo-European colonialism were more ambiguous in societies such as Somalia and Sierra Leone. Yes, colonizers built schools and railways. However, these improvements were not built to develop the country or educate its citizens, but to rule. This heterogeneity makes, for instance, identifying the causal effect of colonialism a fool's errand.[60] Entire disciplines frame themselves around uncovering and debating the effects of colonial histories.

Although different areas of the postcolonial world have had different experiences with colonialism, perceptions of these states are similar. Citizens of Western countries generally perceive postcolonial states to be poor, dangerous, and unstable, and Western states have contributed to those perceptions for centuries. These perceptions that are bound up with material effects help construct racial hierarchy in the postcolonial international order. As I describe in chapter 3, Western states used ideas of "civilization" and "tutelage" grounded in "scientific" racism to justify their imperial ambitions. To continuously reinforce perceptions of non-White inferiority among Anglo-European citizens, colonial states created "aesthetic 'contact zones'" that provided "live examples" of inferior non-White populations throughout the world that needed European help to achieve civilization.[61] An infamous example comes from the 1889 Paris Exposition Universelle's "village nègre" in which hundreds of Africans were compelled to demonstrate what life was "really like" in the colonies.[62] Modern perceptions of inferiority find their roots in these early events.

To be clear, I do not adjudicate long-standing debates about colonialism here, nor do I claim that this chapter represents a comprehensive or definitive account. Rather, this section provides the broad contours of how colonialism affected the places that the West colonized, and how this history created postcolonial subjects that many now perceive to be inferior or undesirable.

60. Heldring and Robinson 2012.

61. Buzan and Lawson 2015, 134.

62. E. Rosenberg 2012, 886–902.

The effects of colonialism fall into several categories, but I focus on the economic and political consequences. After reviewing each of these categories, in the next section I test the proposition that increased migration from former colonies is associated with more restrictive immigration policies in Western states.

Economic Consequences

Evaluations of foreign countries often depend on how rich or poor we perceive that country to be, and these perceptions of economic performance are influential. When we perceive a country to be rich or developed, we often overlook other characteristics that are less than desirable. For example, according to YouGov, only 32 percent of survey respondents have a negative view of Qatar despite its horrific human rights record and support for terrorist groups. Instead, respondents view the country as "safe and cultural," enjoy its "good restaurants," and only lament its "bad traffic."[63] In this ranking, Qatar compares favorably with Romania, and it is not a stretch to assume that the country's wealth, investments abroad, and other forms of soft power—such as sportswashing[64]—contribute to this perception. When respondents think a country is rich, they are more likely to view it as desirable and safe, regardless of its other ills.

This logic applies to immigration politics. Recent work shows that public opinion strongly favors accepting high-skilled immigrants from richer countries,[65] and this trend has persisted since the nineteenth century.[66] The key point for this analysis is that economic development is not randomly or evenly distributed throughout the world, nor is it within the control of any single migrant from that country. However, citizens and leaders use the economic performance of a migrant's country as a proxy for her potential contribution to their society even though one's birth country is a lottery.[67] As a case in point, the "new economic case" for migration restrictions is that migrants from underdeveloped countries will transmit underlying characteristics that are responsible for that underdevelopment and low productivity to their new countries.[68] Economists refer to this argument as the epidemiological model

63. https://today.yougov.com/topics/travel/explore/country/Qatar.

64. Brannagan and Giulianotti 2015.

65. Bansak, Hainmueller, and Hangartner 2016; Hainmueller and Hopkins 2015.

66. Zolberg 2008.

67. Shachar 2009.

68. I adopt this framing from Clemens and Pritchett 2019.

because it claims that immigrants spread low productivity from poor countries to rich countries like a disease.[69] The epidemiological model is influential because it is intuitive. It draws a simple analogy between migration and disease, and it raises familiar concerns about the institutional effects of immigration.[70] Ultimately, if migrant populations transmit too many of their perverse traits—"human capital, culture, genes, institutions, and language"[71]—they will impoverish destination countries.[72]

This is a classic economic argument, and it plays into the prevailing sentiment in many countries. But the argument is fallacious because it uses country-level outcomes to make inferences about the people within those countries. Such reasoning represents another example of the *ecological fallacy*—a logical fallacy that occurs when one uses group-level data to make inferences about the nature of the individuals who compose that group. Human beings make ecological fallacies all the time, particularly when it comes to evaluating prospective immigrants. That is what this chapter is about; concerns about the diffusion of individual-level characteristics that determine low productivity are logically necessary for arguments against immigrants from poor countries.

But what makes some countries richer than others? What makes some people more productive than others? And what role did colonialism play in this process? Since decolonization, scholars have lamented the lack of economic development in the postcolonial world, most notably sub-Saharan Africa. Most economists assume that low development persists because states lack free markets and strong institutions, and suffer from red tape and inefficiency.[73] But recent influential studies point to the slave trade and colonialism as explanations for underdevelopment.[74] These studies find that colonial histories and the identity of the colonizer are important predictors of later economic growth. However, colonialism was a very heterogeneous process; it took different forms throughout the world and therefore had very different effects. For instance, Heldring and Robinson argue that it is difficult to imagine a counterfactual world in which the United States and Canada would have

69. Algan and Cahuc 2013.

70. Isaac 1947.

71. Putterman and Weil 2010, 1677.

72. Collier 2013.

73. Moyo 2009; Sachs 2005.

74. Acemoglu, Johnson, and Robinson 2001; Nunn 2008.

higher GDP per capita if they had not been colonized.[75] At the same time, it is equally difficult to believe that Botswana or Ghana would not have higher levels of economic development if they had not been colonized. Although Botswana has experienced recent economic success, this progress has been in spite of colonization, not because of it.[76] All in all, the literature proposes several mechanisms through which colonialism inhibited future economic development.

First, the prevailing argument among scholars of an earlier generation was that European colonialism harmed colonial economies by looting resources,[77] and this argument persists in many circles.[78] British industrialization depended on expropriated land and (often slave) labor from its colonies, and these extractions funded more than half the country's domestic budget and paid for all the signifiers of modern development.[79] Belgian rule over the Congo is the most infamous case of this exploitation, and our best estimates reveal that this expropriation created a surplus of unemployed labor[80] and may have reduced African living standards by half.[81] Second, the colonial state was the primary engine of foreign domination throughout the global South, and that variation in institutional forms produced different growth trajectories after independence. Acemoglu, Johnson, and Robinson provide the most influential explanation. They argue that areas with less deadly disease environments had greater European settlement, which led to growth-promoting institutions to protect property rights during colonial rule. In colonies with higher death tolls, European settlement was lower, so they did not have the same incentive and instead established extractive, rent-seeking institutions that have not led to economic development after decolonization.[82] Others have built in this institutional argument to claim that other differences in colonial institutions had important effects on postcolonial economic development. Third, and along these same lines, others have pointed to the perverse effects of specific colonial institutions, such as agricultural marketing boards and other market-based institutions, on

75. Heldring and Robinson 2012.
76. Leith 2005.
77. Rodney 2018.
78. Chang 2010; M. Davis 2002.
79. Beckert 2015.
80. M. Davis 2002; Patnaik and Patnaik 2016.
81. Mosley 1983; F. Wilson 1972; Zwart 2011.
82. Acemoglu, Johnson, and Robinson 2001, 2005.

postcolonial economic development.[83] Fourth, Western colonialism was not limited to direct colonization and expropriation. For instance, from 1820 to 1950, Britain and France forced China to sign unequal postwar treaties that imposed neocolonial arrangements that often were accompanied by Western extraterritorial control. During this "century of humiliation," Chinese GDP fell from the ninety to the twentieth percentile globally,[84] and Western views of "deviant" Chinese culture continue to produce modern perceptions of a society inherently susceptible to subterfuge at the hands of Communists and other enemies of the West.[85]

These mechanisms are not necessarily competing; colonialism was a broad process that looked different throughout the world. Regardless, the balance of the evidence suggests that colonial incursions of various forms had negative effects on the later economic development of postcolonial states and perceptions thereof. Moreover, even in those places that benefited from colonialism—through European technology—colonizers made little effort to ensure that these benefits endured. In many cases, these benefits were restricted to the colonial period; after European colonizers left, any positive effects faded away while the negative effects of racism, discrimination, and inequality remained.

A NOTE ON DEPENDENCY THEORIES

Some readers may consider the discussion above faithful to long-standing economic theories of dependency and underdevelopment. Indeed, I argue that one can attribute many modern rationales for restricting immigrants to the histories of European imperialism and neocolonial relationships. Whether or not we can identify a direct effect of colonialism, European imperialism impacts the global South and perceptions thereof. Immigrants from certain countries are deemed undesirable, and some analysts worry that they will transmit the culture that maintains their underdevelopment to Western states.[86] I connect these claims to histories of domination; imperial enterprise had material effects and continues to condition how many Westerners think of these places. Scholars made similar arguments about Latin America, Africa, India, and the Caribbean throughout the 1960s,

83. Bates 1981.
84. Maddison 1998, 164.
85. Del Visco 2019.
86. Algan and Cahuc 2013.

1970s, and 1980s, and this approach attracted widespread attention and debate.[87]

It would be remiss of me to ignore this debate because it reveals that structural theories of underdevelopment are anything but settled science. Critics of this approach argue, first, that dependency theory is imprecise and tautological and it therefore can only critique the capitalist system in general, rather than specific colonial practices.[88] Second, others contend that structural theories of underdevelopment and dependence deprive global South states of agency. In other words, this critique suggests that these theories "are based on invidious comparison between African states in crisis and idealized and tendentiously characterized states elsewhere."[89] Third, some suggest that dependency theories overemphasize economics, politics, and the nation-state, while ignoring how colonialism affected the social relations within states and issues of race and gender.[90] A final group of scholars disputes these theories on empirical grounds, noting that some former colonies in the global periphery have transitioned to the economic center.[91]

These refutations are significant because they reveal important weaknesses in using dependency theory and other theories of structural underdevelopment as a general theory about the world economy. However, this debate does not usurp the argument that I present above. To be sure, grand social theories like dependency theory are not causal panaceas, and the literature that addresses these neo-Marxian approaches rightfully addresses their limitations. But my argument is simple and does not rely on adopting the entire dependency theory approach into one's theory of the international system. Instead, I make two arguments. First, imperialism had material consequences on the lives and livelihoods of those affected. Second, these consequences plausibly carry over to the present day both materially and perceptually.[92] Developed states continue to appropriate labor and resources from the rest of the world, and in 2015 this sum amounted to 10.1 billion tons of raw material and 182 million person-years of labor.[93] This is why I highlight Western racism toward states that have experienced economic development,

87. See, e.g., Amin 1976; Beckford 1972; Booth 1985; and Ganguli 1965.

88. Lall 1975.

89. Mkandawire 2001, 290.

90. Bonilla and Girling 1973; Chase-Dunn 1982; Grosfoguel 2000.

91. Amsden 2003.

92. Hickel, Sullivan, and Zoomkawala 2021.

93. Dorninger et al. 2021.

explore the myriad effects of colonialism, and describe various differences in the historical record throughout the world. Moreover, my theory in this book explicitly considers the construction of race and racism in the international system and how these modern processes connect to the formation of the postcolonial state and social relations therein. As such, this project adopts a modern constructivism to avoid the ills of past theories of underdevelopment, recognize the importance of race to international migration processes, and still take a global historical approach that identifies why many throughout the world still consider immigrants from the global South undesirable. In the next section, I continue this line in noting the political consequences of Anglo-European colonialism.

Political Consequences

The effects of colonialism on postcolonial economic development were tightly bound up with political institutions. It is impossible to talk about the consequences of colonialism without discussing how economics and politics were implicated in the same process. After all, most colonies served the economic interests of the metropole, and the actions of colonial powers reflected this relationship. The implication of this interdependence is that the mechanisms that accentuated economic underdevelopment in former colonies caused and were caused by the effects of colonialization on political institutions. Therefore, it makes sense to consider how colonialism affected the politics of former colonies because these consequences affect our perception of the "stability" and "desirability" of migrants from the non-White world.

The main perception of postcolonial political institutions is that they are corrupt or despotic. There are many paths to corruption and despotism, and there is certainly a debate over the respective causes and consequences of each. However, no explanation is complete without highlighting that colonial powers often drew arbitrary boundaries to denote their territorial possessions. In every case, these new boundaries did not take precolonial politics or settlement patterns into consideration, and as a result created colonial states that divided and consolidated existing communities. Colonial rule over these arbitrary boundaries led to tiny and ineffective postcolonial states that had little to no control over large swaths of their territory. Moreover, these new states lacked social cohesion, divided existing societies, or combined groups that were often antagonistic. As Lange and Dawson explain, the British combined three hundred different linguistic groups to create the colonial Nigerian state.[94]

To create cheap institutions of political control, colonizers picked specific local leaders to serve as regional extensions of the colonial state. Europeans gave these local leaders power in exchange for their collaboration, which led to the abuse of those powers. For example, the British created a system of paramount chiefs in Sierra Leone to support their system of indirect rule. This system created a political hierarchy that had never before existed in Sierra Leone and led to political despotism. After independence, these states lacked a national identity and a stable social contract, and the electorate was fragmented. This manufactured despotism produced postindependence political instability, and in many cases a one-party state. When states lack a connection to their society, they must resort to coercion and corrupt partnership with local elites to extract the resources necessary to function. Therefore, the result of colonial rule was often a state that was "despotically strong, infrastructurally weak, and hardly integrated."[95] There are many examples of postcolonial states with these characteristics that have promoted violence and civil war, such as the Democratic Republic of Congo, Somalia, and elsewhere. In Sierra Leone, political exclusion and animosity toward the British-imposed colonial chiefs led to a bloody ten-year civil war.[96]

Championing local leaders through indirect rule was only one way colonial rulers promoted instability and violence within their states. In addition to catalyzing despotism, colonialism produced and reified group identities that led to violent ethnic conflict after independence. This process had important historical and sociological bases. Recall that the ideology of scientific racism that underpinned colonialism was based on the ideas of racial hierarchy and stratification: one could rationally divide populations into groups, and these groups possessed natural communal identities. As a result, colonizers began categorizing their subjects along racial and ethnic lines, and this explicit ordering of society made differences among groups more salient.[97] Some scholars have seen this process as a deliberate strategy to divide and

94. Lange and Dawson 2009, 789.

95. Lange and Dawson, 790

96. Heldring and Robinson 2012; Keen 2005.

97. Baber 2004; King 1999; Mamdani 2001.

rule colonial possessions. If colonizers could divide their subjects into antagonistic groups, then they would be easier to dominate. A society with salient and opposed ethnic identities would be more preoccupied with fighting each other for the spoils of the colonial state than opposing colonial rule. British India is a prominent example of this strategy. There is substantial evidence that Hindu nationalism only emerged as a comprehensive ethnic identity during the colonial period. What is more, the British promoted this identity, and some scholars suggest that they deliberately pitted Muslims and Hindus against each other through unequal treatment.[98] This division within the Indian state has been the basis of postcolonial strife and violence, for example, with Pakistan.[99]

Colonial rule produced societal conditions and weak institutions that made violence more likely, and these mechanisms affected each other. Indeed, the strength of the state and its institutions affected its ability to combat this civil conflict, and the form of the postcolonial state made civil war more likely.[100] States need a robust administrative and coercive capacity to stem the tide of political violence. This discussion illuminates how colonialism destabilized the political capacity of postcolonial states and created the conditions for violence that weak states could not control. In this way, colonialism created a reinforcing cycle of political instability and violence.

In many cases, colonial powers categorized indigenous populations for ease of administration. This process created salient identities and the potential for in-group conflict. This division coincided with the promotion of certain local leaders that led to corruption and the further institutionalization of antagonistic identities, as some groups received privileged positions in the colonial administration. These ethnic grievances and political corruption produced postcolonial states that were divided, prone to violence, yet incapable of addressing that violence due to their weakness and instability. Cross-national studies of colonialism provide further evidence for these mechanisms and show that colonial histories are associated with communal conflict.[101] The important implication of this work is that there is some evidence to confirm popular perceptions of postcolonial states. Even though the evidence linking colonialism to weak institutions may, for example, only

98. King 1999; Nanday 1983; Pennington 2004.

99. Baber 2004; Breuilly 1993.

100. Henderson 2015.

101. Henderson 2015; Lange and Dawson 2009.

apply to colonies under indirect rule, the stigma of instability is attached to all postcolonial states.

The political instability and violence that often arises from division and despotism is a key consequence of colonialism. Beyond the obvious consequences for the victims, political violence broadcasts a state's instability and precarity to the world. As a result, the rest of the world comes to view that state as dangerous. The implication for immigration is clear: immigrants from these parts of the world may themselves be dangerous. This perception has important consequences for immigration policymaking and structural inequality in the color-blind international system.

Colonial Histories and Migration Policy

Race and racial differences are social constructs, but inequalities based on social constructs are still inequalities. This chapter has delved deeper into the relationship between colonial histories and modern perceptions of inferiority and undesirability. Although there is nothing biologically real about race, colonialism affected certain areas of the world that happened to be inhabited by those we perceive as non-White. These effects often created the conditions within colonies of all forms that fomented economic underdevelopment, political instability, and violence. Politicians and publics are free to view these latter effects as objectively undesirable: one does not need to be an overt racist to view violence and poverty in a negative light. Structural inequalities emerge and persist when those in power do not analyze the histories that created these conditions and use aggregate conditions within states to make inferences about the quality of prospective immigrants.

Importantly, the modern construction of racial undesirability does not depend on facts or objectivity; it is about perceptions. Even for states like China that have experienced tremendous economic growth since the 1960s, the West still stigmatizes these cultures as undesirable, unassimilable, dirty, or "other," which leads to racism, anti-immigrant violence, and prejudice.[102] These beliefs about non-White immigrants and states from the global South persist despite evidence to the contrary and have reared their head during the COVID-19 pandemic.[103] Encounters during the colonial period and the rise

102. Prashad 2001; Puri 2005; Philip Yang 1999, 2000.

103. Gover, Harper, and Langton 2020; Reny and Barreto 2020.

of global capitalism produced long-standing prejudices that persist in the current day and continue the construction of undesirability, even when the facts suggest otherwise. Social constructions are a moving target.

The modern politics of immigration policymaking is rife with this sort of behavior, and the openness of Western publics to various types of immigration reveals the connection between colonial histories and modern restrictions. Public opinion scholars have noted for several decades that elites respond to their constituents and activate anti-immigrant sentiment, and recent survey research shows that Western publics remain antagonistic toward migrants whom they consider to be security threats or economically desperate.[104] The Western response to so-called economic migrants is an indicative example of this behavior: citizens of rich countries do not view migrants who are seeking better economic opportunities as worthy of admission.[105] In this way, citizens of the global North marginalize the economic needs and insecurities of citizens of postcolonial states—needs that their own countries helped produce. They perceive economic migrants from undesirable countries of the world as an undue drain on the country's resources. This suggests an implicit, yet predominant, trend in the public sentiments of rich countries to ascribe economic insecurity as a deserved status for those living in poor countries. In other words, although many emigrated in the past in search of economic opportunities,[106] Western publics perceive these past migrations as legitimate and current migration from postcolonial states in search of a better life as illegitimate.

In the next section, I conduct a cross-sectional analysis of this phenomenon. Specifically, I test whether Western states enact increasingly restrictive immigration policies after they receive an influx of immigrants from postcolonial states. This evidence shows a connection between inflows of migrants from countries that have experienced the effects of colonialism—economic precarity, political instability, and violence—and the impetus to enact more punitive immigration policies. As such, the empirical capstone of this chapter sustains the argument that colonialism produced the conditions that Western states consider undesirable in the present day. In other words, this evidence shows how racial inequalities persist in the modern international system and the role that colonial histories play.

104. Hainmueller and Hopkins 2015; Hopkins 2014; Kustov, Laaker, and Reller 2021.

105. Bansak, Hainmueller, and Hangartner 2016, 218.

106. Zolberg 2008.

Analysis

In the previous chapter, I use linear regression to see whether states enact more restrictive immigration policies in years after they receive racially different immigration flows. The approach was simple, yet the results were definitive. In the final section of this chapter, I use a similar strategy to infer whether Anglo-European states enact more restrictive immigration policies when they receive increased immigration flows from postcolonial states. The goal of this analysis is to amass multiple types of evidence that the history of colonialism helped construct those from the postcolonial world as undesirable and unfit for membership in Western societies. This is the pernicious aspect of modern racism and racial inequality: leaders point to "objective" criteria that Anglo-European states had a hand in perpetuating over the course of hundreds of years. By compiling these various types of evidence, I am able to test the *Colonial Legacy hypothesis* from chapter 3:

> *When states receive increased immigration flows from former colonies, they should respond with an increase in immigration policy restrictiveness. This association should be stronger for the former colonizers.*

In this analysis, the main dependent variable is the same as in the model from chapter 5: the changes in a state's immigration policy restrictiveness in a given year. As such, the unit of analysis is the destination country–year; this analysis is monadic. A value of zero indicates no change, positive values indicate a restrictive change, and negative values indicate less restrictive changes. The natural log of this variable is approximately normally distributed, which makes various flavors of ordinary linear regression appropriate. To reiterate, data on immigration policy changes is scarce, and scholars have only gained traction on this important data paucity in the last decade or so. In this analysis, I use the DEMIG policy dataset, which has information on immigration policy changes for forty-five states from the eighteenth century through 2013.[107] The full set of country-years in the dataset is found in table 5.4. The scope of this dataset leads to a rich analysis because the states included are not simply either colonizers or members of the Anglo-European core; the scope is wider.

Throughout history, states such as Indonesia, South Africa, and Ukraine were either colonized or subjected to some variety of external control. In some parts of this analysis, I group all these states together because the theoretical

107. DEMIG 2015.

mechanism should apply broadly. Colonial incursions affected the material contexts and perceptions of the global South and reinforced ideologies of danger and undesirablity, and this effect should carry through regardless of whether a given state colonized others. In other parts of the analysis, I parse whether there are different associations for states that either were colonizers or are members of the OECD.

The main independent variable in this analysis is similar to those in chapter 5. As such, I restrict this analysis to the period from 1960 to 2013. Although the immigration policy data extend further back in history, the immigration data only begin in 1960. To create this variable, I add up each state's immigration flows during a given time period and record the proportion of those flows that came from a postcolonial state. I use the proportion of postcolonial immigrants rather than the raw number because all countries have different baselines for immigration; this logic motivates the baseline model of migration in the previous chapter. Using the proportion of postcolonial inflows accounts for the degree to which the average citizen or elite considers the immigration flows to be composed of migrants from former colonies. Of course, whether they do so accurately is another story.

I also use a set of controls similar to those in the previous chapter, and I standardize them to aid in interpretation by subtracting the mean and dividing by two standard deviations. I include these controls to account for other economic, political, and social factors that may affect both a state's immigration policy restrictiveness and its propensity to attract immigrants from the postcolonial world. The economic variables are whether a state experienced a negative GDP shock in a given year,[108] the log inflation rate, and the percentage of a state's GDP that comes from trade. I use the World Bank database to compile or construct these indicators.[109] I include a dichotomous variable that indicates whether a given state is at war in a given year. This variable includes civil conflicts and international wars, and I use data from PRIO to construct this indicator.[110] Finally, I include the liberal democracy index from the Varieties of Democracy (V-Dem) project to measure a state's level of democracy.[111] Again, this measure of democracy is appropriate because it

108. These results are robust to other GDP variables, such as GDP growth and GDP per capita levels.

109. World Bank 2019.

110. Gleditsch et al. 2002.

111. Coppedge et al. 2019.

better captures the multidimensional, latent nature of democracy, and it is a continuous measure of this complex structure.

The main results of this analysis are in table 6.1. In model (1) and model (2), a state's change in immigration policy restrictiveness is the dependent variable; model (1) includes fixed effects for destination country and year, and model (2) includes random effects for destination country and year. In model (3), I also include random effects, but in this model the dependent variable is an indicator for whether a state enacted a restrictive immigration policy shock. I define a shock in the same manner as in the other analyses above, consistent with how Neilsen et al. construct their measure of foreign aid shocks.[112] I compare the immigration policy restrictiveness in a given year with the level of restrictiveness in the previous year. If this difference is in the top 85 percent of all differences in a given year, I code that state as having implemented a restriction shock.

The results in all three models are consistent with the theory that states enact more restrictive immigration policies when faced with immigration flows from postcolonial states. In each model, the coefficient is positive and significant at every conventional level of significance. In models (1) and (2), increasing the proportion of immigrants a state receives from one standard deviation below the mean to one standard deviation above is associated with a 20 percent increase in immigration policy restrictiveness. In model (3), that same change in the composition of immigration flows is associated with a 20 percent increase in the probability that a state enacts a restrictive immigration policy shock. It is important to reiterate that these magnitudes are substantively large considering that the modal change in immigration policy restrictiveness in a given year is zero. Importantly, this relationship is consistent across all models, which signifies that this result is not a by-product of the construction of the dependent variable or the decision to use random or fixed effects.

In addition to the relationship between postcolonial inflows and restrictiveness, a few other results stand out. First, in models (1) and (2), there is a positive relationship between negative GDP shocks, inflation rate, and conflict and immigration policy restrictiveness. In other words, countries that experience negative shocks to their GDP, higher inflation rates, and either subnational or interstate violence are more likely to enact restrictive immigration policies. At first blush, it is not clear whether these relationships are

112. Nielsen et al. 2011.

TABLE 6.1. Are immigration flows from former colonies associated with greater migration policy restrictiveness? (1960–2013)

	Dependent Variable		
	Immigration Policy		Restrictive Policy Shock
	Linear Mixed Effects (1)	*Fixed Effects* (2)	*Generalized Linear Mixed Effects* (3)
Log Postcolonial Inflow	0.201***	0.197***	0.752***
	(0.053, 0.349)	(0.055, 0.339)	(0.310, 1.194)
Negative GDP Shock	0.102*	0.119**	0.256
	(−0.010, 0.215)	(0.030, 0.209)	(−0.125, 0.637)
Log Inflation	0.262***	0.258***	−0.692***
	(0.149, 0.375)	(0.084, 0.433)	(−1.110, −0.274)
Conflict	0.281*	0.318**	0.255
	(−0.008, 0.571)	(0.057, 0.580)	(−0.839, 1.348)
Liberal Democracy	−1.020***	−1.040***	−0.170
	(−1.204, −0.835)	(−1.351, −0.730)	(−0.654, 0.315)
Trade Openness	−1.960***	−2.052***	0.523**
	(−2.174, −1.747)	(−2.419, −1.684)	(0.100, 0.946)
Constant	−1.056***		−2.432***
	(−1.536, −0.576)		(−2.708, −2.156)
Random Effects	X		X
Fixed Effects		X	
Observations	1,584	1,584	1,584
R^2		0.805	
Adjusted R^2		0.792	
Log Likelihood	−2,142.334		−494.021
Akaike Inference Criteria	4,304.668		1,006.041
Bayesian Inference Criteria	4,358.345		1,054.351
Residual Standard Error		0.888 (df = 1489)	

Note: *$p < 0.1$; **$p < 0.05$; ***$p < 0.01$.

consistent with or contrary to expectations. On the one hand, some may argue that states that are at war or have experienced economic downturns will be more likely to accept more immigrants because they provide cheap labor and a larger tax base.[113] In this account, one would expect the coefficients to be negative, so the result in table 6.1 is surprising. On the other hand, conflict and economic precarity create the xenophobia, fear, and anxiety that have produced waves of anti-immigration sentiment in the past.[114] This position is consistent with these results.

Second, in models (1) and (2), I estimate a significant, negative relationship between liberal democracy and immigration policy restrictiveness. This result is similar to what we saw in the previous chapter, and it accords with existing arguments about the openness of liberal democracies.[115] It is important to highlight this pattern because it provides further evidence against the argument that liberal democracies must be closed to outsiders to protect their extensive freedoms.[116] However, this analysis does not repudiate the argument that liberal democracies trade openness to outsiders for internal freedoms. Instead, this theory suggests that liberal democracy may moderate the effect of postcolonial inflows on immigration policy. Democracies may have more liberal immigration policies than autocracies, on average, but strong liberal democracies may implement restrictive policies in response to inflows from undesirable immigrants.

To test this argument, I estimate the effect of postcolonial immigration inflows on immigration policy restrictiveness for three different groups of countries: autocracies, weak liberal democracies, and strong liberal democracies.[117] To do so, I rely on the same nonlinear interaction model as I use in chapter 5. This binning estimator allows one to reveal nonlinear interaction effects and is superior to traditional linear models with interaction terms because it does not require strong linear-additive assumptions.[118] In figure 6.1, we can see how the effect of immigration flows from former colonies varies by political regime. Autocracies and weak liberal democracies do not appear to enact strict immigration policies after they receive more postcolonial inflows.

113. Rudolph 2003.

114. Zolberg 2008.

115. Joppke 2005.

116. Hollifield 2004; Weyl 2018.

117. To draw these distinctions, I use the V-Dem liberal democracy index to split the countries into terciles.

118. Hainmueller, Mummolo, and Xu 2019.

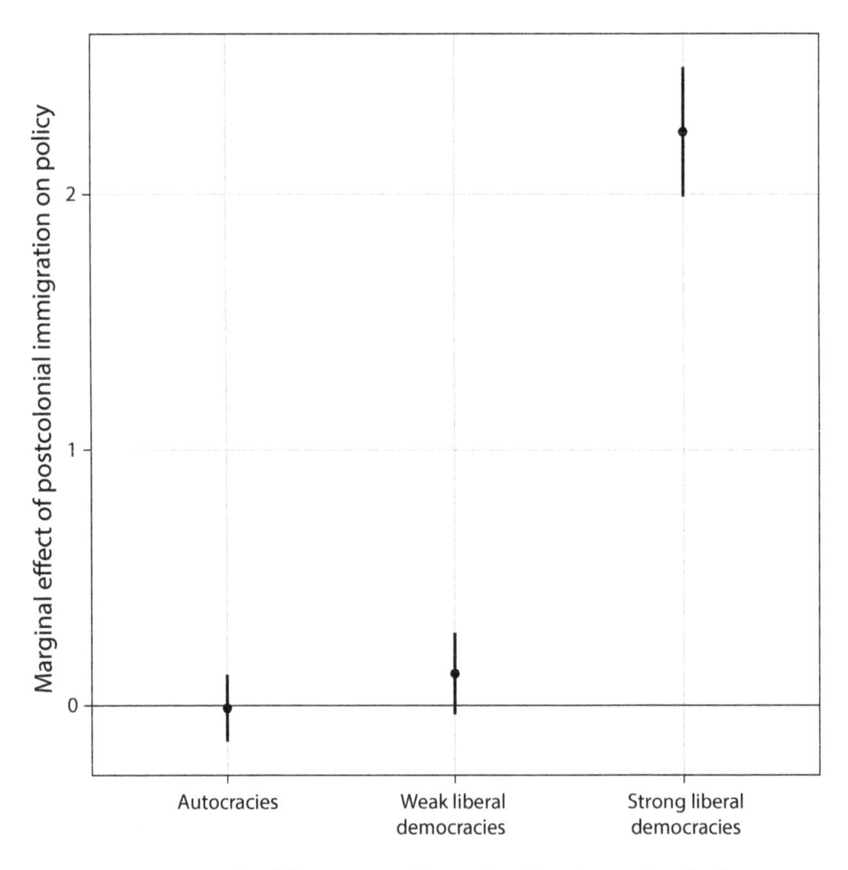

FIGURE 6.1. Liberal democracy moderates the effect of postcolonial inflows on restrictive policies.

However, this ambiguity vanishes for strong liberal democracies. When these states receive immigration flows from former colonies, they sharply respond with more restrictive immigration policies. To be specific, this model estimates that a one standard deviation increase in the proportion of immigrants from postcolonial states is associated with over two new restrictive immigration policies in strong liberal democracies. This is a strong association. Taken together with the results from the previous chapter, it is clear that liberal democracies have an uneven relationship with immigration policy restrictiveness. While liberal democracies are less restrictive on average, strong liberal democracies respond to undesirable immigrants with impunity.

Finally, there are two important contradictions between models (1) and (2) and model (3). In the former, there is a positive relationship between inflation and policy restrictiveness and a negative association between trade openness and restrictiveness. These coefficients are flipped in the latter model. On balance, it is not clear whether this reversal is an artifact either of the sample of countries that make up the DEMIG policy dataset—mostly stable liberal democracies with some outliers—or of any of the modeling decisions. In either case, the main result of interest—that between postcolonial immigration flows and restrictions—is consistent, as well as substantively and statistically significant.

Are Former Colonizers More Restrictive?

It is important to consider whether being a colonizer affects a state's relationship to immigration flows from former colonies. Colonizers, by definition, are directly responsible for the effects of colonialism in these countries. Accordingly, the theory I outline in previous chapters implies that former colonial powers will have been inculcated with the ideology that former colonies are dangerous, poor, and violent. These states are the most susceptible to ideologies of postcolonial inferiority because their national histories and "dispatches from abroad" are so entangled with the need to justify that the non-White world requires pacification and improvement.

To be clear, this theory does not imply that former colonizers will have more restrictive immigration policies on average. Rather, the theory suggests that former colonizers will react to inflows from former colonial subjects with restrictive immigration laws. Colonial powers construct their subjects as inferior to justify their rule. Although explicit colonial rule may fade, these states will be the most likely to construct former colonized peoples as inferior and undesirable because they have such an intimate connection with these constructions. It is unlikely that there will be no consequences from countries using racist justifications for colonialism and spreading these among their population for hundreds of years.

To test this argument, I conduct a simplified regression analysis, the results of which are in table 6.2. Model (1) uses the whole sample and is a simple regression of immigration policy on an indicator of whether a destination state is a colonizer. Model (2) includes a linear interaction between the colonizer variable and the proportion of a state's postcolonial immigration inflow to test whether colonizers are more sensitive to these inflows. Models (3) and (4) replicate model (1), but model (3) is run only on the sample of former colonizers—Belgium, Denmark, France, Germany, Italy, Japan, the

TABLE 6.2. Effect of colonial histories

	Dependent Variable:			
	Immigration Policy			
	(1)	(2)	(3)	(4)
Colonizer	0.257**	−0.325		
	(0.058, 0.456)	(−0.834, 0.184)		
Log Postcolonial Inflow		−0.589***	1.954***	−0.571***
		(−0.829, −0.350)	(1.166, 2.741)	(−0.799, −0.343)
Colonizer X Postcolonial Inflow		2.777***		
		(1.956, 3.599)		
Fixed Effects	X	X	X	X
Full Sample	X	X		
Colonizer Sample			X	
Noncolonizer Sample				X
Observations	1,742	1,742	524	1,218
R^2	0.099	0.159	0.139	0.212
Adjusted R^2	0.093	0.152	0.121	0.205
Residual Standard Error	1.920 (df = 1730)	1.857 (df = 1728)	1.977 (df = 512)	1.761 (df = 1206)

Note: $^{*}p < 0.1$; $^{**}p < 0.05$; $^{***}p < 0.01$.

Netherlands, Portugal, Russia, Spain, the United Kingdom, and the United States—and model (4) is run on the noncolonizers such as Indonesia. I include fixed effects for a given year in each of the models and cluster the standard errors. The clearest result is that colonizers do have more restrictive immigration policies; the positive and significant coefficient in models (1) and (3) show this association. At the same time, noncolonizers have less restrictive policies and are less likely to enact a restrictive immigration policy change (model (4)). Finally, model (2) investigates whether colonial histories moderate the effect of postcolonial immigration flows on restrictive immigration policies. In other words, do colonizers enact more restrictive immigration policies when they receive immigrants from former colonies? The results answer this question with a clear "yes."

However, as I note above, this interactive model imposes strict assumptions that are often not satisfied in political science data. Namely, the moderating effect of postcolonial immigration flows on the effect of colonial history and restrictive policy may not be linear. Figure 6.2 uses the same binning estimator as figure 6.1 above. This analysis shows that colonizers only enact more restrictive immigration policies than noncolonizers when they receive relatively large inflows from postcolonial states. In other words, states that were not colonizers are more likely to implement restrictive immigration policies when they receive low to intermediate proportions of immigration flows from the postcolonial world. However, when comparing states that receive high proportions of their immigration flows from postcolonial states, it is clear that colonizers dramatically respond by enacting more restrictive policies than states that were not colonizers.

Examining differences between colonizers and noncolonizers is one way of revealing the effect of heterogeneity. In so doing, I show that these groups of states have different baselines in immigration policy restrictiveness and respond to immigrants from former colonies in different ways. In addition to the models in table 6.2 and figure 6.2, I take advantage of a multilevel approach to reveal this heterogeneity. Specifically, I rerun model (1) from table 6.2 with random slopes for the destination country. This model allows each destination country to have its own estimated effect of postcolonial inflows on immigration policy. In table 6.3, I present the ten countries with the largest effect, and it is evident that former colonizers (United Kingdom, United States, Portugal) are well represented; however, this pattern is not absolute. Other states like Israel, Australia, and the Slovak Republic also lie in the top ten, but their presence is not surprising. There are many paths to restrictive

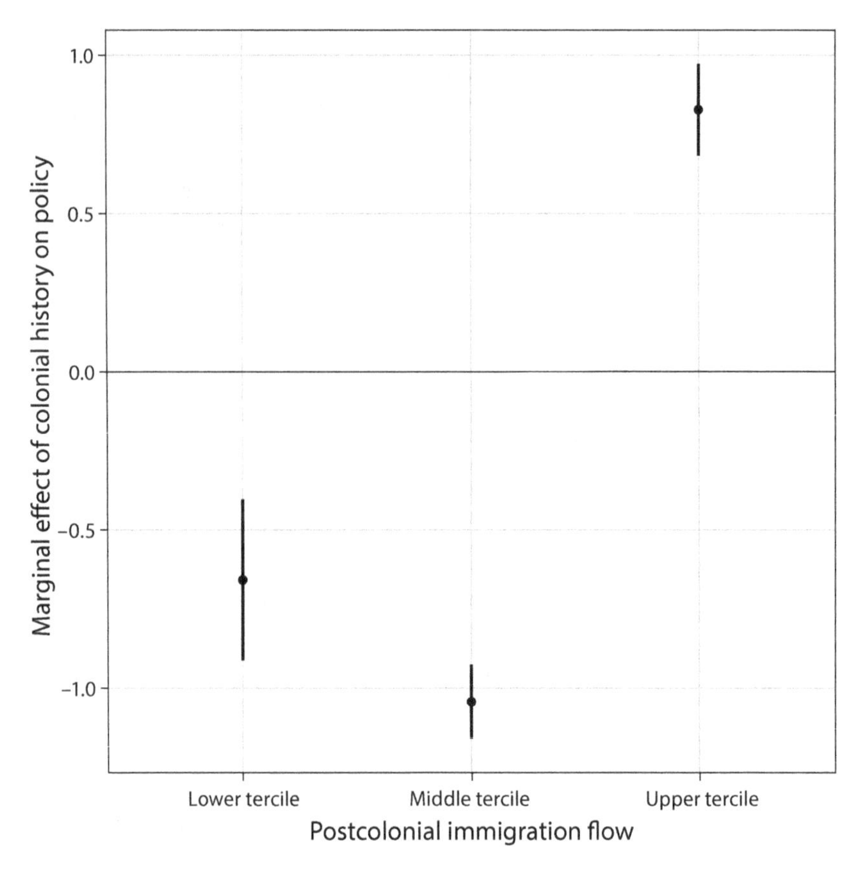

FIGURE 6.2. Postcolonial immigration inflows moderate the effect of being a colonizer on policy restrictiveness. States are divided into equal terciles based on their level of postcolonial immigration inflow to show this nonlinear interaction effect.

immigration policies, and there are many paths to a restrictive reaction to certain types of immigration flows. This table and this analysis simply show that, on average, the conclusion that colonizers are more reactive to postcolonial immigration flows carries through, *even when one does not use an interactive model.* In this analysis, I do not impose any structure on the model: I do not interact the colonizer dummy variable with the postcolonial immigration flow variable. I do not explicitly divide the sample into two groups and look at the different effects within those groups. Instead, the data themselves reveal the same patterns as the other more restrictive approaches, with fewer assumptions.

TABLE 6.3. Countries with the largest positive effect of postcolonial inflows on immigration policy

	Country	(Intercept)	Postcolonial Inflow
1	United Kingdom	−4.92	10.37
2	Netherlands	−1.08	4.25
3	United States	−0.61	4.05
4	Portugal	−2.90	2.65
5	Israel	1.48	2.62
6	Greece	−2.20	2.24
7	Australia	−3.64	2.13
8	Denmark	0.09	1.73
9	Germany	−2.56	1.53
10	Slovak Republic	−1.25	1.48

To conclude this analysis, I use the random slopes model to show predicted differences between a colonizer (United Kingdom) and a noncolonizer (Iceland). I simulate from the fitted regression model that I use in table 6.3 to estimate how each of these countries would react to different proportions of postcolonial immigration flows. The results are in figure 6.3. In this figure, I plot the standard deviation change in the proportion of immigrants from postcolonial states on the x-axis. For example, a value of 0.5 indicates that a country received a 0.5 standard deviation increase in the proportion of immigrants from postcolonial states in a given period. For each of these values, I plot the corresponding number of restrictive (or less restrictive) immigration policies the model predicts each country would enact in a given year. So for a hypothetical 0.5 standard deviation increase in the proportion of postcolonial migrants, the model predicts that the United Kingdom would enact approximately five policies in a given year that are more restrictive, while it predicts that Iceland would enact approximately one policy that is more lenient.

Figure 6.3 makes the differences between these two types of countries stark. On the one hand, for hypothetical decreases in the proportion of immigrants from former colonies, the model predicts that Iceland ambiguously enacts more restrictive immigration policies, while the United Kingdom severely decreases its immigration policy restrictiveness. On the other hand, when these states receive increased numbers of immigrants from postcolonial states, the model predicts Iceland ambiguously decreases its restrictiveness while the United Kingdom becomes far more restrictive. These predicted quantities corroborate the other findings from this chapter, and draw in

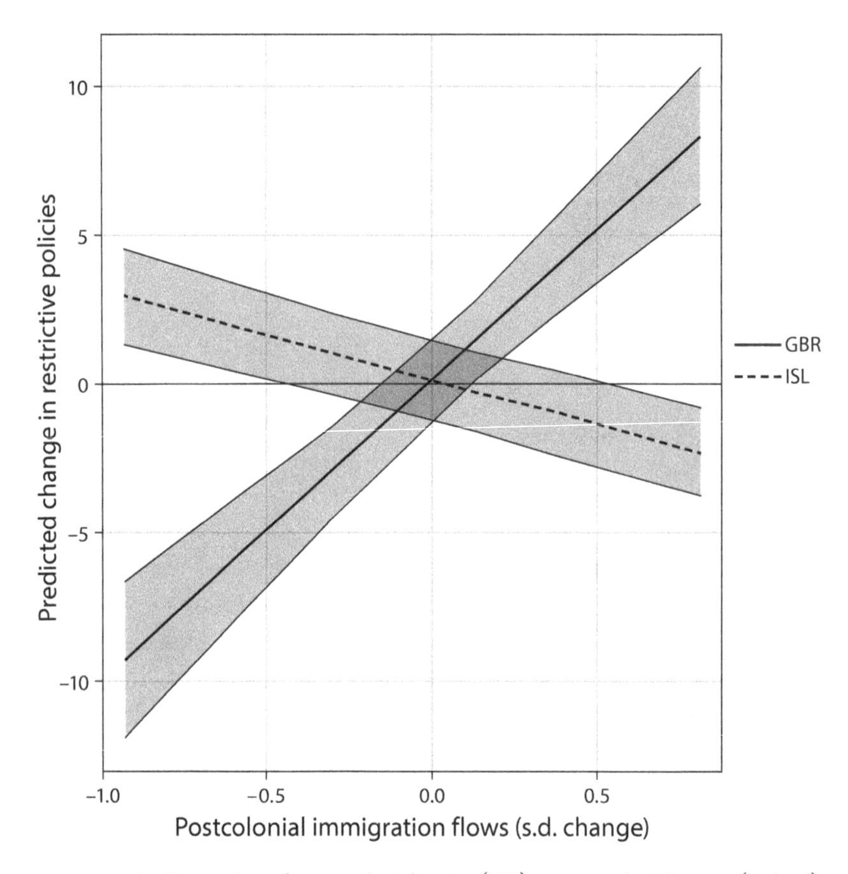

FIGURE 6.3. Comparing a former colonial power (UK) to a noncolonial power (Iceland). At low levels of immigration from postcolonial states, the UK is less restrictive than Iceland, but this relationship flips at above-average levels. Iceland's immigration policy is not sensitive to changes in the composition of immigrants.

greater relief how historical differences matter. The United Kingdom—one of the most notorious colonizers in world history—is incredibly sensitive to immigration flows from former colonies while Iceland appears far less sensitive. To be sure, this is not a causal model and the model is ignorant of what we do not include: these countries are quite different, receive different numbers of immigrants, and so on. This figure simply layers on additional evidence that supports the theory that states react to inflows from former colonies, but that there are important differences in these reactions. Taken together, this evidence clearly delineates how colonial histories continue to affect former colonial subjects, even in an international system that is nominally equal and color-blind.

Discussion

In this chapter, I elaborate on my argument that the history of European colonialism created the conditions in postcolonial states that the West now so naturally decries as undesirable. Colonialism was extractive and exploitative; colonial possessions were meant to serve the metropole. This exploitation affected colonial states in several ways. In one conventional example, colonizers used their colonial possessions as geysers of natural resources and strategic geography, which either harmed existing political institutions or prevented states from experiencing their own political development. In other examples, colonial rules propped up intermediaries that consolidated their rule and created authoritarian regimes, reinforced (or created) ethnic cleavages that spiraled into war, carried out "civilizing missions," and built infrastructure only for the purposes of benefiting the colonial power. In each of these cases, colonialism produced underdevelopment, weak states, and violence that persisted for decades. While the effects of colonial rule transcend this mere description, it is clear that European imperialism had a hand in perpetuating cycles of underdevelopment, instability, and violence—and perceptions thereof—that continue to have important effects in the modern day in many regions of the world.

The effects of colonialism go beyond the mere damaged institutions and economies of colonial subjects. As Frantz Fanon describes, colonialism degraded and dehumanized the colonial subject, which left a deep, psychological impact. The West used the ideology of scientific racism to degrade colonial subjects and their cultural practices and reduce their status to that of undomesticated animals.[119] Europeans used the tag of "primitive" or "underdeveloped" on the non-White world for centuries to warrant the destruction of cultural institutions and the assimilation of colonial society into European culture. During colonization, this dehumanization allowed for continued colonial exploitation due to "a belief in fatality [which] removes all blame from the oppressor."[120] Over the course of his work, Fanon goes to great lengths to diagnose and examine the structural effects of this psychological trauma on colonized peoples.

However, colonization not only left devastating psychological damage on the colonized but also affected the West's perception of these parts of the world. Although the effect on the colonizer's psyche and perception is of less

119. Fanon 1963, 32–33.
120. Fanon, 42.

moral importance, these effects have deep implications for the structure of racial inequality in the modern, color-blind international system. Namely, after centuries of being told that, for example, Africa was the "dark" and "mysterious" continent, it is no wonder that citizens of the West continue to perceive it as such. These stunted perceptions affect how leaders and citizens of the West perceive immigrants and refugees from the non-White, postcolonial world. Scholars like Paul Collier, Robert Kaplan, and David Miller decry the "cultural" consequences of immigration for a reason: they perceive non-Anglo-European culture as inherently incompatible with practices in the West.[121] These perceptions did not arise out of thin air. Rather, scholars and laypersons alike are imbued with an ideology of colonial, non-White inferiority that continues to affect how the West interprets the "objective" conditions in the postcolonial world. And in states that have overcome these effects, long-standing perceptions of inferiority linked to the colonial period continue to structure the relationship between the global North and South.

I show that this often ignored dimension of international history continues to affect the ostensibly postracial process of international migration. Specifically, I show that migrants from postcolonial states are less free to migrate than those from the rest of the world. This inequality also extends to immigration policymaking, as Anglo-European countries have shown themselves to be more willing to enact restrictive immigration policies after they encounter increased migration from the postcolonial world. Although Margaret Peters argues that racism cannot explain variation in immigration policy restrictiveness because it has been consistently present in Western society,[122] this analysis shows that the *exposure* to those the racists deem undesirable is what springs states into action.

Conclusion

This chapter pairs with the analysis in chapter 5 to demonstrate the persistence of racial inequality in international migration. In these analyses, I use several strategies of inference to overcome the inherent issues associated with studying race and migration in an observational setting. These issues notwithstanding, the evidence shows that migrants from the poor, non-White global South—defined in several ways—are less free to migrate. Although the

121. Collier 2013; Kaplan 1994; D. Miller 2016.

122. Peters 2015, 114.

explicit immigration laws of Anglo-European states no longer discriminate on the basis of race, ethnicity, or religion, I find that immigration policy restrictiveness has increased in response to increased immigration from the regions of the world that were previously restricted on racial grounds. To be sure, these immigration flows are not randomly assigned, nor measured without error; however, the weight of this corroborating evidence unmasks a structure of color-blind White supremacy in the ability to move around the globe. This evidence may catch few in some circles by surprise; critical race scholars and their comrades have made claims about the persistence of a "global apartheid" for several decades.[123] Yet, it is vital to use the language of the mainstream to expose the inequalities in nominally equal international processes. For many laypersons and scholars of international migration, the removal of racist laws was the end of the story. This analysis shows that, on the contrary, changing the laws was only the beginning.

In the final empirical chapter of this book, I expand the scope of study beyond the Anglo-European world. To be specific, I look for additional evidence for how racial inequalities in movement persist and expand in the postcolonial period. In chapter 3, I theorize how the spread of the institution of sovereignty to the postcolonial world has an important hand in the expansion of this inequality. This is not an exercise in blaming the victim, nor is it an admonishment of independence movements. Rather, this final piece of analysis argues that the late-modern nation-state emerged as an institution whose purpose was to exclude outsiders and manage their populations. Restriction defines what it means to be a state, and the "victory" of the postcolonial nation-state form over other alternative movements codified these restrictions throughout the world.[124] The ideology of bordering and restriction has retrenched and strengthened since decolonization. This hegemony explains how international racial inequality has expanded in the postcolonial world, and it is to this process I turn in the next chapter.

123. Köhler 1978; Nevins 2012; Richmond 1994.

124. Getachew 2019; Wilder 2015.

7

The Expansion of Closure in the Modern International Order

THIS CHAPTER BUILDS on the two previous chapters which examine how racial bias in international migration persists in a color-blind world. Taken together, chapters 5 and 6 imply that Western states continue to enact policies that disproportionately impact immigrants of color and that they enact these policies when faced with increased immigration from the non-White, postcolonial world. These conclusions reveal a dimension of international inequality that few in the mainstream discipline of international relations have considered, and they shine a light on how simply removing racist laws and institutions is not sufficient to produce equality. If the story ended here, this book would unmask the structural inequality that continues to stare the non-White world in the face, and we could proceed to theorize the costs and ethics of this structure and its consequences for the study of international politics. However, this final empirical chapter unpacks the ironically tragic dimension of the postcolonial international system and its patterns of migration.

This dimension goes beyond the actions of Anglo-European states and how they respond to the "undesirable" world that their colonial incursions created. Going beyond, I consider how colonialism, processes of decolonization, and their effects continue to reproduce and *enhance* extant international racial inequality. This perspective runs counter to the conventional ignorance of persistent racial hierarchies in mainstream international relations scholarship.[1] However, it accords with existing scholarship on

1. See Grovogui 1996; Henderson 2013; Krishna 2001; Nisancioglu 2019; and Shilliam 2013; see also Vitalis 2015, for critiques of this ignorance.

how colonialism affected and continues to affect the global South and its institutions.[2]

This conventional ignorance of racial inequality pervades the study of international politics: realists argue that modern hierarchies boil down to imbalances in the capabilities of states,[3] while institutionalists claim that some states rationally choose to enter into hierarchical arrangements,[4] and English School scholars highlight the expansion or globalization of international society and its institutions after decolonization.[5] In each of these perspectives, persistent racial hierarchy in international politics is either epiphenomenal or invisible because the presumption is that postcolonial states are either equal (English School scholars and laypersons); unequal due to their own insufficient capabilities (realists); or hierarchical by choice (institutionalists). While English School, critical, and interpretavist scholars have begun facing the persistent inequalities in the modern international society,[6] the latter two approaches presume that postcolonial states are now free to act as they see fit, or at least in a way consistent with their material power. Therefore, any instances of inequality in international politics reduce to choice: some states either have implicitly chosen not to walk the path toward building up their capabilities, which has left them perpetually inferior out of no fault of the West, or they are free to choose their own arrangements with other states and institutions, some of which are hierarchical.

Postcolonial states, however, are rarely free to choose their own arrangements, and there are many examples of how Western states imposed restrictive conditions on their colonial subjects prior to decolonization. Freedom with conditions is the state of play in the international system, and this arrangement has forced non-White states of the global South to "earn" their equality in ways that were not required of their Western counterparts in previous eras. I describe some examples of these conditionalities in chapter 6.

In the naive account of global history, decolonization and the end of de jure racism in the international system ought to allay historical inequalities. Above, I show that we are still a long way from racial equality in international migration patterns, but I have left out half of the story. In chapters 2 and 3, I lay

2. See, e.g., Henderson 2015; Mamdani 1990; Mkandawire 2010; and Van de Walle 2009.

3. Krasner 1999, 3.

4. Cooley and Spruyt 2009; Lake 2009.

5. Dunne and Reus-Smit 2017, 29–31.

6. Anghie 2007; Keene 2002; Reus-Smit 2013; Spanu 2019; Suzuki 2005.

out how the emergence of the modern, rational nation-state was entwined with racist immigration laws. Modern states required larger tax bases and standing armies, which led to the fomentation of nationalism. Modern states offered up political participation and other rights in exchange for taxes for public goods and military service, which made states more legitimate and powerful. Nationalism, xenophobia, and jingoism spread because ambitious leaders took advantage of mobilized and crystallized national publics. This development coincided with the rise of scientific racism and eugenics, which catalyzed the creation of discriminatory immigration policies.[7] This is a historical institutionalist account that corresponds well with the historical record and explains the rapid rise of modern states, populism, ethnic cleavages, and racist immigration controls in the Anglo-European world during the nineteenth century. This theory also helps explain why we see the persistence of restrictive immigration policies in the Anglo-European world: the desire to restrict undesirables never went away, and undesirability is correlated with existing constructions of racial difference that fit the purpose of state building. But this account does not explain why we see *increased* inequality in migration in chapter 5.

In this chapter, I lay out the second half of the story, which addresses what happened during and after decolonization and explains why we see more inequality, rather than less. In short, decolonization was not a simple process: colonizers resisted and only acquiesced to independence after their subjects agreed to severe conditions. This conditionality was endemic throughout the postcolonial world, and it reflects the differences between non-White, post-1960 decolonization and earlier examples. Anglo-Europeans imposed the colonial state on their subjects, which greatly differed from the European state-building experience. That Anglo-European and postcolonial states experienced independence differently is an important and often overlooked feature of international history.

Decolonization transformed the international system, but it did not transform the norms of international politics. The institution of sovereignty was still paramount: decolonization did not lead to the drastic rethinking of the state form that many postcolonial thinkers desired.[8] The existing institutions of the international system persisted, and these norms of behavior imparted what it meant to be a modern nation-state. "Proper" nation-states

7. Kroneberg and Wimmer 2012; Wimmer 2013.

8. Cf. Getachew 2019; Wilder 2015.

had similar institutions—foreign ministries, standing armies, flags, and so on—and decolonization led to the diffusion of the Western model of how to be a state to the postcolonial world. I adopt this account of decolonization from the world polity theory of John W. Meyer and his collaborators.[9] World polity theory is powerful because it picks up where the institutionalist approach leaves off and describes the hegemony of the nation-state model in the postcolonial era in compelling and convincing terms.[10]

However, an account of decolonization that depends solely on world polity theory misses a key point. Namely, world polity theory has a fuzzy view of state agency, which makes it uncomfortable to describe the trajectory of postcolonial states. World polity theory suggests that world cultural norms diffuse throughout the world, and that actors interpret their adoption of these existing models and institutions as self-interested rationality.[11] Implicitly then, the world polity theorists would claim that postcolonial states *chose* to emulate Western nation-states. Such a story misrepresents the "freedom" that former colonies possessed after gaining independence; it ignores the continued, structural power of the West and disregards how colonizers imposed domestic governance institutions on their colonial subjects.[12] The adoption of Western models of the nation-state were clearly not free choices, as they often ran directly against those who wished to organize the postcolonial world in a different manner. Applying world polity theory to decolonization without reflection can resemble victim-blaming.

In turn, I lean on the work of Antonio Gramsci to highlight how the hegemony of the model of the Western nation-state shaped and shoved the emergence of postcolonial states. I argue that postcolonial states were embedded in a Western world culture that reflected continued Anglo-European hegemony in the international system. Independence and decolonization were processes that created the perpetual need for new states to do more to perform their legitimate statehood. In the case of border control and immigration policy, Western states pushed the postcolonial world into institutional models that emphasized that proper nation-states firmly control their borders. This adoption of Western bordering practices often reflected the exact opposite of historical precedent. In fact, freedom of movement existed throughout

9. Meyer et al. 1997.

10. Wimmer and Feinstein 2016, 615.

11. Meyer et al. 1997, 168.

12. Henderson 2015.

much of the postcolonial world, particularly in sub-Saharan Africa and the Ottoman Empire,[13] prior to the nineteenth century. Colonizers imposed arbitrary boundaries, broke up centuries-long norms, and conditionally accepted postcolonial states as members of the international system. To appease these latter conditions and perform their legitimacy within the context of Western hegemony, postcolonial states enacted strict bordering policies. This epitomizes the dark side of norm diffusion that I highlight in chapter 6.

Take the African continent, for example. When Europeans arrived and colonized Africa, they created the first hard boundaries in the continent's history, which led to new citizenship laws and border controls that tied individuals to specific, geographically defined polities. For the first time, people would not be able to move as they pleased, a freedom that was central to life in the precolonial period.[14] However, after independence, the closing and policing of international borders became an "important symbol of sovereignty."[15] This trend produced more closure and inequality in postcolonial patterns in international migration, as postcolonial states adopted Western models of border control that entrenched the norms of boundary-making.

In this way, postcolonial states are not "racist" when they control their borders. These states are victims of Western imperialism and hegemony, both of which force their hand in perpetuating this behavior. This ambiguity in postcolonial agency is important to acknowledge because it reveals how policies we observe are not truly free choices and depend on a history of exploitation. Most postcolonial states are located near other postcolonial states. This means that most postcolonial states live in a neighborhood of other states that also experienced the brunt of colonialism. As a result, when they enact restrictive policies to perform their sovereignty and protect their borders, they increase restrictions on non-White migrants because most migrants that postcolonial states encounter are also from the global South.[16] In this way, they inadvertently reproduce the same exclusions that occur in the West.[17] So, while the leaders of postcolonial states are technically complicit in

13. Kasaba 2009.

14. Herbst 2000, 227.

15. Herbst, 228.

16. Abel and Sander 2014; Abel 2018.

17. To be sure, free movement zones do exist in a few regions of the global South, but these zones would only dispel my argument here if they were ubiquitous or the standard, rather than limited exceptions.

their adoption of strict border controls, these actions take place in an international system that requires non-White states to constantly perform their legitimacy. One cannot understand the postcolonial rise of restrictiveness in international migration without appreciating the history of imperialism.

The chapter proceeds as follows. In the next section, I describe existing accounts of decolonization and the globalization of the international society. I pay close attention to how these theories ignore the imposition of nation-state institutions on the postcolonial world, and how these state-level policies reinforce international hierarchy. Next, I elaborate on world polity theory and how it helps us explain the expansion of Western models of nation-statehood throughout the world. Following that, I critique the conventional world polity account of how the nation-state form diffused to the postcolonial world. To do so, I discuss Gramsci's concept of hegemony and the effect of continued Anglo-European dominance in the international system on newly independent states' behavior in international institutions. Given this theoretical framework, I elaborate on my account of how and why restrictions on movement quickly emerged in former colonies and discuss it in relation to others. Then I warrant this argument with quantitative evidence that shows the expansion of restrictive bordering practices throughout the postcolonial world. The final section concludes with the implications of this increased restrictiveness on the international system and its inhabitants.

The Hegemony of the Nation-State

When former colonies gained independence, they resembled existing members of the international system rather than some other type of polity. This was not a surprise. Over the past two-hundred years, the nation-state has become the dominant political form in the international system. It has outlived and surpassed kingdoms, empires, sultanates, city-states, and duchies, and the sheer dominance of one type of political organization is remarkable given previous eras of international history. Naturally, there is a debate over how the hegemony of the nation-state emerged. On the one hand, historical institutionalists claim that the first nation-states succeeded because they offered a radically different bargain with their populations. The state would exchange political participation for military service and public goods for taxes. This bargain strengthened and legitimized these states, and it mollified popular resistance to incursions such as tax collection. Moreover, these states could now mobilize massive numbers of citizens for military service because the population had a personal stake in the state's destiny. Nationalism, its sense of "we-feeling," and the idea of the national state was a natural consequence of this embrace of previously disparate populations.[18] This bargain spread as the Industrial Revolution took hold and more states pursued the high-modernist goals of the period. As I describe in chapter 2, nationalism, the politicization of race and ethnicity, and populism were different outcomes of a general process of political modernization.[19] Taken together, these different rationales explain the rise of nationalism and why the nation-state spread over the past two-hundred years.[20]

On the other hand, world polity theorists argue that historical institutionalists cannot explain why a non-nation-state was more likely to be replaced by a nation-state rather than another type of political form during the twentieth-century. In other words, historical institutionalism may adeptly describe the particular historical process that produced the European nation-state, but it cannot explain why nation-states became hegemonic during the twentieth-century. World polity theorists argue that existing states passed along behavioral norms to newly independent states in international organizations. New states become sovereign when existing states recognize their legitimacy. That recognition occurs after extensive communication within those organizations and involves existing states sharing the nation-state template. In so doing, existing states advance the spread of a particular form of statehood.[21] The importance of recognition and the intersubjective construction of new states is similar to the English School account of how the international society expanded or globalized during the same period.[22] Unsurprisingly, given the relative plausibility of each account, there is mixed evidence for each, and it is clear that neither provides a covering law explanation of this vast period of international history.[23]

This debate is relevant to the larger argument of this book because it is a debate over *expansion*: Why did the nation-state spread throughout the world when it is not obvious that it is functional for every state in every region of the world? Given that a variety of types of political organization flourished

18. Buzan and Lawson 2015, 114.

19. Kroneberg and Wimmer 2012, 179.

20. There is a large literature on the historical institutionalist account. For recent work, see Kroneberg and Wimmer 2012; Hiers and Wimmer 2013; A. D. Smith 1998; and Wimmer 2013.

21. Li and Hicks 2016; McNeely 1995; Meyer et al. 1997; Strang 1991.

22. Bull and Watson 1984; Dunne and Reus-Smit 2017.

23. Li and Hicks 2016; Wimmer and Feinstein 2016.

prior to the colonial period, why did we see no reversion to these precolonial forms? Why were anticolonial, anti-nation-state movements, such as Negritude, unsuccessful? The implication of the institutionalist/world polity debate is that something about the trajectory of international history made it more likely that former colonies would resemble Western nation-states than another type of polity. Whether one believes this was a bottom-up (institutionalist) or a top-down (world polity theory) process delineates the sides.

In chapter 2, I lean on an institutionalist account of the emergence of modern, Anglo-European nation-states. The pernicious aspect of the transformation of the Anglo-European world was that the ideology of progress that motivates states to perfect, centralize, and modernize was the same ideology that fostered xenophobia, racism and eugenics, and colonial expansion. The historical moment that produced the Second Industrial Revolution also begot the period of "scientific" White supremacy in which racist immigration restrictions played an integral part. The emergence of the modern nation-state occurred when long-standing Anglo-European states transformed with little direct influence from others. While nationalism and other ideologies of progress diffused across Europe, there was no extant model of how a modern nation-state should behave. These practices simply (or complexly) emerged out of a confluence of historical events. However, decolonization and the production of new *postcolonial* polities took place during a different time and under different auspices.

Postcolonial polities emerged in the international system exclusively out of previously subordinate relationships with existing states. In many cases, this emergence occurred out of bloody wars of liberation (such as in Algeria) or out of larger imperial dissolutions (such as the Ottoman Empire) or when colonial subjects allowed former colonizers to have privileges in their territory (such as continued French monetary control over much of West Africa). These latter cases of independence with conditions track with Kwame Nkrumah's description of neocolonialism whereby "the State which is subject to it is, in theory, independent and has all the outward trappings of international sovereignty. In reality its economic system and thus its political policy is directed from outside."[24] In other words, the decolonization of the non-White world was different because these new states ostensibly joined the same international society as their former masters, but their membership

24. Nkrumah 1965, ix.

was not as equal as advertised. Institutionalism lacks a good account of how the nation-state form spread to the postcolonial world under these conditions because it cannot explain why postcolonial polities adopted the nation-state in particular, in the face of other compelling and popular alternatives, under the careful watch of existing states, many of which happened to be former colonizers.

In short, the Anglo-Europeans constructed a "world society" or "world culture" of how polities should organize themselves, look, and behave in the modern world. Initially, this process was not deliberate; it emerged naturally out of the institutionalist story I describe above. However, two world wars, the defeat of European fascism, and the emergence of established forums for international communication and cooperation—such as the League of Nations and the United Nations—led to the establishment of a dominant world culture that dictated clear norms for how modern polities should organize themselves. While there were fissures over regime type, the evidence shows remarkable isomorphism across nation-states on the eve of decolonization. In the next section, I further elaborate on this world polity theory of decolonization. Specifically, I outline the mechanisms that led to the spread of the Anglo-European nation-state form to the postcolonial world. This discussion sets up the final piece of this book's argument: how this particular version of (hegemonic) decolonization led to the rise of border control and immigration policy restrictiveness and created a more restrictive postcolonial world.

World Culture, Decoupling, and Symbolic Reform

To explain why we see increased racial inequality in movement since decolonization, I begin with world polity theory. World polity theory is powerful because it explains why we observe striking similarities across all nation-states in the international system. These similarities include flags, ministries of education, constitutions, and other institutions. In brief, world polity theory argues that, since the Enlightenment, a world cultural model has emerged that defines popular sovereignty, rational statehood, individual liberties, and equality before the law as key cornerstones for appropriate state behavior and purpose.[25] This template has had an important role in constituting the modern nation-state "since at least the 17th century." As a result, the international

25. Meyer et al. 1997.

sovereign state system has been composed "of formally equal nation-states having similar rationalized identities and purposes."[26] This homogenization has intensified as the number of states in the system has increased.[27]

According to world polity theory, these world cultural templates became global after WWII. During decolonization, newly independent states adopted the same norms and institutions as existing members of the international system, and world polity theory provides a *macrophenomenological* account—not reducible to the individual intentions, circumstances, or histories of states—for how and why certain features of states diffused to the rest of the world. This culture defines the nation-state as a rational and responsible actor, and this is how states present themselves in international forums. The leaders of states represent their polities as purpose-driven organizations that act rationally to achieve clearly delineated goals. The power of world polity theory emerges when one considers that the goals of states in the modern era are remarkably similar. Nearly all states—regardless of regime type—claim they want to achieve economic growth, collective progress, and individual flourishing. States codify these commitments to collective and individual progress in national constitutions,[28] which leads them to pursue similar goals in economic, education, and military policy.[29]

This insight leads to conclusions similar to realist and institutionalist accounts, which suggest, for different reasons, that states should behave and look similarly. Functional requirements of statehood, other powerful states in the system, and domestic cultures ensure that nation-states adopt the same institutions, goals, and interests. However, this is not the case in reality. For example, nearly all constitutions and official state discourses emphasize a commitment to egalitarian citizenship, but actual state policies contradict or run counter to these pronouncements in many cases. This disconnect is called *decoupling*. Decoupling is an important concept because it both provides additional evidence for world polity theory and demonstrates its strength in explaining international development.[30] For if world cultural forms—independent of the individual intentions of states—do not exert causal power, then decoupling would not proliferate throughout the world.

26. Meyer et al., 163.
27. Strang and Meyer 1993.
28. Boli 1987.
29. Meyer et al. 1997, 153.
30. Meyer et al. 1997, 154.

Decoupling occurs because new states adopt the entire suite of proper nation-state behaviors wholesale; they do not pick and choose. However, it is not possible to implement all the institutions of a modern nation-state. Global socialization processes work at different levels and are therefore implemented at different speeds, which can lead to incoherence. Some institutions are easier to implement than others, and many elements are inconsistent with existing local practices and customs, even among those states that were colonized by Europeans. Introducing more ambiguity, some global practices themselves "are highly idealized and internally inconsistent, making them impossible to actualize in practice."[31] The institutions and behavior of modern nation-states were not rationally developed; they emerged out of the historical process I describe above, and this inchoate development led to a patchwork of overlapping, often incompatible practices. In truth, there is no coherent template for postcolonial states to pull off the shelf.

An important consequence of this difficulty is that it is more straightforward for postcolonial states to symbolically adopt certain institutions rather than others. For example, it is much easier to create a governing executive with cabinet ministries, including a ministry for education, than to build schools, organize a national education policy, and create the social services at local, regional, and national levels to support these initiatives. This is not the fault of postcolonial states, nor does it reflect an inherent inability to create an effective national education system. Instead, it is an obvious implication of two factors. First, new states attempted to create an independent nation-state apparatus, including all institutions, in an astoundingly short period of time. While many Anglo-European states developed their modern state form over centuries of chaotic fits and starts without the influence of external colonizers, postcolonial states had no such luck. The effect of European colonialism is a key mechanism for this entire book, and it returns in this chapter's story.

Second, these modern nation-state practices are often at odds with both precolonial and colonial institutions. States in the former group had entirely different political institutions, and the imposition of Western cultural norms on their development was anathema to their previous trajectory. As Henderson notes in the case of Africa, the emergence of "quasi" postcolonial states "ossified Africa's variegated political communities within state structures that were usually inconsistent with the precolonial forms."[32] Some states,

31. Meyer et al., 154.

32. Henderson 2009, 33.

like Somalia and South Sudan, did not develop centralized institutions and instead had strong local governance structures; while others, like Nigeria, Sierra Leone, and Uganda, had a mixture of local and centralized institutions. In post-Ottoman Turkey, the nation-state apparatus has remained at odds with nomadic tribes to the present day.[33] Thus, Anglo-European institutions were not obviously functional for these states, and it is unsurprising that the transmission of externally defined identities and practices led to significant decoupling.

Postcolonial institutions resembled colonial institutions, and the bargain between the postcolonial elites and their former colonizers ensured the continuity of the repressive colonial domestic economy. Not only did colonial domination affect the economic, political, and institutional starting points of postcolonial states, but their economies also deliberately "focused less on internal industrial development and more on the often brutal extraction of resources, exploitation of labor, and maintenance of dependent relations in international trade . . . to benefit the metropole and its domestic agents."[34] This continuity was ubiquitous in postcolonial Africa, Asia, and Latin America,[35] and its inequality baked in the decoupling process and explains the most pernicious aspect of this account for the case of international migration: the implementation of symbolic reform and policies. As a result, codifying general principles in law or planning for future progress and policies occurs in the absence of state capacity. This takes place when states engage in extensive national planning programs and codify general principles of their commitment to human flourishing and progress. These general plans and statements signal to the rest of the world that the state is committed to these tenets, but in the absence of state capacity, they function as symbols. Symbolic adoption occurs throughout the international system. For example, Hafner-Burton and Tsutsui provide evidence that signing global human rights accords did not actually improve human rights records in the developing world and in the most abusive countries.[36] States feel compelled to conform to global cultural standards, but in many cases, they lack the ability or will to implement reform. Symbolic gestures and reform fill this gap and serve the purpose of signaling a state's acquiescence to the global culture.

33. Kasaba 2009, ch. 5.

34. Henderson 2015, 112.

35. McKean 2020; Robinson 2008; Suwandi, Jonna, and Foster 2019.

36. Hafner-Burton and Tsutsui 2005.

It would be a mistake, however, to interpret decoupling as a sort of hypocrisy whereby postcolonial states signal their commitment to norms without actually implementing real change. Decoupling shows the power of world cultural forms. When states implement policies that are ill suited for local circumstances or that go against domestic interests, they demonstrate the socializing power of global culture. To interpret decoupling and symbolic reforms as hypocritical requires a pessimistic, almost subversive, view of postcolonial states. One needs to think that new states deliberately decide to implement symbolic policies to deceive the rest of the world. This assumption is implicit and unstated in world polity theory. My goal is to elaborate on this fact without discrediting the theoretical enterprise: world polity theory has great explanatory power and it is vital for this book's story, but it is incomplete.

As an alternative, consider the history of decolonization and how the particular circumstances of postcolonial states may force their hand and lead to decoupling and symbolic policies. As I show later in this chapter, restrictive dispositions toward migrants and refugees are a quintessential example of such symbolism throughout the postcolonial world. These modern realities of migration policy are anathema to the precolonial migration patterns and realities, and the decolonization process plays a significant role in this shift. As I previously describe, Western states conditionally acquiesced to decolonization, which contradicts how previous expansions occurred. This shift introduced a conditionality to membership in the international society that did not previously apply to Anglo-European states. The conditionality of membership in the international society creates the perpetual need for postcolonial states to perform their legitimate statehood, thereby demonstrating their sovereign authority.

One important way of doing so is through strict immigration policies, as the closing and policing of international borders has become an important symbol of sovereignty. However, it is not clear how states can implement effective and restrictive immigration policies under the best of conditions and with the largest pool of resources. This ambiguity has led scholars to debate whether immigration policies work at all.[37] Postcolonial states, particularly those in Africa, were now sovereign over large territories, but they lacked the resources necessary to govern them. Accordingly, these states enact strict, yet symbolic, policies to demonstrate their sovereign authority. These symbolic

37. Czaika and Haas 2013.

policies, such as the creation of border fences and strict visa policies, allow the state to perform its sovereign authority in a policy realm that is increasingly relevant for demonstrating legitimate statehood.[38] In the next section, I elaborate on this point and describe how and why postcolonial states have become increasingly restrictive and antagonistic toward their counterparts in the non-White world.

Instead of assuming the worst intentions, I bring in an additional perspective—the social theory of hegemony—to provide an account of how and why this decoupling and symbolic reform occurs in the postcolonial international system. This perspective ties in the aforementioned account of decolonization to larger accounts of how dominance persists, often covertly, in nominally equal societies. Appreciating the effect of Anglo-European hegemony and the direct effect of colonization allows one to explain, in this case, the rise of racial bias in migration and border restrictions in the postcolonial world without forcing non-White states to be self-defeating. In many ways, an ancillary theory of hegemony completes the historical account of perpetual inequality in the international system that stretches from the precolonial through the postcolonial periods.

Hegemony and Socialization within International Society

World polity theory is simple, and it is appealing because it does not require one to believe that existing states directly imposed their way of life on the rest of the world. Instead, this global culture of behavior and institutions diffused without the explicit intention of Western or non-Western states. Meyer and his colleagues argue that conventional realist and institutionalist arguments about the nature of the international system can account for a world in which states are antagonistic and unequal or in which they cooperate, but they cannot explain "a world in which national states, subject to only modest coercion or control, adopt standard identities and structural forms."[39] Proponents

38. Other scholars have stressed the symbolic nature—or "security theater"—that borders provide (Andreas 2012). This work often portrays such symbolic politics as a panacea against public anxieties about migration (Mainwaring and Silverman 2017). This chapter demonstrates that a need to signal legitimacy and proper sovereign statehood to *external* audiences also drives symbolic politics, which is a departure from the extant literature. I thank an anonymous reviewer for highlighting this contribution.

39. Meyer et al. 1997, 174.

point to instances of decoupling to claim that this global culture plays a strong causal role because, without such an effect, it is unlikely that all states would implement isomorphic policies and institutions.

Despite its explanatory power, world polity theory fails in an important way. World polity theory emphasizes that one can gain fundamental insight into the behavior of actors—states, in this case—by examining the blueprints from which they derive their behavior. However, it fails to address *why* and *how* new actors adopt those blueprints in the first place. In other words, the standard world polity account presupposes that actors either passively acquiesce or enthusiastically adopt dominant institutions and standards of behavior. By their own admission, world polity theorists "de-emphasize the role of coercive power in creating and maintaining institutions."[40] This absence is understandable because world polity theory is a response to political realists and institutionalists who either ignore norms and emphasize the role of direct coercion or refuse to assign any causal power beyond the individual actor. World polity theory is an explanatory advance on other alternatives because it highlights that some changes and patterns of diffusion in the social world are structural and happen without such violence. But these accounts are mostly descriptive and do not purport to provide a mechanism for how this diffusion actually occurs. While some world polity theorists claim that a search for such mechanisms is futile because cultural processes are so "complex,"[41] there has been some effort in recent years to expand the theory to account for how, for instance, membership in international governmental organizations helps behavioral norms and institutions diffuse without direct coercion.[42]

However, does the absence of *violent* coercion imply that there was *no* coercion? World polity theory implicitly assumes that direct coercion is the only way that states can exercise power in the international system. This assumption is limiting because it precludes one from studying the myriad ways that power functions in any social system. A state's scope of action is not only limited by another actor directly; there are other examples of more diffuse, structural constraints that also constrain behavior. Accordingly, as Michael Barnett and Raymond Duvall claim, analysts of international politics need a conception of power that allows one to understand how and why some actors have "power over" others (direct coercion), as well as the

40. Schofer et al. 2012, 62.

41. Schofer et al., 65.

42. Frank, Hardinge, and Wosick-Correa 2009.

"enduring structures and processes of global life that enable and constrain the ability of actors to shape their fates and their futures."[43] This latter form of power is *constitutive*. Constitutive relations of power involve how social relations determine what actions and practices actors are allowed to undertake, particularly within institutional arrangements. For instance, world systems theory suggests that structures of capitalist production produce three types of states—core, periphery, and semiperiphery—and these positions in the world economy generate particular identities and interests. A chief implication is that states in the periphery often adopt ideological conceptions of self-interest that perpetuate their exploitation.[44] Such a *hegemonic* story can help us complete the picture of how the nation-state form diffused and its implications for international migration in the global South.

Hegemony and the Nation-State

This version of power draws on the work of Antonio Gramsci, and it is missing from extant world polity approaches to socialization.[45] In short, the structure of the social system in which one is embedded determines actors' capacities and leads them to think ideologically. This social structure—the taken-for-granted rhythms of everyday life—shapes how actors, particularly subordinate ones, view their interests and desires. This ideological thinking serves the dominant class (or actors in the system) and is one way Gramsci defines *hegemony*—predominance by consent. To be specific, Gramsci theorizes how dominant classes in capitalist society exercise political and moral leadership over others by winning them over with concessions. This leadership is all-encompassing; the dominant class sets the moral, political, and intellectual baseline assumptions of society through a common world-view. In this account, a hegemonic social order is powerful because it defines what is normal and legitimate in society. Gramsci sees the institutions of civil society as the dimension of the capitalist state that produces concessions among the subaltern, makes capitalism more palatable, and reproduces hegemony. In this way, Gramsci describes how this civil society promotes behavior within the subordinate classes that is consistent with the hegemonic order, such as the Protestant work ethic, thereby damning most institutions of modern life. The working class comes to believe that serving a corporation is a

43. Barnett and Duvall 2005, 41.

44. Wallerstein 2011.

45. This section draws on Gramsci 1971. See also Cammett 1967.

privilege and rejects labor organizing because it runs counter to the natural order of society. Hegemony is powerful because society's putatively benign institutions lead the subaltern to consent to, and often revel in, their own domination.

This definition may confuse those familiar with international politics because Gramsci and most international relations scholars define hegemony differently. On the one hand, the former defines hegemony as a practice of power that relies on the consent of those in subordinate classes. Dominant actors do not rule through direct coercion; they rule with passive acquiescence. On the other hand, most international relations scholars consider a state hegemonic if it has the overwhelming ability to influence other states and dominate the rules and arrangements of international politics.[46] This definition implies direct control or coercion because a state can be hegemonic *without* the consent of others. Despite this difference in definition, and although Gramsci has little to say about international politics, his concepts have led others to consider the role of hegemony in various areas of the international society and its institutions.[47]

Given Gramsci's definition, one can see how the nation-state form and the existing arrangements of the international society became hegemonic during and after decolonization. Throughout the early and mid-twentieth-century, existing Anglo-European states founded the international society on the basis of new international institutions. The predominance of these institutions was decisive because existing states built them on the principle of national self-determination, which led them to codify the nation-state as the international system's fundamental building block. If a polity wanted to reap the financial benefits of membership in an international organization, it needed to resemble a nation-state. Incentives and insistence, not direct violence, led to acquiescence. For example, membership in the United Nations General Assembly was open to any independent nation-state but unavailable to any other type of polity. This condition for membership that seems benign on the

46. This account is most closely associated with hegemonic stability theory (HST). There are several competing versions of HST (long cycle theory, power transition theory, etc.), but the basic claim is that international systems remain stable when they have a single, dominant hegemon. The hegemon dictates the various institutional arrangements of international politics, and so long as there are no challengers and the hegemon retains its preponderance of power, there is little conflict. See, e.g., Gilpin 1981; Kindleberger 1986; Modelski 1987; and Organski 1958.

47. See, e.g., Cox 1983; Morton 2007; and Murphy 1998.

surface led tiny, "invented" states, such as Lesotho and the Gambia, to become full members of the UN, while "larger units like the Zulu or Ashanti groups, which were previously organized as empires," were not.[48] All of this took place despite villages, city-states, and empires being ubiquitous, legitimate ways to organize a political community prior to European colonialism.

These developments ensured that Anglo-European states did not need to coerce former colonies—in the conventional military or economic sense—into adopting the nation-state form. Colonizers and their allies did not meet, as they did in Berlin in 1884–1885, to formally codify their intentions to make postcolonial states nation-states. Rather, colonizers' *behavior* during the colonial period and their creation of the modern international society codified the postcolonial international order as one in which nation-states were the only legitimate political form. Although we observe transnational initiatives, like the East African Community and the unification of Tanganyika and Zanzibar, the fact remains that the former is a transnational union of nation-states and the latter emerged as a nation-state as well (Tanzania).

Of note in the latter case, the motto of the Tanganyika African National Union (TANU)—the revolutionary vanguard in Julius Nyerere's political project in Tanzania—was *Uhuru na Umoja* (Freedom and Unity). Even Nyerere, a staunch revolutionary political theorist and activist, saw *national* unity as the best way forward after independence. Nyerere's political thought emphasized the coherence between precolonial, tribal life (what he calls "tribal socialism") and his vision for a postindependence, nation-state-centric socialism as the best way to organize society.[49] This history suggests that the hegemony of the nation-state form emerged from the interaction between domestic (postcolonial state) and international (institution and society) levels.

On the one hand, as Thandika Mkandawire notes, "the end of colonialism left an institutional and infrastructural residue that still plays a major role."[50] At the domestic level, postcolonial ruling classes replaced traditional institutions with "a form of extremely arbitrary rule that is more reflective of colonial regimes."[51] As a result, the postcolonial policy became a state that often reproduced the same authoritarianism that was rampant during the colonial

48. Herbst 2000, 101.

49. Nyerere 1987.

50. Mkandawire 2010, 1648.

51. Henderson 2015, 132.

period. This continuity reinforced the taken-for-granted preeminence of the "corrupt" postcolonial state that dominates modern discourses about Africa, the Middle East, and Latin America.[52]

This replacement of the colonial state with the postcolonial form epitomizes the ubiquity of Gramscian hegemony at the domestic level during this period. Mahmood Mamdani describes how colonial powers began co-opting nationalism as a counter-ideology in the 1940s as a way of detaching nationalism from democratic struggles and representing it as the "defense of *state* interests"[53] (emphasis mine). Colonizers could now represent any movement that purported to transcend or replace the state as divisive and counter to the national interest. However, the co-option of this ideology required transitioning from a colonial to an independent *state* that could then be associated with the interests of the "national" population. Consequentially, the political reforms of the 1940s that begot the postcolonial institutions of the 1950s and 1960s have their roots in the counter-ideology that colonizers used to subvert local, nonstate popular movements. There were two important consequences of this period that ensured that the nation-state form would remain paramount and affixed in the postcolonial hegemony: "the production of a one-dimensional history of the 'national movement' on the one hand, the delegitimation of all contemporary democratic struggles as detracting from national unity on the other."[54] Colonizers imparted domestic institutions and ensured that the Westphalian state—subordinate to the nation—would remain the only obvious way to organize their polity after independence.

On the other hand, Anglo-Europeans both created the new institutions of the international society on the basis of the nation-state and drew artificial borders during the colonial period that made it obvious to create a new nation-state based on those boundaries. While Anglo-Europeans did not produce a white paper articulating their intention to ensure postcolonial polities resembled nation-states, it is clear that the institutions and the associated rules that they created established hegemony at the level of the international system. To reiterate, Western states used their own standpoint and experience

52. This discussion is closely related to the work on neopatrimonialism in postcolonial African states. Henderson 2015 (129–138) describes how colonial powers imparted forms of domestic governance on postcolonial states. The result was a *neopatrimonialism*—rule vested in a single leader that is characterized by patronage, power, and status—that emerged directly out of colonialism.

53. Mamdani 1990, 51–52.

54. Mamdani 1990, 55.

to guide the creation of the new international order and its institutions. In turn, this post-WWII hegemony "was sufficiently expansive to project itself onto the world scale,"[55] and restricted the forms of states that were permissible in the international system.[56] Therefore, decolonization is an example of Gramscian hegemony because the dominant class—in this case, the Anglo-European states—"won over" (albeit implicitly) the subaltern by granting independence and membership in the international system. However, these concessions only occurred within the existing framework that those dominant states created and on the basis of domestic institutions that they left behind.

Postcolonial Hegemony and Transnational Resistance Movements

How does this hegemonic account accord with the Pan-African/Asian/Islamic movements that were at the forefront of the struggle against imperialism? Recent scholarship throughout the social sciences, humanities, and adjacent disciplines highlights the importance of movements such as Pan-Africanism and Pan-Islamism as examples of transnational movements that organized against imperialism and Westphalian sovereignty.[57] This literature combats the "unworldly Eurocentrism" of most scholars who do not consider non-Western intellectual resources and political practices,[58] and it reveals the importance of transnational resistance to Western models of sovereignty (i.e., the nation-state).[59] These scholars may take issue with my description of the emergence of the postcolonial state because it implies that these important movements diminished in their influence over actual institutions.

Despite the importance of many in these movements in *conceiving* of alternative modes of sovereignty, they could not break the monopoly of the nation-state form. Colonizers were willing to cede control of their possessions to postcolonial rulers who would uphold the nation-state and national boundaries.[60] National sovereignty and hierarchy that facilitated "dependence and domination" reigned even though decolonization may have been "a project

55. Cox 1987, 226.
56. Rupert 1995.
57. See, e.g., Aydin 2007; Shilliam 2006.
58. Valdez 2019, 4–5.
59. Getachew 2019.
60. Apter and Coleman 1962.

of reordering the world that sought to create a domination-free and egalitarian international order."[61] There are several explanations for the failure of these movements to achieve their ultimate aims. The most notable explanation involves internal debate and fragmentation that ultimately led to the victory of the pro-sovereignty cohort over those who rejected Westphalian sovereignty, like Marcus Garvey.[62] In short, this debate boiled down to differences between those like Du Bois, who sought to replace colonial rule in Africa with the "talented tenth" that had benefited from Western education, and those like Garvey, whose movement had mass appeal and rejected traditional sovereignty.[63]

The split between the Casablanca and Monrovia groups of postcolonial states epitomized this division. While the Monrovia group (Liberia, Nigeria, and most of Francophone West Africa) insisted on maintaining a strong version of Westphalian sovereignty and national borders, the Casablanca group (Algeria, Tanzania, Libya, Mali, Morocco, Ghana, Egypt, and Guinea) was more open to versions of federal cooperation that rejected the preeminence of the nation-state.[64] The establishment of the Organization of African Unity (OAU) in 1963 brought this schism to a close, but in so doing, it cemented the the postcolonial incorporation into the Westphalian international system. In fact, resolving the sovereignty issue was the only way to end the impasse. To do so, leaders included the principle of "non-interference in the internal affairs of individual states" in its constitution.[65] As Andrews notes, the Casablanca group's acquiescence "blunted the radicalism of the OAU by promoting colonial state nationhood," and this reflects the general condition of other forms of non-Western resistance in the postcolonial international system.[66]

This account of the failure of unified group movements to resist the pull of Westphalian sovereignty is consistent with the work of Henderson and others who note that colonizers imposed colonial domestic institutions on postcolonial states.[67] Indeed, Adogamhe argues that "the dilemma of post-colonial

61. Getachew 2019, 2, 4.
62. Shilliam 2006.
63. Andrews 2017, 2504.
64. Andrews 2017; Guyatt 2016.
65. M'Buyinga 1982, 176.
66. Andrews 2017, 2506.
67. Henderson 2015.

states have not really abandoned the colonial logic of oppression and domination as well as the exploitative and the predatory politics that are inimical to unity and development. One major obstacle to integration is the fear of losing state sovereignty."[68] Basing unity on sovereignty weakens the collective, and this fear of losing sovereignty reflects the hegemony of the Anglo-European international order.

What about the movements that remained and continued to challenge Western hegemony and dominance in the international system? Colonial subjugation through racialized dispossession and violence produced an international division of labor between the industrialized core and the commodity-exporting periphery. Colonial legacies often left postcolonial states in a state of structural vulnerability: many were dependent on exporting a narrow range of commodities and importing manufactured goods and technology. Despite considerable variation among the postcolonial economies of Africa, Asia, Latin America, and the Middle East, this structural inequality and vulnerability provided the impetus for several movements, such as the New International Economic Order, the Non-Aligned Movement, and the Group of 77. These movements were influential, and they responded to the unjust structures of the postcolonial international system from within that system.

Faced with the influence of these movements, the United States, United Kingdom, France, and other Western powers resisted the attempts by the postcolonial coalition to reform the international order.[69] Put in terms of my argument, Western powers tolerated these movements for a time as they reinforced the nation-state as the legitimate political form in the international system. However, when the movements became too influential, the West subverted them and strengthened the interests of private international capital. While I do not dispute the importance of these non-Western movements, I argue that they remained embedded within the Western hegemony of the postcolonial state system. Once postcolonial states became ensnared in the hegemonic Westphalian order, their attempts to resist the hierarchy of that order from within was diminished *because of its hegemonic power*. Rules, institutions, and raw power aligned to prevent any significant insurrections. This is how hegemonic orders work: those that dominate construct the order to elicit acquiescence, but retain the right to respond with institutional force once certain features outlive their purpose.

68. Adogamhe 2008, 27.
69. Mortimer 1984.

To summarize, the hegemony of the nation-state was so strong that it was able to overcome existing transnational political movements because its ideology co-opted so many postcolonial leaders and counter-ideologies. Although former colonizers created a new international order that encouraged nation-state formation, nationalist and revolutionary leaders, such as Ho, Mao, and Nehru, also embraced the state as the only legitimate means of organizing a polity in the postcolonial period.[70] Moreover, most of the leaders who attended the fifth Pan-African Congress in 1945 that set out to unify the postcolonial world did not ultimately seek a revolutionary new form of political organization. Although Europeans viewed many of these leaders—Kenyatta, Lumumba, Machel, Mugabe, and Touré—as dangerous revolutionaries, these leaders upheld the Westphalian order and declined to pursue alternative political forms, at least on the eve of decolonization.[71] Rather, Western hegemony overwhelmed other innovative ways of thinking about political organization in the postcolonial world,[72] and led to the consolidation of nation-states and universal membership in international organizations. Notably, the one leader who remained staunchly revolutionary (in the transnational, nonstatist sense), Kwame Nkrumah, was deposed by a Western-backed coup in 1966. Sometimes direct violence and coercion is necessary to maintain hegemonic orders.

Institutions and the Hegemony of World Culture

The role of international organizations in upholding hegemony is vital because the expansion of world culture takes place primarily in these international forums.[73] Indeed, much of the recent work applying world polity theory investigates the effect of international governmental organizations on state behavior.[74] Scholars argue that the precipitous increase in the number and scope of international organizations promotes increased connections

70. Herbst 2000, 100.

71. Herbst, 100. Of course, this could be *because* the hegemony of the nation-state had already set in and caused this acquiescence. See Kenyatta 1965; Lumumba 1962; Mugabe 1983; and Touré 1978.

72. The fifth Pan-African Congress in 1945 is the primary example of Africans coming together to consider innovative, alternative forms of organizing the postcolonial world. See, e.g., Du Bois 1947.

73. Boli and Thomas 1997.

74. Hughes et al. 2009.

among states, leading to dense networks of cooperation, the diffusion of expertise, and ultimately the transmission of global culture.[75] There is substantial evidence for this IO effect, and recent work has linked international organization membership with the structure of national education systems,[76] environmental legislation,[77] women's rights,[78] and scientific expertise.[79]

The IO effect is a natural implication of the hegemonic diffusion of the nation-state form during decolonization. When former colonies became independent, they remained embedded in an Anglo-European hegemony. Anglo-European states granted independence to former colonies after imposing the institutions of the colonial state. This process is analogous to how Gramsci describes the dominant classes promoting consent among the subaltern. Moreover, when independence occurred, former colonies maintained the nation-state form to reap the further benefits of membership in the international society, such as UN membership. Evidence that norms of behavior coalesce when states are members of the same organizations closes the causal circle. Former colonies had far less room to maneuver than initially appeared because they were ensconced in a hegemonic world culture that encouraged the nation-state form after former colonizers implemented colonial institutions and membership in organizations, both of which installed norms of proper state behavior. This is one way the hegemonic expansion of world culture occurs.[80]

The remaining implications of world polity theory still accord with this hegemonic story. In fact, they become more acute, and this acuity has important implications for the rest of this chapter. Recall that states often use symbolic or general policies to signal their commitment to global norms of appropriate behavior when they lack the necessary resources. States with fewer resources change their behavior not only when they freely accept global

75. Boli and Thomas 1997; Meyer et al. 1997.

76. Schafer 1999.

77. Frank, Hironaka, and Schofer 2000.

78. Paxton, Hughes, and Green 2006.

79. Finnemore 1993.

80. This argument applies widely to different types of international institutions and finds common cause with extant work. For instance, Kathy Powers shows that African leaders have constructed more regional trade agreements (RTAs) than the leaders from any other region (Powers 2004, 375). Henderson builds on this finding and argues that membership in RTAs conveys "international legitimacy" to postcolonial African regimes that allowed them to secure resources from the international community (Henderson 2015, 241–242).

norms bur also when they are compelled to do so. As discussed above, a perverse aspect of decolonization is that postcolonial states faced far more conditionalities for membership in the international society than their counterparts in the global North. These conditions for independence and membership in the international society allegedly arose out of fear that former colonies would become failed states without greater intervention from the Anglo-European world. These extra conditions have led scholars to raise concerns about the racist undertones of this Western management of putative equals.[81]

Roland Paris calls this process "the globalization of the very idea of what a state should look like and how it should act," and it reflects the continuity between the colonial and postcolonial periods.[82] Conditions for membership in international institutions, humanitarian intervention, and other Western impositions convey norms of "civilized" behavior on the postcolonial world. When institutions like the UN, the IMF, and the World Bank make financial aid and membership contingent on economic liberalization, political liberalization, and democratization programs, they argue that these conditionalities are in the best interest of the obligated state.[83] As such, even though Western states argue that conditionalities and structural adjustment programs are to the postcolonial state's benefit, the "civilizing mission" quality of these programs reflects a White supremacy that runs counter to the beneficence of their stated aims. The superficial forms of sovereignty/suzerainty that emerged during the twentieth century—trusteeships, mandates, satellite states—show the high bar that non-White states were forced to face at the onset of their emergence from colonialism.

This high bar shows the continuity between these postcolonial "civilizing missions" and recent psychological scholarship on the effects of anti-Black racism. Victims of anti-Black racism in the United States report feeling anxiety about having to overcompensate for their inferior status in society, leading to a racial trauma that shares symptoms with post-traumatic stress disorder.[84] Likewise, postcolonial conditionalities provide a high bar for non-White states and require them to prove to the rest of the world that they are proper and legitimate sovereigns. This need to constantly perform leads postcolonial states to institute the norms of existing states in a more extreme manner

81. Gruffydd Jones 2013; Shah 2009.

82. Paris 2002, 638.

83. Islam and Morrison 1996; Jeffries 1993.

84. Mosley et al. 2021.

because they feel obligated to overcompensate for their inferior status. In short, Anglo-Europeans not only imposed the nation-state form on postcolonial states; the added pressure to constantly justify their own sovereignty leads former colonies to adopt more extreme policies.

To be clear, I do not intend to blame postcolonial states for enacting restrictive policies, nor am I arguing that they are somehow racists or equally culpable. Rather, postcolonial states are victims of a hierarchical, postcolonial international system, within which they are placed in a structural position of inferiority that requires them to overcompensate and enact more extreme policies to reap important benefits and maintain their legitimacy in the eyes of the world. This is how Gramscian hegemony works in modern international politics.

Do International Institutions Really *Affect Behavior?*

This argument relies on a key mechanism: the constitutive effect of international institutions on state behavior. If international institutions do not socialize states or incentivize them to change their behavior, then it is unlikely that requiring postcolonial states to join the key institutions of the international society will have had the power I suggest. It might just be the case that postcolonial states are just states that want to survive in the same dangerous international system as everyone else. This skepticism is reflected in John Mearsheimer's long-standing belief in the "false promise" of international institutions.[85]

Like most realists, Mearsheimer argues that the international system is anarchic, which means it is composed of independent political units that are not beholden to any supranational authority. The upshot is that states must act in a self-help manner because they cannot "call the police" if another state acts in a nefarious way. Postcolonial states simply live in a dangerous world in which states can never know the intentions of other states, and they must balance against powerful states to protect themselves.[86] In the realist account, the structural incentives of the international system socialize postcolonial states to become the same perfectly competitive firms as every other state. This means that states must engage in practices of *realpolitik*—balancing, bandwagoning, war-fighting, and relative gains-seeking—instead of accepting the norms of the international system, such as the rule of law, and institutional

85. Mearsheimer 1994.
86. Waltz 1979, 111–114.

constraints on their behavior. Therefore, the realist critique maintains that states are impervious to international norms and institutions; an instrumental, self-help logic informs all of their international behavior, and states only use (or work through) institutions when they think they will materially benefit from doing so. Institutions and norms have no power of their own, and they conform to state interests, often under threat of sanctions from powerful states.

But then what explains the relative prevalence of institutional cooperation in the contemporary international system? And why do powerful states acquiesce to the norms of behavior that supranational entities endorse? Mearsheimer concedes that cooperation is possible when states do not feel threatened, and that "some states are especially friendly for historical or ideological reasons."[87] But as Wendt argues, this claim entirely begs the question of why states would be this friendly if we truly lived in a dangerous, realist world.[88] Constructivists maintain that many aspects of realist explanations for cooperation—that states are status quo powers or sovereign—rely on social factors. For example, as Wendt claims, most realists assume the importance and preeminence of sovereignty without acknowledging its institutional character.[89] As we have seen in previous chapters, sovereignty is an institution of mutual recognition: states are not sovereign members of the international system unless existing members recognize them as such.

This social approach to international politics has led many to claim that international institutions socialize states and affect their behavior.[90] In other words, when states join institutions, they are inducted into its rules and norms. These scholars presume that states shift from acting solely according to their material interests—what some call a logic of consequences—and toward acting in accordance with the behavior that their new community deems appropriate, regardless of whether they agree. This latter logic is called the logic of appropriateness. So even if a state would be strictly richer or more powerful from acting differently, the institution socializes them into acting suboptimally or differently than they otherwise would act. Jeffrey Checkel calls replacing instrumental calculations with "conscious role-playing" Type

87. Mearsheimer 1994, 79.

88. Wendt 1995, 79.

89. Wendt 1995, 79, fn 24.

90. Barnett and Finnemore 2004; Chayes and Chayes 1998; Checkel 2005; Finnemore 1993; Haas 1990.

I internalization or socialization.[91] In some cases, states go beyond following community norms because they are appropriate and begin adopting them because they view them as the right thing to do. In this Type II socialization, states begin to "adopt the interests or even possibly the identity, of the community of which they are a part."[92] Following the story from this book, when postcolonial states join the institutions of the international system, including sovereignty itself, their membership leads to Type I socialization because not following norms of behavior will lead to censure or opprobrium.[93] While some states may experience Type II socialization, this is not required because the thinner form still produces changes in behavior.

This latter point is important because it obviates the critique that institutions have no true power to socialize states. One is not wedded to the strong argument that socialization requires changing identities (Type II); simply changing one's behavior out of fear of the consequences counts as socialization (Type I) too. This position dovetails with over a half century of scholarship that demonstrates that powerful states subject themselves to institutional oversight, even in security affairs.[94] Indeed, powerful states continue to delegate authority to institutions even though they have the least to gain because they provide reassuring "hands-tying" mechanisms, credible commitments, specialized expertise, and the efficiency of centralized information provision, and they allow them to signal their intentions.[95] In these cases, it is irrelevant whether states follow the dictates of institutions because their identities change or because doing so is in their material self-interest. Strategic choice and socialization are not either-or propositions: the interaction between the two is ubiquitous throughout the international system.[96] The important fact is that membership in institutions changes behavior. Even if one rejects the Type II socializing power of international institutions, the empirical and theoretical record supports the claim that institutions affect state behavior.

Acknowledging this record illuminates how membership in the institutions of the international society can reinforce inequalities between the

91. Checkel 2005, 804.

92. Checkel, 804.

93. Johnston 2001.

94. See, e.g. Axelrod 1981; and Keohane and Nye 1977.

95. Abbott and Snidal 1998; Ikenberry 2001; Nielson and Tierney 2003; North and Weingast 1989; A. Thompson 2015.

96. Johnston 2005, 1014.

Anglo-European core and the postcolonial world. Moreover, it shows how my argument fits in with existing scholarship on the international relations of the postcolonial world. The most prominent example of this scholarship and the most important in the context of my claims is Errol Henderson's recent book, *African Realism? International Relations Theory and Africa's Wars in the Postcolonial Era*.[97] In this work, Henderson adopts a realist perspective on the international system in his theory of how colonialism affected postcolonial domestic and international relations. Domestically, the crux of his argument is that colonial powers homogenized postcolonial states when they imposed their domestic forms of governance. "The carryover of the repressive apparatus of the colonial state with a military more attuned to repression than foreign war is readily apparent, as is the continuity of the colonial domestic economy."[98] These effects created neopatrimonial relations within African states that explain why African states often fight civil wars but rarely fight international ones.

For Henderson, the international socialization of postcolonial states was a combination of two processes. First, "colonialism socialized the entities that would become Africa's postcolonial states into a global system as politically marginal, economically dependent, and socially peripheral tributaries of their European metropoles in an oligarchically ordered, capitalist-dominated, white supremacist global order."[99] This took place during the colonial period. Second, he argues that the socialization of African states in the *postcolonial* era resembles the story that "Waltz largely describes," and that these states "were conditioned and constrained by the homogenizing impact of the prevalent [Cold War foreign policy] practices."[100] So postcolonial states were affected both by their colonial experiences and the standard dictates of the Waltzian international system.

Henderson's discussion of postcolonial socialization at the international level epitomizes the complex politics of the Cold War. My take is that we are explaining different aspects of the same process. While Henderson focuses on how this socialization affects armed conflict, military intervention, and regional trade, I theorize how the socialization of postcolonial states into color-blind institutions *during the modern period* produces more inequality

97. Henderson 2015.
98. Henderson 2015, 112.
99. Henderson 2015, 111.
100. Henderson, 112, 145.

in international migration, rather than less. In fact, Henderson already acknowledges international institutions' important homogenizing role by claiming that postcolonial states' imitation of the practices of the international order "were evident in postcolonial African states' international diplomacy, trade relations, [and] *membership in international organizations*"[101] (emphasis mine). I simply add that the homogenizing impact of the Cold War (and contemporary) foreign policy practices produces inequality too. I explore the coercive imposition of the nation-state form and how these taken-for-granted aspects of membership in the sovereign state system are also engines of Western hegemony that reproduce international racial inequality through coercing or encouraging postcolonial states to behave in certain ways. Even if these institutions do not socialize postcolonial states in the Type II sense, they still affect behavior such as states' restrictive bordering practices.[102]

Hegemonic Diffusion, the IO Effect, and Border Control

Border control is one example of this extremity. And in the remainder of this chapter, I show that postcolonial states have embraced border fence construction as an important signal of their competence. At face value, the diffusion of the nation-state form and physical border controls appear puzzling because these developments run counter to both centuries of precolonial history and experiences during colonialism. As I note above, the freedom of movement was a norm in most of the non-Western world. Precolonial practices were often organized around different types of polities, such as villages and empires, and people were largely free to move as they pleased. In empires and during the colonial period, administrators drew arbitrary boundaries that often bisected existing patterns of movement and political arrangements. When colonizers drew these boundaries, they also enacted citizenship laws and policies that marked the first time individuals were tied to specific polities, particularly on the African continent. Yet, even during colonialism, most colonial subjects were free to move *within* empires to suit the labor needs of plantations, mines, and public administration. Therefore, decolonization was a jarring shift away from precedent. For example, almost overnight, French

101. Henderson, 112.

102. To be sure, restrictive bordering practices are only one possible way postcolonial states demonstrate their sovereignty and legitimacy. Future work should tie this discussion of international migration and bordering practices to a larger discussion of the postcolonial state.

West Africa changed from a region of free movement to an amalgam of dozens of nation-states that were now committed to defining who could enter their territory.[103]

This transition did not take place because former colonies simply emulated existing states. Rather, the nation-state form globalized because of the power of persistent Anglo-European hegemony in the international system. This hegemony was perverse because former colonies were pushed to become nation-states to, for instance, reap the benefits of membership in international institutions. But membership in the institutions of the international society came with conditions, and newly independent states were forced to continuously prove that they were competent and legitimate.[104] This need to demonstrate legitimacy changed the nature of migration in the postcolonial world. Consistent with the logic of world polity theory, postcolonial states began building physical fences along their borders shortly after decolonization as they began interacting with Anglo-European states in international forums. These physical barriers are quintessential examples of symbolic reform, particularly on the African continent where nation-states govern vast, sparsely inhabited territory. Many states have borders that are thousands of miles long, which makes it impossible to prevent unauthorized crossing. However, these borders, limited as they are, signal to the rest of the world that the state is a legitimate sovereign authority. Symbolic expressions of authority accomplished more than signaling legitimacy to the Anglo-European world. They also allowed rulers to codify their authority at home. New leaders had no incentive to organize their new national boundaries around the territory they actually controlled. Doing so would lead to a dramatic reduction in their authority because, as in the colonial period, most states lacked the administrative capacity to rule over their entire territory. However, border fences exuded authority and warranted the maintenance of existing boundaries, despite the unevenness of real sovereign authority. This history is important because it affirms the interdependence between colonialism (the drawing of arbitrary borders), decolonization (the globalization of the nation-state form), and postcolonialism (the need to perform sovereignty).

There are many examples of postcolonial states using border walls in this way to symbolically perform their duty as sovereign states in the

103. Gould 1974.

104. One prominent example is how the International Monetary Fund imposes conditions on its members when they apply for aid (Cox 1996; Stone 2008).

service of the national interest. Importantly, these examples are not limited to one region of the global South. States have used border fences to protect their national security and to affirm their independence in south Asia (India/Bangladesh and India/Pakistan borders), central Asia (Turkmenistan/Uzbekistan/Kyrgyzstan), sub-Saharan Africa (Botswana/Zimbabwe and South Africa/Zimbabwe), Latin America (Argentina/Paraguay), and the Arabian Peninsula (UAE/Oman and Saudi Arabia/Yemen). In these (and other) cases, the stated government rationale for building these walls is to assert state power at its frontier, remove border ambiguity, and protect the state from "dangerous" security threats. To take one example, India uses narratives of "infiltrators" and "threats" to justify the 2,500-mile barrier on the Bangladeshi border. These narratives emerged after the Partition in 1947, and they universally involve protecting the sanctity of Indian sovereignty from unlawful threats.[105] Similarly, post-Soviet states in central Asia relied on similar justifications to build extensive border fences after their independence in the 1990s. Turkmen president Saparmurat Niyazov argued "as we [Turkmenistan, Uzbekistan, and Kazakhstan] all are sovereign states, we cannot keep the borders open any more" to jolt his government to complete its 1,700-kilometer border fence.[106] All in all, it is clear that postcolonial states rely on the physical border fence to perform their legitimate sovereignty, corroborate the international acknowledgment of their borders, and safeguard their national interest. They make this choice despite the economic incentives to refrain from doing so. In fact, these economic incentives take a backseat to the power of symbolism. Nick Mangwana, spokesman for Zimbabwe's government, lays bare this calculus while recognizing South Africa's sovereign right to erect a new fence on their shared border: "Some people build durawalls around their houses, fields or properties and some put up fences. This is a choice people make on how to *show* their boundaries"[107] (emphasis mine).

One may interpret this argument as suggesting that postcolonial states learned that they should control their borders from existing states. This misrepresents the logic of hegemony within world polity theory. I do not suggest that representatives from former colonies sat with leaders from their former colonizers and wrote down the rules for how to be a sovereign state. It

105. McDuie-Ra 2014, 83–84.

106. Burke 2001.

107. Muronzi 2020.

is unlikely that any conversations at the United Nations regarding a state's legitimacy specifically involve border control. Rather, as I note above, international organizations are social environments, and actors that enter social environments rarely remain the same.[108] Newly independent states enter international organizations that are replete with rules and incentives to conform to certain standards of behavior. These standards allow international organizations—with rules defined by the most powerful states—to influence newly sovereign states and catalyze Type I socialization.[109] This argument is constitutive, not causal.

Border controls fall naturally out of this arrangement. When newly independent states become members of the same international organizations as Anglo-European states, they are pushed to perform their sovereign statehood on several fronts. The explicit rules of the international society and implicit norms of statehood create the incentives for new states to appear as legitimate sovereigns. Doing so consolidates power at home and creates an air of legitimacy abroad, both within institutions and elsewhere. What is more, the growing menu of international organizations both ratchets up the cumulative social pressure to perform sovereignty and creates more obligations and conditions for membership in the international society. As the breadth of state obligations expands, so too does the need for states to appear legitimate and strong. Shared membership in international organizations, while not directly compelling states to build up border controls, allows the logic and demands of modern, sovereign statehood to quickly expand throughout the world. One can see this process in figure 7.1. Figure 7.1(A) plots the number of international organizations in which postcolonial states shared membership with the extant Anglo-European order, and 7.1(B) plots the total number of border fences built by those postcolonial states during the same period. This figure presents descriptive evidence of an association between organization membership and increased border control, other than the post-Soviet admission period from 1990 to 2000. In the next section, I dig deeper into this relationship.

Importantly, this embrace of border control and fencing had knock-on effects within postcolonial states that continue to resonate today. Most clearly,

108. See, e.g., Finnemore 1996; Lewis 1998; and Wendt 1994. Constructivists posit that international organizations affect state interests and preferences. Member states interact on a constant basis, which leads them to take on new identities and interests.

109. Martin and Simmons 1998.

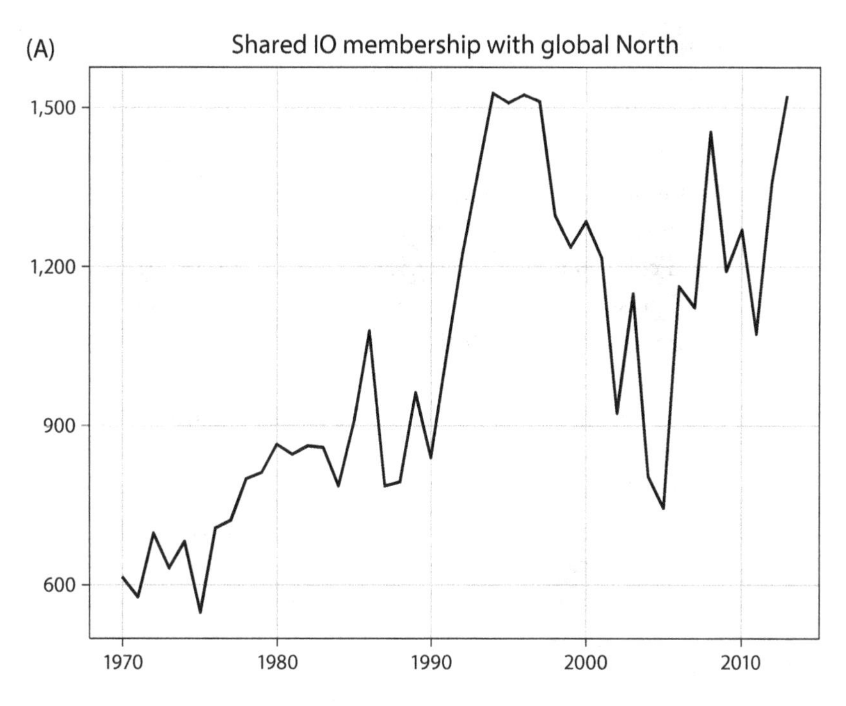

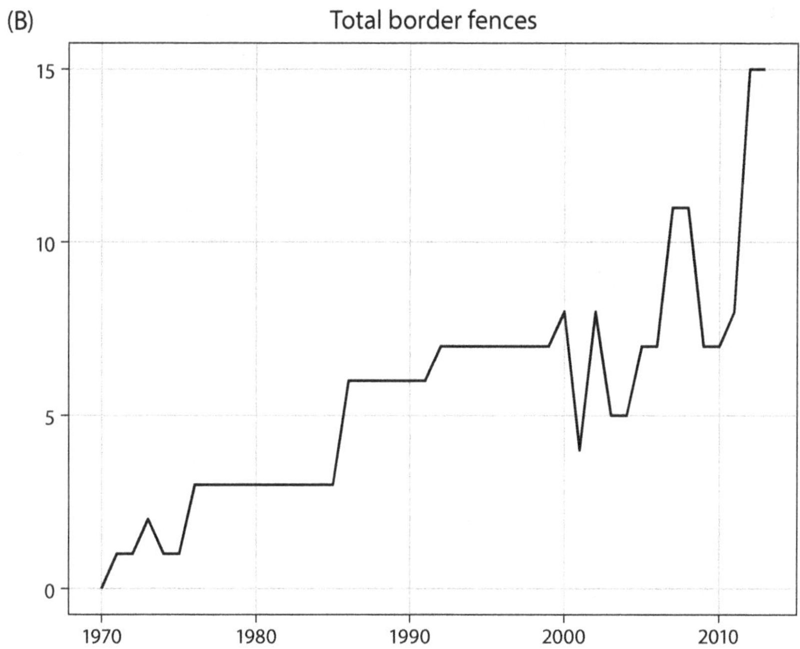

FIGURE 7.1. IO membership (A) and the proliferation of border fences (B).

the creation of new nation-states and prioritizing border control as an important symbol of sovereignty catalyzed strong anti-immigrant sentiments. Citizens in the postcolonial world exhibit a similar vitriol for immigrants and refugees as Western states. This similarity is striking because of the historical legacies of free movement throughout most of the postcolonial world. For example, in West Africa, a region where free movement was the rule during the precolonial and colonial periods, immigrants and refugees face tremendous opposition and persecution.[110] This anti-immigrant sentiment and violence is pervasive throughout Africa, particularly against Somalis, Zimbabweans, and others.[111] Two-thirds of migrants from sub-Saharan Africa move to other countries within the region,[112] so despite the proliferation of border fences and other controls to limit migrants, movement still occurs. Just as in the West, opportunistic politicians politicize this immigration for their own gain, which has led to increased anti-immigrant sentiment and violence.[113] This transition from ubiquitous free movement to politicized, symbolically restricted movement took place within a generation, and the consequences are clear. Symbolic policies, such as border fences, that perform sovereignty are not benign. Migration will still occur in the postcolonial world because fences are unlikely to stem the tide; however, publics will seize on these inflows and the rhetoric of politicians, thereby increasing the demand for restrictive policies and violence.

This is the ironic tragedy of persistent racial bias in international migration in the color-blind era. Non-White migrants face stricter policies not only at home but also within the global South. There is nothing natural or inherent about these conditions in the postcolonial world. They emerged out of Anglo-European hegemony within the existing international society. In the next section, I show evidence that this increased closure is a function of this hegemonic diffusion of world culture.

Border Fences and the Expansion of Closure

To study the diffusion of border restrictions, I rely on a similar empirical strategy as that used in previous chapters. Namely, I use linear regression to infer whether the norms of the world polity—strict border controls—have

110. Buehler, Fabbe, and Han 2020; Cogley, Doces, and Whitaker 2018.

111. Charman and Piper 2012; Whitaker 2017.

112. Gonzalez-Garcia 2016.

113. Landau 2010; Mosselson 2010.

diffused to the postcolonial world. World polity theorists and their critics have used a similar approach to test the empirical implications of their theories over the past two decades.[114]

Recall that my argument is that the nation-state form spread to the postcolonial world because of Anglo-European hegemony. The nation-state is the "obvious" way to organize a polity, and newly independent states were forced to adopt this form to join international organizations and reap the associated benefits. This argument builds on Henderson's related account of the effects of White supremacy and colonialism on postcolonial states in Africa. While Henderson provides a compelling argument that the direct, oppressive effects of colonialism produce neopatrimonialism,[115] I focus on how Western hegemony operates in plain sight in the supposedly equal processes of the Waltzian international system. In this chapter, I explore the coercive imposition of the nation-state form and how these taken-for-granted aspects of membership in the sovereign state system are also engines of Western hegemony that reproduce international racial inequality through coercing or encouraging postcolonial states to behave in certain ways. The rub is that Waltz's "like units" assumption is not value-free; the socialization process he describes perpetuates international racial inequality and is accelerated through the putatively equality-enhancing institutions of the liberal international order. These organizations are the main conduit through which the norms of world culture, such as strict border controls, spread to the postcolonial world. To be sure, there are other ways that norms diffuse in the international system that do not rely on formal international forums. However, participation in international organizations requires states to behave according to the same principles, encourages conversations and collaboration among elites, and provides the institutional background that fosters convergence. Studies of religious groups, political town halls, and other organizations consistently show that institutions and their leaders change the behavior of group members through both active and passive means.[116]

In other words, I contend that postcolonial states would not restrict their borders to the observed degree in the absence of Western hegemony. Postcolonial states need to constantly demonstrate to the West that they are legitimate sovereign states, and adopting existing norms is the easiest way to do so. These states often rely on symbolic policies because doing so signals

114. Li and Hicks 2016; Wimmer and Feinstein 2016.

115. Henderson 2015.

116. Hoffmann and Miller 1997; Minozzi et al. 2015.

the adoption of a global norm.[117] Therefore, I expect postcolonial states to be more willing to enact restrictive policies, on average, and I presume that those that share membership in more international organizations with states from the global North will be even more restrictive. Accordingly, I provide several forms of evidence that sharing membership in international organizations with Anglo-European states correlates with the adoption of symbolic border control policies: the construction of border fences. In so doing, I test the *Expansion of Closure hypothesis* from chapter 3:

> *Postcolonial states will be more likely to build border fences. Postcolonial states that participate in more international institutions should also build more border fences.*

Analysis

Europe's 2015 migrant "crisis," President Donald Trump's call to build a wall on the US-Mexico border, and the general rise of anti-immigrant populism throughout the Western world have led to a recent surge in scholarship on border fence construction.[118] This scholarship provides clear lessons for studying why states build walls and guides this analysis, its data, and its modeling approach.

Border fences are different from mere borders because the former have a physical appearance, often designed "to enhance border control."[119] The physical nature of border fences gives them their symbolic power. As such, I begin with Carter and Poast's data on border walls that covers the period from 1800 to 2014 and use Nazli Avdan's work to extend the data to 2016.[120] However, because this chapter is all about decolonization, I limit this analysis to the postcolonial period (1960–2016). In constructing their data, Carter and Poast use John Keegan's definition of a strategic defense to identify fortified borders throughout the world.[121] This definition is flexible enough to identify the myriad forms of borders that states have constructed throughout the twentieth and twenty-first centuries,[122] but it is also agnostic about why the state built the border wall. This ambivalence allows the authors to include all physical border defenses and walls without investigating intentions. In this analysis,

117. Sibley 1995, 32.

118. Avdan and Gelpi 2017; Carter and Poast 2017, 2020; Hassner and Wittenberg 2015.

119. Hassner and Wittenberg 2015, 162.

120. Carter and Poast 2017; Avdan 2018.

121. Carter and Poast 2017, 11, citing Keegan 1993, 142.

122. Carter and Poast 2017, 11.

TABLE 7.1. Raw count of border fences by region, 2014

World Region	Fences
Sub-Saharan Africa	26
Europe & central Asia	25
South Asia	15
Middle East & North Africa	12
North America	8
East Asia & Pacific	6
Latin America & Caribbean	0
Former colony	63
Colonizer	29

the main dependent variable is an indicator (0/1) for whether a state built a border fence in a given year.

Data and Variables

Raw statistics on border fences are found in table 7.1. One can see that the total number of fences built is unevenly distributed across the regions of the world. Indeed, one of the advantages of this analysis when compared to those in the previous chapter is that these data have global coverage. Sub-Saharan Africa and Europe/central Asia have built the most border fences, while states in East Asia and Latin America/the Caribbean have built very few. Of course, one must attribute some of this variance to geography. Island nations have a water border that does not require a fence to defend. In addition, the global distribution of border fences shows that countries in sub-Saharan Africa and throughout the global South (e.g., Middle East and North Africa, South Asia) are more prone to this symbolic form of migration control. A further interesting pattern emerges when one compares the number of fences built by former colonies and former colonizers. In the bottom section of table 7.1, one can see that former colonies have built roughly twice the number of fences as former colonizers. These raw differences, combined with the regional patterns, provide descriptive evidence that newly independent members of the international system are more likely to build border fences.

Although it is difficult to pin down the precise motivations for why states build border fences, we can use linear regression to dig further into these patterns and test the implications of our theory.[123] Because the dependent

123. Carter and Poast 2017; Hassner and Wittenberg 2015.

variable is binary—0 if a country did not build a wall in a given year and 1 if it did—I use logistic regression in the first part of this analysis. Logistic regression allows one to estimate the association between independent variables and the probability that a country builds a border fence in a given year.[124]

In this analysis, the main independent variable of interest is the number of international organizations a given country shares membership in with OECD countries. Elsewhere, scholars investigate if shared membership in international organizations is associated with conflict or trade.[125] These analyses are usually dyadic; the unit of analysis is a pair of countries in a given year, and the goal is to see whether a relational variable, such as shared IO membership, is associated with another relational variable, such as war. Here, the unit of analysis is monadic—a single country in a given year. To create this shared IO variable from dyadic datasets, I add up the number of international organizations in which a given country shares membership with OECD countries in a given year. This monadic variable allows us to estimate the relationship between sharing international forums with existing, rich members of the international society and the probability of border fence construction. Specifically, the Expansion of Closure hypothesis suggests that we should see a positive association between the number of IOs a country participates in with OECD states and the probability of border construction. This research design is the conventional method for testing the implications of world polity theory.[126]

Beyond the main association, the Expansion of Closure hypothesis implies an interactive relationship between IO membership and whether a state is a former colony. In the story above, Western hegemony forces postcolonial states to adopt the norms of the international system, and this effect should be strongest for those postcolonial states that share membership in more IOs with states in the global North. In other words, the association between shared IO membership and border fence construction should be conditional on whether a state was also a colony. I accommodate this aspect of the theory in two ways. In the regression models, I include an indicator for whether a country was a former colony. In several models, I interact this indicator with the shared IO variable to see whether the relationship between shared IOs

124. In the interest of space, I do not describe the mechanics of logistic regression. For more detail, see, e.g., Gelman and Hill 2006, chs. 5–6, and Long 1997.

125. Ingram, Robinson, and Busch 2005; Kinne 2013.

126. Li and Hicks 2016.

and the probability of wall construction is, consistent with the main hypothesis, greater for former colonies. In other models, I use this variable to run the noninteractive models on distinct subsamples of colonial and postcolonial states.

I also include several independent variables in this analysis, several of which will be familiar. The first is the liberal democracy index from the Varieties of Democracy (V-Dem) project.[127] Liberal democracies tend to be freer, more open societies; however, some posit that states must trade off internal freedoms for border control because citizens will not be receptive to granting freedoms to outsiders.[128] Further, states should be more likely to build border fences if they or their neighbors experience violence or instability. The second and third independent variables capture this conventional wisdom. The second variable is an indicator for whether the state is engaged in a militarized interstate dispute (MID) in a given year, and it comes from the Correlates of War project.[129] This variable is important because extant work demonstrates that colonial experience and political violence are interdependent.[130] The third variable is an indicator for whether there is conflict near its border. These data are from the Major Episodes of Political Violence and Conflict Regions dataset collected by the Center for Systemic Peace.[131] The fourth independent variable deals with economic shocks and how they are likely related to border fence construction. On the one hand, countries that experience negative economic shocks may be more likely to build border fences to ameliorate its citizens' fears of outside competition. On the other hand, poorer countries lack the resources to build border walls. To attend to these dynamics, I construct a GDP shock measure that notes whether a given country has experienced a sharp decline in its economic production. To create the GDP shock variable, I calculate the change in GDP for each country-year ($GDP_t - GDP_{t-1}$), and then define the bottom 15 percentage of these changes as GDP shocks.[132] Finally, the increased fear of terrorist attacks in the post-9/11 world are associated with greater public support for border walls and immigration controls.[133] To account for this relationship, I include

127. Coppedge et al. 2019.
128. Weyl 2018.
129. Palmer et al. 2020.
130. Ravlo, Gleditsch, and Dorussen 2003.
131. Marshall 2019.
132. Nielsen et al. 2011.
133. Hetherington and Suhay 2011; Neal 2009.

a lagged measure of terrorist attacks because countries that previously experienced such attacks should be more likely to build walls in subsequent years. This measure is from the Global Terrorism database.[134]

Border Fences Emerge with IO Membership

The results of the main analysis are found in table 7.2. I report six models in this table. The first three models are logistic regressions with random effects for year and country. The final three models are linear probability models with random effects for year and country. The logistic regressions (models (1)–(3)) are the main models in this analysis because they are best suited to model a binary dependent variable. However, some scholars prefer to use linear regression to model limited dependent variables because linear regression recovers the correct marginal effects and is much easier to implement and interpret.[135] Accordingly, I use a linear probability model to replicate the main logistic regressions in models (4)–(6). The main results are consistent regardless of whether one uses logistic regression or a linear probability model. This consistency is paramount because it strengthens the internal validity of these results.[136]

In each of these models, I standardize each of the continuous independent variables such that the coefficient represents the effect of moving from one standard deviation below the mean to one standard deviation above. The main coefficient of interest is shared IOs, which estimates the association between the number of memberships in IOs shared with countries in the global North and the probability of building a border fence in a given year. In model (1), I report this association, which suggests a strong positive relationship between the two variables. In other words, the more IOs a country shares with rich states, the greater the probability that it will build a border fence. To be specific, a hypothetical shift from one standard deviation below the mean to one standard deviation above the mean is associated with a large

134. National Consortium for the Study of Terrorism and Responses to Terrorism (START) 2019.

135. "The upshot of this discussion is that while a nonlinear model may fit the CEF for LDVs more closely than a linear model, when it comes to marginal effects this probably matters little" (Angrist and Pischke 2008, 80).

136. I also use the linear probability models to check the robustness of the results because the dependent variable is zero inflated: there are many more 0s than 1s in the dataset, which can bias estimated coefficients (King and Zeng 2001). The consistent results across the logistic regressions and linear probability models ameliorates these concerns.

TABLE 7.2. Regression models of new border fence construction

	Dependent Variable					
	New Border Fence					
	(1)	(2)	(3)	(4)	(5)	(6)
Shared IOs	4.118***	2.836***	1.997**	0.092***	0.198***	0.046
	(0.640)	(1.085)	(0.780)	(0.032)	(0.047)	(0.035)
Former Colony			−1.795**			0.035
			(0.839)			(0.046)
Liberal Democracy Index	−3.989***	−1.824	−4.146***	−0.069***	−0.068*	−0.101***
	(0.590)	(1.134)	(0.589)	(0.027)	(0.035)	(0.028)
Militarized Interstate Dispute (MID)	1.024**	1.190**	1.193***	0.090***	0.153***	0.102***
	(0.449)	(0.576)	(0.453)	(0.034)	(0.050)	(0.034)
Conflict on Border	−0.136	0.348	−0.213	−0.077***	−0.048	−0.086***
	(0.341)	(0.674)	(0.357)	(0.024)	(0.036)	(0.024)
Negative GDP Shock	1.747***	4.452***	2.482***	0.038	−0.031	0.045
	(0.642)	(1.272)	(0.706)	(0.043)	(0.056)	(0.043)
Lagged Terrorist Attacks	0.257	−0.168	0.076	0.035**	0.049**	0.032**
	(0.288)	(0.330)	(0.299)	(0.016)	(0.021)	(0.016)
Shared IOs X Former Colony			3.009***			0.120***
			(0.850)			(0.033)
Constant	−2.905***	−3.288*	−1.301	0.062***	0.094***	0.054
	(1.030)	(1.854)	(1.456)	(0.023)	(0.031)	(0.035)
Sample	Full	Fmr. col.	Full	Full	Fmr. col.	Full
Model	Logit	Logit	Logit	LPM	LPM	LPM
Year RE	X	X	X	X	X	X
Country RE	X	X	X	X	X	X
Observations	1,194	668	1,194	1,194	668	1,194
Log Likelihood	−199.273	−111.838	−192.942	65.391	−17.387	67.553
Akaike Inference Criteria	414.546	239.677	405.883	−110.782	54.775	−111.106
Bayesian Inference Criteria	455.226	275.711	456.734	−59.931	99.818	−50.085

Note: $^{*}p<0.1$; $^{**}p<0.05$; $^{***}p<0.01$.

increase in the probability that a country builds a border fence in a given year. Model (1) includes the other independent variables noted above, but this model does not include the interaction between shared IOs and former colonial status. Its purpose is to provide initial evidence of the main relationship of interest.

This association lends strong descriptive evidence that the norms of sovereign statehood permeate international institutions. At the same time, this model reveals other important relationships. The model estimates that liberal democracies are less likely to build border fences, which corroborates prior expectations. States that experience negative economic shocks are also more likely to build fences, perhaps as a reaction to the desire of elites and citizens to protect domestic workers and industries. In addition, there is a strong positive relationship between participating in a militarized interstate dispute and building fences in subsequent years. This pattern lends credence to the lay idea that states build up their border fences to protect themselves from external threats. However, contrary to expectations, we do not see a significant relationship between nearby violent conflicts or lagged terrorist attacks and the likelihood of building a border fence. Of course, it could be the case that all three conflict variables are correlated and the effect of violence on border construction is soaked up by the MID variable.

Shared IOs and Border Fences in Former Colonies

Model (1) of table 7.2 provides initial evidence for several of the mechanisms of interest; however, the purpose of this chapter is to discern whether former colonies build border fences to signal their adoption of global norms of sovereignty. The implication of such a relationship would be that the postcolonial world is increasingly unequal and restrictive for non-White migrants from the global South due to the effects of Western hegemony.

To begin unpacking this relationship, I report regional random intercepts from model (1) in table 7.3. One can interpret these intercepts as a region's baseline likelihood of building a border fence in a model that accounts for each of the independent variables of interest. In table 7.3, one can see that the baseline likelihood of building a border fence is highest in South Asia, sub-Saharan Africa, and the Middle East and North Africa, even though these regions do not have the highest raw numbers of border fences. Instead, these intercepts signify how the relative likelihood of building a border fence in a given year varies by region, given the distribution of other factors, such as political regime type. This table provides a basic illustration that non-White

TABLE 7.3. Regional random intercepts for baseline likelihood of building a border fence (model (2))

	World Region	(Intercept)
1	South Asia	5.34
2	Sub-Saharan Africa	3.21
3	Middle East & North Africa	1.28
4	North America	−0.60
5	East Asia & Pacific	−2.56
6	Europe & Central Asia	−3.26
7	Latin America & Caribbean	−3.42

states of the global South are more likely to adopt the symbolic power of physical borders to signal their sovereignty, even after controlling for economic, political, and military factors.

The random intercepts in table 7.3 are a useful way of estimating baseline differences across regions, but they do not explicitly address the question of whether world cultural norms diffuse to former colonies in international organizations. To do so, I conduct several tests. First, I replicate model (1) but restrict the analysis to those countries that were former colonies. The results of this analysis are in model (2) of table 7.2. One can see that the relationship between shared IOs and border fence construction is similarly strong and positive. Yet, this approach is not ideal because it requires me to disregard nearly half of the data to run the model on this subsample.

To ameliorate these concerns, I return to the full dataset. In model (3) of table 7.2, I include an indicator variable for whether a state was a former colony and interact this indicator with the shared IOs variable. In so doing, I test whether the relationship between shared IO membership and border fence construction is larger or smaller for former colonies. The Expansion of Closure Hypothesis implies the former. This model also tests whether the number of shared IOs moderates the association between being a former colony and the probability of border fence construction.

The results are found in model (3). To be specific, model (3) includes the interaction between shared IOs and former colonies, as well as all the other independent variables of interest. These results are consistent with the preliminary results above and support the Expansion of Closure hypothesis. Taking the control variables first, one can see a strong coherence between model (1) and model (3): liberal democracies are less likely to build border fences, while states that experience negative economic shocks and that are engaged in militarized interstate disputes are more likely to build fences.

The more germane results are found in the interpretation of the interaction in model (3). Strictly looking at the table, one can see that, consistent with the theory and hypothesis, the effect of shared membership in IOs with states from the global North on the likelihood of border fence construction is stronger for former colonies. To put a finer point on it, the coefficient on shared IO membership is the estimated effect of sharing IO membership on the probability of fence construction for a state that was not a former colony. The simple heuristic of the "divide-by-four rule" leads to the following inference: moving from sharing one standard deviation below the mean to one standard deviation above is associated with a 50 percentage increase in the the probability of building a border fence.[137] For former colonies, adding the shared IO and interaction coefficients together shows that the marginal effect of sharing IO membership on the probability of border fence construction is vastly larger for the victims of Anglo-European colonialism. This result is consistent with the theory that former colonies are more susceptible to the diffusion of global culture within international organizations, and they are more likely to build border fences in response to this pressure.

Importantly, we can also test the other side of this interaction: if colonial history moderates the effect of sharing IO membership on border fence construction, then sharing IO membership moderates the effect of colonial history on border fence construction too. While one can use the same logic to assert that this moderation occurs, the substantive implications of this interaction are more difficult to interpret because the shared IO variable is continuous. To aid in interpretation, I plot both interactions in figure 7.2. Figure 7.2(A) shows the aforementioned moderating effect of colonial history. Figure 7.2(B) demonstrates the moderating effect of shared IOs. One can see that states that were former colonies are more likely to build border fences *if they share an above average number of IO memberships with Western states.* The interpretation of this interaction effect is important because (1) it reveals the care one must take in interpreting these models, and (2) the result provides further evidence for the Expansion of Closure hypothesis. Postcolonial states can reject or resist the influence of Anglo-European hegemony—they have agency—but the unequal structure of the international system carries through as these states are increasingly wrapped up in its institutions.

Although these results are clear, the reader may still be uncertain because regression output—particularly output from logistic regression—is difficult

137. Gelman and Hill 2006, 42.

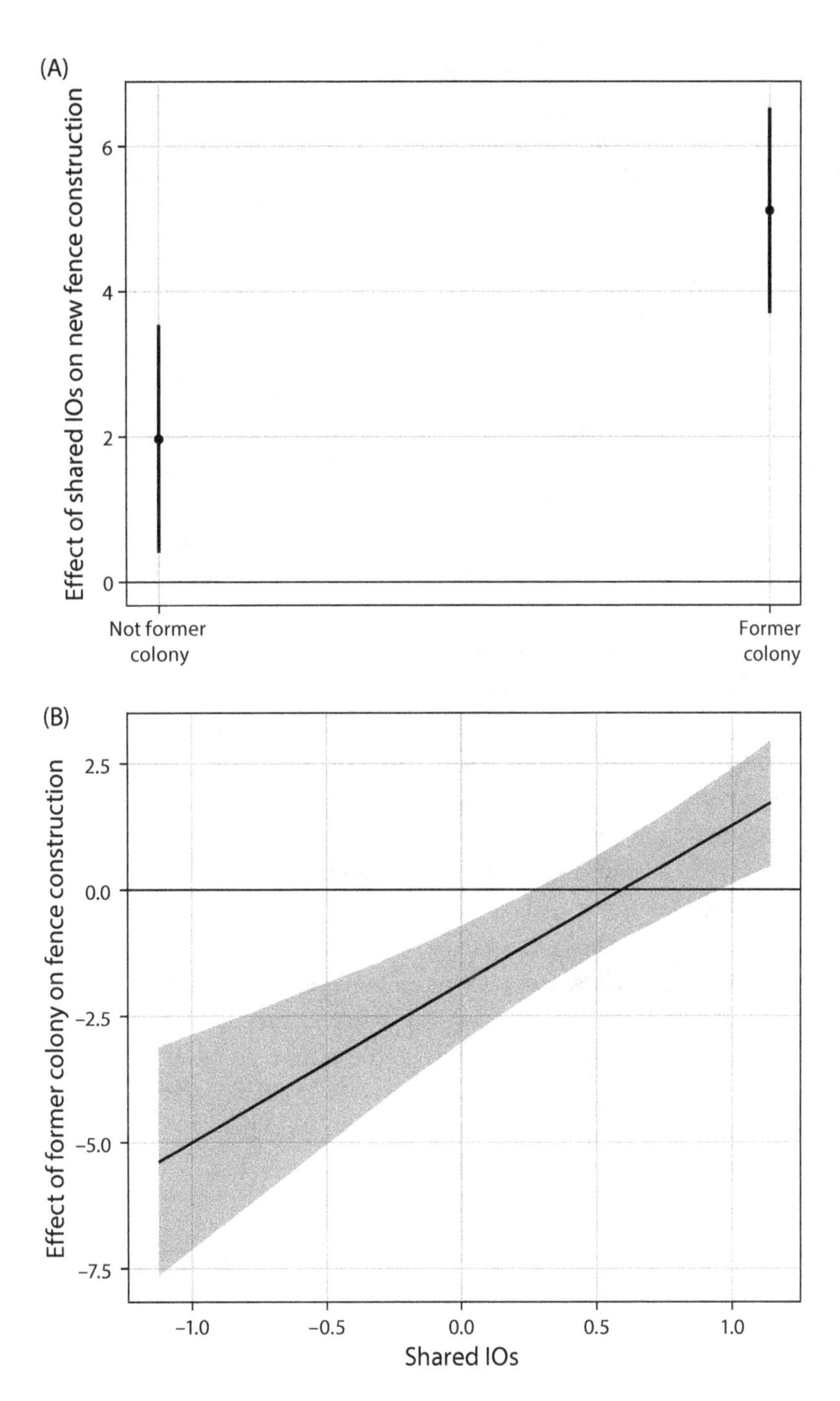

FIGURE 7.2. Interaction plots of the moderating effects of shared membership in IOs and former colonial status (model (3), table 7.2). (A) Postcolonial states have larger associations between shared IO membership and fence construction. (B) Similar moderating effect of IO membership on the effect of being a former colony on fence construction.

to interpret. To provide an additional lens through which one can interpret this evidence, I use predictive simulation to present substantive comparisons between colonizers and former colonies. Specifically, I use model (3) in table 7.2 to plot how the predicted probability of building a border fence changes as the number of shared IOs changes for a former colony and a former colonizer with the values of the other variables set at their average or modal values. In other words, I assume that the two hypothetical states are identical: average levels of liberal democracy, not engaged in an MID, no conflict on their border, not experiencing a negative economic shock, and did not experience a terrorist attack in the previous year. The only factors that vary are colonial status, region, and the number of shared IO memberships. These are the least provocative conditions imaginable because I assume the states have average institutions and are not experiencing any economic or security emergencies.

These conditions lay bare the importance of the institutions of the international order. Indeed, figure 7.3 puts a finer point on the profound substantive differences between colonies and colonizers that I estimate in model (3). On the one hand, one can see that the probability of building a border fence tepidly increases for former colonizers as the number of shared IOs increases. On the other hand, the predicted probability of building a border fence sharply increases for former colonies as the number of shared IOs increases beyond the mean value. So, under normal conditions, our colonizer behaves as expected: the probability of fence construction is inelastic with respect to the number of shared IOs. The pattern makes sense because we expect members of the Anglo-European core to be rule setters rather than rule takers. On the flip side, the probability of fence construction is tremendously elastic with respect to the number of shared IOs for former colonies, revealing the significant structural influence Western hegemony has over their behavior when they are strong participants in that order.

Discussion

This analysis shows that former colonies that are members of international organizations with existing members of the international society are more likely to build border fences. Each of the models above tells the same story: although sharing IO membership with states of the global North is not randomly assigned, there is a clear, positive association linking these international forums with border wall construction. These patterns are necessary to

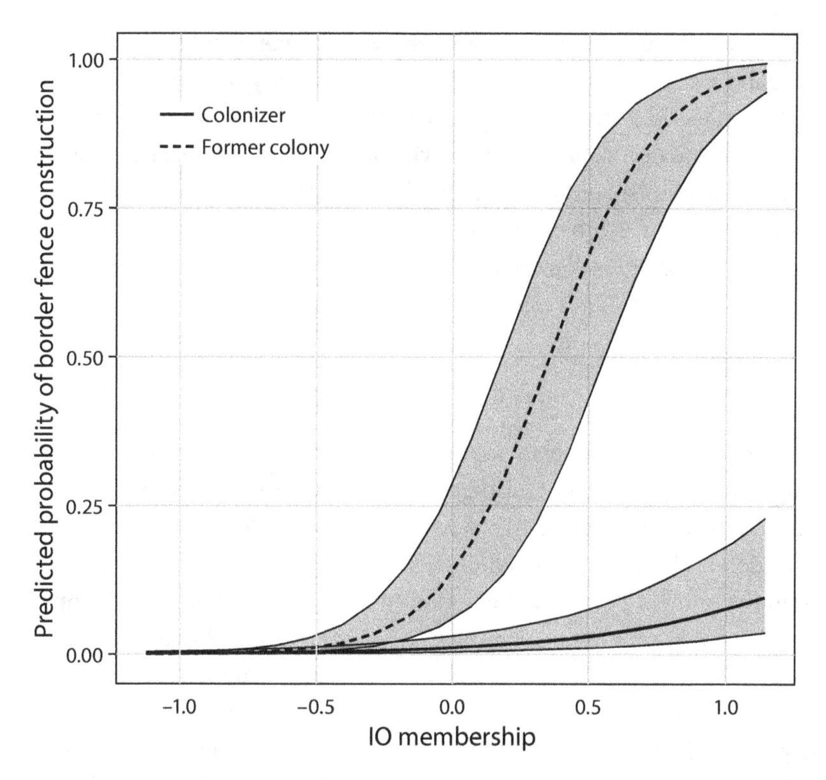

FIGURE 7.3. Comparing the simulated probability of building a fence between a former colony in sub-Saharan Africa and a European colonizer. Results are presented with 95 percent predictive intervals. This figure shows that former colonies are more likely to build border fences when they share membership in more IOs with Anglo-European states. All other variables are held at their mean or mode.

corroborate the theory that the norms of the international society—what it means to be a state—expanded to postcolonial states.

This analysis is certainly not the final word. A skeptic may argue that the relationship between shared IOs and border wall construction is spurious. However, that critic must make a convincing case that some other omitted variable affected both the number of IOs a country shares with states in the global North and the likelihood of building a border fence in a given year. The lack of any obvious variable and the robustness of these results dampen concerns regarding internal validity.

To summarize, the purpose of this analysis is to provide cross-national evidence that the hegemonic norms of international society diffuse to the global South, and that former colonies respond by building border fences to signal their sovereignty to the rest of the world. One should not interpret this analysis as definitive proof of world polity theory or of an intentional adoption of world culture on the part of former colonies. Instead, one should take these results as the best available evidence that newly independent states that participate in shared international forums with Anglo-European states are more likely to exhibit behavior consistent with the imposition of the norms that those Anglo-European states set. This globalization has important implications for racial inequality in the international system.

Conclusion

In the previous two chapters, I found evidence that racial inequality persists in international migration and that Western states enact restrictive immigration policies in response to inflows from racially different, postcolonial populations. These chapters demonstrate that colonialism not only affected the non-White world during the period of colonial rule, but it also continues to have important effects through the present day. Colonialism created the conditions in the non-White global South that politicians, elites, and citizens of the Anglo-European world now claim are objective reasons to deny entry into their state. In this way, modern racism in international politics does not depend on the overt racism of White Australia or the Chinese Exclusion Act. Racism is an ideology that ranks human beings under the assumption that some are inferior to others, but it does not require one to be intentionally or mindfully racist in a vulgar way. Rather, racism—and racial inequality—often emerges in the modern day when people uncritically accept commonsense narratives, such as "immigrants from country X will put our country in danger," without considering those narratives' origins and the West's role in creating them. This type of racism leads Western states to securitize migrants and enact restrictive, objective immigration policies even in a color-blind era.

In this chapter, I push this story a step further and complete the historical circle that links colonialism, decolonization, and our current era. This final piece is perhaps the most nefarious dimension of modern racial inequality because it explains why we observe in chapter 5 that racial inequality *increased* in the postcolonial era. During decolonization, the nation-state form globalized to former colonies because the nation-state was an important part of the "common sense" of international politics, and because colonizers grafted their own domestic impositions during the imperial period. What is more, Anglo-European states expanded the international society and its institutions to include these new states, which led to the further diffusion of global norms throughout the postcolonial world. However, former colonizers often did so while imposing new conditions on membership at the same time. These myriad conditionalities created the perpetual need for postcolonial states to perform their legitimate statehood to justify their membership in the international society. One important way of doing so has been through border control, as the closing and policing of international borders has become an important symbol that a state is legitimate and powerful. As such, I provide evidence that postcolonial states have increasingly built border walls—the most symbolic method of border control—and that this process is most associated with sharing membership in international organizations with Western states.

Hierarchies need not be explicit or institutional: racial inequality in international migration persists because the hegemony of sovereignty and the nation-state form catalyzes restrictiveness and closure within the non-White world. The implication of this analysis is that Anglo-European hegemony not only continues to justify increasingly restrictive immigration policies in Western states but also promotes restrictions and anti-immigrant sentiment within the global South. These restrictions within the global South are not based on racism, but they increase racial inequality at the aggregate level of the international system because non-White migrants experience even more barriers to movement than they did before. Although the freedom of movement prevailed throughout the world prior to Western incursions, the hegemony of Anglo-European world culture tipped the hand of postcolonial states and has made them an integral piece of the system of racial inequality. Accordingly, the prospects for mitigating this racial inequality and restrictions on movement remain minute, as long as border control remains the hallmark of the legitimate sovereign state.

8

Conclusion
Reflections on the Future

IN THE PREVIOUS seven chapters, I have done five things. First, I theorized the nature of racism in the modern, color-blind international system. This discussion is important because it warrants an examination of how racial inequality in international migration can remain despite the end of explicitly discriminatory policies. Second, I dispelled the conventional wisdom that border control and the right to exclude foreigners are inherent, timeless features of sovereign states. Third, I argued that the right of border control only emerged with the advent of the modern nation-state, industrial capitalism, and scientific racism. Elites used this right to justify restricting racially undesirable immigrants during a period when rising nationalism, chauvinism, and racism bonded the modern nation-state together. Fourth, I tracked how Anglo-European colonialism affected the economic, social, and institutional development of the non-White world during this same period. The legacy of colonialism produced modern non-White migrants that the West now rejects as objectively undesirable. Finally, I unpacked how decolonization and the expansion of the international society led to more closure and racial inequality as postcolonial states, embedded in Anglo-European hegemony, adopted the nation-state form and as such are required to constantly perform their sovereignty via symbolic means, such as building border walls.

The dominant thread running throughout this book is that many of the current conflicts surrounding migration originate in Anglo-European colonialism. The international politics of the modern day have roots in the international politics of past days, in which explicit racism, colonialism, and White supremacy played preeminent roles. Yet, I do not absolve individual instances of prejudice of their role in perpetuating contemporary racial inequalities.

Explicit racism and discrimination still occur with alarming frequency in our ostensibly color-blind international society, and we should highlight and repudiate the moral failing of racists. However, the argument and evidence in this book shines a light on the historical and structural antecedents that feed into both racism and racial inequality in international politics in general and international migration in particular.

From this perspective, this book dovetails with recent efforts to reunite international relations with its history and argue that the orthodox discipline places far too little emphasis on how (relatively) recent history—colonialism, scientific racism, the rise of industrial capitalism, and so on—continue to affect modern politics in, for instance, Western perceptions of the global South.[1] This call is ironic because many mainstream scholars of international security use historical case studies from this era to warrant their theories.[2] Accordingly, a central premise of this book is that scholars of international politics should pay closer attention to international and economic history and not analyze contemporary IR in a vacuum. Having thrown down this gauntlet, the task of this final chapter is to reflect on the specific implications for the politics of international migration and the general implications for the international politics of the twenty-first century.

To do so, I begin with a discussion of modern racism and how I think it will continue to affect international politics, prior to launching into a broader discussion of the nature of sovereignty and the state. Ultimately, I come to two conclusions about the future of international politics. The first conclusion is pessimistic: the legacy of colonialism will continue to reproduce existing racial inequalities in the international system. The effects of colonialism will both reinforce the racist beliefs of overt racists and provide fodder for those who may not be old-fashioned racists, but want to ensure, for example, that the state only admits objectively desirable migrants. As long as states and their leaders consider border control to be a fundamental aspect of sovereignty, this aspect of modern racism will endure. The second conclusion is more optimistic: states did not always conceive of sovereignty in this way, which implies that we can reconceive sovereignty to mean something else in the future. Such a redefinition is not utopian; rather, it implies that an ambitious postsovereignty cosmopolitanism is not a requirement for

1. Buzan and Lawson 2015; Hobson 2012; Mitzen 2013.

2. See, e.g., Friedman and Long 2015; Gilli and Gilli 2019; Hassner 2020; and Rapport 2020.

a more humane migration regime that will improve aggregate global well-being. However, the cases of climate migration and other areas of international cooperation temper expectations about the future prospects of such a shift.

Implications for International Racial Inequality

Contemporary Racism and the Public

Racial inequality in international migration persists despite the end of racial quotas and other forms of explicit discrimination. This book shines a light on the nature of race and racism in the modern international system, and it speaks to how similar inequalities may exist in other areas of international politics. In chapter 1, I define race and racism in an international context, describe why they are difficult to study, and justify why inequalities in international migration are *racial* inequalities. In so doing, I adopt Alain Locke's vision of race as an "ethnic fiction" that has no biological basis and operates through the privileging of certain cultural traits over others. Naturally, these cultural traits are highly correlated with geographic areas, which warrants the analysis later in the book. One complication I highlight is that Anglo-European states have largely legislated old-fashioned racism out of international politics. Unlike previous eras, leaders no longer use racial inferiority, inherent backwardness, or savagery to justify colonialism, land seizures, or trusteeship.

One may see this transition as a positive development; however, Lisa Tilley and Robbie Shilliam note that the transition to legal color blindness coincided with leaders and citizens equating racism with overt racist acts.[3] In this way, the transition to color blindness absolves many people and institutions of confronting the nature of racial inequality beyond acts of individual prejudice. Yes, it was overtly racist for states to distribute public goods on the basis of race and for the international society to justify colonialism and trusteeship on the same basis. But now a modern skeptic of racism may contend that laws forbid this prejudice, and any residual inequalities, achievement gaps, or income differences must be explained by individual behavioral deficiencies.[4] This perspective misses how people and states that were either racialized as White or as members of the dominant racial order (such as Anglo-European colonizers) received "material benefits from the racial order"

3. Tilley and Shilliam 2018.

4. Tilley and Shilliam 2018, 538.

during the period of explicit racism.[5] Not only did these benefits entrench those at the top of the racial hierarchy as dominant and desirable, it also has led them to "struggle to maintain their privileges."[6] In this way, the transition from explicit racism to "color blindness" has obfuscated the continued importance of race in society, and therefore has blinded many within the international relations academy and society to racial inequalities in property ownership, wealth accumulation, debt, precarity to environmental changes, and elsewhere.[7]

This blindness occurs both within states and at the level of the international system and is indicative of how modern racism operates. In many ways, modern racism is more complex and insidious than old-fashioned racism because of how easy it is for a skeptic to ignore its associated inequalities. These inequalities that remain after the transition to color blindness are the consequences of a *residual racism*—the privileging of certain groups over others on the basis of putatively obvious, yet supposedly objective, characteristics that are taken to be inherent. What is more, modern racism takes many forms. We still see instances of explicit racism and discrimination throughout the world, but we also have racists who conceal their true beliefs, symbolic racists, people who are racist because they are misinformed or misled, and those who may be well informed but miss how they have benefited from a system (like colonialism) that caused the things they fear or consider undesirable. The upshot of these myriad forms of racism is that nearly all citizens of the modern world contribute to the persistence of racial inequality within and between states, and many of those participants have the incentive or inclination to ignore, minimize, or dispute the relevance of race and racism to those inequalities. So, even though scholars often highlight the power of structural racism that "creates uneven access to the goods and services of society through institutional norms, rules, and roles that favor whites and disfavor ethnoracial minorities,"[8] *people* are responsible for perpetuating this structure when they either ignore or reject its existence.

The role of individuals reveals itself most often when scholars analyze the persistence of racism within states, but people also play a role in perpetuating global racial inequalities. In this book, I focus on racial inequality in

5. Bonilla-Silva 2006, 15.

6. Bonilla-Silva, 15.

7. Bonilla-Silva 2006; Goldberg 2009; Spence 2012.

8. Sewell 2016, 408.

international migration. International migration—like most areas of international politics—depends on domestic politics, policymaking, and elite and public opinion because the migration policies of states shape global patterns of movement. In short, migration policy is a dimension of foreign policy,[9] and even the staunchest structural realists appreciate the close relationship between domestic politics and foreign policymaking.[10] Above, I argue that states continue to restrict immigrants on the basis of desirability, which is a standard that correlates with race because Anglo-European colonialism, exploitation, and explicit racism created the conditions that make the non-White world seem undesirable. *To whom* do migrants from the non-White world seem undesirable? The citizens of Anglo-European countries are the engine of policies that restrict immigration to only the best and the brightest.

Prior to decolonization, these Anglo-Europeans often opposed immigration on explicitly racist grounds, as Aristide Zolberg and others reveal.[11] Although this era was rotten with overt racism, one could argue that it was easier to identify and therefore solve. If racists are visible, then they provide a clear target for protest, information campaigns, and other forms of mediation. In the color-blind era, the situation is not as simple. Of course, overt racists who reject non-White immigrants as biologically inferior still walk among us. However, they are joined by others who harbor different types of racism that are more difficult to identify and combat. We see "ignorant" racists who oppose racially different immigration because they have incorrect perceptions and information about immigrants. These perceptions drive baseless views that hoards of undesirable non-White immigrants are at the gates. Indeed, there is substantial evidence that many voters in Western states are highly misinformed about the size, composition, and characteristics of immigrant populations.[12] In the case of the United States, recent evidence suggests that political conservatives and their media drive these effects.[13]

In addition, we can speak of "reluctant" racists who may consider immigrants from the non-White world undesirable *because* of the selective, yet reliable, information that they consume. Those in this group often have accurate information about migrants from postcolonial spaces—migrants from

9. Rudolph 2003.

10. Mearsheimer 2019; Waltz 1967; M. C. Williams 2009.

11. FitzGerald and Cook-Martin 2014; Lake and Reynolds 2008; Zolberg 2008.

12. Blinder 2015; Citrin and Sides 2008; Herda 2010, 2015.

13. Herda 2019.

sub-Saharan Africa are poorer, on average, than those from western Europe—yet they ignore the history of explicit racism and domination that made them this way. Reluctant racists also selectively consume information, but this information is overly myopic, rather than bunk. This perspective is rife in the literature on the new economic case for migrant restrictions, which worries that migrants from poor countries will transmit the culture that makes their home country poor to their new homeland. Although Michael Clemens, Lant Pritchett, and others have debunked these fears over the last two decades,[14] there are still those that rely on neoclassical economic theory to reject the desirability of migrants from the global South.[15]

Solving this multifaceted type of racism will be difficult for four reasons. First, politicians have strong incentives to misrepresent the relative danger of immigrants. These incentives are the stuff of securitization theory, which describes how leaders use speech acts to call out security threats and justify extraordinary policy measures.[16] In both democratic and nondemocratic societies, leaders have the incentive to lie and misrepresent the relative danger of immigrants because of the potential electoral benefits.[17] Second, there is strong evidence that correcting misperceptions about the size and composition of immigrant flows has only limited effects on people's attitudes toward immigrants.[18] People often have fact-resistant worldviews, which suggests that complete or nonmisleading information may change perceptions but not behavior.[19] Third, recent trends in media consumption and dissemination suggest that these issues will only grow in the coming years. Indeed, political polarization has risen throughout the Anglo-European world, particularly in the United States. Recent media consolidation and the tendency to only consume information that confirms one's prior beliefs only increase

14. Clemens 2011; Clemens and Pritchett 2019; Clemens, Montenegro, and Pritchett 2019.

15. Paul Collier bluntly argues that "one reason poor countries are poor is that they are short of effective organization" and "migrants are essentially escaping from countries with dysfunctional social models" (Collier 2013, 33–34). He then argues that "uncomfortable as it may be . . . migrants bring their culture with them" to draw the connection between state institutions and the citizens that are trying to escape them (Collier, 68). This argument exemplifies the sort of color-blind racist thinking that is pervasive among well-informed citizens of Western states. Collier would balk at claims of racism and respond that he is just responding to "facts."

16. Aradau 2004; Bourbeau 2011; Buzan, Wæver, and De Wilde 1998.

17. Hurwitz and Peffley 2005; Lupia and Menning 2009.

18. Hopkins, Sides, and Citrin 2019.

19. Nyhan et al. 2019.

groupthink tendencies and will entrench misinformation that will amplify these information-based antecedents of modern racism.[20] Finally, these issues are related to the problems of color-blind racism that Eduardo Bonilla-Silva reveals.[21] Because a minute (yet growing) number of people in the modern world admit to their racism, those in the other categories are likely to claim that they do not "see race," are just responding to objective information, or "are not racist but. . . ." This is how nonovert forms of racism hide in plain sight. This book and its theory and evidence push these insights up to the level of the international system to reveal how color-blind racism within states can produce racial inequality among them. Taken together, these consequences suggest that color-blind racism, particularly against non-White immigrants, is difficult to address and may be difficult to ameliorate despite others' best intentions.

Sovereignty and Border Control

Given the discussion in the previous section, the main cause for pessimism regarding modern racial equality is that racist beliefs and policies are able to hide in plain sight. Although overt racists still plague Western societies, they are not the primary culprits of modern White supremacy. Rather, ordinary citizens who do not view themselves as racist, and would vehemently reject such a label, are the silent engines of modern racial inequality. Those in this group hold views about certain people and places that lead them to support certain policies that restrict those people from their society. In short, this first implication suggests that international racial inequality—in migration and otherwise—lies at the feet of citizens and their beliefs.

However, the leaders of states and the ideology of the modern nation-state also plays an important role. Above, I briefly highlight that politicians have the incentive to construct migrants as security threats to gain popular support. While this issue certainly speaks to the problem of public opinion, it reveals a deeper issue associated with the evolving relationship between the modern nation-state and the institution of sovereignty. In chapter 2, I note that border control and the right to restrict foreigners are not inherent, timeless rights of nation-states. In other words, when nation-states emerged as institutional competitors to city-states, empires, and duchies, there was no presumption that border control and strict population management defined what it meant

20. Martin and McCrain 2019.

21. Bonilla-Silva 2006, 2012.

to be a state. Instead, this belief emerged in the nineteenth century as settler colonial states began encountering racially undesirable immigrants from the non-White world. The emergence of the plenary power doctrine in the United States both exemplified this shift and sent a strong signal to the rest of the world: real states control their borders and populating well should be the state's top priority.

Although overtly racist references to "populating well" have receded somewhat since decolonization, the idea that states have the sovereign duty and right to control their borders has become an even stronger ideology. This ideology has taken hold within both the popular consciousness and the academy. In the case of the former, one need not search long to find examples of politicians, commentators, and citizens arguing that states have the right to close their borders to guard against the misappropriation of the benefits of membership in their society. Indeed, it is common to hear commentators, such as former Arkansas (US) governor Mike Huckabee, question, "What morality prioritizes the right of a Honduran to cross the border, over the right of an American . . . to feed her family?"[22] There is no subtext here: the argument is that states *must* control their borders to maintain their legitimacy and to ensure that their public goods are not dispersed to unworthy nonmembers.

In the latter case, philosophical work questions whether democratic societies are robust to large inflows of immigrants. Although liberal and democratic theories are grounded in principles of freedom and equality, democracy requires citizens to participate in institutionalized political processes, so political communities must be bounded to distinguish members from nonmembers. This necessity calls for the existence of hard borders, and it presumes that citizens will not participate in a democracy if there is not a clear sense of the other members of their polity.[23] This ideology emerged during the twentieth century, and it presumes democracies cannot survive without hard borders and strict notions of sovereignty because, otherwise, ordinary people will not participate.[24] Scholars and commentators continue to assert this claim despite growing evidence that deliberative democracy can succeed in diverse, polarized societies.[25]

22. Majors 2018.
23. Abizadeh 2008, 43.
24. Mouffe 2000, 39.
25. Minozzi et al. 2020; Neblo 2017.

This ideology reinforces the problem of securitization I note above. The problem when everyone assumes that democracies require borders or that proper states defend their borders is that these sentiments ensure that leaders will always have the linguistic resource of "a border that must be defended" from "the other people beyond it." This is a powerful resource and gives politicians the incentive to use immigration policy and the figure of the migrant as fodder to prop up domestic political support. Politicians are motivated to win reelection,[26] and appeals to fear are a quick way for politicians to get the public onside and win support for their policies, even when they are bad.[27] So in a world where electoral democracy is hegemonic, a large proportion of people live under political regimes in which it is expedient for politicians to securitize to provoke fear-based responses. Because immigrants are such a natural target due to their otherness, and strong borders have come to define what it means to be a modern state, it is easy to see how and why politicians are motivated to securitize migrants.

An additional, related implication of securitization and the linguistic resource of borders is that pervasive anti-immigrant sentiment can be an issue that ties political coalitions together. In other words, securitizing immigrants and restrictive policy positions become convenient political bargaining chips. This behavior is pervasive throughout the world, and it spans the ideological spectrum. For example, in January 2020, the Austrian Green party was in negotiations to join a government with the right-wing ÖVP. The Greens were willing to govern with such a vehemently anti-immigrant party in exchange for more progressive environmental legislation and for the opportunity to join the government.[28] This example of strange bedfellows suggests that opposition to immigration and the militarization of immigration policy will always be a prime candidate for cross-party cooperation. Because opposition to immigration can be found on both the right and the left,[29] similar grand political bargains are likely throughout the rest of the world, particularly as anthropomorphic climate change becomes more severe. The commonsense notion that real states have strong borders and that democratic communities must distinguish and protect themselves from outsiders only furthers this concern.

26. Mayhew 1974.

27. Lupia and Menning 2009.

28. Schuetze and Bennhold 2020.

29. King and Valdez 2011.

However, although sovereignty now means that states control hard borders and have the right and obligation to exclude foreigners, this book shows that this has not always been the case. The history of state sovereignty shows that it is a malleable ideology. Leaders did not originally conceive of sovereignty to include border control. This dimension of sovereignty has only become common sense recently. Many behave as if sovereignty is a transcendental concept even though it is not; it is socially and historically constructed. As such, we may be able to reconceive of what sovereignty means and reconsider the relationship between borders and the state. Whether this will require jettisoning nations from the nation-state or an exogeneous shock remains to be seen.[30]

Responsibility

Like all expositions of racial inequality, this book raises the question of who or what is responsible for the racial inequality in international migration. This question is complicated for two reasons that imply that racial inequality may persist unabated because states and people will continue to pass the buck of responsibility. First, as I write above, people rarely see themselves as racist under color-blind racism. Second, the historical and structural dimension of this story encourages citizens and leaders to absolve themselves of responsibility and pin remaining inequality on "history."

The first issue is related to extant issues with color-blind racism. These issues will be familiar to the reader who has made it this far. To be succinct, nonovert racists in the modern international system do not think they harbor racist beliefs. These "nonracists" instead argue that they simply respond to objective facts when they support, for example, "a total and complete shutdown" on immigration from Muslim-majority countries "until our country's representatives can figure out what is going on."[31] Although the example to which I allude is extreme, it is indicative of the sort of thinking that is pervasive throughout the world. Now that explicit racism has been legislated out of societies, it is straightforward to contend that any remaining racial disparities are a function of behavioral deficiencies on the part of affected groups.[32] Of course, this reasoning reproduces another important form of racism that I have discussed at length. Be that as it may, such exercises in motivated reasoning are responsible for a lack of action to combat persistent inequalities within states, and there is reason to believe that this tendency will scale up to racial

30. Deudney 2007; Stevens 2011.

31. J. Johnson 2015.

32. Shilliam 2018; Tilley and Shilliam 2018.

inequalities in the international system. This is especially true considering the domestic antecedents of racial inequality in international migration.

Second, and related, this book's historical theory and explanation may catalyze this buck-passing tendency. I argue that colonialism and the era of explicit racism created today's undesirable non-White migrants. One may agree with this argument and its unfortunate implications, but argue that contemporary states must nevertheless do what is in their best interest. This issue is related to Michael Neblo's taxonomy of subjects in the modern racism debate.[33] Neblo uses a battery of race-related questions to identify one's type as either an open racist, racial progressive, principled conservative, racial resenter, or apolitical. Although this study comes from the United States, its implications are far-reaching and related to this book because it highlights the multifaceted nature of modern racism and how nonracist principles or objective facts mask or confound underlying racist views. One of the more interesting results of this study is that those identified as principled conservatives both admitted that racial inequality exists and opposed affirmative action and other progressive means to address it. The key to resolving this impasse is that these conservatives are "focused on 'history' as the main cause, with current discrimination by whites, or lack of effort by blacks as decidedly less important."[34] One cannot go back and fix history.

This connection to extant work in the American context is important because it highlights the potential pitfalls of this book's implications. If principled citizens and leaders can simply point to history as the most decisive cause of modern inequality, then they absolve themselves of current responsibility. This concern is particularly acute if they engage in conventional realist reasoning and argue that leaders have a duty to protect the state's national interest above all else. This implication has larger knock-on effects for similar and adjacent scholarship that is historically informed.[35] One can reveal the historical roots of a given phenomenon, but that history may provide an excuse for many to shirk responsibility. Structure and history are convenient targets for those who wish to deflect blame.[36] Future work at the intersection of ethics, international politics, and public engagement must address this pathology.

33. Neblo 2009.

34. Neblo 2009, 37.

35. Buzan and Lawson 2015.

36. However, see I. Young 2006 for an alternative view. Young argues that focusing on blame absolves stakeholders from identifying who or what is responsible and fixing those underlying issues. Individual blame is too easy to deflect.

Implications for International Migration

Future Immigration Policies

Evidence that Western states continue to enact strict immigration policies after they receive inflows from racially different populations will be dispiriting for people who are in favor of more open borders, because it is symptomatic of a larger disconnect between empirical evidence and political reality in the politics of immigration. Many immigration scholars consider immigration policy to be a function of domestic interest groups, economic conditions, and business interests.[37] Accordingly, concern about economic (fiscal and wage) effects is one major component of anti-immigration sentiment throughout the world.[38] Most economists act as if these concerns dwarf all others. However, recall that there is more or less a consensus that low-skilled immigration does not negatively affect native wages or public finances.[39] In an objective, *homo economicus* world, leaders and citizens of immigrant-receiving countries would absorb this evidence and update their beliefs accordingly. Doing so would lead them to concede that societies accept far too few immigrants and that they could reap tremendous economic benefits from more open immigration policies.[40]

So there must be something else going on here that explains anti-immigrant public opinion and increasingly restrictive immigration policies. Why are citizens motivated to ignore this evidence? I contend that cultural and social (read: racial) considerations lie at the heart of most anti-immigrant feelings and that many people use economic concerns as either explicit or implicit smoke screens for their real fears.[41] This smoke screen is plausible because the end of overtly racist immigration policies throughout the world was one of the most drastic changes in global governance during the twentieth century. Prior to World War II, states as varied as the United States and Panama used biological racism to warrant their immigration policies, and it is staggering that these laws disappeared in such a short period of time.

The surprising part of this rapid shift toward color blindness is that it occurred at all. Fitzgerald and Cook-Martin argue that liberalism and

37. Freeman 1995.

38. Dancygier and Donnelly 2013; Mayda 2006; Scheve and Slaughter 2001.

39. Card and Krueger 1990; Card 2012; Dustmann and Frattini 2014; Ortega and Peri 2013.

40. Clemens and Pritchett 2019.

41. See Peters 2017, 226–228, for an argument that immigration policies will likely remain restrictive that is based on economic and firm considerations.

democracy, contrary to popular belief, were engines of racist immigration policies during the nineteenth and early twentieth centuries.[42] Classical liberalism emphasized the rights and liberties of individuals, as well as the freedom of political participation, religion, movement, and exchange. However, as I note above, mass political participation coheres liberal democracies, and these states define themselves in terms of excluded others to bolster collective identity and participation. Unsurprisingly, this shift coincided with the admission of border control as inherent to state sovereignty. Until recently, racism was the chief ideology that justified most exclusions. Famously, John Stuart Mill wrote in the *New York Times* in 1870 that mass Chinese immigration would harm the "more civilized and improved portion of mankind."[43] Simply put, liberal democracy bolsters and is bolstered by racism and other prejudice. If racism exists in any form, the exclusionary predilections of liberal democracy will amplify that prejudice. Indeed, the potent combination of overt, latent, and color-blind racism and the taken-for-granted nature of state sovereignty will likely ensure that restrictive immigration policies are here to stay.

I do not think it is likely that citizens and policymakers—in the West or elsewhere—will overcome these fact-resistant beliefs for three reasons. First, cultural and economic concerns lie at the heart of anti-immigrant sentiment. People do not want more immigrants because they fear that they "won't assimilate," are "too different," or will reap undeserved fiscal benefits, regardless of whether these fears are warranted.[44] Ultimately, these motivated beliefs will lead citizens and elites to oppose immigration, even when they are in dire need. For example, Poland has experienced a severe labor shortage since 2015 across most sectors of its economy. If it does not change its immigration stance, then it will have one million vacant jobs by 2030.[45] However, the right-wing Law and Justice Party won election that same year on a staunchly anti-immigrant platform. Poland is one of the most anti-immigrant countries in Europe, and acute labor market needs have not reduced these sentiments. This case is illustrative of how "cultural" concerns outstrip rational ones. Moreover, the extant public opinion literature corroborates this insight

42. FitzGerald and Cook-Martin 2014, 3.

43. Mill 1861, 65.

44. Critics of so-called mass immigration often quickly transition from unsubstantiated fears about assimilation to conclusions about terrorism or other danger. See Horowitz 2017.

45. Pronczuk 2019.

and shows that cultural and religious concerns drive public anti-immigrant sentiment.[46]

Second, democracy and mass political participation permit citizens to lean on racism and other prejudices to make electoral decisions. This issue is related to a point I have belabored throughout this book. Incumbent leaders and others vying to take their place have strong incentives to engage in dog whistle racism to appeal to these sentiments.[47] The leaders and citizens do not need to be overtly racist: anti-immigrant laws are popular because they seem as though they simply prioritize those in one's own country over outsiders. Given the fact-resistant disposition toward the realities of immigration laid out above, this creates a congruence. A politician who pushes policies for prejudiced reasons and one who is merely trying to do right by their citizens can end up supporting similar immigration policies because both couch their policies in terms of the national interest.

Finally, famous recent attempts at removing barriers to movement have coincided with further increases in restrictiveness elsewhere. The politics of the Schengen Area, a European area of free movement without border or passport controls, exemplifies this concern. Schengen is the quintessential example of a borderless world, but it should not be held up as a model for the future. Not only does the Schengen Area exist in Europe, where long histories of conflict have catalyzed postwar reconciliation, but it also has led to "Fortress Europe." When these European countries decided to abolish internal borders, they strengthened their external borders at the same time.[48] Although Schengen and other borderless regions may increase the local freedom of movement, they are unlikely to decrease racial inequality in migration because they reproduce the same inequality between the North and South.

What would it take for states to change course and enact more open immigration policies? All in all, the prospects for a global shift in immigration policy restrictiveness are bleak because of these reasons and colonialism's effects on the psyche of those appraising immigrants throughout the world. Save for a catastrophic exogenous shock, one of which I discuss below, it is more likely that the world will become more restrictive rather than less. Even globalization, which scholars previously credited with creating a borderless,

46. Adida, Lo, and Platas 2019; Bansak, Hainmueller, and Hangartner 2016; Hainmueller and Hopkins 2015.

47. López 2015.

48. Rudolph 2005, 11.

interconnected world,[49] will likely produce more restrictiveness because firms will not have the incentive to lobby for more open policies,[50] and the knock-on costs of globalization felt by the West's oft-lamented White working class will spur calls for further protectionism and restrictions.[51]

Migration and the Global Climate Crisis

Climate change is one such exogeneous shock. For thousands of years, human beings have lived in a narrow temperature band from approximately 11 degrees to 15 degrees Celsius.[52] This fact is not surprising—all species have what is called a "climate niche." What is surprising is that over the next fifty years, "1 to 3 billion people are projected to be left outside the climate conditions that have served humanity well over the past 6000 y[ears]."[53] These changing conditions have already affected millions of people throughout the world, particularly in the global South.[54] Anthropogenic climate change is one of the greatest threats to human civilization, and although climate refugees are a symptom of a more acute sickness, these movements have the potential to impact the lives of over a billion people long before our climate becomes existentially inhospitable.

The fact that most first-wave climate refugees are from the global South puts the onus on the North to act. These rich countries have two choices. On the one hand, they can choose to open their borders to those from the fastest-warming countries, thereby alleviating pressure both abroad (by allowing people to escape inhospitable climates) and at home (by alleviating demographic decline). On the other hand, they can choose to further retrench and keep their borders closed to outsiders, thereby trapping millions of climate refugees in overburdened, inhospitable, and increasingly precarious regions of the world.[55]

Given the discussion above, the likeliest outcome is a mixture of the two. At first, certain Northern countries that have already been at the forefront

49. Held et al. 1999.

50. Peters 2017.

51. Hozić and True 2017; Shilliam 2018.

52. Xu et al. 2020, 11350.

53. Xu et al., 11350

54. Biermann and Boas 2010; Farbotko and Lazrus 2012; Wennersten and Robbins 2017.

55. See Malm 2021 for a bleak take on how the climate crisis will amplify far-right solutions that include closing the border to protect the nation.

of climate activism, such as Norway and Sweden, will likely lead the way on admitting these refugees. At the same time, I expect that the same cultural fears will hamstring the rest of the Anglo-European world into paralysis. Only after a dramatic event, such as mass starvation, death, or destruction that scientists can conclusively pin on climate change, will the rest fall in line.

Even then, these remaining countries—I am thinking of the United States—will have their own issues with climate change (rising tides, extreme weather, etc.), which could lead to further backlash against outsiders. After all, don't we have a greater obligation to protect our citizens before we help foreigners? The logic of exclusion, sovereignty, and responsibility appears once more. If the Anglo-European world's collective response to the refugees fleeing the Syrian Civil War is a preview of what is to come,[56] then we should worry about the tendency for rich countries to close ranks when presented with potential inflows of non-White migrants, regardless of the impetus for their movement. This border hardening could trap millions of people, making them more desperate and precarious as the global South experiences forced urbanization and the other effects of climate change.

The best outcome for humanity will require both immense goodwill and international cooperation. The former requires fostering a sense of cosmopolitan empathy—the idea that one is a citizen of the world and therefore holds all people in the same regard[57]—among a sufficiently large percentage of those in the global North, which is no simple task.[58] The latter requires states to overcome not only the well-worn issues associated with international cooperation but also their own status quo bias in international migration.[59] Receiving states are allowed under international law to determine their level and type of immigrants for admission, which will lead to less radical solutions because states must bargain over the distribution of a largely undesirable entity—the non-White migrant. All of this must take place during an inevitable period of climate change–induced instability, which will undoubtedly affect the likelihood that the best outcome occurs.

56. Adida, Lo, and Platas 2019; Hangartner et al. 2019.

57. Nussbaum 1996.

58. Cosmopolitanism is often associated with the protection of universal human values and prioritizes "respect, tolerance, and responsibility for the human community" (Pichler 2009, 707). Climate change and climate refugees certainly fall under this umbrella.

59. Money and Lockhart 2018, 6.

A BRIEF REFLECTION ON PANDEMICS

In addition to the obvious implications for the politics surrounding the global climate crisis, I must briefly acknowledge an important elephant in the room: the COVID-19 pandemic that began in 2020. I completed and edited this manuscript almost entirely during the pandemic's most dire months, which saw the world unevenly grind to a screeching halt. Nonessential international travel—most of it anyway—stopped, and many people throughout the world experienced some degree of lockdown during which they could not leave their homes other than to do necessary shopping and exercise.

Unsurprisingly, academics almost immediately began considering what the pandemic's implications for the international order might be.[60] COVID-19 presented the most dramatic exogenous shock to the international system since WWII, and it is still unclear how international cooperation might change after it is over. Whether states organize a universal vaccine passport to regulate international travel, retrench, or simply return to normal remains anyone's guess.

However, one clear effect of the pandemic has been the closing and increased restriction of international borders. As some scholars have noted, this increasingly restrictive border orientation reflects how countries chose to "externalize" the virus, rather than deal with it domestically.[61] The pandemic, particularly in the early months, produced immense anxiety, and many states took the opportunity to continue what they had already intended to do: restrict their borders to prevent undesirables from entering. It is simply easier to close one's borders, close ranks, and think myopically in the face of such a nebulous, invisible threat.

By most measures, these efforts have been successful, and I presume that the migrants that have experienced the most harm remain those from the non-White global South. Perhaps the response to COVID-19 provides a sneak peek of the ultimate response to global climate change. If so, it is likely that the social forces and structural ignorance of history that I describe in this book will only increase in strength. While Piketty believes that another economic depression or world war are the sole hopes for alleviating the incessant increases in income inequality throughout the world,[62] the pandemic shows

60. See, e.g., Barnett 2020; Lipscy 2020.

61. Kenwick and Simmons 2020.

62. Piketty 2014.

that similar shocks will likely only enhance racial inequality, surveillance, precarity, othering, and antagonism in international politics.[63]

Prospects for International Cooperation

The case of climate refugees raises a larger issue: there has been little international cooperation on migration. This paucity is jarring when one compares international migration to other areas, such as trade, capital markets, aviation, and law enforcement. For example, while the World Trade Organization and a host of preferential trade agreements regulate international trade, states limit cooperation on migration to a few guest worker regimes and a handful of small regional zones of free movement. Indeed, the legal rules that govern the right to move to another country, establish permanent residence, obtain citizenship rights, and secure employment are almost completely outside the scope of international cooperation. The only significant case of cooperation over migration in recent years is the deal between the European Union and Turkey to stop refugees from the Middle East from traveling to Europe to seek asylum. Seen in this light, the future climate-induced refugee crisis looms large because this case demonstrates that cooperation is only available when it involves (1) an integrated, supranational bloc of countries (European Union) and (2) a deal to restrict migrants from traveling to that bloc.

This narrow scope of cooperation is surprising in light of the modern economic theory of trade agreements. In this theory, states maximize their own interests and ignore the welfare of foreigners. So, when an importing country imposes a tariff, exporting countries reduce their prices in response, which improves the importer's terms of trade. Foreigners bear these costs, so importing countries ignore this negative externality when they set their tariffs. As a result, tariffs are too high and inefficient from a global perspective. This is why international cooperation is so important, and this logic applies to all markets, including migration.[64] As such, there is a role for international migration agreements to prevent these inefficiencies, even if states are self-interested. Any economic adviser to a Western government will be familiar with this standard logic, which raises the question of why such cooperation is absent.

63. Dionne and Turkmen 2020; Greitens 2020.

64. Sykes 2013, 321.

The standard explanations for why international cooperation on international migration does not exist will be familiar. First, modern international law gives states extensive discretion over the admission of foreigners,[65] and migration policy remains "the last major redoubt of unfettered national sovereignty."[66] Second, the supposed costs and benefits of international migration are unevenly distributed within states. Immigration may either be a boon or bust depending on one's sector of the economy, which affects policymaking at the national level.[67] Finally, the perceived costs and benefits of international migration are unevenly distributed between states. The countries that must cooperate on international migration are those that think they stand to lose the most from increased immigration, regardless of whether those perceptions match reality.[68] This asymmetry in interests between the global North and global South ensures that states have little room for potential agreement.

As I have argued in this book, racism is an unstated antecedent of this lack of cooperation. Faced with the dearth of international cooperation, economists argue that states care about the *distribution* of national income rather than its overall size. This suggestion has significant implications when states consider the effect of increased immigration from poor, unproductive, and otherwise undesirable immigrants. In this way, this book's argument rears its head once again because perceptions, rather than the reality, of immigration are doing the work here. Armed with the best available evidence about the positive effects and ultimate necessity of increasing immigration, states still do not cooperate because they fear the costs of admitting undesirable immigrants. Although some political theorists argue that international cooperation is necessary or moral,[69] recent empirical work shows that the cooperation that does exist reproduces the fears and interests of rich, Western states.[70] Taken together with this book's analysis, further cooperation is unlikely because migration is different than other types of international flows. Cooperating to promote free trade, for example, does not conjure the same fears of being overrun by racialized, undesirable others. This lack of

65. Opeskin 2012.

66. Martin 1989, 547.

67. Dancygier and Donnelly 2013; Freeman 2006.

68. Sykes 2013, 317.

69. Hidalgo 2016.

70. Geiger and Pécoud 2014.

cooperation will ultimately have important implications for global efforts to address the issue of climate refugees and other related issues.

Implications for the Study of International Politics

Race, Racism, and Contemporary International Relations

Over the past several years, international relations scholars have reacquainted themselves with the imperialist origins of the field.[71] Doing so has revealed to the mainstream that scholars first developed the discipline of international relations to address the concerns of administering racially undesirable, colonial populations. This history is both simple and complex, and the upshot is that international relations theories have White supremacist histories that often obscure the earliest contributions of Black scholars like Du Bois, Locke, and Merze Tate.[72] This type of historical reckoning extends to adjacent fields, such as political theory, and it is indicative of a larger trend whereby contemporary scholars wrestle with how their field's origins may affect current scholarship and teaching.[73]

This book is a direct descendant of this initiative: I use the history of explicit racism and colonialism in the international system to describe why inequality persists in international migration despite the end of racial quotas. Where I differ, however, is in the application of the lessons of the recent turn to racism in the international system. Most of this recent scholarship either qualitatively examines how race and racism emerge in certain cases,[74] theorizes the transnational stratum of race and racial inequality,[75] or considers how race and racism affected international relations historically.[76] Instead, I use quantitative methods to test a historical theory of why inequality persists in the modern international system, which is an appeal that few IR scholars have made.[77]

To put it differently, this book operates at the intersection of existing approaches. I am indebted to the historical accounts of the field's origins and

71. Anievas, Manchanda, and Shilliam 2015; Rutazibwa 2020; Vitalis 2015.

72. Henderson 2013, 2017; Hobson 2012.

73. Rutazibwa 2020.

74. Búzás 2018; Hozić and True 2017; Owens 2017; Rajaram 2018; Shilliam 2018.

75. Gruffydd Jones 2008; Nisancioglu 2019; D. Thompson 2013; Tilley and Shilliam 2018.

76. Búzás 2013; Klotz 1995; Lake and Reynolds 2008; Vucetic 2011.

77. Henderson 2015 remains an important exception, and this book is indebted to his model of using quantitative methods to study race and colonialism in international politics.

how explicit racism shaped international politics in the nineteenth and early twentieth centuries. Moreover, I take onboard the nuanced theories of structural racism in the constitution of international order. However, I do so in the service of a systematic analysis that speaks to how race and racism affect international politics today. To do so, I use quantitative methods, which some argue are incapable of blending with critical theory.[78] I admit that quantifying and measuring have important power, but measurement and quantitative methods have the advantage of being the tools of the orthodoxy. I use these tools to expose contemporary racial inequality to those who question the validity of qualitative or historical methods.[79] This choice is pragmatic, and although some may scoff at this admission, it is important to expose and communicate the existence of inequality in a way that will be taken seriously by the mainstream. Otherwise, critique will only spiral into further critique and further subdisciplinary infighting.[80]

Accordingly, I hope this book, its approach, and its argument provide a model for future work on racism and other inequalities in international politics. One does not need to choose between doing work that exposes inequalities, structural or otherwise, in international politics and doing quantitative work. In fact, this conflates debates over epistemology with those over ontology, which is counterproductive for studying the social world.[81] International politics is a social science that focuses on politics "in the wild," and it is necessary to use all the tools—historical, theoretical, qualitative, and quantitative—to study its complex nature. Accordingly, my midrange approach[82] merely subjects a politically important aspect of the modern international system to inquiry, and it uses the methods appropriate for warranting its conclusions. I leave further work to other scholars who may use other tools.

Political Economy, International Theory, and History

Along these same lines, this project also has important implications for the study of international political economy (IPE). Currently, there are two dominant strands of IPE scholarship. The first is open economy politics (OEP),

78. Aradau and Huysmans 2014.

79. The skeptical reader should note that W.E.B. Du Bois conducted one of the first quantitative studies in social science to uncover racial inequalities in Philadelphia (Du Bois 1899). This fact should ameliorate concerns of any universal imperialism of quantitative methods.

80. Baele and Bettiza 2021; Latour 2004.

81. Wendt 1999, 6.

82. Lake 2013.

which rose to prominence in the mid-1990s in the American academy during the shift away from grand theories, such as Marxism, and toward falsifiable, midrange theories.[83] Proponents developed OEP as a rational choice approach that begins with a distribution of preferences among individuals and then aggregates those preferences across interest groups to examine the international implications. As such, this approach is strongly wedded to positivism, empiricism, and the scientific method. The key innovation of OEP is to use narrow hypothesis testing to research each component of the object under study—such as trade policy—in isolation from the others. A full picture emerges and science accumulates when scholars "pool our knowledge of the different parts."[84]

The second school is more prominent in the British IR academy. This alternative, English-speaking approach to IPE is distinct from the former because it is less wedded to the standard scientific tenets of OEP. What is more, those in British IPE are far more willing to engage with scholars and debates in other disciplines (beyond political science and economics), such as law, philosophy, history, and sociology. These scholars also prioritize normative questions in addition to empirical ones, while those who use the OEP approach tend to ignore these nonempirical issues.[85] A recent, quintessential example of this second approach is the special issue of *New Political Economy* on raced markets, edited by Lisa Tilley and Robbie Shilliam.[86] In this special issue, scholars tackle subjects as diverse as race and racism in the international system, neocolonialism, the plight of refugees as surplus value, and neoliberal welfare regimes. While nothing prevents OEP scholars from studying these issues with their methods, they rarely do so.

This book is unique among those that examine aspects of the international political economy because it combines the two approaches. In so doing, it highlights how one can study an object of the international political economy and international migration, yet not be wedded either to positivist, quantitative hypothesis testing or to normative and multidisciplinary perspectives. While scholastic cultures emerge for good reasons—preferential attachment, different interests in different places, and so on—nothing prevents one from beginning a project with an ostensibly "American" approach, developing a historically informed theory that draws on critical scholarship, using the latest

83. Oatley 2017, 2.
84. Lake 2011, 472.
85. Cohen 2007, 199.
86. Tilley and Shilliam 2007.

statistical techniques to test the implications of that theory, and then drawing out the normative implications of the results. In many ways, this implication for the study of IPE is similar to the implication for the study of IR. Scholars ought to use all the tools at their disposal, rather than limit their possibilities. While I would never begrudge someone for choosing not to learn method X or approach Y, using the full range of the IR and IPE toolbox is more likely to produce insights that are interpretable and significant to both scholastic "cultures" and the wider world.[87]

Lessons for Paradigm Warriors

Some readers will be surprised to find a concluding section on the implications of this book for the supposedly discredited and irrelevant paradigms of IR theory: realism, liberalism, and constructivism. Indeed, there has been significant debate since the 1990s about whether IR paradigms matter in the post–Cold War era and whether scholars should act as if they matter at all.[88] While some, like John Mearsheimer and Stephen Walt, lament the "end" of theorizing—grand, paradigm-based theorizing—in mainstream international relations, others, like David Lake, say "good riddance": that work did nothing for our knowledge of international politics beyond navel-gazing. There are two ironies in this debate. The first irony is that both sides claim that the other's approach will not produce cumulative knowledge. Mearsheimer and Walt think narrow hypothesis testing will not produce cumulative knowledge because it will lead to thousands of narrow, often contradictory findings that others will never press scholars to explain.[89] Lake claims that reifying paradigms and grand theories is dangerous because its implied interparadigm competition produces extreme arguments in which adherents to each paradigm use the time periods and evidence that conform to the logic of their theories.[90] This argument suggests that scholars will go

87. Moreover, although some on the "British" side may scoff, I chose to use the tools of mainstream social science for a reason beyond the obvious inferential ones I note above. My goal is to unmask the racial inequality the mainstream ignores. To do so, I amassed evidence that was interpretable to the majority of scholars. I admit that this choice has moral and gatekeeping implications, and I do not shy away from the orthodox, American, and Northern biases in this analysis.

88. Lake 2011; Mearsheimer and Walt 2013.

89. Mearsheimer and Walt 2013, 444.

90. Lake 2011, 469–470.

round and round and never accumulate knowledge about actual international politics.

Regardless of what John Mearsheimer, Stephen Walt, or David Lake claims, IR paradigms *do* still matter. In fact, in the most recent Teaching, Research, and International Policy (TRIP) survey from 2017, 73 percent of IR scholars identified their scholarship with a paradigm, and 54 percent identified with the classic choices of realism, liberalism, or constructivism.[91] Moreover, as Lake admits, most undergraduate IR courses and PhD field seminars organize the discipline around these main schools.[92] In turn, although it was not my initial intention, this book does have important implications for scholars in each camp.

First, as I note in the introduction to this chapter, realists need to think more historically. A realist may protest that they *do* take history seriously. After all, their case studies are from the Concert of Europe and the War of the Triple Alliance. However, scholars use these historical events to test timeless, covering law theories, and they often commit the sin of selecting on the dependent variable to do so.[93] Historically informed theories are not the same as theories that involve historical processes. Second, this book reveals something that some IR liberals likely already know—namely, that they should be careful what they wish for regarding the intervening role of international institutions. While institutions may be well suited as information-providing mechanisms, they also play a role in fostering international norms that can have deleterious knock-on effects for non-Anglo-European states.[94] Finally, this book's theory, evidence, and implications demonstrate to constructivists that just because something is socially constructed, it does not mean that it is not morally wrong, bad, or sticky. For example, this book corroborates the argument that the institution of sovereignty is a social construct. The constructivists' initial impulse will be to note how the fact of social construction means that states can reconstruct its meaning to produce more positive outcomes. "Anarchy is what states make of it,"[95] after all. However, social constructions, like the connection between sovereignty and border control,

91. Maliniak et al. 2017.

92. Lake 2011, 467.

93. Ashworth et al. 2008.

94. In addition, political theorists have commented on the problems of "liberal imperialism" for many years (Mantena 2010). In short, the tenets of liberal internationalism *produced* scientific racism, colonialism, and other violent Western incursions into the non-White world.

95. Wendt 1992.

often resist change and can have unfortunate effects, in this example, on racial inequality when they globalize throughout the world. English School scholars, Marxists, feminists, and others should draw their own conclusions, but all in all, this book calls for all scholars to think wider when considering how they do their scholarship and the politics on which they focus that scholarship.

Doing so will, for instance, provide some conceptual clarity on foundational debates in international relations scholarship, such as whether sovereignty exists, or resembles an "organized hypocrisy," or is merely being eroded.[96] This book shows that sovereign states are informed by changing conceptions of what sovereignty means and that these concepts can become common sense even though they are not immutable. Liberals and constructivists (and some realists, like Stephen Krasner) have shown that states are no longer ideal-typical sovereigns, but this fact does not mean sovereignty or the state are eroding. Instead, sovereign states shape and adapt to what sovereignty means in their current context. Against those who argue that sovereignty has different components and show how states can be sovereign in one area but not in others, I argue that states can be fully sovereign *in their historical context*. When the norms of sovereignty change, then the nature of the state changes too. This argument allows us to hold two things in our head simultaneously. States do not have all the attributes that some realists attribute to them, but they are still powerful institutions with tanks, guns, and warheads. In other words, modern states are not mere reifications just because they do not resemble nineteenth-century sovereigns.[97] Rather, the state adapts. States are not withering away, and we should interpret that adaptation accordingly.[98]

96. Krasner 1999; Rudolph 2005; Sassen 1996; Strange 1994.

97. Ringmar 1996.

98. Many scholars have argued in the past three decades that sovereignty is complex and not withering away. Instead, states "bargain" or "trade off" different dimensions of sovereignty to suit their interests (Barkin 2001; Barkin and Cronin 1994; Krasner 1999; Rudolph 2005). This line of thinking is useful, but it overstates the importance of, for example, delegating some authority over trade to the WTO, and it ignores that states still do have immense power and authority over their populations and in certain areas (like migration). This is not a question of trade-offs; it is a question of how to study the ways international norms of behavior interact with the state's perpetual domestic power.

Conclusion

Every country in the world is too closed to immigration. Without realizing I was doing so, I began considering the ideas behind this book the summer after my first year of college when I was working for a United States senator. The media, his constituents, colleagues, and most opponents lionized my boss for his ideological consistency, commitment to his state, and desire to do right by its citizens. Admittedly, this was a time in my life when I was quite ignorant about the complexities of the world's problems, but I was eager to see how leaders made important decisions.

When I worked for the senator, there was a contentious debate over the United States' health care system. My boss's position was simple: there is liberty in free choice. The US should allow all citizens to purchase health care policies across state lines, thereby reducing the inefficiencies that inflate prices. As a rising college sophomore who had taken some introductory economics, this proposal made sense to me. After all, one of my professors proclaimed that modern markets have generated more wealth and reduced more poverty than any other innovation in human history. Too much micromanagement and "conscious direction," after all, is "the road to serfdom."[99]

However, as my work continued that summer, I was confused that many staunch advocates of free markets seemed perfectly willing to advocate for intervention to get what they wanted. Unfortunately for my own citation count, I was not the first person to make this observation.[100] Yet, this experience was staggering for many reasons because it exposed, among other things, the ubiquity of motivated reasoning: few people have principles; they merely have aims that they are motivated to pursue at any cost. I started to view other areas of US and international politics through this lens. In line with this book's themes and argument, I was astounded that many of the people who were so keen to push for free markets, trade, and capital flows were so adamant that we should tighten immigration policies and admit only "the best and brightest." As a Jewish American, this suggestion seemed bizarre because almost all of my ancestors and their non-Jewish immigrant counterparts would have been (and were!) considered undesirable by the American public and leaders of their

99. F. Hayak 2001 [1944], 21.
100. F. A. Hayak 1960, 401.

day.[101] As I laid out in the preface, my family's story could have unfolded differently had many American citizens and policymakers gotten their way and completely restricted immigration from undesirable and unassimilable Jews at the beginning of the twentieth century.

It was only years later, during my last years of graduate school, that I came to realize that discrimination and prejudice play a massive role both in how states make decisions and in the constitution of the international system. I saw many world leaders, who advocated for free markets on the one hand and for immigration restrictions on cultural or desirability grounds on the other, attribute assumptions and stereotypes about groups of people to actual people. Scholars call this type of flawed reasoning the ecological fallacy, and it is pervasive in what some call symbolic, color-blind, or dog whistle racism.[102] Leaders and citizens rarely say overtly racist things, but they use group-based assumptions to infer individual desirability all the time, whether or not they realize it. This is why modern racism is hard to study. Indeed, some readers may be shouting at this page, "I don't want more immigration, but I'm not a racist! My reasons are objective." To these skeptics I respond: Remember, attributing blame is complex and so is the modern world. The point of this book is to expose the deep roots of why people engage in this attribution and how it is a reinforcing cycle that leads to increasingly restrictive immigration policies throughout the world.

Unfortunately, I do not see an easy way forward; there are no simple policy recommendations of the sort one finds in the last chapter of international relations books. The damages of colonialism and explicit racism happened: leaders and citizens view migrants from the non-White world as dangerous, unproductive, or undesirable for a reason. That's why they want to restrict them from their country. This history melds with the recent past and present in a difficult way to make it unlikely that everyone will suddenly perceive their own beliefs as immoral, no matter how inefficient they are for the free market of labor. Therefore, my hope is that readers, scholars, students, practitioners, friends, and enemies will engage with the argument and lessons of this book and, regardless of how they come down on its conclusions, go forward with the appreciation that real people and real lives are at stake in international politics. The line between desirable and undesirable is in the eye of the beholder, and drawing that line has consequences.

101. Brodkin 1998; Zolberg 2008.

102. Bonilla-Silva 2006; Kinder and Sears 1981; López 2015.

APPENDIX

A. Baseline Model Details

I took great care to avoid the technical details of the baseline model in the main text. I left them out because not all readers will be well versed in the techniques of Bayesian inference, nor will some readers care to know all the gory details. However, this ambivalence does not mean that the details are particularly complicated. Yes, the computer code is a bit involved, and the underlying algorithm is a literal physics simulation, but the logic is not rocket science.

Here is the gist. Very often, the things we want to model in the social world are not the result of a pure process. They are mixtures or combinations of multiple processes. These mixtures imply that an observation has multiple causes, which requires one to use multiple probability distributions to model it. Technically speaking, this means we use more than one likelihood to model the same outcome variable.

Count variables are uniquely prone to this issue. The problem is that counts of 0 can often arise in more than one way. Consider the example of international migration. If we observe a zero in the data, then there was no migration between two states. However, we could see that zero either because the rate of migration is very low *or* because migration is structurally impossible between the two states. We are never sure which is the case; we observe a zero either way. Figure A.1 demonstrates the zero inflation of the bilateral migration data.

Recall, the goal of this model is to generate the best possible predictions between every pair of states in the world. As such, it is necessary to model (1) the possibility that any observed zero in the data can occur because migrants either are structurally incapable of migrating between two countries or are able to migrate but do not, and (2) the observed, positive migration flows in the data. This model requires two steps. First, I model the probability of migration between any two states (π), by allowing it to vary by year. I imagine

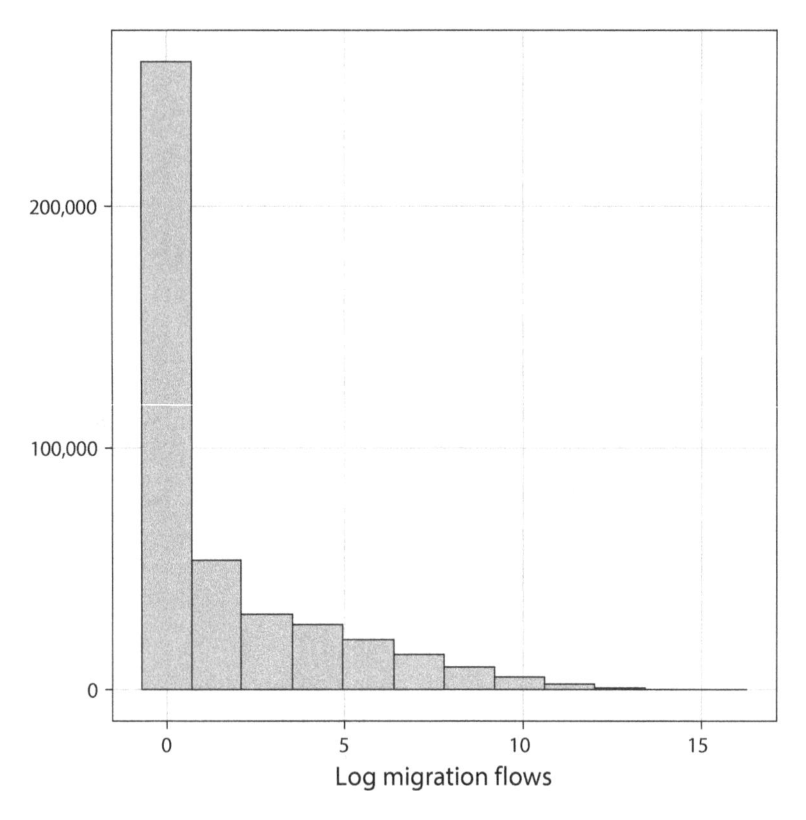

FIGURE A.1. Distribution of migration flows, 1960–2015. This distribution is highly zero inflated and requires a more complicated modeling strategy to account for both the preponderance of zeros and the distribution of positive flows.

that the overall probability of migration between any two states in the world ought to vary across time periods. Second, I model the positive flows with a Weibull distribution. The Weibull distribution is a positive, continuous distribution that is characterized by two parameters: a "shape" parameter, α, and a "scale" parameter, σ ($y \in [0, \infty), \alpha \in \mathbb{R}, \sigma \in \mathbb{R}$). While the Weibull distribution is normally reserved for survival analysis,[1] it gives a good approximation of the natural logarithm of the positive migration flows between states over our time period.

In this model, the scale, or spread, of the migration flows as a linear model ($\sigma = \mu = X\beta$). However, because σ must be positive, I exponentiate the

1. Box-Steffensmeier and Zorn 2001.

TABLE A.1. Baseline model results

	Dependent Variable:
	Migration Flow
Log Migrant Stock	0.924***
	(0.898, 0.949)
Contiguous	1.564***
	(1.484, 1.643)
Log Bilateral Distance	−1.056***
	(−1.084, −1.028)
GDP Difference	0.330***
	(0.231, 0.430)
Log GDPc Origin	0.613***
	(0.529, 0.698)
Log GDPc Origin Squared	−0.026***
	(−0.030, −0.022)
Log Population Destination	−1.502***
	(−1.570, −1.434)
Colony	0.326***
	(0.237, 0.415)
Common Currency	−1.042***
	(−1.120, −0.964)
Common Language	0.652***
	(0.618, 0.686)
Political Violence Origin	−0.036***
	(−0.046, −0.026)
Liberal Democracy Origin	−0.375***
	(−0.465, −0.286)
Liberal Democracy Destination	0.638***
	(0.544, 0.733)
Education Origin	−0.005***
	(−0.006, −0.004)
Constant	2.701***
	(1.966, 3.436)
Observations	162,152
Log Likelihood	−348,299.000
Akaike Inference Criteria	696,635.900
Bayesian Inference Criteria	696,825.800

Note: *p<0.1; **p<0.05; ***p<0.01.

linear predictor. The independent variables typically used in empirical models of migration enter through the linear predictor, μ. In addition, I expect there to be variation in how these variables affect the distribution of migration flows because flows are grouped within dyads. To capture this structure of the data, I multiply the linear predictor in this model by a scalar, θ, that varies by dyad—these are random effects. In essence, I include a different σ for each dyad in the dataset. Therefore, $\sigma_{i,j} = e^{\mu} \times \theta_{i,j}$. This technique accounts for the unique structure of migration data and leads to an accurate model of the data-generating process.[2]

The formal specification of the model follows, where y_i is the migration flow from state A to state B. I estimate this model in R using Stan. Stan is a programming language that implements Bayesian statistical inference. It primarily uses Hamiltonian Monte Carlo to estimate models. For more details, see the Stan user's manual.[3]

$$p(y_i|\pi, \alpha, \sigma) = \begin{cases} \text{Bernoulli}\ (1 \mid \pi) & \text{if } y_i = 0 \\ \text{Bernoulli}\ (0 \mid \pi) \times \text{Weibull}\ (y_i \mid \alpha,\ \sigma) & \text{if } y_i \geq 0 \end{cases}$$

There are two linear models in this function, and each has a different link function that ensures each has the right support when transformed back into the main likelihood. In this model, the parameters in the linear models need prior distributions, which I assign to be weakly regularizing. This discussion only scratches the surface of the technical details of the model. For a more in-depth treatment, there are several good resources on Bayesian statistics.[4] The results are found in table A.1.

B. Graded Response Model

I also use a fully Bayesian approach to measure immigration policy restrictiveness. As I describe in the main text, all countries have an unobservable disposition toward migration. Some countries want to restrict more than others, and they use policy changes to achieve their desired level of restrictiveness. However, immigration policies are notoriously difficult to implement, which makes it hard to target them for specific goals. For instance, increasing policy restrictiveness in one area may lead to more immigration, as prospective migrants change their strategy. This disconnect between preferences and policies makes it difficult to measure a state's level of policy restrictiveness.

In response, I use a latent variable model to estimate this restrictiveness. I use each state's observed policy changes in each of the four areas (border

2. Gelman and Hill 2006, 244–247.

3. Stan Development Team 2020.

4. Gelman et al. 2014; McElreath 2020.

and land control, integration, exit, and integration) to infer their underlying restrictiveness in a given year. To do so, I implement a Bayesian graded response model. Graded response models are a type of item response theory (IRT) model for categorical predictors. In this case, each policy change is a categorical response, which makes this task similar to modeling the responses to *n* items on a questionnaire. For instance, we have four "items" in each year (four policy dimensions) and the same number of possible "answers" to each (more restrictive, less restrictive, no change).

To be specific, the outcome variable y, the change in restrictiveness for each category, is an ordered category. To account for this structure, I use the *cumulative model*, which assumes

$$P(y = c) = F(\tau_c - \psi) - F(\tau_{c-1} - \psi)$$

In this expression, $\psi \in [0, 1]$ is the probability of "success" (latent restrictiveness), F is the cumulative distribution function, and τ is a vector of $C - 1$ thresholds. In the graded response model, F is the standard logistic distribution. This model is extremely flexible, and I can expand it to estimate country, year, and item (policy area) parameters. This means that I can directly estimate the underlying policy restrictiveness in a given year, for a given country, and a given policy area.

In other words, every one of the distributional parameters ψ can be written as a function of country, item, and year parameters. This model might seem complicated, but it is just another type of generalized linear model. The ultimate model of ψ is

$$\psi = \frac{exp(\theta_s + \zeta_i + \gamma_y)}{1 + exp(\theta_s + \zeta_i + \gamma_y)}$$

which is known as the Rasch model. In this model, we interpret θ_s as each state's estimated immigration policy restrictiveness. So higher values of θ_s suggest that a state is more likely to enact a restrictive policy in a given year regardless of policy area. ζ_i is the overall restrictiveness of each policy area, and γ_y is the aggregate restrictiveness of a given year.

Because the graded response model is just a generalized linear model, I can easily implement it in R using Stan directly or using a package like brms. Regardless, I give each of these three parameters weakly regularizing priors that are a normal distribution with a mean of 0 and a standard deviation of 3.[5]

5. See Bürkner 2019 for much more detail on these models and their implementation in R and Stan.

C. Immigration Policy Analysis

The results in chapter 5 provide clear evidence that states become more restrictive after they receive non-White immigrants. In this appendix, I provide descriptive statistics of the main dependent and independent variables of interest, as well as additional model specifications.

Descriptive Statistics

Plots of the main variables of interest are found in figure C.1 and figure C.2. Figure C.1 shows the distribution of immigration policy restrictiveness from 1960 to 2015. I log the policy restrictiveness variable in each of the models, and this figure reflects that transformation. Figure C.2 presents a distribution of each of the four independent variable measures of racially different immigration flows. The first two histograms show the genetic ancestral measures; the other two histograms give the raw distribution of the percentage of sub-Saharan Africa and non-OECD immigration flows. In the models, I log and standardize each of these variables.

In table C.1, I describe how each of these independent variables varies by region. There are few surprising features in this table: sub-Saharan Africa receives the largest number of immigrants from sub-Saharan Africa, and South Asia and East Asia receive the least. However, sub-Saharan Africa does have the second most genetically diverse immigration flows in the world. This may surprise some readers, but it is likely a function of the ancestral distance measure: sub-Saharan Africa receives most of its immigrants from the global South, which is an incredibly diverse region of the world, despite what many in the West may believe.

Interactions

In this section, I show that the linear-additive assumption does not hold for a standard interaction model. Doing so warrants the use of Hainmueller et al.'s kernel-based interaction technique in chapter 5. The results of this diagnostic test are shown in figure C.3. If the kernel-based technique was not necessary, then the curves would look like lines and would overlap with the diagonal lines in the figure. The diagonal lines are the simple linear-interactive relationship, and the curves are the result of a generalized additive model.

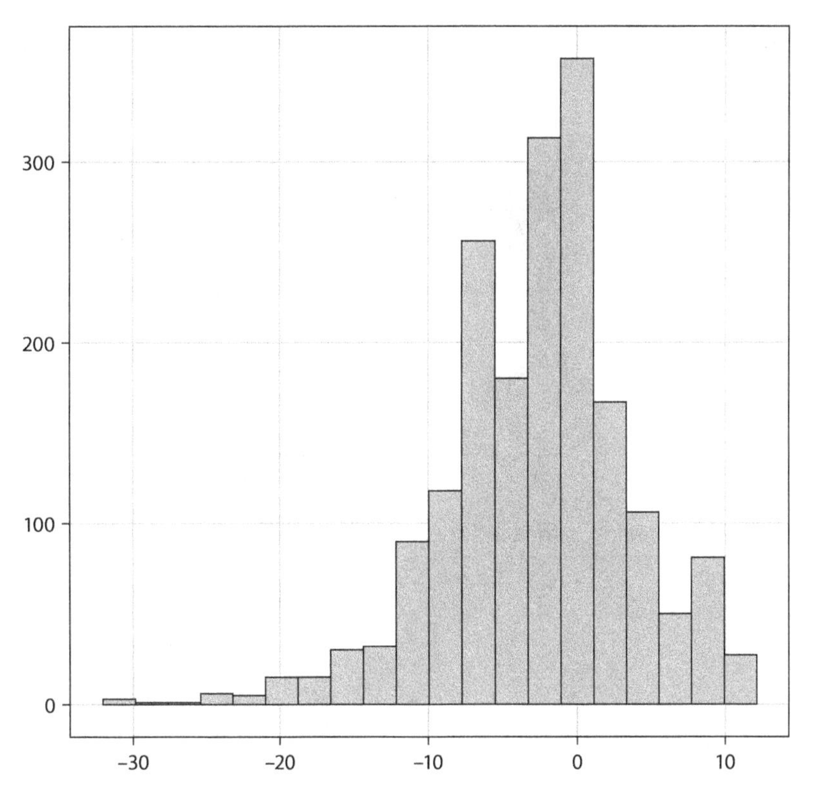

FIGURE C.1. The distribution of aggregate immigration policy restrictiveness, 1960–2015.

Alternative Specifications

In this section, I present several alternative specifications for the models in chapter 5. These models have both spatial and temporal dependence, which require attention. However, there are different strategies for accounting for this dependence. While I use country random effects to account for spatial heterogeneity, I account for temporal effects in two ways. First, I include a lagged dependent variable because past values of immigration policy restrictiveness strongly affect current values. These results are found in table C.2. One can see that the results are consistent with the main results. Using a different specification to account for temporal dependence does not affect the inference that racially different immigration flows, defined in several ways, are associated with immigration policy restrictiveness. Second, I replicate the main text specifications, but instead include a variable that measures whether a destination state was a former colonial power. In these models, I drop the

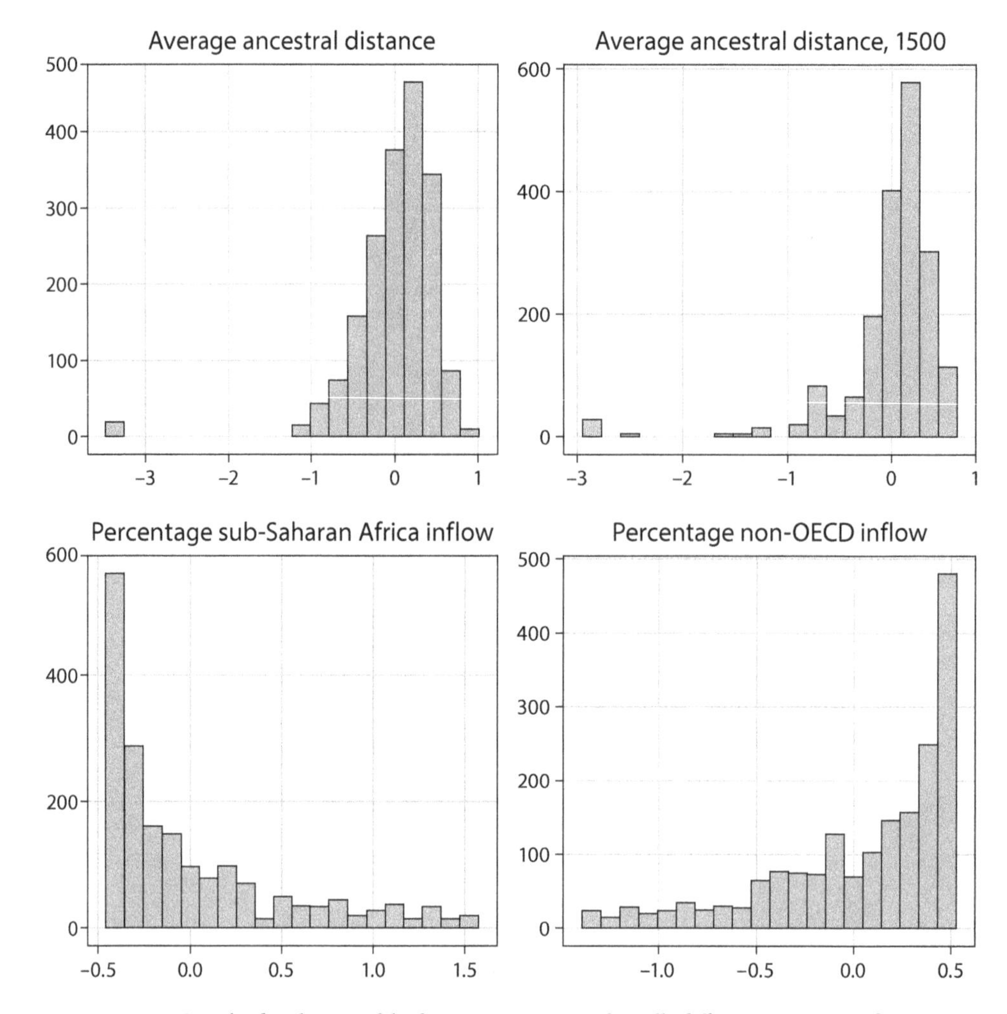

FIGURE C.2. The distribution of the four main measures of racially different immigration flows.

TABLE C.1. Distribution of racially different immigration measures by region

Region	Average Genetic Distance	Average Genetic Distance (1500)	Non-OECD	Sub-Saharan Africa
Latin America & Caribbean	0.05	−0.48	0.89	0.13
East Asia & Pacific	0.23	0.26	0.89	0.06
Europe & Central Asia	−0.05	0.08	0.66	0.22
North America	0.38	0.28	0.80	0.11
South Asia	−0.60	−1.30	0.99	0.03
Middle East & North Africa	−0.23	−0.18	0.82	0.54
Sub-Saharan Africa	0.37	0.01	0.86	0.72

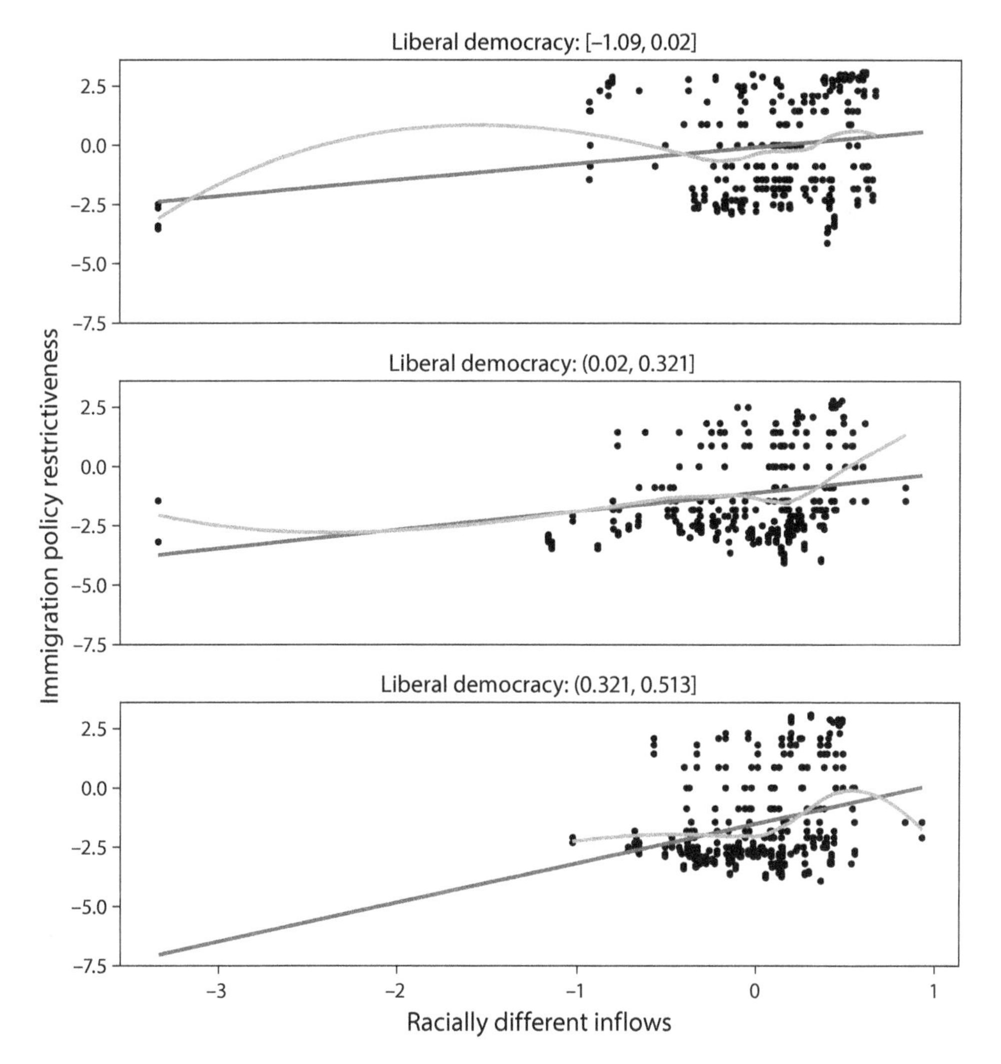

FIGURE C.3. If the linear-additive assumption held, then we would see the curves and lines overlap. However, one can see that there is a nonlinear relationship between racially different inflows in previous periods and immigration policy restrictiveness that varies across the terciles of the liberal democracy variable.

country random effects because they are colinear with the colonial variable. The results are in Table C.3, and they are nearly identical to the main results with one difference: the association between sub-Saharan Africa inflows and policy restrictiveness is no longer significant, which is likely due to the strong correlation between being a former colonial power and receiving immigrants from sub-Saharan Africa.

TABLE C.2. Model specification with lagged dependent variable

	Aggregate Policy Restrictiveness			
	(1)	(2)	(3)	(4)
IHS Average Ancestral Distance	0.133**			
	(0.030, 0.236)			
IHS Average Ancestral Distance (1500)		0.154***		
		(0.049, 0.258)		
IHS Percentage SSA Flow			0.060	
			(−0.055, 0.175)	
IHS Percentage Non-OECD Flow				0.166***
				(0.045, 0.287)
Lag Policy	1.003***	1.005***	1.004***	1.006***
	(0.993, 1.014)	(0.994, 1.015)	(0.994, 1.015)	(0.996, 1.016)
Negative GDP Shock	0.104*	0.092	0.103*	0.108*
	(−0.006, 0.214)	(−0.018, 0.202)	(−0.008, 0.213)	(−0.001, 0.218)
Liberal Democracy	−0.133**	−0.160**	−0.135**	−0.123*
	(−0.264, −0.002)	(−0.294, −0.027)	(−0.267, −0.003)	(−0.252, 0.007)
Inflation Rate	−0.049	−0.048	−0.049	−0.048
	(−0.153, 0.054)	(−0.152, 0.057)	(−0.153, 0.055)	(−0.151, 0.055)
Trade Openness	0.018	0.003	−0.008	0.053
	(−0.107, 0.142)	(−0.124, 0.130)	(−0.133, 0.117)	(−0.075, 0.181)
Conflict	0.066	0.103	0.039	0.014
	(−0.232, 0.365)	(−0.198, 0.405)	(−0.259, 0.338)	(−0.284, 0.312)
(Intercept)	−0.171***	−0.163***	−0.168***	−0.171***
	(−0.248, −0.095)	(−0.241, −0.086)	(−0.244, −0.091)	(−0.246, −0.096)
Country RE	X	X	X	X
N	1,649	1,649	1,649	1,649
Log Likelihood	−2,277.043	−2,276.119	−2,279.618	−2,276.497
Akaike Inference Criteria	4,574.086	4,572.239	4,579.237	4,572.994
Bayesian Inference Criteria	4,628.166	4,626.318	4,633.316	4,627.073

Note: *p < .1; **p < .05; ***p < .01. SSA = sub-Saharan Africa. IHS = inverse hyperbolic sine transformation. The racial distance variables are transformed by the IHS function.

TABLE C.3. Regression models of immigration policy restrictiveness with postcolonial variable

	Log Policy Restrictiveness			
	(1)	(2)	(3)	(4)
IHS Average Ancestral Distance	0.062*			
	(−0.007, 0.132)			
IHS Average Ancestral Distance (1500)		0.081**		
		(0.011, 0.151)		
IHS Percentage SSA Flow			0.035	
			(−0.036, 0.106)	
IHS Percentage Non-OECD Flow				0.099**
				(0.019, 0.180)
Negative GDP Shock	0.063*	0.058	0.063*	0.066*
	(−0.008, 0.135)	(−0.014, 0.130)	(−0.009, 0.134)	(−0.006, 0.137)
Liberal Democracy	−0.124***	−0.139***	−0.125***	−0.126***
	(−0.214, -0.035)	(−0.229, −0.049)	(−0.215, −0.035)	(−0.216, −0.037)
Inflation Rate	−0.048	−0.047	−0.048	−0.046
	(−0.115, 0.018)	(−0.114, 0.020)	(−0.115, 0.019)	(−0.113, 0.021)
Colonial	0.080*	0.083*	0.085*	0.089**
	(−0.009, 0.170)	(−0.007, 0.173)	(−0.005, 0.175)	(0.0004, 0.177)
Trade Openness	0.009	0.001	−0.004	0.026
	(−0.072, 0.090)	(−0.080, 0.082)	(−0.084, 0.076)	(−0.057, 0.109)
Conflict	0.039	0.061	0.027	0.013
	(−0.156, 0.234)	(−0.136, 0.258)	(−0.168, 0.222)	(−0.182, 0.207)
(Intercept)	−0.063	−0.060	−0.059	−0.061
	(−0.145, 0.018)	(−0.142, 0.022)	(−0.141, 0.022)	(−0.142, 0.020)
Year RE	*X*	*X*	*X*	*X*
N	1,686	1,686	1,686	1,686
Log Likelihood	−1,608.392	−1,607.367	−1,609.474	−1,606.908
Akaike Inference Criteria	3,236.784	3,234.734	3,238.949	3,233.816
Bayesian Inference Criteria	3,291.086	3,289.036	3,293.250	3,288.117

Note: $^{*}p < .1$; $^{**}p < .05$; $^{***}p < .01$. SSA = sub-Saharan Africa.

TABLE C.4. Logistic regressions with time trend

	Policy Change			
	(1)	(2)	(3)	(4)
IHS Average Ancestral Distance	0.446**			
	(0.009, 0.884)			
IHS Average Ancestral Distance (1500)		0.575**		
		(0.083, 1.068)		
IHS Percentage SSA Flow			0.477**	
			(0.093, 0.861)	
IHS Percentage Non-OECD Flow				0.784***
				(0.299, 1.268)
Time Trend	0.031***	0.032***	0.034***	0.028***
	(0.029, 0.032)	(0.031, 0.034)	(0.032, 0.036)	(0.027, 0.029)
Negative GDP Shock	0.470**	0.450**	0.472**	0.454**
	(0.101, 0.838)	(0.082, 0.817)	(0.104, 0.839)	(0.082, 0.825)
Liberal Democracy	−0.111	−0.193	−0.053	−0.081
	(−0.627, 0.406)	(−0.713, 0.327)	(−0.567, 0.461)	(−0.606, 0.443)
Inflation Rate	−0.313	−0.299	−0.308	−0.299
	(−0.712, 0.087)	(−0.696, 0.099)	(−0.703, 0.087)	(−0.696, 0.097)
Trade Openness	0.211	0.121	0.057	0.391
	(−0.243, 0.665)	(−0.323, 0.564)	(−0.371, 0.486)	(−0.090, 0.872)
Conflict	0.185	0.298	0.102	0.003
	(−0.916, 1.286)	(−0.814, 1.411)	(−0.988, 1.192)	(−1.098, 1.103)
(Intercept)	−63.233***	−67.144***	−70.438***	−58.156***
	(−66.050, −60.416)	(−69.960, −64.329)	(−74.052, −66.824)	(−60.860, −55.452)
Country RE	X	X	X	X
N	1,686	1,686	1,686	1,686
Log Likelihood	−537.780	−536.877	−537.585	−534.649
Akaike Inference Criteria	1,093.560	1,091.754	1,093.171	1,087.298
Bayesian Inference Criteria	1,142.431	1,140.625	1,142.042	1,136.169

Note: $^{*}p < .1$; $^{**}p < .05$; $^{***}p < .01$. SSA = sub-Saharan Africa.

TABLE C.5. Logistic regressions with lagged dependent variable

	Policy Change			
	(1)	(2)	(3)	(4)
IHS Average Ancestral Distance	0.488**			
	(0.015, 0.961)			
IHS Average Ancestral Distance (1500)		0.470*		
		(−0.041, 0.982)		
IHS Percentage SSA Flow			0.259	
			(−0.163, 0.680)	
IHS Percentage Non-OECD Flow				0.878***
				(0.367, 1.390)
Lag Policy	−0.035*	−0.029	−0.031	−0.028
	(−0.073, 0.003)	(−0.068, 0.010)	(−0.069, 0.007)	(−0.068, 0.011)
Negative GDP Shock	0.336*	0.309	0.320*	0.326*
	(−0.038, 0.710)	(−0.064, 0.682)	(−0.053, 0.693)	(−0.050, 0.701)
Liberal Democracy	0.013	−0.046	0.048	0.051
	(−0.529, 0.556)	(−0.593, 0.500)	(−0.502, 0.599)	(−0.504, 0.605)
Inflation Rate	−0.566***	−0.577***	−0.582***	−0.528**
	(−0.982, −0.150)	(−0.992, −0.162)	(−0.996, −0.168)	(−0.940, −0.115)
Trade Openness	0.419*	0.373	0.316	0.615**
	(−0.074, 0.912)	(−0.115, 0.861)	(−0.168, 0.801)	(0.090, 1.141)
Conflict	0.433	0.492	0.348	0.204
	(−0.674, 1.540)	(−0.625, 1.609)	(−0.751, 1.447)	(−0.901, 1.310)
(Intercept)	−2.535***	−2.514***	−2.505***	−2.566***
	(−2.843, −2.227)	(−2.823, −2.204)	(−2.809, −2.201)	(−2.883, −2.249)
Country RE	X	X	X	X
N	1,649	1,649	1,649	1,649
Log Likelihood	−533.680	−534.126	−535.384	−529.758
Akaike Inference Criteria	1,085.360	1,086.252	1,088.768	1,077.515
Bayesian Inference Criteria	1,134.032	1,134.923	1,137.439	1,126.187

Note: *p < .1; **p < .05; ***p < .01. SSA = sub-Saharan Africa.

In addition, I test whether the results are robust to a different measure of policy restrictiveness. To be specific, I recode the policy restrictiveness measure as a binary variable and test the same associations with a logistic regression. In other words, I code each country-year a "1" if they are more restrictive than they were in the previous year and a "0" otherwise. The logic here is that the continuous immigration policy restrictiveness has too much nuance, and the binary dependent variable better accounts for dramatic shifts in policy disposition year over year. The results are in tables C.4 and C.5. In these tables, I use both methods for accounting for temporal dependence, and the results are consistent. I still find strong evidence that racially different immigration flows are associated with a higher probability of being more restrictive toward migrants than in previous years.

BIBLIOGRAPHY

Aalberts, Tanja E. 2014. "Rethinking the Principle of (Sovereign) Equality as a Standard of Civilisation." *Millennium* 42 (3): 767–789.

Abbott, Kenneth W., and Duncan Snidal. 1998. "Why States Act through Formal International Organizations." *Journal of Conflict Resolution* 42 (1): 3–32.

Abel, Guy J. 2018. "Estimates of Global Bilateral Migration Flows by Gender between 1960 and 2015." *International Migration Review* 52 (3): 809–852. https://doi.org/10.1111/imre.12327.

Abel, Guy J., and Joel E. Cohen. 2019. "Bilateral International Migration Flow Estimates for 200 Countries." *Scientific Data* 6 (1): 1–13.

Abel, Guy J., and Nikola Sander. 2014. "Quantifying Global International Migration Flows." *Science* 343 (6178): 1520–1522. https://doi.org/10.1126/science.1248676.

Abizadeh, Arash. 2008. "Democratic Theory and Border Coercion: No Right to Unilaterally Control Your Own Borders." *Political Theory* 36 (1): 37–65.

Acemoglu, Daron, Simon Johnson, and James A. Robinson. 2001. "The Colonial Origins of Comparative Development: An Empirical Investigation." *American Economic Review* 91 (5): 1369–1401.

Acemoglu, Daron, Simon Johnson, and James A. Robinson. 2005. "The Rise of Europe: Atlantic Trade, Institutional Change, and Economic Growth." *American Economic Review* 95 (3): 546–579.

Acemoglu, Daron, and James A. Robinson. 2012. *Why Nations Fail: The Origins of Power, Prosperity, and Poverty.* New York: Crown Books.

Acharya, Amitav. 2014. "Global International Relations (IR) and Regional Worlds: New Agenda for International Studies." *International Studies Quarterly* 58 (4): 647–659.

Adamson, Fiona B. 2006. "Crossing Borders: International Migration and National Security." *International Security* 31 (1): 165–199.

Adida, Claire L., Adeline Lo, and Melina R. Platas. 2019. "Americans Preferred Syrian Refugees Who Are Female, English-Speaking, and Christian on the Eve of Donald Trump's Election." *PloS One* 14 (10): e0222504.

Adogamhe, Paul G. 2008. "Pan-Africanism Revisited: Vision and Reality of African Unity and Development." *African Review of Integration* 2 (2): 1–34.

Agamben, Giorgio. 1998. *Homo Sacer: Sovereign Power and Bare Life.* Palo Alto, CA: Stanford University Press.

Alarian, Hannah M. 2017. "Citizenship in Hard Times: Intra-EU Naturalisation and the Euro Crisis." *Journal of Ethnic and Migration Studies* 43 (13): 2149–2168.

Alberdi, Juan Bautista. 1899. *Escritos póstumos de J. B. Alberdi: América.* Buenos Aires: Imp. Cruz Hermanos.

Alexander, Titus. 1996. *Unravelling Global Apartheid: An Overview of World Politics.* Cambridge, UK: Polity Press.

Algan, Yann, and Pierre Cahuc. 2013. "Trust and Growth." *Annual Review of Economics* 5 (1): 521–549.

Al Jazeera. 2015. "Poland's President Warns of Refugees Bringing Epidemics." [Online; posted 18-October-2015]. https://www.aljazeera.com/news/2015/10/poland-president-refugees-epidemics-151018162358594.html.

Allan, Bentley B. 2017. "Producing the Climate: States, Scientists, and the Constitution of Global Governance Objects." *International Organization* 71 (1): 131–162.

Allan, Bentley B. 2018. *Scientific Cosmology and International Orders.* Vol. 147. Cambridge, UK: Cambridge University Press.

American Sociological Association. 2003. *The Importance of Collecting Data and Doing Social Scientific Research on Race.* Washington, DC: American Sociological Association.

Amin, Samir. 1976. *Unequal Development: An Essay on the Social Formations of Peripheral Capitalism.* New York: Monthly Review Press.

Amsden, Alice H. 2003. "Comment: Good-Bye Dependency Theory, Hello Dependency Theory." *Studies in Comparative International Development* 38 (1): 32–38.

Anderson, Benedict. 1983. *Imagined Communities: Reflections on the Origin and Spread of Nationalism.* London: Verso.

Anderson, Bridget. 2013. *Us and Them? The Dangerous Politics of Immigration Control.* Oxford, UK: Oxford University Press.

Andreas, Peter. 2012. *Border Games: Policing the U.S.-Mexico Divide.* Ithaca, NY: Cornell University Press.

Andrews, Kehinde. 2017. "Beyond Pan-Africanism: Garveyism, Malcolm X and the End of the Colonial Nation State." *Third World Quarterly* 38 (11): 2501–2516.

Andrews, Sarah, David Leblang, and Sonal S. Pandya. 2018. "Ethnocentrism Reduces Foreign Direct Investment." *Journal of Politics* 80 (2): 697–700.

Angeles, Luis, and Kyriakos C. Neanidis. 2015. "The Persistent Effect of Colonialism on Corruption." *Economica* 82 (326): 319–349.

Anghie, Antony. 2007. *Imperialism, Sovereignty and the Making of International Law.* Cambridge, UK: Cambridge University Press.

Angrist, Joshua D., and Jörn-Steffen Pischke. 2008. *Mostly Harmless Econometrics: An Empiricist's Companion.* Princeton, NJ: Princeton University Press.

Anievas, Alexander, Nivi Manchanda, and Robbie Shilliam. 2015. *Race and Racism in International Relations.* London: Routledge.

Appiah, Anthony. 1992. *In My Father's House: Africa in the Philosophy of Culture.* New York: Oxford University Press.

Appiah, Anthony. 1996. "Race, Culture, Identity: Misunderstood Connections." In *Color Conscious,* edited by Anthony Appiah and Amy Gutmann, 30–105. Princeton, NJ: Princeton University Press.

Apter, D., and J. Coleman. 1962. "Pan-Africanism or Nationalism in Africa." In *Pan-Africanism Reconsidered,* edited by American Society of African Culture, 81–115. Berkeley: University of California Press.

Aradau, Claudia. 2004. "Security and the Democratic Scene: Desecuritization and Emancipation." *Journal of International Relations and Development* 7 (4): 388–413.

Aradau, Claudia, and Jef Huysmans. 2014. "Critical Methods in International Relations: The Politics of Techniques, Devices and Acts." *European Journal of International Relations* 20 (3): 596–619.

Ashworth, Scott, Joshua D. Clinton, Adam Meirowitz, and Kristopher W. Ramsay. 2008. "Design, Inference, and the Strategic Logic of Suicide Terrorism." *American Political Science Review* 102 (2): 269–273.

Avdan, Nazli. 2018. *Visas and Walls: Border Security in the Age of Terrorism.* Philadelphia: University of Pennsylvania Press.

Avdan, Nazli, and Christopher F. Gelpi. 2017. "Do Good Fences Make Good Neighbors? Border Barriers and the Transnational Flow of Terrorist Violence." *International Studies Quarterly* 61 (1): 14–27.

Axelrod, Robert. 1981. "The Emergence of Cooperation among Egoists." *American Political Science Review* 75 (2): 306–318.

Aydin, Cemil. 2007. *The Politics of Anti-Westernism in Asia: Visions of World Order in Pan-Islamic and Pan-Asian Thought.* New York: Columbia University Press.

Ayers, John W., C. Richard Hofstetter, Keith Schnakenberg, and Bohdan Kolody. 2009. "Is Immigration a Racial Issue? Anglo Attitudes on Immigration Policies in a Border County." *Social Science Quarterly* 90 (3): 593–610.

Baber, Zaheer. 2004. " 'Race', Religion and Riots: The 'Racialization' of Communal Identity and Conflict in India." *Sociology* 38 (4): 701–718.

Baele, Stephane J., and Gregorio Bettiza. 2021. " 'Turning' Everywhere in IR: On the Sociological Underpinnings of the Field's Proliferating Turns." *International Theory* 13 (2): 314–340.

Bairoch, Paul. 1982. "The Main Trends in National Economic Disparities since the Industrial Revolution." In *Disparities in Economic Development since the Industrial Revolution,* edited by Paul Bairoch and Lévy-Leboyer, 3–17. London: MacMillan Press.

Bairoch, Paul. 1995. *Economics and World History: Myths and Paradoxes.* Chicago: University of Chicago Press.

Baker, Lee D. 1998. "Columbia University's Franz Boas: He Led the Undoing of Scientific Racism." *Journal of Blacks in Higher Education* 22 (Winter), 89–96.

Balderrama, Francisco E., and Raymond Rodríguez. 2006. *Decade of Betrayal: Mexican Repatriation in the 1930s.* Albuquerque: University of New Mexico Press.

Bansak, Kirk, Jens Hainmueller, and Dominik Hangartner. 2016. "How Economic, Humanitarian, and Religious Concerns Shape European Attitudes toward Asylum Seekers." *Science* 354 (6309): 217–222.

Barder, Alexander D. 2019. "Scientific Racism, Race War and the Global Racial Imaginary." *Third World Quarterly* 40 (2): 207–223.

Barkin, J. Samuel, and Bruce Cronin. 1994. "The State and the Nation: Changing Norms and the Rules of Sovereignty in International Relations." *International Organization* 48 (1): 107–130.

Barkin, Samuel. 2001. "Resilience of the State." *Harvard International Review* 22 (4): 42–46.

Barnett, Michael. 2020. "COVID-19 and the Sacrificial International Order." *International Organization* 74 (S1): E128–E147. https://doi.org/10.1017/S002081832000034X.

Barnett, Michael, and Raymond Duvall. 2005. "Power in International Politics." *International Organization* 59 (1): 39–75.

Barnett, Michael, and Martha Finnemore. 2004. *Rules for the World: International Organizations in Global Politics.* Ithaca, NY: Cornell University Press.

Barraclough, Geoffrey. 1964. *An Introduction to Contemporary History.* London: CA. Watt.

Barro, Robert J. 2001. "Human Capital and Growth." *American Economic Review* 91 (2): 12–17.

Bashford, Allison. 2010. "Internationalism, Cosmopolitanism, and Genetics." In *The Oxford Handbook of the History of Eugenics,* edited by Allison Bashford and Philippa Levine, 154–172. New York: Oxford University Press.

Bates, Robert H. 1981. *Markets and States in Tropical Africa.* Berkeley: University of California Press.

Bayat, Asef. 2000. "From 'Dangerous Classes' to 'Quiet Rebels': Politics of the Urban Subaltern in the Global South." *International Sociology* 15 (3): 533–557.

BBC. 2015. "David Cameron Criticised over Migrant 'Swarm' Language." [Online; posted 30-July-2015]. https://www.bbc.com/news/uk-politics-33716501.

BBC. 2018a. "Australia Considers Visas for White South African Farmers." [Online; posted 14-March-2018]. https://www.bbc.com/news/world-africa-43403408.

BBC. 2018b. "Boris Johnson Faces Criticism over Burka 'Letter Box' Jibe." n.d. [Online; posted 06-August-2018]. https://www.bbc.com/news/uk-politics-45083275.

Bearce, David H., and Andrew F. Hart. 2017. "International Labor Mobility and the Variety of Democratic Political Institutions." *International Organization* 71 (1): 65–95.

Beckert, Sven. 2015. *Empire of Cotton: A Global History.* New York: Vintage.

Beckford, George L. 1972. *Persistent Poverty: Underdevelopment in Plantation Economies of the Third World.* Kingston, Jamaica: University of the West Indies Press.

Beine, Michel, Simone Bertoli, and Jesús Fernández-Huertas Moraga. 2016. "A Practitioners' Guide to Gravity Models of International Migration." *World Economy* 39 (4): 496–512.

Bemporad, Elissa. 2019. *Legacy of Blood: Jews, Pogroms, and Ritual Murder in the Lands of the Soviets.* New York: Oxford University Press.

Benedicto, Ainhoa Ruiz, and Pere Brunet. 2018. *Building Walls: Fear and Securitization in the European Union.* Amsterdam: Transnational Institute.

Berinzon, Maya, and Ryan C. Briggs. 2016. "Legal Families without the Laws: The Fading of Colonial Law in French West Africa." *American Journal of Comparative Law* 64 (2): 329–370.

Bhabha, Homi K. 1990. *Nations and Narration.* London: Routledge.

Bierbrauer, Günter, and Edgar W. Klinger. 2002. "Political Ideology, Perceived Threat, and Justice towards Immigrants." *Social Justice Research* 15 (1): 41–52.

Biermann, Frank, and Ingrid Boas. 2010. "Preparing for a Warmer World: Towards a Global Governance System to Protect Climate Refugees." *Global Environmental Politics* 10 (1): 60–88.

Bjerre, Liv, Marc Helbling, Friederike Römer, and Malisa Zobel. 2014. "Conceptualizing and Measuring Immigration Policies: A Comparative Perspective." *International Migration Review* 49 (3): 555–600.

Blinder, Scott. 2015. "Imagined Immigration: The Impact of Different Meanings of 'Immigrants' in Public Opinion and Policy Debates in Britain." *Political Studies* 63 (1) : 80–100.

Boas, Franz. 1911. *The Mind of Primitive Man: A Course of Lectures Delivered before the Lowell Institute, Boston, Mass., and the National University of Mexico, 1910–1911.* New York: Macmillan.

Bobo, Lawrence D. 2011. "Somewhere between Jim Crow and Post-racialism: Reflections on the Racial Divide in America Today." *Daedalus* 140 (2): 11–36.

Bobo, Lawrence D., James R. Klugel, and Ryan A. Smith. 1997. "Laissez-Faire Racism: The Crystallization of a Kinder, Gentler, Anti-Black Ideology." In *Racial Attitudes in the 1990s,* edited by Jack K. Martin and Steven A. Tuch, 15–39. Westport, CT: Praeger.

Boli, John. 1987. "World Polity Sources of Expanding State Authority and Organizations, 1870–1970." In *Institutional Structure,* edited by George M. Thomas, John W. Meyer, Francisco O. Ramirez, and John Boli, 71–91. Beverly Hills, CA: Sage.

Boli, John, and George M. Thomas. 1997. "World Culture in the World Polity: A Century of International Non-governmental Organization." *American Sociological Review* 62 (2) : 171–190.

Bonilla, Frank, and Robert Girling. 1973. *Structures of Dependency.* Palo Alto, CA: Stanford University Press.

Bonilla-Silva, Eduardo. 2006. *Racism without Racists: Color-Blind Racism and the Persistence of Racial Inequality in the United States.* New York: Rowman & Littlefield.

Bonilla-Silva, Eduardo. 2012. "The Invisible Weight of Whiteness: The Racial Grammar of Everyday Life in Contemporary America." *Ethnic and Racial Studies* 35 (2): 173–194.

Bonjour, Saskia, and Laura Block. 2016. "Ethnicizing Citizenship, Questioning Membership: Explaining the Decreasing Family Migration Rights of Citizens in Europe." *Citizenship Studies* 20 (6–7): 779–794.

Booth, David. 1985. "Marxism and Development Sociology: Interpreting the Impasse." *World Development* 13 (7): 761–787.

Borjas, George J. 1999. *Heaven's Door: Immigration Policy and the American Economy.* Princeton, NJ: Princeton University Press.

Boucher, Anna. 2007. "Skill, Migration and Gender in Australia and Canada: The Case of Gender-Based Analysis." *Australian Journal of Political Science* 42 (3): 383–401.

Boucher, Anna. 2016. *Gender, Migration, and the Global Race for Talent.* Manchester, UK: Manchester University Press.

Boucher, Anna K., and Justin Gest. 2018. *Crossroads: Comparative Immigration Regimes in a World of Demographic Change.* New York: Cambridge University Press.

Bourbeau, Philippe. 2011. *The Securitization of Migration: A Study of Movement and Order.* New York: Routledge.

Bourke, Latika. 2017. "Donald Trump Told Malcolm Turnbull 'You Are worse Than I Am' on Refugees during Call, Leaked Transcript Reveals." ABC News. [Online;

posted 03-August-2017]. https://www.abc.net.au/news/2017-08-04/donald-trump-told-malcolm-turnbull
-refugee-deal-was-stupid/8773368.

Box-Steffensmeier, Janet M., and Christopher J. W. Zorn. 2001. "Duration Models and Proportional Hazards in Political Science." *American Journal of Political Science* 45 (4): 972–988.

Brambor, Thomas, William Roberts Clark, and Matt Golder. 2006. "Understanding Interaction Models: Improving Empirical Analyses." *Political Analysis* 14 (1): 63–82.

Brannagan, Paul Michael, and Richard Giulianotti. 2015. "Soft Power and Soft Disempowerment: Qatar, Global Sport and Football's 2022 World Cup Finals." *Leisure Studies* 34 (6): 703–719.

Braumoeller, Bear F. 2004. "Hypothesis Testing and Multiplicative Interaction Terms." *International Organization* 58 (4): 807–820. https://doi.org/10.1017/s0020818304040251.

Breuilly, John. 1993. *Nationalism and the State*. Chicago: University of Chicago Press.

Breunig, Christian, Xun Cao, and Adam Luedtke. 2012. "Global Migration and Political Regime Type: A Democratic Disadvantage." *British Journal of Political Science* 42 (4): 825–854.

Brodkin, Karen. 1998. *How Jews Became White Folks and What That Says about Race in America*. New Brunswick, NJ: Rutgers University Press.

Brustein, William I. 2003. *Roots of Hate: Anti-Semitism in Europe before the Holocaust*. Cambridge, UK: Cambridge University Press.

Buehler, Matt, Kristin E. Fabbe, and Kyung Joon Han. 2020. "Community-Level Postmaterialism and Anti-migrant Attitudes: An Original Survey on Opposition to Sub-Saharan African Migrants in the Middle East." *International Studies Quarterly*, 64 (3): 669–683.

Bull, Hedley, and Adam Watson. 1984. *The Expansion of International Society*. Oxford, UK: Clarendon Press.

Burke, Justin. 2001. "Turkmen Head Erects Fences; Criticizes Chemicals Industry, Contract Servicemen." Eurasianet. [Online; posted 02-April-2001]. https : //web.archive.org /web/20070706201327/http : //www.eurasianet.org/resource/turkmenistan/hypermail /200104/0000.html.

Bürkner, Paul-Christian. 2019. *Bayesian Item Response Modeling in R with brms and Stan*. eprint: arXiv:1905.09501.

Buzan, Barry. 2008. *People, States & Fear*. Colchester, UK: ECPR Press.

Buzan, Barry, and George Lawson. 2014. "Rethinking Benchmark Dates in International Relations." *European Journal of International Relations* 20 (2): 437–462.

Buzan, Barry, and George Lawson. 2015. *The Global Transformation: History, Modernity and the Making of International Relations*. Cambridge, UK: Cambridge University Press.

Buzan, Barry, Ole Wæver, and Jaap De Wilde. 1998. *Security: A New Framework for Analysis*. London: Lynne Rienner.

Búzás, Zoltán I. 2013. "The Color of Threat: Race, Threat Perception, and the Demise of the Anglo-Japanese Alliance (1902–1923)." *Security Studies* 22 (4): 573–606.

Búzás, Zoltán I. 2018. "Is the Good News about Law Compliance Good News about Norm Compliance? The Case of Racial Equality." *International Organization* 72 (2): 351–385.

Cairns, Alan C. 1999. "Empire, Globalization, and the Fall and Rise of Diversity." In *Citizenship, Diversity, and Pluralism: Canadian and Comparative Perspectives*, edited by Alan C. Cairns,

John C. Courtney, Peter MacKinnon, Hans J. Michelmann, and David E. Smith, 23–57. Montreal: McGill-Queen's University Press.

Cammett, John M. 1967. *Antonio Gramsci and the Origins of Italian Communism*. Palo Alto, CA: Stanford University Press.

Campbell, David. 1992. *Writing Security: United States Foreign Policy and the Politics of Identity*. Minneapolis: University of Minnesota Press.

Caragliu, Andrea, Chiara Del Bo, Henri L. F. de Groot, and Gert-Jan M. Linders. 2013. "Cultural Determinants of Migration." *Annals of Regional Science* 51 (1): 7–32.

Card, David. 2012. "Comment: The Elusive Search for Negative Wage Impacts of Immigration." *Journal of the European Economic Association* 10 (1): 211–215.

Card, David, and Alan Krueger. 1990. "Does School Quality Matter? Returns to Education and the Characteristics of Public Schools in the United States". Technical report. National Bureau of Economic Research.

Carl, N. 2018. "Reasons Why People Voted Leave or Remain." Centre for Social Investigation. [Online; posted 24-April-2018]. http://csi.nuff.ox.ac.uk/wp-content/uploads/2018/05/Carl_Reasons_Voting.pdf.

Carter, David B., and Paul Poast. 2017. "Why Do States Build Walls? Political Economy, Security, and Border Stability." *Journal of Conflict Resolution* 61 (2): 239–270.

Carter, David B., and Paul Poast. 2020. "Barriers to Trade: How Border Walls Affect Trade Relations." *International Organization* 74 (1): 165–185.

Castles, Stephen. 2004. "Why Migration Policies Fail." *Ethnic and Racial Studies* 27 (2): 205–227.

Cavallar, Georg. 2008. "Vitoria, Grotius, Pufendorf, Wolff and Vattel: Accomplices of European Colonialism and Exploitation or True Cosmopolitans?" *Journal of the History of International Law* 10 (2): 181–209.

Cavallar, Georg. 2009. "Immigration and Sovereignty: Normative Approaches in the History of International Legal Theory (Pufendorf–Vattel–Bluntschli–Verdross)." *Austrian Review of International and European Law* 11 (1): 3–22.

Cavalli-Sforza, Luigi Luca, Paolo Menozzi, and Alberto Piazza. 1994. *The History and Geography of Human Genes*. Princeton, NJ: Princeton University Press.

Césaire, Aimé. 2000. *Discourse on Colonialism*. New York: Monthly Review Press.

Chang, Ha-Joon. 2010. *Bad Samaritans: The Myth of Free Trade and the Secret History of Capitalism*. New York: Bloomsbury Press.

Charman, Andrew, and Laurence Piper. 2012. "Xenophobia, Criminality and Violent Entrepreneurship: Violence against Somali Shopkeepers in Delft South, Cape Town, South Africa." *South African Review of Sociology* 43 (3): 81–105.

Chase-Dunn, Christopher K. 1982. "A World-System Perspective on Dependency and Development in Latin America." *Latin American Research Review* 17 (1): 166–171.

Chatham House. "What Do Europeans Think about Muslim Immigration?" 2017. [Online; posted 07-February-2017]. https://www.chathamhouse.org/expert/comment/what-do-europeans-think-about-muslim-immigration%7D.

Chayes, Abram, and Antonia Handler Chayes. 1998. *The New Sovereignty: Compliance with International Regulatory Agreements*. Cambridge, MA: Harvard University Press.

Checkel, Jeffrey T. 2005. "International Institutions and Socialization in Europe: Introduction and Framework." *International Organization* 59 (4): 801–826.

Chetail, Vincent. 2016. "Sovereignty and Migration in the Doctrine of the Law of Nations: An Intellectual History of Hospitality from Vitoria to Vattel." *European Journal of International Law* 27 (4): 901–922.

Chibber, Vivek. 2013. *Locked in Place: State Building and Late Industrialization in India.* Princeton, NJ: Princeton University Press.

Chimni, Bupinder S. 2006. "The World Trade Organization, Democracy and Development: A View from the South." *Journal of World Trade* 40 (1): 5–36.

Chiswick, Barry R., and Paul W. Miller. 1995. "The Endogeneity between Language and Earnings: International Analyses." *Journal of Labor Economics* 13 (2): 246–288.

Cienski, Jan. 2015. "Migrants Carry 'Parasites and Protozoa,' Warns Polish Opposition Leader." Politico. [Online; posted 14-October-2015]. https://www.politico.eu/article/migrants-asylum-poland-kaczynski-election/.

Citrin, Jack, and John Sides. 2008. "Immigration and the Imagined Community in Europe and the United States." *Political Studies* 56 (1): 33–56.

Clark, Kenneth B., Isidor Chein, and Stuart W. Cook. 2004. "The Effects of Segregation and the Consequences of Desegregation: A (September 1952) Social Science Statement in the Brown v. Board of Education of Topeka Supreme Court Case." *American Psychologist* 59 (6): 495–501.

Clark, Tom S., and Drew A. Linzer. 2015. "Should I Use Fixed or Random Effects?" *Political Science Research and Methods* 3 (2): 399–408.

Clemens, Michael A. 2011. "Economics and Emigration: Trillion-Dollar Bills on the Sidewalk?" *Journal of Economic Perspectives* 25 (3): 83–106.

Clemens, Michael A., Claudio E. Montenegro, and Lant Pritchett. 2019. "The Place Premium: Bounding the Price Equivalent of Migration Barriers." *Review of Economics and Statistics* 101 (2): 201–213.

Clemens, Michael A., and Lant Pritchett. 2019. "The New Economic Case for Migration Restrictions: An Assessment." *Journal of Development Economics* 138: 153–164.

Cleveland, Sarah H. 2002. "Powers Inherent in Sovereignty: Indians, Aliens, Territories, and the Nineteenth Century Origins of Plenary Power over Foreign Affairs." *Texas Law Review* 81: 1–284.

Clinton, Joshua, Simon Jackman, and Douglas Rivers. 2004. "The Statistical Analysis of Roll Call Data." *American Political Science Review* 98 (2): 355–370.

Cogley, Nathaniel Terence, John Andrew Doces, and Beth Elise Whitaker. 2018. "Which Immigrants Should Be Naturalized? Which Should Be Deported? Evidence from a Survey Experiment in Côte d'Ivoire." *Political Research Quarterly* 72 (3): 653–668.

Cohen, Benjamin J. 2007. "The Transatlantic Divide: Why Are American and British IPE So Different?" *Review of International Political Economy* 14 (2): 197–219.

Coleman, Mathew. 2005. "US Statecraft and the US-Mexico Border as Security/Economy Nexus." *Political Geography* 24 (2): 185–209.

Collier, Paul. 2013. *Exodus: How Migration Is Changing Our World.* Oxford, UK: Oxford University Press.

Cooley, Alexander, and Hendrick Spruyt. 2009. *Contracting States: Sovereign Transfers in International Relations.* Princeton, NJ: Princeton University Press.

Cooper, Frederick. 1996. *Decolonization and African Society: The Labor Question in French and British Africa.* Cambridge, UK: Cambridge University Press.

Coppedge, Michael, John Gerring, Staffan I. Lindberg, Svend-Erik Skaaning, and Jan Teorell. 2019. Varieties of Democracy (V-Dem) project, "Varieties of Democracy: Codebook v9."

Cornelius, Wayne A., and Takeyuki Tsuda. 2004. "Controlling Immigration: The Limits of Government Intervention." In *Controlling Immigration: A Global Perspective,* edited by Wayne Cornelius, 3–45. Stanford, CA Stanford University Press.

Cornell, Stephen, and Douglas Hartmann. 2006. *Ethnicity and Race: Making Identities in a Changing World.* New York: Sage Publications.

Corstange, Daniel. 2009. "Sensitive Questions, Truthful Answers? Modeling the List Experiment with LISTIT." *Political Analysis* 17 (1): 45–63.

Cox, Robert W. 1983. "Gramsci, Hegemony and International Relations: An Essay in Method." *Millennium* 12 (2): 162–175.

Cox, Robert W. 1987. *Production, Power and World Order: Social Forces in the Making of History.* New York: Columbia University Press.

Cox, Robert W. 1996. "The Global Political Economy and Social Choice." In *Approaches to World Order,* edited by Robert W. Cox and Timothy J. Sinclair, 191–208. Cambridge, UK: Cambridge University Press.

Czaika, Mathias, and Hein de Haas. 2013. "The Effectiveness of Immigration Policies." *Population and Development Review* 39 (3): 487–508.

Czaika, Mathias, and Hein de Haas. 2014. "The Globalization of Migration: Has the World Become More Migratory?" *International Migration Review* 48 (2): 283–323.

Dancygier, Rafaela M., and Michael J. Donnelly. 2013. "Sectoral Economies, Economic Contexts, and Attitudes toward Immigration." *Journal of Politics* 75 (1): 17–35.

Dauvergne, Catherine. 2019. "Gendering Islamophobia to Better Understand Immigration Laws." *Journal of Ethnic and Migration Studies,* 1–16.

Davis, Julie Hirschfeld, Sheryl Gay Stolberg, and Thomas Kaplan. 2018. "Trump Alarms Lawmakers with Disparaging Words for Haiti and Africa." *New York Times* (January 11, 2018): A1.

Davis, Mike. 2000. "The Origin of the Third World." *Antipode* 32 (1): 48–89.

Davis, Mike. 2002. *Late Victorian Holocausts: El Niño Famines and the Making of the Third World.* London: Verso Books.

Davis, Rebecca. 2018. "What the Latest Crime States Suggest about Farm Murders." *Daily Maverick.* [Online; posted 1-September-2018]. https://www.dailymaverick.co.za/article/2018-09-13-what-the-latest-crime-stats-suggest-about-farm-murders/.

Deace, Steve. 2017. "Video Exposes Truthful Evidence That Our Leaders Won't." *Washington Times.* [Online; posted 17-November-2015]. https://www.washingtontimes.com/news/2015/nov/17/steve-deace-video-exposes-truthful-evidence-our-le/.

De Haas, Hein, Katharina Natter, and Simona Vezzoli. 2015. "Conceptualizing and Measuring Migration Policy Change." *Comparative Migration Studies* 3 (1): 1–21.

Haas, Hein de, Katharina Natter, and Simona Vezzoli. 2018. "Growing Restrictiveness or Changing Selection? The Nature and Evolution of Migration Policies." *International Migration Review* 52 (2): 324–367.

Del Visco, Stephen. 2019. "Yellow Peril, Red Scare: Race and Communism in National Review." *Ethnic and Racial Studies* 42 (4): 626–644.

DEMIG 2015. *DEMIG POLICY, Version 1.3, Online Edition.* Oxford, UK: International Migration Institute, University of Oxford.

Dennison, James, and Andrew Geddes. 2019. "A Rising Tide? The Salience of Immigration and the Rise of Anti-immigration Political Parties in Western Europe." *Political Quarterly* 90 (1): 107–116.

Dernbach, Andrea, and Paul Starzmann. 2018. "What's in the New German Immigration Law?" Euractiv. [Online; posted 08-October-2018]. https://www.euractiv.com/section/central-europe/news/was-steht-im-neuen-einwanderungsgesetz.

Deudney, Daniel. 2007. *Bounding Power: Republican Security Theory from the Polis to the Global Village.* Princeton, NJ: Princeton University Press.

Dikötter, Frank. 1998. "Race Culture: Recent Perspectives on the History of Eugenics." *American Historical Review* 103 (2): 467–478.

Dionne, Kim Yi, and Fulya Felicity Turkmen. 2020. "The Politics of Pandemic Othering: Putting COVID-19 in Global and Historical Context." *International Organization* 74 (S1): E213–E230. https://doi.org/10.1017/S0020818320000405.

Doherty, Ben. 2018. "Australia's Immigration Policy Is Meant to be Blind to Race, but Is It?" *Guardian.* [Online; posted 05-April-2018]. https://www.theguardian.com/australia-news/2018/apr/05/australia-says-its-immigration-policy-is-blind-to-race-what-do-the-facts-show.

Dorninger, Christian, Alf Hornborg, David J. Abson, Henrik Von Wehrden, Anke Schaffartzik, Stefan Giljum, John-Oliver Engler, Robert L. Feller, Klaus Hubacek, and Hanspeter Wieland. 2021. "Global Patterns of Ecologically Unequal Exchange: Implications for Sustainability in the 21st Century." *Ecological Economics* 179: 106824.

Doty, Roxanne Lynn. 1993. "The Bounds of 'Race' in International Relations." *Millennium—Journal of International Studies* 22 (3): 443–461.

Doty, Roxanne Lynn. 1999. "Racism, Desire, and the Politics of Immigration." *Millennium* 28 (3): 585–606.

Douglas, Karen Manges, Rogelio Sáenz, and Aurelia Lorena Murga. 2015. "Immigration in the Era of Color-Blind Racism." *American Behavioral Scientist* 59 (11): 1429–1451.

Du Bois, William Edward Burghardt. 1899. *The Philadelphia Negro: A Social Study.* Boston: Ginn & Co.

Du Bois, William Edward Burghardt. 1915. "The African Roots of War." *Atlantic Monthly* 115 (5): 707–714.

Du Bois, William Edward Burghardt. 1943. "The Realities in Africa." *Foreign Affairs* 21 (4): 721–732.

Du Bois, William Edward Burghardt. 1947. *The World and Africa.* New York: Viking Press.

Du Bois, William Edward Burghardt. 1996. "The Present Outlook for the Darker Races of Mankind (1900)." In *The Oxford W.E.B. Du Bois Reader,* edited by Eric J. Sundquist, 47–54. Oxford, UK: Oxford University Press.

Du Bois, William Edward Burghardt. 2007 [1940]. *Dusk of Dawn.* Oxford, UK: Oxford University Press.

Duncan, Otis Dudley, and Beverly Duncan. 1955. "A Methodological Analysis of Segregation Indexes." *American Sociological Review* 20 (2): 210–217.

Dunn, Kevin M., Natascha Klocker, and Tanya Salabay. 2007. "Contemporary Racism and Islamaphobia in Australia: Racializing Religion." *Ethnicities* 7 (4): 564–589.

Dunne, Tim, and Christian Reus-Smit. 2017. *The Globalization of International Society*. Oxford, UK: Oxford University Press.

Dustmann, Christian, and Tommaso Frattini. 2014. "The Fiscal Effects of Immigration to the UK." *Economic Journal* 124 (580): F593–F643.

Dziedzic, Stephen. 2018. "Malcolm Turnbull Says Australia Is an Option for South Africans Who Fear Persecution." ABC News. [Online; posted 03-April-2018]. https://www.abc.net.au/news/2018-04-03/peter-dutton-escalates-row-with-south-africa/9615496.

Easterly, William, and Ross Levine. 1997. "Africa's Growth Tragedy: Policies and Ethnic Divisions." *Quarterly Journal of Economics* 112 (4): 1203–1250.

Ellermann, Antje, and Agustín Goenaga. 2019. "Discrimination and Policies of Immigrant Selection in Liberal States." *Politics & Society* 47 (1): 87–116.

Elrick, Jennifer, and Elke Winter. 2018. "Managing the National Status Group: Immigration Policy in Germany." *International Migration* 56 (4): 19–32.

Elster, Jon. 1985. *Making Sense of Marx*. Cambridge, UK: Cambridge University Press.

Emerick, Charles Franklin. 1910. "A Neglected Factor in Race Suicide." *Political Science Quarterly* 25 (4): 638–655.

Epstein, Gil S. 2008. "Herd and Network Effects in Migration Decision-Making." *Journal of Ethnic and Migration Studies* 34 (4): 567–583.

Faist, Thomas. 2000. *The Volume and Dynamics of International Migration and Transnational Social Spaces*. Oxford, UK: Oxford University Press.

Fanon, Frantz. 1963. *The Wretched of the Earth*. New York: Grove Press.

Farbotko, Carol, and Heather Lazrus. 2012. "The First Climate Refugees? Contesting Global Narratives of Climate Change in Tuvalu." *Global Environmental Change* 22 (2): 382–390.

Feagin, Joe R. 2006. *Systemic Racism*. New York: Routledge.

Feenstra, Robert C., Robert Inklaar, and Marcel P. Timmer. 2015. "The Next Generation of the Penn World Table." *American Economic Review* 105 (10): 3150–3182.

Fields, Barbara J. 1990. "Slavery, Race and Ideology in the United States of America." *New Left Review* 181 (1): 95–118.

Financial Times, Editorial Board. 2020. "Nigeria Is at Risk of Becoming a Failed State." [Online; posted 22-December-2020]. https://www.ft.com/content/9abc218d-3881-4bfd-8951-e76336cde94f.

Finnemore, Martha. 1993. "International Organizations as Teachers of Norms: The United Nations Educational, Scientific, and Cultural Organization and Science Policy." *International Organization* 47 (4): 565–597.

Finnemore, Martha. 1996. *National Interests in International Society*. Ithaca, NY: Cornell University Press.

Finnemore, Martha, and Kathryn Sikkink. 1998. "International Norm Dynamics and Political Change." *International Organization* 52 (4): 887–917.

FitzGerald, David, and David Cook-Martin. 2014. *Culling the Masses*. Cambridge, MA: Harvard University Press.

Fitzgerald, Jennifer, David Leblang, and Jessica C. Teets. 2014. "Defying the Law of Gravity: The Political Economy of International Migration." *World Politics* 66 (3): 406–445.

Flitton, Daniel. 2014. "We're a Weird Mob of Unfriendly Racists: Monash University Report." *Sydney Morning Herald.* [Online; posted 24-March-2014]. https://www.smh.com.au/national/were-a-weird-mob-of-unfriendly-racists-monash-university-report-20140323-35buu.html.

Ford, Robert. 2011. "Acceptable and Unacceptable Immigrants: How Opposition to Immigration in Britain Is Affected by Migrants' Region of Origin." *Journal of Ethnic and Migration Studies* 37 (7): 1017–1037.

Frank, David John, Tara Hardinge, and Kassia Wosick-Correa. 2009. "The Global Dimensions of Rape-Law Reform: A Cross-National Study of Policy Outcomes." *American Sociological Review* 74 (2): 272–290.

Frank, David John, Ann Hironaka, and Evan Schofer. 2000. "The Nation-State and the Natural Environment over the Twentieth Century." *American Sociological Review* 61 (1): 96–116.

Frankema, Ewout, and Marlous Van Waijenburg. 2012. "Structural Impediments to African Growth? New Evidence from Real Wages in British Africa, 1880–1965." *Journal of Economic History* 72 (4): 895–926.

Fredrickson, George M. 2002. *Racism: A Short History.* Princeton, NJ: Princeton University Press.

Freeman, Gary P. 1995. "Modes of Immigration Politics in Liberal Democratic States." *International Migration Review* 29 (4): 881–902.

Freeman, Gary P. 2006. "National Models, Policy Types, and the Politics of Immigration in Liberal Democracies." *West European Politics* 29 (2): 227–247.

Freeman, Gary P. 2011. "Comparative Analysis of Immigration Politics: A Retrospective." *American Behavioral Scientist* 55 (12): 1541–1560.

Friedman, Max Paul, and Tom Long. 2015. "Soft Balancing in the Americas: Latin American Opposition to U.S. Intervention, 1898–1936." *International Security* 40 (1): 120–156.

Ganguli, Birendranath N. 1965. "Dadabhai Naoroji and the Mechanism of 'External Drain.'" *Indian Economic & Social History Review* 2 (2): 85–102.

Garcia y Griego, Manuel. 1994. "Canada: Flexibility and Control in Immigration and Refugee Policy." In *Controlling Immigration: A Global Perspective,* edited by 119–140. Palo Alto, CA: Stanford University Press.

Geiger, Martin, and Antoine Pécoud. 2014. "International Organisations and the Politics of Migration." *Journal of Ethnic and Migration Studies* 40 (6): 865–887.

Gellner, Ernest. 2008. *Nations and Nationalism.* Oxford, UK: Blackwell.

Gelman, Andrew, John B. Carlin, Hal S. Stern, and Donald B. Rubin. 2014. *Bayesian Data Analysis, Third Edition.* New York: Taylor & Francis.

Gelman, Andrew, and Jennifer Hill. 2006. *Data Analysis Using Regression and Multilevel/Hierarchical Models.* Cambridge, UK: Cambridge University Press.

Gest, Justin. 2018. "Points-Based Immigration Was Meant to Reduce Racial Bias. It Doesn't." *Guardian.* [Online; posted 19-January-2018]. https://www.theguardian.com/commentisfree/2018/jan/19/points-based-immigration-racism.

Getachew, Adom. 2019. *Worldmaking after Empire: The Rise and Fall of Self-Determination.* Princeton, NJ: Princeton University Press.

Getmanski, Anne, Guy Grossman, and Austin L. Wright. 2019. "Border Walls and Smuggling Spillovers." *Quarterly Journal of Political Science* 14 (3): 329–347.

Geuss, Raymond. 2008. *Philosophy and Real Politics.* Princeton, NJ: Princeton University Press.

Gibbs, Raymond W. 2001. "Intentions as Emergent Products of Social Interactions." In *Intentions and Intentionality: Foundations of Social Cognition,* edited by Bertram F. Malle, Louis J. Moses, and Dare A. Baldwin, 105–122. Cambridge, MA: MIT Press.

Gilli, Andrea, and Mauro Gilli. 2019. "Why China Has Not Caught Up Yet: Military-Technological Superiority and the Limits of Imitation, Reverse Engineering, and Cyber Espionage." *International Security* 43 (3): 141–189.

Gilpin, Robert. 1981. *War and Change in World Politics.* Cambridge, UK: Cambridge University Press.

Gleditsch, Nils Petter, Peter Wallensteen, Mikael Eriksson, Margareta Sollenberg, and Håvard Strand. 2002. "Armed Conflict 1946–2001: A New Dataset." *Journal of Peace Research* 39 (5): 615–637.

Goldberg, David Theo. 2009. *The Threat of Race: Reflections on Racial Neoliberalism.* Malden, MA: Wiley-Blackwell.

Goldstein, Judith L., Douglas Rivers, and Michael Tomz. 2007. "Institutions in International Relations: Understanding the Effects of the GATT and the WTO on World Trade." *International Organization* 61 (1): 37–67.

Gong, Gerrit W. 1984. *The Standard of "Civilization" in International Society.* Oxford, UK: Clarendon Press.

Gonzalez-Garcia, Jesus. 2016. *Sub-Saharan African Migration: Patterns and Spillover.* Washington, DC: International Monetary Fund.

Goodwin, Matthew, and Caitlin Milazzo. 2017. "Taking Back Control? Investigating the Role of Immigration in the 2016 Vote for Brexit." *British Journal of Politics and International Relations* 19 (3): 450–464.

Gould, W.T.S. 1974. "International Migration in Tropical Africa: A Bibliographical Review." *International Migration Review* 8 (3): 347–365.

Goutor, David. 2007. "Constructing the 'Great Menace': Canadian Labour's Opposition to Asian Immigration, 1880–1914." *Canadian Historical Review* 88 (4): 549–576.

Gover, Angela R., Shannon B. Harper, and Lynn Langton. 2020. "Anti-Asian Hate Crime during the COVID-19 Pandemic: Exploring the Reproduction of Inequality." *American Journal of Criminal Justice* 45 (4): 647–667.

Gowa, Joanne, and Raymond Hicks. 2013. "Politics, Institutions, and Trade: Lessons of the Interwar Era." *International Organization* 67 (3): 439–467.

Gramsci, Antonio. 1971. *Selections from the Prison Notebooks.* New York: International Publishers.

Grant, Madison. 1924. *The Passing of the Great Race.* London: G. Bell & Sons.

Gratton, Brian. 2018. "Race or Politics?: Henry Cabot Lodge and the Origins of the Immigration Restriction Movement in the United States." *Journal of Policy History* 30 (1): 128–157.

Greenhill, Brian. 2016. *Transmitting Rights: International Organizations and the Diffusion of Human Rights Practices.* New York: Oxford University Press.

Greitens, Sheena Chestnut. 2020. "Surveillance, Security, and Liberal Democracy in the Post-COVID World." *International Organization* 74 (S1): E169–E190. https://doi.org/10.1017/S0020818320000417.

Grogger, Jeffrey, and Gordon H. Hanson. 2011. "Income Maximization and the Selection and Sorting of International Migrants." *Journal of Development Economics* 95 (1): 42–57.

Grosfoguel, Ramon. 2000. "Developmentalism, Modernity, and Dependency Theory in Latin America." *Nepantla: Views from South* 1 (2): 347–374.

Grotius, Hugo, and Richard Tuck. 2005. *The Rights of War and Peace.* Indianapolis, IN: Liberty Fund Inc.

Grovogui, Siba N. 1996. *Sovereigns, Quasi Sovereigns, and Africans: Race and Self-Determination in International Law.* Minneapolis: University of Minnesota Press.

Grovogui, Siba N. 2001. "Come to Africa: A Hermeneutics of Race in International Theory." *Alternatives: Global, Local, Political* 26 (4): 425–448.

Grovogui, Siba N. 2002. "Regimes of Sovereignty: International Morality and the African Condition." *European Journal of International Relations* 8 (3): 315–338.

Gruffydd Jones, Branwen. 2008. "Race in the Ontology of International Order." *Political Studies* 56 (4): 907–927.

Gruffydd Jones, Branwen. 2013. " 'Good Governance' and 'State Failure': Genealogies of Imperial Discourse." *Cambridge Review of International Affairs* 26 (1): 49–70.

Guiso, Luigi, Paola Sapienza, and Luigi Zingales. 2009. "Cultural Biases in Economic Exchange?" *Quarterly Journal of Economics* 124 (3): 1095–1131.

Gutiérrez Rodríguez, Encarnación. 2018. "The Coloniality of Migration and the 'Refugee Crisis': On the Asylum-Migration Nexus, the Transatlantic White European Settler Colonialism-Migration and Racial Capitalism." *Refuge* 34 (1): 16–28.

Guyatt, N. 2016. *Bind Us Apart: How Enlightened Americans Invented Racial Segregation.* Oxford, UK: Oxford University Press.

Haas, Ernst B. 1990. *When Knowledge Is Power: Three Models of Change in International Organizations.* Berkeley: University of California Press.

Hafner-Burton, Emilie M., and Kiyoteru Tsutsui. 2005. "Human Rights in a Globalizing World: The Paradox of Empty Promises." *American Journal of Sociology* 110 (5): 1373–1411.

Hainmueller, Jens, and Michael J. Hiscox. 2006. "Learning to Love Globalization: Education and Individual Attitudes toward International Trade." *International Organization* 60 (2): 469–498.

Hainmueller, Jens, and Daniel J. Hopkins. 2015. "The Hidden American Immigration Consensus: A Conjoint Analysis of Attitudes toward Immigrants." *American Journal of Political Science* 59 (3): 529–548.

Hainmueller, Jens, Jonathan Mummolo, and Yiqing Xu. 2019. "How Much Should We Trust Estimates from Multiplicative Interaction Models? Simple Tools to Improve Empirical Practice." *Political Analysis* 27 (4): 163–192.

Halliday, Fred. 1999. *Revolution and World Politics: The Rise and Fall of the Sixth Great Power.* Durham, NC: Duke University Press.

Hangartner, Dominik, Elias Dinas, Moritz Marbach, Konstantinos Matakos, and Dimitrios Xefteris. 2019. "Does Exposure to the Refugee Crisis Make Natives More Hostile?" *American Political Science Review* 113 (2): 442–455.

Hannaford, Ivan. 1996. *Race: The History of an Idea in the West.* Baltimore, MD: Johns Hopkins University Press.

Hansen, Hans Krause, and Tony Porter. 2012. "What Do Numbers Do in Transnational Governance?" *International Political Sociology* 6 (4): 409–426.

Hansen, Randall, and Shalini Randeria. 2016. "Tensions of Refugee Politics in Europe." *Science* 353 (6303): 994–995.

Hassner, Ron E. 2020. "The Cost of Torture: Evidence from the Spanish Inquisition." *Security Studies* 29 (3): 457–492.

Hassner, Ron E., and Jason Wittenberg. 2015. "Barriers to Entry: Who Builds Fortified Boundaries and Why?" *International Security* 40 (1): 157–190.

Hathaway, James. 1994. "Three Critical Questions about the Study of Immigration Control." In *Controlling Immigration: A Global Perspective,* edited by Wayne Cornelius, Philip Martin, and James Hollifield, 49–51. Stanford, CA Stanford University Press.

Hatton, Timothy J., and Jeffrey G. Williamson. 2005. "What Fundamentals Drive World Migration?" In *Poverty, International Migration and Asylum,* edited by George J. Borjas and Jeff Crisp, 15–38. London: Palgrave Macmillan.

Hawkins, Freda. 1991. *Critical Years in Immigration: Canada and Australia Compared.* Kingston, ON: McGill-Queen's University Press.

Hayak, F. A. 1960. *The Constitution of Liberty.* Chicago: University of Chicago Press.

Hayak, F. A. 2001 [1944]. *The Road to Serfdom.* 2nd ed. London: Routledge.

Hayter, Teresa. 2000. *Open Borders: The Case against Immigration Controls.* London: Pluto Press.

Hayter, Teresa. 2001. "Open Borders: The Case against Immigration Controls." *Capital & Class* 25 (3): 149–156.

Heale, Michael J. 2009. "Anatomy of a Scare: Yellow Peril Politics in America, 1980–1993." *Journal of American Studies* 23 (1): 19–47.

Held, David, Anthony McGrew, David Goldblatt, and Jonathan Perraton. 1999. *Global Transformations: Politics, Economics and Culture.* Palo Alto, CA: Stanford University Press.

Heldring, Leander, and James A. Robinson. 2012. "Colonialism and Economic Development in Africa." Working paper, series 18566. National Bureau of Economic Research. https://doi.org/10.3386/w18566.

Henderson, Errol A. 2009. "Disturbing the Peace: African Warfare, Political Inversion and the Universality of the Democratic Peace Thesis." *British Journal of Political Science* 39 (1): 25–58.

Henderson, Errol A. 2013. "Hidden in Plain Sight: Racism in International Relations Theory." *Cambridge Review of International Affairs* 26 (1): 71–92.

Henderson, Errol A. 2015. *African Realism? International Relations Theory and Africa's Wars in the Postcolonial Era.* London: Rowman & Littlefield.

Henderson, Errol A. 2017. "The Revolution Will Not Be Theorised: Du Bois, Locke, and the Howard School's Challenge to White Supremacist IR Theory." *Millennium—Journal of International Studies* 45 (3): 492–510.

Herbst, Jeffrey. 2000. *States and Power in Africa: Comparative Lessons in Authority and Control.* Princeton, NJ: Princeton University Press.

Herda, Daniel. 2010. "How Many Immigrants? Foreign-Born Population Innumeracy in Europe." *Public Opinion Quarterly* 74 (4): 674–695.

Herda, Daniel. 2015. "Beyond Innumeracy: Heuristic Decision-Making and Qualitative Misperceptions about Immigrants in Finland." *Ethnic and Racial Studies* 38 (9) : 1627–1645.

Herda, Daniel. 2019. "Tracking Ignorance: Examining Changes in Immigrant Population Innumeracy in the United States from 2005 to 2013." *Migration Letters* 16 (2): 329–339.

Hesse, Barnor. 2007. "Racialized Modernity: An Analytics of White Mythologies." *Ethnic and Racial Studies* 30 (4): 643–663.

Hetherington, Marc, and Elizabeth Suhay. 2011. "Authoritarianism, Threat, and Americans' Support for the War on Terror." *American Journal of Political Science* 55 (3): 546–560.

Hickel, Jason, Dylan Sullivan, and Huzaifa Zoomkawala. 2021. "Plunder in the Post-colonial Era: Quantifying Drain from the Global South through Unequal Exchange, 1960–2018." *New Political Economy*, 1–18.

Hidalgo, Javier. 2016. "The Case for the International Governance of Immigration." *International Theory* 8 (1): 140–170.

Hiers, Wesley, and Andreas Wimmer. 2013. "Is Nationalism the Cause or Consequence of the End of Empire?" In *Nationalism and War*, edited by J. A. Hall and S. Malesevic, 212–254. Cambridge, UK: Cambridge University Press.

Hitler, Adolf. 2016. In *Mein Kampf. Eine kritische Edition*, edited by Christian Hartmann, Thomas Vordermayer, Othmar Plöckinger, and Roman Töppel. Munich: Institut für Zeitgeschichte.

Hobson, John M. 2004. *The Eastern Origins of Western Civilisation*. Cambridge, UK: Cambridge University Press.

Hobson, John M. 2012. *The Eurocentric Conception of World Politics: Western International Theory, 1760–2010*. Cambridge, UK: Cambridge University Press.

Hoffmann, John P., and Alan S. Miller. 1997. "Social and Political Attitudes among Religious Groups: Convergence and Divergence over Time." *Journal for the Scientific Study of Religion* 36 (1): 52–70.

Hogan, Jackie, and Kristin Haltinner. 2015. "Floods, Invaders, and Parasites: Immigration Threat Narratives and Right-Wing Populism in the USA, UK and Australia." *Journal of Intercultural Studies* 36 (5): 520–543.

Hollifield, James F. 2004. "The Emerging Migration State." *International Migration Review* 38, no. 3,: 885–912.

Holt, Thomas C. 2000. *The Problem of Race in the Twenty-First Century*. Cambridge, MA: Harvard University Press.

Hopkins, Daniel J. 2014. "One Language, Two Meanings: Partisanship and Responses to Spanish." *Political Communication* 31 (3): 421–445.

Hopkins, Daniel J., John Sides, and Jack Citrin. 2019. "The Muted Consequences of Correct Information about Immigration." *Journal of Politics* 81 (1): 315–320.

Horowitz, Daniel. 2017. "178,000 Bangladeshi Immigrants and the Threats of Non-assimilation." *Conservative Review*. [Online; posted 11-December-2017]. https://www.conservativereview.com/news/178000-bangladeshi-immigrants-the-threats-of-non-assimilation/.

Hozić, Aida A and Jacqui True. 2017. "Brexit as a Scandal: Gender and Global Trumpism." *Review of International Political Economy* 24 (2): 270–287.

Hubbell, Andrew. 2001. "A View of the Slave Trade from the Margin: Souroudougou in the Late Nineteenth-Century Slave Trade of the Niger Bend." *Journal of African History* 42 (1): 25–47.

Hughes, Melanie M. 2013. "The Intersection of Gender and Minority Status in National Legislatures: The Minority Women Legislative Index." *Legislative Studies Quarterly* 38 (4): 489–516.

Hughes, Melanie M., Lindsey Peterson, Jill Ann Harrison, and Pamela Paxton. 2009. "Power and Relation in the World Polity: The INGO Network Country Score, 1978–1998." *Social Forces* 87 (4): 1711–1742.

Hunt, Michael H. 2009. *Ideology and U.S. Foreign Policy*. New Haven, CT: Yale University Press.

Huntington, Samuel H. 1968. *Political Order in Changing Society*. Ithaca, NY: Cornell University Press.

Hurwitz, Jon, and Mark Peffley. 2005. "Playing the Race Card in the Post–Willie Horton Era: The Impact of Racialized Code Words on Support for Punitive Crime Policy." *Public Opinion Quarterly* 69 (1): 99–112.

Huth, Paul K., Sarah E. Croco, and Benjamin J. Appel. 2011. "Does International Law Promote the Peaceful Settlement of International Disputes? Evidence from the Study of Territorial Conflicts since 1945." *American Political Science Review* 105 (2): 415–436.

ICISS 2001. *The Responsibility to Protect: Report of the International Commission on Intervention and State Sovereignty*. Ottawa: International Development Research Centre.

Ikenberry, G. John. 2001. *After Victory: Institutions, Strategic Restraint, and the Rebuilding of Order after Major Wars*. Princeton, NJ: Princeton University Press.

Imai, Kosuke, and In Song Kim. 2019. "When Should We Use Unit Fixed Effects Regression Models for Causal Inference with Longitudinal Data?" *American Journal of Political Science* 63 (2): 467–490.

Ingram, Paul, Jeffrey Robinson, and Marc L. Busch. 2005. "The Intergovernmental Network of World Trade: IGO Connectedness, Governance, and Embeddedness." *American Journal of Sociology* 111 (3): 824–858.

Isaac, Julius. 1947. *Economics of Migration*. London: Routledge, Trench, Trubner & Co.

Islam, Nasir, and David R. Morrison. 1996. "Introduction: Governance, Democracy and Human Rights." *Canadian Journal of Development Studies/Revue canadienne d'études du développement* 17 (4): 5–18.

Jakobi, Anja. 2009. *International Organizations and Lifelong Learning: From Global Agendas to Policy Diffusion*. New York: Springer.

James, C. L. R. 2001. *The Black Jacobins: Toussaint L'Ouverture and the San Domingo Revolution*. London: Penguin UK.

James, Harold. 2001. *The End of Globalization: Lessons from the Great Depression*. Cambridge, MA: Harvard University Press.

Jeffries, Richard. 1993. "The State, Structural Adjustment and Good Government in Africa." *Journal of Commonwealth & Comparative Politics* 31 (1): 20–35.

Johnson, Jenna. 2015. "Trump Calls for 'Total and Complete Shutdown of Muslims Entering the United States.'" *Washington Post*. [Online; posted 15-December-2015]. https://www.washingtonpost.com/news/post-politics/wp/2015/12/07/donald-trump-calls-for-total-and-complete-shutdown-of-muslims-entering-the-united-states/.

Johnson, Kevin R. 2000. "Race Matters: Immigration Law and Policy Scholarship, Law in the Ivory Tower, and the Legal Indifference of the Race Critique." *University of Illinois Law Review* 2000 (2): 525–558.

Johnston, Alastair Iain. 2001. "Treating International Institutions as Social Environments." *International Studies Quarterly* 45 (4): 487–515.

Johnston, Alastair Iain. 2005. "Conclusions and Extensions: Toward Mid-range Theorizing and beyond Europe." *International Organization* 59 (4): 1013–1044.

Joly, Danièle. 1987. "Associations amongst the Pakistani Population in Britain." In *Immigrant Associations in Europe,* edited by John Rex, Danièle Joly, and Czarina Wilpert, 62–87. Farnham, UK: Gower Publishing.

Joppke, Christian. 2005. *Selecting by Origin: Ethnic Migration in the Liberal State.* Cambridge, MA: Harvard University Press.

Junn, Jane, and Natalie Masuoka. 2008. "Asian American Identity: Shared Racial Status and Political Context." *Perspectives on Politics* 6 (4): 729–740.

Kant, Immanuel. 1777. "Of the Different Human Races." In *The Idea of Race,* edited by Robert Bernasconi and Tommy L. Lott, 8–22. Indianapolis, IN: Hackett.

Kaplan, Robert D. 1994. "The Coming Anarchy." *Atlantic Monthly* 273 (2): 44–76.

Karemera, David, Victor Iwuagwu Oguledo, and Bobby Davis. 2000. "A Gravity Model Analysis of International Migration to North America." *Applied Economics* 32 (13): 1745–1755.

Karnitsching, Matthew. 2015. "Orbán Says Migrants Threaten 'Christian' Europe." Politico. [Online; posted 03-September-2015]. https : //www.politico.eu/article/orban-migrants-threaten-christian-europe-identity-refugees-asylum-crisis/.

Kasaba, Resat. 2009. *A Movable Empire: Ottoman Nomads, Migrants, and Refugees.* Seattle: University of Washington Press.

Kaufman, Michael T. 1998. "Stokely Carmichael, Rights Leader Who Coined 'Black Power,' Dies at 57." *New York Times.* [Online; posted 16-November-1998]. https://www.nytimes.com/1998/11/16/us/stokely-carmichael-rights-leader-who-coined-black-power-dies-at-57.html.

Keck, Margaret E., and Kathryn Sikkink. 1999. "Transnational Advocacy Networks in International and Regional Politics." *International Social Science Journal* 51 (159): 89–101.

Keegan, John. 1993. *A History of Warfare.* New York: Random House.

Keen, David. 2005. *Conflict and Collusion in Sierra Leone.* New York: Palgrave.

Keene, Edward. 2002. *Beyond the Anarchical Society: Grotius, Colonialism and Order in World Politics.* Cambridge, UK: Cambridge University Press.

Keene, Edward. 2014. "The Standard of 'Civilisation', the Expansion Thesis and the 19th-Century International Social Space." *Millennium* 42 (3): 651–673.

Kendi, Ibram X. 2016. *Stamped from the Beginning: The Definitive History of Racist Ideas in America.* New York: Nation Books.

Kendi, Ibram X. 2020. "Stop Blaming Black People for Dying of the Coronavirus." *Atlantic, op-ed, April 14, 2020,* https : //www.theatlantic.com/ideas/archive/2020/04/race-and-blame/609946/.

Kennan, John, and James R. Walker. 2011. "The Effect of Expected Income on Individual Migration Decisions." *Econometrica* 79 (1): 211–251.

Kenwick, Michael R., and Beth A. Simmons. 2020. "Pandemic Response as Border Politics." *International Organization* 74 (S1): E36–E58. https://doi.org/10.1017/S0020818320000363.

Kenyatta, Jomo. 1965. *Facing Mt. Kenya.* New York: Vintage Books.

Keohane, Robert O., and Joseph S. Nye Jr. 1977. *Power and Interdependence.* New York: Little, Brown & Co.

Kevles, Daniel. 1995. *In the Name of Eugenics: Genetics and the Uses of Human Heredity.* Cambridge, MA: Harvard University Press.

Kim, Claire Jean. 1999. "The Racial Triangulation of Asian Americans." *Politics & Society* 27 (1): 105–138.

Kinder, Donald R., and David O. Sears. 1981. "Prejudice and Politics: Symbolic Racism versus Racial Threats to the Good Life." *Journal of Personality and Social Psychology* 40 (3): 414–431.

Kindleberger, Charles P. 1986. *The World in Depression, 1929–1939.* Berkeley: University of California Press.

King, Desmond, and Inés Valdez. 2011. "From Workers to Enemies: National Security, State Building, and America's War on Illegal Immigrants." In *Narrating Peoplehood amid Diversity: Historical and Theoretical Perspectives,* edited by Michael Böss, 145–182. Aarhus, Denmark: Aarhus University Press.

King, Gary, and Langche Zeng. 2001. "Explaining Rare Events in International Relations." *International Organization* 55 (3): 693–715.

King, Richard. 1999. "Orientalism and the Modern Myth of 'Hinduism.' " *Numen* 46 (2): 146–185.

Kinne, Brandon J. 2013. "Igo Membership, Network Convergence, and Credible Signaling in Militarized Disputes." *Journal of Peace Research* 50 (6): 659–676.

Kitimbo, Adrian. 2015. "Is It Time for Open Borders in Southern Africa? The Case for Free Labour Movement in SADC." In *Africans Investing in Africa,* edited by Terrance McNamee, Mark Pearson, and Wiebe Boer, 85–99. New York: Palgrave Macmillan.

Klotz, Audie. 1995. "Norms Reconstituting Interests: Global Racial Equality and U.S. Sanctions against South Africa." *International Organization* 49 (3): 451–478.

Knudsen, Knud. 1997. "Scandinavian Neighbours with Different Character? Attitudes toward Immigrants and National Identity in Norway and Sweden." *Acta Sociologica* 40 (3): 223–243.

Koch, Svea. 2015. "A Typology of Political Conditionality beyond Aid: Conceptual Horizons Based on Lessons from the European Union." *World Development* 75 (1): 97–108.

Köhler, Gernot. 1978. "Global Apartheid." *Alternatives: Global, Local, Political* 4 (2): 263–275.

Köhler, Gernot. 1995. "The Three Meanings of Global Apartheid: Empirical, Normative, Existential." *Alternatives* 20 (3): 403–413.

Kohli, Aarti, Peter L. Markowitz, and Lisa Chavez. 2011. "Secure Communities by the Numbers: An Analysis of Demographics and Due Process." Technical report. Warren Institute on Law and Social Policy.

Kohli, Aarti, Peter L. Markowitz, and Lisa Chavez. 2018. "Australia's Offshore Humanitarian Program: 2017–18." Australian Department of Home Affairs.

Koyama, Hitomi, and Barry Buzan. 2019. "Rethinking Japan in Mainstream International Relations." *International Relations of the Asia-Pacific* 19 (2): 185–212.

Kramer, Paul A. 2006. "Race-Making and Colonial Violence in the U.S. Empire: The Philippine-American War as Race War." *Diplomatic History* 30 (2): 169–210.

Krasner, Stephen D. 1999. *Sovereignty: Organized Hypocrisy.* Princeton, NJ: Princeton University Press.

Krishna, Sankaran. 2001. "Race, Amnesia, and the Education of International Relations." *Alternatives: Global, Local, Political* 26 (4): 401–424.

Kroneberg, Clemens, and Andreas Wimmer. 2012. "Struggling over the Boundaries of Belonging: A Formal Model of Nation Building, Ethnic Closure, and Populism." *American Journal of Sociology* 118 (1): 176–230.

Kuklinski, James H., Michael D. Cobb, and Martin Gilens. 1997. "Racial Attitudes and the 'New South.' " *Journal of Politics* 59 (2): 323–349.

Kupiszewska, D., and B. Nowok. 2008. "Comparability of Statistics on International Migration Flows in the European Union." In *International Migration in Europe: Data, Models and Estimates.* London: Wiley.

Kustov, Alexander, Dillon Laaker, and Cassidy Reller. 2021. "The Stability of Immigration Attitudes: Evidence and Implications." *Journal of Politics* 84 (4): 1478–1494.

Lake, David A. 2009. *Hierarchy in International Relations.* Ithaca, NY: Cornell University Press.

Lake, David A. 2011. "Why 'Isms' Are Evil: Theory, Epistemology, and Academic Sects as Impediments to Understanding and Progress." *International Studies Quarterly* 55 (2): 465–480.

Lake, David A. 2013. "Theory Is Dead, Long Live Theory: The End of the Great Debates and the Rise of Eclecticism in International Relations." *European Journal of International Relations* 19 (3): 567–587.

Lake, Marilyn, and Henry Reynolds. 2008. *Drawing the Global Colour Line: White Men's Countries and the Question of Racial Equality.* New York: Cambridge University Press.

Lall, Sanjaya. 1975. "Is 'Dependence' a Useful Concept in Analysing Underdevelopment?" *World Development* 3 (11-12): 799–810.

Landau, L. B. 2010. "Loving the Alien? Citizenship, Law, and the Future in South Africa's Demonic Society." *African Affairs* 109 (435): 213–230.

Lange, Matthew, and Andrew Dawson. 2009. "Dividing and Ruling the World? A Statistical Test of the Effects of Colonialism on Postcolonial Civil Violence." *Social Forces* 88 (2): 785–817.

Langton, Kenneth P., and M. Kent Jennings. 1968. "Political Socialization and the High School Civics Curriculum in the United States." *American Political Science Review* 62 (3): 852–867.

Latour, Bruno. 2004. "Why Has Critique Run Out of Steam? From Matters of Fact to Matters of Concern." *Critical Inquiry* 30 (2): 225–248.

Law, Anna O. 1996. "Race, Ethnicity, and National Origins in Public Policy—When Should It Matter." *Georgetown Immigration Law Journal* 10: 71–76.

Leith, Clark J. 2005. *Why Botswana Prospered.* Montreal: McGill University Press.

Lewis, Jeffrey. 1998. "Is the 'Hard Bargaining' Image of the Council Misleading? The Committee of Permanent Representatives and the Local Elections Directive." *JCMS: Journal of Common Market Studies* 36 (4): 479–504.

Li, Xue, and Alexander Hicks. 2016. "World Polity Matters: Another Look at the Rise of the Nation-State across the World, 1816 to 2001." *American Sociological Review* 81 (3): 596–607.

Lindberg, Staffan I., Michael Coppedge, John Gerring, and Jan Teorell. 2014. "V-Dem: A New Way to Measure Democracy." *Journal of Democracy* 25 (3): 159–169.

Lipscy, Phillip Y. 2020. "COVID-19 and the Politics of Crisis." *International Organization* 74 (S1): E98–E127. https://doi.org/10.1017/S0020818320000375.

Locke, Alain L. 1916. *Race Contacts and Interracial Relations: Lectures on the Theory and Practice of Race.* Washington, DC: Howard University Press.

Locke, Alain L. 1924a. "The Concept of Race as Applied to Social Culture." In *The Philosophy of Alain Locke: Harlem Renaissance and Beyond,* edited by Leonard Harris, 187–199. Philadelphia: Temple University Press.

Locke, Alain L. 1924b. "The Problem of Race Classification." In *The Philosophy of Alain Locke: Harlem Renaissance and Beyond,* edited by Leonard Harris, 163–174. Philadelphia: Temple University Press.

Locke, Alain L. 1925. "Enter the New Negro." *Survey Graphic* 6 (6): 631–634.

Long, J. Scott. 1997. *Regression Models for Categorical and Limited Dependent Variables.* New York: Sage Publications.

López, Ian Haney. 2015. *Dog Whistle Politics: How Coded Racial Appeals Have Reinvented Racism and Wrecked the Middle Class.* New York: Oxford University Press.

Lovejoy, Paul E. 2000. *Transformations in Slavery.* Cambridge, UK: Cambridge University Press.

Lumumba, Patrice. 1962. *Congo, My Country.* New York: Frederick A. Praeger.

Lupia, Arthur, and Jesse O. Menning. 2009. "When Can Politicians Scare Citizens into Supporting Bad Policies?" *American Journal of Political Science* 53 (1): 90–106.

MacDonald, John S., and Leatrice D. MacDonald. 1964. "Chain Migration Ethnic Neighborhood Formation and Social Networks." *Milbank Memorial Fund Quarterly* 42 (1): 82–97.

MacMaster, Neil. 2001. *Racism in Europe: 1870–2000.* New York: Palgrave.

Maddison, Angus. 1995. *Monitoring the Global Economy.* Paris: OECD Publishing.

Maddison, Angus. 1998. *Chinese Economic Performance in the Long Run.* Paris: OECD Publishing.

Maguire, Amy, and Amy Elton. 2017. "Dutton's Demonisation of Refugees Is the Latest Play in a Zero-Sum Game." *Conversation.* [Online; posted 20-November-2017]. https://theconversation.com/duttons-demonisation-of-refugees-is-the-latest-play-in-a-zero-sum-game-69043.

Mahadi, Abdullahi. 1992. "The Aftermath of the Jihad in the Central sudan as a Major Factor in the Volume of the Trans-Saharan Slave Trade in the Nineteenth Century." *Slavery and Abolition* 13 (1): 111–128.

Mainwaring, Cetta, and Stephanie J. Silverman. 2017. "Detention-as-Spectacle." *International Political Sociology* 11 (1): 21–38.

Majors, Bruce. 2018. "Open Borders Are Not Libertarian So Long as America Is a Welfare State." Federalist. [Online; posted 02-August-2018]. https://thefederalist.com/2018/08/02/open-borders-not-libertarian-long-america-welfare-state/.

Maliniak, Daniel, Susan Peterson, Ryan Powers, and Michael J. Tierney. 2017. *TRIP 2017 Faculty Survey. Teaching, Research, and International Policy Project.* Williamsburg, VA Global Research Institute. https://trip.wm.edu/.

Mallinson, Claire. 2017. "Rohingya Crisis: Australia Can't Stay Silent on Myanmar's Apartheid." ABC News. [Online; posted 30-November-2017]. https://www.abc.net.au/news/2017-12-01/myanmar-treatment-of-rohingya-apartheid-amnesty-international/9206562.

Mallon, Ron. 2006. " 'Race': Normative, Not Metaphysical or Semantic." *Ethics* 116 (3): 525–551.

Mallon, Ron. 2007. "A Field Guide to Social Construction." *Philosophy Compass* 2 (1): 93–108.

Malm, Andreas. 2021. *White Skin, Black Fuel: On the Danger of Fossil Fascism*. London: Verso Press.

Mamdani, Mahmood. 1990. "State and Civil Society in Contemporary Africa: Reconceptualizing the Birth of State Nationalism and the Defeat of Popular Movements." *Africa Development/Afrique et développement* 15 (3/4): 47–70.

Mamdani, Mahmood. 2001. *When Victims Become Killers*. Princeton, NJ Princeton University Press.

Mann, Michael. 1988. *States, War and Capitalism: Studies in Political Sociology*. Oxford, UK: Blackwell.

Mann, Michael. 2004. *Fascists*. London: Cambridge University Press.

Mann, Michael. 2012. *The Sources of Social Power, Vol. 3: Global Empires and Revolution, 1890–1945*. London: Cambridge University Press.

Manners, Ian. 2002. "Normative Power Europe: A Contradiction in Terms?" *JCMS: Journal of Common Market Studies* 40 (2): 235–258.

Manning, Patrick. 1990. *Slavery and African Life*. Cambridge, UK: Cambridge University Press.

Manning, Roger B. 1986. "Rural Societies in Early Modern Europe: A Review." *Sixteenth Century Journal* 17 (3): 353–360.

Mantena, Karuna. 2010. "The Crisis of Liberal Imperialism." *Histoire@ Politique* 11 (2): 1–23.

Marshall, Monty G. 2019. "Major Episodes of Political Violence (MEPV) and Conflict Regions, 1946–2018." Center for Systemic Peace, http://www.systemicpeace.org/inscr/inscr.htm.

Martin, David A. 1989. "Effects of International Law on Migration Policy and Practice: The Uses of Hypocrisy." *International Migration Review* 23 (3): 547–578.

Martin, Gregory J., and Joshua McCrain. 2019. "Local News and National Politics." *American Political Science Review* 113 (2): 372–384.

Martin, Lisa L., and Beth A. Simmons. 1998. "Theories and Empirical Studies of International Institutions." *International Organization* 52 (4): 729–757.

Martin, S., and E. Ferris. 2017. "Border Security, Migration Governance, and Sovereignty." In *Ideas to Inform International Cooperation on Safe, Orderly and Regular Migration*. Geneva: IOM

Massey, Douglas S., Gretchen A. Condran, and Nancy A. Denton. 1987. "The Effect of Residential Segregation on Black Social and Economic Well-Being." *Social Forces* 66 (1): 29–56.

Massey, Douglas S., and Nancy A. Denton. 1988. "The Dimensions of Residential Segregation." *Social Forces* 67 (2): 281–315.

Massey, Douglas S., and Felipe García España. 1987. "The Social Process of International Migration." *Science* 237 (4816): 733–738.

Massey, Douglas S., Jonathan Rothwell, and Thurston Domina. 2009. "The Changing Bases of Segregation in the United States." *Annals of the American Academy of Political and Social Science* 626 (1): 74–90.

Mau, Steffen, Fabian Gülzau, Lena Laube, and Natascha Zaun. 2015. "The Global Mobility Divide: How Visa Policies Have Evolved over Time." *Journal of Ethnic and Migration Studies* 41 (8): 1192–1213.

Mayda, Anna Maria. 2006. "Who Is against Immigration? A Cross-Country Investigation of Individual Attitudes toward Immigrants." *Review of Economics and Statistics* 88 (3): 510–530.

Mayda, Anna Maria. 2008. "Why Are People More Pro-trade Than Pro-migration?" *Economics Letters* 101 (3): 160–163.

Mayer, T., and S. Zignago. 2005. "Market Access in Global and Regional Trade." CEPII working paper 2. http://www.cepii.fr/PDF_PUB/wp/2005/wp2005-02.pdf.

Mayhew, David R. 1974. *Congress: The Electoral Connection*. New Haven, CT: Yale University Press.

M'Buyinga, Elenga. 1982. *Pan Africanism or Neo-colonialism? The Bankruptcy of the OAU* London: Zed Books.

McAlexander, Richard J. 2020. "How Are Immigration and Terrorism Related? An Analysis of Right-and Left-Wing Terrorism in Western Europe, 1980–2004." *Journal of Global Security Studies* 5 (1): 179–195.

McDuie-Ra, Duncan. 2014. "The India-Bangladesh Border Fence: Narratives and Political Possibilities." *Journal of Borderlands Studies* 29 (1): 81–94.

McElreath, Richard. 2020. *Statistical Rethinking: A Bayesian Course with Examples in R and STAN*. Boca Raton, FL: Chapman & Hall/CRC.

McKean, Benjamin L. 2020. *Disorienting Neoliberalism: Global Justice and the Outer Limit of Market Freedom*. New York: Oxford University Press.

McKeown, Adam M. 2008. *Melancholy Order: Asian Migration and the Globalization of Borders*. New York: Columbia University Press.

McNeely, Connie L. 1995. *Constructing the Nation-State: International Organization and Prescriptive Action*. Westport, CT: Greenwood Press.

McNeill, J. R. 2010. *Mosquito Empires*. Cambridge, UK: Cambridge University Press.

McPherson, Lionel K. 2015. "Deflating 'Race.' " *Journal of the American Philosophical Association* 1 (4): 674–693.

Mearsheimer, John J. 1994. "The False Promise of International Institutions." *International Security* 19 (3): 5–49.

Mearsheimer, John J. 2019. *The Great Delusion: Liberal Dreams and International Realities*. New Haven, CT: Yale University Press.

Mearsheimer, John J., and Stephen M. Walt. 2013. "Leaving Theory Behind: Why Simplistic Hypothesis Testing Is Bad for International Relations." *European Journal of International Relations* 19 (3): 427–457.

Meseguer, Covadonga, and Achim Kemmerling. 2018. "What Do You Fear? Anti-immigrant Sentiment in Latin America." *International Migration Review* 52 (1): 236–272.

Meyer, John W., John Boli, George M. Thomas, and Francisco O. Ramirez. 1997. "World Society and the Nation-State." *American Journal of Sociology* 103 (1): 144–181.

Milanovic, Branko. 2019. *Capitalism, Alone: The Future of the System That Rules the World*. Cambridge, MA: Harvard University Press.

Miles, Robert. 1989. *Racism*. London: Routledge.

Miles, William F. S. 2014. *Scars of Partition: Postcolonial Legacies in French and British Borderlands.* Lincoln: University of Nebraska Press.

Mill, John Stewart. 1861. *Considerations on Representative Government.* New York: Harper.

Miller, David. 2016. *Strangers in Our Midst.* Cambridge, MA: Harvard University Press.

Miller, John Franklin. 1882. "1882 Chinese Exclusion Act Congressional Debate." In *Congressional Record,* vol. 14, 1.

Mills, Charles W. 1998. *Blackness Visible: Essays on Philosophy and Race.* Ithaca, NY: Cornell University Press.

Mills, Charles W. 2015. "Global White Ignorance." In *Routledge International Handbook of Ignorance Studies,* edited by Matthias Gross and Linsey McGoey, 217–227. Abingdon, UK: Routledge. https://doi.org/10.4324/9781315867762.

Mills, Charles W. 2018. " 'But What Are You *Really*'." In *Blackness Visible: Essays on Philosophy and Race,* edited by Charles W. Mills, 41–66. Ithaca, NY: Cornell University Press.

Mills, Melinda, Gerhard G. Van de Bunt, and Jeanne De Bruijn. 2006. "Comparative Research: Persistent Problems and Promising Solutions." *International Sociology* 21 (5): 619–631.

Minozzi, William, Michael A. Neblo, Kevin M. Esterling, and David M. J. Lazer. 2015. "Field Experiment Evidence of Substantive, Attributional, and Behavioral Persuasion by Members of Congress in Online Town Halls." *Proceedings of the National Academy of Sciences* 112 (13): 3937–3942.

Minozzi, William, Hyunjin Song, David M. J. Lazer, Michael A. Neblo, and Katherine Ognyanova. 2020. "The Incidental Pundit: Who Talks Politics with Whom, and Why?" *American Journal of Political Science* 64 (1): 135–151.

Mitzen, Jennifer. 2013. *Power in Concert: The Nineteenth-Century Origins of Global Governance.* Chicago: University of Chicago Press.

Mkandawire, Thandika. 2001. "Thinking about Developmental States in Africa." *Cambridge Journal of Economics* 25 (3): 289–314. https://doi.org/10.1093/cje/25.3.289.

Mkandawire, Thandika. 2010. "On Tax Efforts and Colonial Heritage in Africa." *Journal of Development Studies* 46 (10): 1647–1669.

Mkandawire, Thandika. 2015. "Neopatrimonialism and the Political Economy of Economic Performance in Africa: Critical Reflections." *World Politics* 67: 563.

Modelski, George. 1987. *Long Cycles in World Politics.* London: MacMillan Press.

Money, Jeannette. 1999. *Fences and Neighbors: The Political Geography of Immigration Control.* Ithaca, NY: Cornell University Press.

Money, Jeannette, and Sarah P. Lockhart. 2018. *Migration and the Structure of International Cooperation.* Athens: University of Georgia Press.

Moradi, Alexander. 2008. "Confronting Colonial Legacies—Lessons from Human Development in Ghana and Kenya, 1880–2000." *Journal of International Development* 20 (8): 1107–1121.

Morgenthau, Hans J. 1951. *In Defense of the National Interest.* New York: Knopf.

Morning, Ann. 2008. "Ethnic Classification in Global Perspective: A Cross-National Survey of the 2000 Census Round." *Population Research and Policy Review* 27 (2): 239–272.

Mortimer, Robert A. 1984. *The Third World Coalition in International Politics.* Boulder, CO: Westview Press.

Morton, Adam David. 2007. "Waiting for Gramsci: State Formation, Passive Revolution and the International." *Millennium* 35 (3): 597–621.

Mosley, Della V., Candice N. Hargons, Carolyn Meiller, Blanka Angyal, Paris Wheeler, Candice Davis, and Danelle Stevens-Watkins. 2021. "Critical Consciousness of Anti-Black Racism: A Practical Model to Prevent and Resist Racial Trauma." *Journal of Counseling Psychology* 68 (1): 1–16.

Mosley, Paul. 1983. *The Settler Economies: Studies in the Economic History of Kenya and Southern Rhodesia, 1900–1963*. New York: Cambridge University Press.

Mosselson, Aidan. 2010. " 'There Is No Difference between Citizens and Non-citizens Anymore': Violent Xenophobia, Citizenship and the Politics of Belonging in Post-apartheid South Africa." *Journal of Southern African Studies* 36 (3): 641–655.

Mouffe, Chantal. 2000. *The Democratic Paradox*. London: Verso.

Mountford, Andrew. 1997. "Can a Brain Drain Be Good for Growth in the Source Economy?" *Journal of Development Economics* 53 (2): 287–303.

Moyo, Dambisa. 2009. *Dead Aid: Why Aid Is Not Working and How There Is a Better Way for Africa*. New York: Farrar, Straus & Giroux.

Mugabe, Robert. 1983. *Our War of Liberation*. Gweru, Zimbabwe: Mambo Press.

Muller, Edward N. 1985. "Income Inequality, Regime Repressiveness, and Political Violence." *American Sociological Review* 50 (1): 47–61.

Mullings, Leith. 2005. "Interrogating Racism: Toward an Antiracist Anthropology." *Annual Review of Anthropology* 34: 667–693.

Muronzi, Chris. 2020. "Zimbabwe Unfazed by South Africa Plan to Erect Border Fence." Al Jazeera. [Online; posted 21-March-2020]. aljazeera.com/news/2020/3/21/zimbabwe-unfa zed-by-south-africa-plan-to-erect-border-fence.

Murphy, Craig N. 1998. "Understanding IR: Understanding Gramsci." *Review of International Studies* 24 (3): 417–425.

Murray, Mark. 2019. "Support for Free Trade Reaches New High in NBC/WSJ poll." NBC News. [Online; posted 08-August-2019]. https : //www.documentcloud.org/documents /6297116-NBCWSJ-August-2019-Poll.html.

Musterd, Sako, and Ronald Van Kempen. 2009. "Segregation and Housing of Minority Ethnic Groups in Western European Cities." *Tijdschrift voor economische en sociale geografie* 100 (4): 559–566.

Muthu, Sankar. 2003. *Enlightenment against Empire*. Princeton, NJ: Princeton University Press.

Nanday, Ashis. 1983. *Intimate Enemy: Loss and Recovery of Self under Colonialism*. New York: Oxford University Press.

Narkowicz, Kasia. 2018. " 'Refugees Not Welcome Here': State, Church and Civil Society Responses to the Refugee Crisis in Poland." *International Journal of Politics, Culture, and Society* 31 (4): 357–373.

National Consortium for the Study of Terrorism and Responses to Terrorism (START) 2019. "Global Terrorism Database (GTD)" University of Maryland. https://www.start.umd.edu /gtd.

N'Diaye, Pap. 2006. "Questions de couleur. Histoire, idéologie et pratiques du colorisme." In *De la question sociale à la question raciale? Représenter la société française*, edited by Éric Fassin and Didier Fassin, 37–54. Paris: La Découverte.

N'Diaye, Pap. 2008. *La condition noire: Essai sur une minorité française.* Paris: Calmann-Lévy.

Neal, Andrew W. 2009. "Securitization and Risk at the EU Border: The Origins of FRONTEX" *JCMS: Journal of Common Market Studies* 47 (2): 333–356.

Neblo, Michael A. 2009. "Three-Fifths a Racist: A Typology for Analyzing Public Opinion about Race." *Political Behavior* 31 (1): 31–51.

Neblo, Michael A. 2017. *Deliberative Democracy between Theory and Practice.* New York: Cambridge University Press.

Neuringer, Sheldon Morris. 1980 [1969]. *American Jewry and United States Immigration Policy, 1881–1953.* New York: ARNO Press.

Nevins, Joseph. 2002. *Operation Gatekeeper: The Rise of the "Illegal Alien" and the Making of the US-Mexico Boundary.* New York: Routledge.

Nevins, Joseph. 2012. "Policing Mobility: Maintaining Global Apartheid from South Africa to the United States." In *Beyond Walls and Cages: Prisons, Borders, and Global Crisis,* edited by Jenna M. Loyd, Matt Mitchelson, and Andrew Burridge, 19–26. Athens: University of Georgia Press.

Ngai, Mae M. 1999. "The Architecture of Race in American Immigration Law: A Reexamination of the Immigration Act of 1924." *Journal of American History* 86 (1): 67. https://doi.org/10.2307/2567407.

Ngai, Mae M. 2003. "The Strange Career of the Illegal Alien: Immigration Restriction and Deportation policy in the United States, 1921–1965." *Law and History Review* 21 (1): 69–107.

Nielsen, Richard A., Michael G. Findley, Zachary S. Davis, Tara Candland, and Daniel L. Nielson. 2011. "Foreign Aid Shocks as a Cause of Violent Armed Conflict." *American Journal of Political Science* 55 (2): 219–232.

Nielson, Daniel L., and Michael J. Tierney. 2003. "Delegation to International Organizations: Agency Theory and World Bank Environmental Reform." *International Organization* 57 (2): 241–276.

Nisancioglu, Kerem. 2019. "Racial Sovereignty." *European Journal of International Relations,* 1–25.

Nkrumah, Kwame. 1965. *Neo-colonialism: The Last Stage of Imperialism.* New York: International Publishers.

North, Douglass C., and Barry R. Weingast. 1989. "Constitutions and Commitment: The Evolution of Institutions Governing Public Choice in Seventeenth-Century England." *Journal of Economic History* 49 (4): 803–832.

Nunn, Nathan. 2008. "The Long-Term Effects of Africa's Slave Trades." *Quarterly Journal of Economics* 123 (1): 139–176.

Nussbaum, Martha C. 1996. "Patriotism and Cosmopolitanism." In *For Love of Country: Debating the Limits of Patriotism,* edited by Joshua Cohen, 3–17. Boston: Beacon Press.

Nyerere, Julius K. 1987. "Ujamaa: The Basis of African Socialism." *Journal of Pan African Studies* 1 (1): 4–11.

Nyhan, Brendan, Ethan Porter, Jason Reifler, and Thomas Wood. 2019. "Taking Fact-Checks Literally but Not Seriously? The Effects of Journalistic Fact-Checking on Factual Beliefs and Candidate Favorability." *Political Behavior* 42 (3): 939–960.

Oatley, Thomas. 2017. "Open Economy Politics and Trade Policy." *Review of International Political Economy* 24 (4): 699–717.

Obasogie, Osagie K. 2014. *Blinded by Sight: Seeing Race through the Eyes of the Blind.* Stanford, CA: Stanford University Press.

Olson, Mancur. 1993. "Dictatorship, Democracy, and Development." *American Political Science Review* 87 (3): 567–576.

Omi, Michael, and Howard Winant. 1994. *Racial Formation in the United States: From the 1960s to the 1990s.* New York: Routledge.

Opeskin, Brian. 2012. "Managing International Migration in Australia: Human Rights and the 'Last Major Redoubt of Unfettered National Sovereignty.'" *International Migration Review* 46 (3): 551–585.

Orgad, Liav, and Theodore Ruthizer. 2009. "Race, Religion and Nationality in Immigration Selection: 120 Years after the Chinese Exclusion Case." *Constitutional Commentary* 26: 237.

Organski, Abramo F. K. 1958. *World Politics.* New York: Knopf.

Ortega, Francesc, and Giovanni Peri. 2009. "The Causes and Effects of International Migrations: Evidence from OECD Countries 1980–2005." Technical report. National Bureau of Economic Research. http://www.nber.org/papers/w14833.pdf.

Ortega, Francesc, and Giovanni Peri. 2013. "The Effect of Income and Immigration Policies on International Migration." *Migration Studies* 1 (1): 47–74.

Owens, Patricia. 2017. "Racism in the Theory Canon: Hannah Arendt and 'the One Great Crime in Which America Was Never Involved.'" *Millennium* 45 (3): 403–424.

Palladini, Fiammetta. 2008. "Pufendorf Disciple of Hobbes: The Nature of Man and the State of Nature: The Doctrine of Socialitas." *History of European Ideas* 34 (1): 26–60.

Pallister-Wilkins, Polly. 2011. "The Separation Wall: A Symbol of Power and a Site of Resistance?" *Antipode* 43 (5): 1851–1882.

Palmer, Glenn, Roseanne W. McManus, Vito D'Orazio, Michael R. Kenwick, Mikaela Karstens, Chase Bloch, Nick Dietrich, Kayla Kahn, Kellan Ritter, and Michael J. Soules. 2020. "The MID5 Dataset, 2011–2014: Procedures, Coding Rules, and Description." Working paper. Correlates of War project. https://correlatesofwar.org/data-sets/MIDs/mid-5-data-and-supporting-materials.zip/view.

Paris, Roland. 2002. "International Peacebuilding and the 'Mission Civilisatrice.'" *Review of International Studies* 28 (4): 637–656.

Patnaik, Utsa, and Prabhat Patnaik. 2016. *A Theory of Imperialism.* New York: Columbia University Press.

Paxton, Pamela, Melanie M. Hughes, and Jennifer L. Green. 2006. "The International Women's Movement and Women's Political Representation, 1893–2003." *American Sociological Review* 71 (6): 898–920.

Pearson, Charles H. 1893. *National Life and Character: A Forecast.* New York: Macmillan.

Pennington, Brian. 2004. *Was Hinduism Invented? Britons, Indians, and the Colonial Construction of Religion.* New York: Oxford University Press.

Persaud, Randolph B., and Rob B. J. Walker. 2001. "Apertura: Race in International Relations." *Alternatives* 26 (4): 373–376.

Peters, Margaret E. 2015. "Open Trade, Closed Borders: Immigration in the Era of Globalization." *World Politics* 67 (1): 114–154.

Peters, Margaret E. 2017. *Trading Barriers: Immigration and the Remaking of Globalization.* Princeton, NJ: Princeton University Press.

Phelan, Jo C., Bruce G. Link, and Naumi M. Feldman. 2013. "The Genomic Revolution and Beliefs about Essential Racial Differences: A Backdoor to Eugenics?" *American Sociological Review* 78 (2): 167–191.

Philpott, Daniel. 2001. *Revolutions in Sovereignty: How Ideas Shaped Modern International Relations.* Princeton, NJ: Princeton University Press.

Pichler, Florian. 2009. "'Down-to-Earth' Cosmopolitanism: Subjective and Objective Measurements of Cosmopolitanism in Survey Research." *Current Sociology* 57 (5): 704–732.

Piketty, Thomas. 2014. *Capital in the 21st Century.* Cambridge, MA: Harvard University Press.

Piketty, Thomas. 2020. *Capital and Ideology.* Cambridge, MA: Harvard University Press.

Popper, Karl R. 1962. *Conjectures and Refutations: The Growth of Scientific Knowledge.* New York: Basic Books.

Powell, Walter W., and Paul J. DiMaggio. 1991. *The New Institutionalism in Organizational Analysis.* Chicago: University of Chicago Press.

Powers, Kathy L. 2004. "Regional Trade Agreements as Military Alliances." *International Interactions* 30 (4): 373–395.

Poynting, Scott, and Victoria Mason. 2007. "The Resistible Rise of Islamophobia: Anti-Muslim Racism in the UK and Australia before 11 September 2001." *Journal of Sociology* 43 (1): 61–86.

Prashad, Vijay. 2001. *The Karma of Brown Folk.* Minneapolis: University of Minnesota Press.

Price, Richard, and Christian Reus-Smit. 1998. "Dangerous Liaisons? Critical International Theory and Constructivism." *European Journal of International Relations* 4 (3): 259–294.

Pronczuk, Monika. 2019. "Poland's Immigrant Stance at Odds with Need for Workers." *Financial Times.* [Online; posted 05-August-2019]. https://www.ft.com/content/2dd225a8-a498-11e9-974c-ad1c6ab5efd1.

Pufendorf, Samuel von. 1703 [1672]. *The Law of Nature and Nations or a General System of the Most Important Principles of Morality, Jurisprudence and Politics.* Oxford, UK: L. Litchfield. https://books.google.com/books?id=SZcoAQAAMAAJ.

Puri, Sunita. 2005. "Rhetoric v. Reality: The Effect of 'Multiculturalism' on Doctors' Responses to Battered South Asian Women in the United States and Britain." *Patterns of Prejudice* 39 (4): 416–430.

Putterman, Louis, and David N. Weil. 2010. "Post-1500 Population Flows and the Long-Run Determinants of Economic Growth and Inequality." *Quarterly Journal of Economics* 125 (4): 1627–1682.

Rajaram, Prem Kumar. 2018. "Refugees as Surplus Population: Race, Migration and Capitalist Value Regimes." *New Political Economy* 23 (5): 627–639.

Rapport, Aaron. 2020. "Threat Perceptions and Hidden Profiles in Alliances: Revisiting Suez." *Security Studies* 29 (2): 199–230.

Ravenstein, E. G. 1885. "The Laws of Migration." *Journal of the Statistical Society of London* 48 (2): 167–235.

Ravenstein, E. G. 1889. "The Laws of Migration." *Journal of the Statistical Society of London* 52 (2): 241–305.

Ravlo, Hilde, Nils Petter Gleditsch, and Han Dorussen. 2003. "Colonial War and the Democratic Peace." *Journal of Conflict Resolution* 47 (4): 520–548.

Ray, Victor. 2019. "A Theory of Racialized Organizations." *American Sociological Review* 84 (1): 26–53.

Rejai, Mostafa, and Cynthia H. Enloe. 1969. "Nation-States and State-Nations." *International Studies Quarterly* 13 (2): 140–158.

Reny, Tyler T., and Matt A. Barreto. 2020. "Xenophobia in the Time of Pandemic: Othering, Anti-Asian Attitudes, and COVID-19." *Politics, Groups, and Identities*, 1–24.

Reus-Smit, Christian. 2013. *Individual Rights and the Making of the International System*. London: Cambridge University Press.

Rezai, Mohammad R., Laura C. Maclagan, Linda R. Donovan, and Jack V. Tu. 2013. "Classification of Canadian Immigrants into Visible Minority Groups Using Country of Birth and Mother Tongue." *Open Medicine* 7 (4): e85–e93.

Richmond, Anthony H. 1994. *Global Apartheid: Refugees, Racism, and the New World Order*. New York: Oxford University Press.

Ringmar, Erik. 1996. "On the Ontological Status of the State." *European Journal of International Relations* 2 (4): 439–466.

Robinson, William I. 2008. *Latin America and Global Capitalism: A Critical Globalization Perspective*. Baltimore: Johns Hopkins University Press.

Rodney, Walter. 2018. *How Europe Underdeveloped Africa*. Brooklyn, NY: Verso.

Rogers, Andrei. 2010. "Requiem for the Net Migrant." *Geographical Analysis* 22 (4): 283–300.

Rosenberg, Andrew S. 2019. "Measuring Racial Bias in International Migration Flows." *International Studies Quarterly* 63 (4): 837–845.

Rosenberg, Emily S. 2012. "Transnational Currents in a Shrinking World." In *A World Connecting, 1870–1945*, edited by Emily S. Rosenberg, 813–996. Cambridge, MA: Belknap Press.

Rosière, Stéphane, and Reece Jones. 2012. "Teichopolitics: Re-considering Globalisation through the Role of Walls and Fences." *Geopolitics* 17 (1): 217–234.

Rudolph, Christopher. 2003. "Security and the Political Economy of International Migration." *American Political Science Review* 97 (4): 603–620.

Rudolph, Christopher. 2005. "Sovereignty and Territorial Borders in a Global Age." *International Studies Review* 7 (1): 1–20.

Ruggie, John Gerard. 1998. "What Makes the World Hang Together? Neo-utilitarianism and the Social Constructivist Challenge." *International Organization* 52 (4): 855–885.

Ruhs, Martin. 2013. *The Price of Rights: Regulating International Labor Migration*. Princeton, NJ: Princeton University Press.

Ruhs, Martin, and Philip Martin. 2008. "Numbers vs. Rights: Trade-Offs and Guest Worker Programs." *International Migration Review* 42 (1): 249–265.

Rupert, Mark. 1995. *Producing Hegemony: The Politics of Mass Production and American Global Power*. Cambridge, UK: Cambridge University Press.

Rutazibwa, Olivia U. 2020. "Hidden in Plain Sight: Coloniality, Capitalism and Race/ism as Far as the Eye Can See." *Millennium: Journal of International Studies* 48 (2): 221–241.

Rydgren, Jens. 2008. "Immigration Sceptics, Xenophobes or Racists? Radical Right-Wing Voting in Six West European Countries." *European Journal of Political Research* 47 (6): 737–765.

Sabaratnam, Meera. 2020. "Is IR Theory White? Racialised Subject-Positioning in Three Canonical Texts." *Millennium* 49 (1): 3–31.

Sachs, Jeffrey. 2005. *The End of Poverty: How We Can Make It Happen in Our Lifetime.* London: Penguin.

Safi, Michael. 2017. "Myanmar Treatment of Rohingya Looks Like 'Textbook Ethnic Cleansing,' Says UN." *Guardian.* [Online; posted 11-September-2017]. https://www.theguardian.com/world/2017/sep/11/un-myanmars-treatment-of-rohingya-textbook-example-of-ethnic-cleansing.

Salam, Reihan. 2016. "Why Are Immigration Advocates So Quick to Play the Race Card?" *National Review.* [Online; posted 01-July-2016]. https://www.nationalreview.com/2016/07/immigration-racism-education-less-skilled-mexican-asian-european/.

Samejima, Fumiko. 1997. "Graded Response Model." In *Handbook of Modern Item Response Theory,* edited by Wim J. van der Linden and Ronald K. Hambleton, 85–100. New York: Springer.

Sassen, Saskia. 1995. "Immigration and Local Labour Markets." In *The Economic Sociology of Immigration,* edited by A. Portes, 87–127. New York: Russell Sage Foundation.

Sassen, Saskia. 1996. *Losing Control? Sovereignty in the Age of Globalization.* New York: Columbia University Press.

Savage, I. Richard, and Karl W. Deutsch. 1960. "A Statistical Model of the Gross Analysis of Transaction Flows." *Econometrica* 28 (3): 551–572.

Schafer, Mark J. 1999. "International Nongovernmental Organizations and Third World Education in 1990: A Cross-National Study." *Sociology of Education* 72 (2): 69–88.

Schaffer, Gavin. 2007. " 'Scientific' Racism Again?: Reginald Gates, the *Mankind Quarterly* and the Question of 'Race' in Science after the Second World War." *Journal of American Studies* 41 (2): 253–278.

Schelling, Thomas C. 1971. "Dynamic Models of Segregation." *Journal of Mathematical Sociology* 1 (2): 143–186.

Scheve, Kenneth F., and Matthew J. Slaughter. 2001. "Labor Market Competition and Individual Preferences over Immigration Policy." *Review of Economics and Statistics* 83 (1): 133–145.

Schofer, Evan, Ann Hironaka, David John Frank, and Wesley Longhofer. 2012. "Sociological Institutionalism and World Society." In *The Wiley-Blackwell Companion to Political Sociology,* edited by Edwin Amenta, Kate Nash, and Alan Scott, 57–68. Chichester, UK: Wiley-Blackwell.

Schon, Justin. 2019. "Motivation and Opportunity for Conflict-Induced Migration: An Analysis of Syrian Migration Timing." *Journal of Peace Research* 56 (1): 12–27.

Schuetze, Christopher F., and Katrin Bennhold. 2020. "Head-Scarf Ban and Carbon Taxes: Austria Gets an Unlikely Government." *New York Times.* [Online; posted 08-January-2020]. https://www.nytimes.com/2020/01/02/world/europe/austria-kurz-greens-coalition-government.html.

Scott, James C. 1998. *Seeing Like a State.* New Haven, CT: Yale University Press.

Searle, John R. 1995. *The Construction of Social Reality.* New York: Free Press.

Secretary of State for the Home Department. 2018. "The UK's Future Skills-Based Immigration System." UK Parliament. https://assets.publishing.service.gov.uk/government/uploads

/system/uploads/attachment_data/file/766465/The-UKs-future-skills-based -immigration-system-print-ready.pdf.

Semyonov, Moshe, Rebeca Raijman, and Anastasia Gorodzeisky. 2006. "The Rise of Anti-foreigner Sentiment in European Societies, 1988–2000." *American Sociological Review* 71 (3): 426–449.

Sewell, Abigail A. 2016. "The Racism-Race Reification Process: A Mesolevel Political Economic Framework for Understanding Racial Health Disparities." *Sociology of Race and Ethnicity* 2 (4): 402–432.

Shachar, Ayelet. 2009. *The Birthright Lottery: Citizenship and Global Inequality.* Cambridge, MA: Harvard University Press.

Shah, Kamil. 2009. "The Failure of State Building and the Promise of State Failure: Reinterpreting the Security-Development Nexus in Haiti." *Third World Quarterly* 30 (1): 17–34.

Shanks, Cheryl. 2001. *Immigration and the Politics of American Sovereignty, 1890–1990.* Ann Arbor: University of Michigan Press.

Sharma, Nandita. 2020. *Home Rule: National Sovereignty and the Separation of Natives and Migrants.* Durham, NC: Duke University Press.

Shelby, Tommie. 2003. "Ideology, Racism, and Critical Social Theory." *Philosophical Forum* 34 (2): 153–188.

Shelby, Tommie. 2014. "Racism, Moralism, and Social Criticism." *Du Bois Review: Social Science Research on Race* 11 (1): 57–74.

Shilliam, Robbie. 2006. "What about Marcus Garvey? Race and the Transformation of Sovereignty Debate." *Review of International Studies* 32 (3): 379–400.

Shilliam, Robbie. 2013. "Race and Research Agendas." *Cambridge Review of International Affairs* 26 (1): 152–158.

Shilliam, Robbie. 2018. *Race and the Undeserving Poor.* Newcastle-upon-Tyne, UK: Agenda Publishing.

Shin, Adrian J. 2017. "Tyrants and Migrants Authoritarian Immigration Policy." *Comparative Political Studies* 50 (1): 14–40.

Shweder, Richard A. 1991. *Thinking Through Cultures: Expeditions in Cultural Psychology.* Cambridge, MA: Harvard University Press.

Sibley, David. 1995. *Geographies of Exclusion.* London: Routledge.

Silva, J. M. C., Manuel Caravana Santos, and Silvana Tenreyro. 2006. "The Log of Gravity." *Review of Economics and Statistics* 88 (4): 641–658.

Simon, Patrick. 2015. "The Choice of Ignorance: The Debate on Ethnic and Racial Statistics in France." In *Social Statistics and Ethnic Diversity,* edited by Patrick Simon, Victor Piché, and Amélie A. Gagnon, 65–88. New York: Springer.

Sjaastad, Larry A. 1962. "The Costs and Returns of Human Migration." *Journal of Political Economy* 70 (5): 80–93.

Smith, Anthony D. 1998. *Nationalism and Modernism: A Critical Survey of Recent Theories of Nations and Nationalism.* London: Routledge.

Smith, Stephen D. 2020. "Since We're Debating Labels, Stop Calling It Anti-Semitism. It's Jew Hatred." *Forward.* [Online; posted 07-July-2020]. https://forward.com/opinion/450209/since-were-debating-labels-stop-calling-it-anti-semitism-its-jew-hatred/.

Sommerer, Thomas, and Jonas Tallberg. 2019. "Diffusion across International Organizations: Connectivity and Convergence." *International Organization* 73 (2): 399–433.

Spanu, Maja. 2019. "The Hierarchical Society: The Politics of Self-Determination and the Constitution of New States after 1919." *European Journal of International Relations* 26 (2): 372–396.

Spence, Lester K. 2012. "The Neoliberal Turn in Black Politics." *Souls* 14 (3–4): 139–159.

Spencer, Herbert. 1896. *The Principles of Biology*. Vol. 1. New York: D. Appleton.

Spolaore, Enrico, and Romain Wacziarg. 2009. "The Diffusion of Development." *Quarterly Journal of Economics* 124 (2): 469–529.

Spolaore, Enrico, and Romain Wacziarg. 2016. "Globalization and Exchange Rate Policy." In *The Palgrave Handbook of Economics and Language*, edited by Victor Ginsburgh and Shlomo Weber, 221–231. London: Palgrave Macmillan.

Spolaore, Enrico, and Romain Wacziarg. 2018. "Ancestry and Development: New Evidence." *Journal of Applied Econometrics* 33 (5): 748–762.

Stan Development Team. 2020. "Stan Modeling Language Users Guide and Reference Manual, Version 2.24," https://mc-stan.org/users/documentation/.

Stevens, Jacqueline. 2011. *States without Nations: Citizenship for Mortals*. New York: Columbia University Press.

Stewart, Jeffrey. 1992. "Introduction." In *Alain Locke [1916]. Race Contacts and Interracial Relations: Lectures on the Theory and Practice of Race*, edited by Jeffrey Stewart, xix–lix. Washington, DC: Howard University Press.

Stone, Randall W. 2008. "The Scope of IMF Conditionality." *International Organization* 62 (4): 589–620.

Strang, David. 1990. "From Dependency to Sovereignty: An Event History Analysis of Decolonization 1870–1987." *American Sociological Review* 55 (6): 846–860.

Strang, David. 1991. "Global Patterns of Decolonization, 1500–1987." *International Studies Quarterly* 35 (4): 429.

Strang, David, and John W. Meyer. 1993. "Institutional Conditions for Diffusion." *Theory and Society* 22 (4): 487–511.

Strange, Susan. 1994. "Wake Up, Krasner! The World Has Changed." *Review of International Political Economy* 1 (2): 209–219.

Stumpf, Juliet. 2006. "The Crimmigration Crisis: Immigrants, Crime, and Sovereign Power." *American University Law Review* 56: 367–419.

Sullivan, Shannon, and Nancy Tuana. 2007. *Race and Epistemologies of Ignorance*. Albany, NY: SUNY Press.

Suwandi, Intan, R. Jamil Jonna, and John Bellamy Foster. 2019. "Global Commodity Chains and the New Imperialism." *Monthly Review* 70 (10): 1–24. https://doi.org/10.14452/mr-070-10-2019-03_1.

Suzuki, Shogo. 2005. "Japan's Socialization into Janus-Faced European International Society." *European Journal of International Relations* 11 (1): 137–164.

Suzuki, Shogo. 2009. *Civilization and Empire: China and Japan's Encounter with European International Society*. London: Routledge.

Sykes, Alan O. 2013. "International Cooperation on Migration: Theory and Practice." *University of Chicago Law Review* 80: 315–340.

Tannenwald, Nina. 1999. "The Nuclear Taboo: The United States and the Normative Basis of Nuclear Non-use." *International Organization* 53 (3): 433–468.

Tannock, Stuart. 2011. "Points of Prejudice: Education-Based Discrimination in Canada's Immigration System." *Antipode* 43 (4): 1330–1356.

Tessler, Hannah, Meera Choi, and Grace Kao. 2020. "The Anxiety of Being Asian American: Hate Crimes and Negative Biases during the COVID-19 Pandemic." *American Journal of Criminal Justice* 45 (4): 636–646.

Thomas, Chantal. 1999. "Causes of Inequality in the International Economic Order: Critical Race Theory and Postcolonial Development." *Transnational Law and Contemporary Problems* 9: 1.

Thomas, George M., John W. Meyer, Francisco O. Ramirez, and John Boli. 1987. *Institutional Structure: Constituting State, Society, and Individual.* Beverly Hills, CA: Sage.

Thompson, Alexander. 2015. *Channels of Power: The UN Security Council and US Statecraft in Iraq.* Ithaca, NY: Cornell University Press.

Thompson, Debra. 2013. "Through, against and beyond the Racial State: The Transnational Stratum of Race." *Cambridge Review of International Affairs* 26 (1): 133–151.

Thompson, Warren S. 1917. "Race Suicide in the United States." *Scientific Monthly* 5 (1): 22–35.

Tilley, Lisa, and Robbie Shilliam. 2007. "Special Issue: Raced Markets." *New Political Economy* 23 (5): 531–639.

Tilley, Lisa, and Robbie Shilliam. 2018. "Raced Markets: An Introduction." *New Political Economy* 23 (5): 534–543.

Tinbergen, Jan. 1962. *Shaping the World Economy: Suggestions for an International Economic Policy.* New York: Twentieth Century Fund.

Todaro, Michael P. 1969. "A Model of Labor Migration and Urban Unemployment in Less Developed Countries." *American Economic Review* 59 (1): 138–148.

Torpey, John. 1998. "Coming and Going: On the State Monopolization of the Legitimate 'Means of Movement.'" *Sociological Theory* 16 (3): 239–259.

Torpey, John. 2000. *The Invention of the Passport: Surveillance, Citizenship and the State.* Cambridge, UK: Cambridge University Press.

Touré, Ahmed Sékou. 1978. *Strategy and Tactics of the Revolution.* Conakry, Guinea: Press Office.

Trauner, Joan B. 1978. "The Chinese as Medical Scapegoats in San Francisco, 1870–1905." *California History* 57 (1): 70–87.

Treier, Shawn, and Simon Jackman. 2008. "Democracy as a Latent Variable." *American Journal of Political Science* 52 (1): 201–217.

Ture, Kwame, and Charles V. Hamilton. 1967. *Black Power: The Politics of Liberation.* New York: Vintage Books.

Valdez, Inés. 2019. *Transnational Cosmopolitanism: Kant, Du Bois, and Justice as a Political Craft.* Cambridge, UK: Cambridge University Press.

Van de Walle, Nicolas. 2009. "The Institutional Origins of Inequality in Sub-Saharan Africa." *Annual Review of Political Science* 12: 307–327.

Vattel, Emer de. 2009. *The Law of Nations, or, Principles of the Law of Nature, Applied to the Conduct and Affairs of Nations and Sovereigns.* Indianapolis, IN: Liberty Fund.

Virdee, Satnam, and Brendan McGeever. 2017. "Racism, Crisis, Brexit." *Ethnic and Racial Studies* 41 (10): 1802–1819.

Vitalis, Robert. 2000. "The Graceful and Generous Liberal Gesture: Making Racism Invisible in American International Relations." *Millennium—Journal of International Studies* 29 (2): 331–356.

Vitalis, Robert. 2010. "The Noble American Science of Imperial Relations and Its Laws of Race Development." *Comparative Studies in Society and History* 52 (4): 909–938.

Vitalis, Robert. 2015. *White World Order, Black Power Politics: The Birth of American International Relations.* Ithaca, NY: Cornell University Press.

Vitoria, F. de, A. Pagden, and L. Lawrence. 1991. *Vitoria: Political Writings.* Cambridge, UK: Cambridge University Press.

Vucetic, Srdjan. 2011. *The Anglosphere: A Genealogy of a Racialized Identity in International Relations.* Stanford, CA: Stanford University Press.

Wallerstein, Immanuel. 2011. *The Modern World-System I: Capitalist Agriculture and the Origins of the European World-Economy in the Sixteenth Century.* Berkeley: University of California Press.

Waltz, Kenneth N. 1967. *Foreign Policy and Democratic Politics: The American and British Experience.* New York: Little, Brown & Co.

Waltz, Kenneth N. 1979. *Theory of International Politics.* Reading, MA: Addison-Wesley.

Ware, Leland. 2015. "Color-Blind Racism in France: Bias against Ethnic Minority Immigrants." *Washington University Journal of Law & Policy* 46: 185–244.

Wendt, Alexander. 1992. "Anarchy Is What States Make of It: The Social Construction of Power Politics." *International Organization* 46 (2): 391–425.

Wendt, Alexander. 1994. "Collective Identity Formation and the International State." *American Political Science Review* 88 (2): 384–396.

Wendt, Alexander. 1995. "Constructing International Politics." *International Security* 20 (1): 71.

Wendt, Alexander. 1999. *Social Theory of International Politics.* Cambridge, UK: Cambridge University Press.

Wendt, Alexander. 2000. "On the Via Media: A Response to the Critics." *Review of International Studies* 26 (1): 165–180.

Wendt, Alexander. 2001. "Driving with the Rearview Mirror: On the Rational Science of Institutional Design." *International Organization* 55 (4): 1019–1049.

Wennersten, John R., and Denise Robbins. 2017. *Rising Tides: Climate Refugees in the Twenty-First Century.* Bloomington: Indiana University Press.

Weyl, E. Glen. 2018. "The Openness-Equality Trade-Off in Global Redistribution." *Economic Journal* 128 (612): F1–F36.

Whitaker, Beth Elise. 2017. "Migration within Africa and Beyond." *African Studies Review* 60 (2): 209–220.

White, Michael J. 1983. "The Measurement of Spatial Segregation." *American Journal of Sociology* 88 (5): 1008–1018.

White House. 2019. "Remarks by President Trump on Modernizing Our Immigration System for a Stronger America." [Online; posted 16-May-2019]. https://www.whitehouse.gov/briefings-statements/remarks-president-trump-modernizing-immigration-system-stronger-america/.

Whitman, James Q. 2017. *Hitler's American Model: The United States and the Making of Race Law*. Princeton, NJ: Princeton University Press.

Wilder, Gary. 2015. *Freedom Time: Negritude, Decolonization, and the Future of the World*. Durham, NC: Duke University Press.

Williams, David R., and Chiquita Collins. 2001. "Racial Residential Segregation: A Fundamental Cause of Racial Disparities in Health." *Public Health Reports* 116 (5): 404.

Williams, David R., Risa Lavizzo-Mourey, and Rueben C. Warren. 1994. "The Concept of Race and Health Status in America." *Public Health Reports* 109 (1): 26–41.

Williams, Eric. 2021. *Capitalism and Slavery*. Chapel Hill: University of North Carolina Press.

Williams, Michael C. 2009. "Waltz, Realism and Democracy." *International Relations* 23 (3): 328–340.

Wilson, Francis. 1972. *Labour in the South African Gold Mines, 1911–1969*. Cambridge, UK: Cambridge University Press.

Wilson, Philip K 2002. "Harry Laughlin's Eugenic Crusade to Control the 'Socially Inadequate' in Progressive Era America." *Patterns of Prejudice* 36 (1): 49–67.

Wilson, William J. 1973. *Power, Racism, and Privilege: Race Relations in Theoretical and Sociohistorical Perspectives*. New York: Free Press.

Wimmer, Andreas. 2013. *Waves of War: Nationalism, State-Formation, and Ethnic Exclusion in the Modern World*. Cambridge, UK: Cambridge University Press.

Wimmer, Andreas, and Yuval Feinstein. 2016. "Still No Robust Evidence for World Polity Theory." *American Sociological Review* 81 (3): 608–615.

Wolff, Christian von, and J. H. Drake. 1934. *Jus Gentium Methodo Scientifica Pertractatum*. Oxford, UK: Clarendon Press.

World Bank. 2019. "Trade Openness". Data retrieved from World Development Indicators. https://data.worldbank.org/indicator/NE.TRD.GNFS.ZS.

Wren, Karen. 2001. "Cultural Racism: Something Rotten in the State of Denmark?" *Social & Cultural Geography* 2 (2): 141–162.

Xu, Chi, Timothy A. Kohler, Timothy M. Lenton, Jens-Christian Svenning, and Marten Scheffer. 2020. "Future of the Human Climate Niche." *Proceedings of the National Academy of Sciences* 117 (21): 11350–11355. eprint: https://www.pnas.org/content/117/21/11350.full.pdf.

Yang, Peidong. 2018. "Desiring 'Foreign Talent': Lack and Lacan in Anti-immigrant Sentiments in Singapore." *Journal of Ethnic and Migration Studies* 44 (6): 1015–1031.

Yang, Philip Q. 1999. "Sojourners or Settlers: Post-1965 Chinese Immigrants." *Journal of Asian American Studies* 2 (1): 61–91.

Yang, Philip Q. 2000. "The 'Sojourner Hypothesis' Revisited." *Diaspora: Journal of Transnational Studies* 9 (2): 235–258.

Young, Crawford. 1994. *The African Colonial State in Comparative Perspective*. New Haven, CT: Yale University Press.

Young, Iris. 2006. "Katrina: Too Much Blame, Not Enough Responsibility." *Dissent* 53 (1): 41–46.

Yudell, Michael, Dorothy Roberts, Rob DeSalle, and Sarah Tishkoff. 2016. "Taking Race Out of Human Genetics." *Science* 351 (6273): 564–565.

Zarakol, Ayşe. 2017. *Hierarchies in World Politics*. Cambridge, UK: Cambridge University Press.

Zarni, Maung, and Alice Cowley. 2014. "The Slow-Burning Genocide of Myanmar's Rohingya." *Pacific Rim Law & Policy Journal* 23: 681–752.

Zolberg, Aristide R. 2008. *A Nation by Design: Immigration Policy in the Fashioning of America.* Cambridge, MA: Harvard University Press.

Zwart, Pim de. 2011. "South African Living Standards in Global Perspective, 1835–1910." *Economic History of Developing Regions* 26 (1): 49–74.

INDEX

References to figures and tables are indicated by "f" and "t" following the page numbers.

Aalberts, Tanja E., 188
Abel, Guy, 112, 112n46, 124, 125, 159
Acemoglu, Daron, 74, 195
Adogamhe, Paul G., 238–39
Africa: anti-immigrant sentiment in, 252; arbitrary creation of borders in, 222, 247–48; border controls in, 80–81; border fences in, 248–49, 255, 255*t*; Casablanca group vs. Monrovia group, 239; civil wars in, 246; colonial institutions in, 74; colonialism's negative effects on, 177, 215–16; corruption in, 236; creation of nation-states in, 80, 80n53, 228–29; deindustrialization of, 76; effect of slave trade on, 69–70, 71n28; emigration underflows from, 136–37; free movement in, 248, 252; living standards in, 195; noncolonized areas in, 74, 78; symbolic reforms and policies in, 230, 248. *See also* colonialism; decolonization and postcolonial world; non-White world; sub-Saharan Africa; *specific countries*
Agamben, Giorgio, 48n56
Algerian war of liberation, 225
Allan, Bentley, 12
American Sociological Association, 101
Amish, 14–15
Amsterdam Institute for Social Research immigration policy dataset, 146. *See also* DEMIG policy dataset
ancestral distance measure, 155–60, 160n80, 162*t*, 164, 166, 168n100, 169–70, 169*t*, 302*f*, 302*t*
Andrews, Kehinde, 238
Anghie, Antony, 11
Anglo-European countries: anti-immigrant populism in, 254; climate change and, 283; and colonialism, 72; defined, 5n30; domestic labor in, 53; and "high modernism," 45, 47, 58–59, 60; and modern racial imperialism, 91, 270–71; political polarization in, 273; and racial hierarchy, 25–26, 100, 103, 177, 220; and systems of global governance, 11, 223, 225. *See also* colonialism; color blindness; decolonization and the postcolonial world; global North; hegemony; scientific racism
antimiscegenation laws, 48
antiracists, 99, 103–4, 172, 176, 182, 184–85
anti-Semitism, xv, xv*n*2
Appiah, Anthony, 98
Asia: border fences in, 249, 255, 255*t*, 260, 261*t*; deindustrialization of, 75; immigration to the US from, 54–55, 108; and "Peter Pan theory," 78. *See also* central Asia; *specific countries*
assimilation, refusal of, xviii, 54, 65, 280
Australia: Asian immigration to, 55; border controls in, 36; and Migration Act (1966), 166; neutrality of national interest in, 67; restrictive immigration policies

Australia (*continued*)
in, 61, 211, 213*t*; and Rohingya, 2–3, 2n8; "White Australia" policies, 1–3, 4, 6, 17, 56, 166, 266
Austrian Green party, 276
autocracies and authoritarianism: colonial promotion of, 73, 215; of postcolonial rulers, 235–36; restrictive immigration policies and, 207, 208*f*
Avdan, Nazli, 254

Barbour, Philip, 52
Barnett, Michael, 232–33
Barraclough, Geoffrey, 55
baseline model of migration, 87–88, 117, 121, 125, 126–30; colonial and cultural ties, effects of, 129; construction of, 126–27; details of, 295–98, 296*f*, 297*t*; economic and political conditions, effects of, 128–29; economic gravity model and, 130–31; fixed effects vs. random effects, 132n47; geographic barriers, effects of, 127; political violence, effects of, 129–30; purpose of, 126, 131–32, 171; random effects, use of, 132, 132n47, 165, 205; as regression model, 130, 163*t*, 164–65; social networks, effects of, 127–28; statistical model, 130–32
Bayesian approach, 118, 151, 152n70, 153
Belgium, 209–11; exploitation of Congo by, 195
Bernier, François, 16
bias. *See* measurement of racial bias; migration bias; racial bias
Boas, Franz, 102
Bonilla-Silva, Eduardo, 274
border control: in DEMIG policy dataset, 146, 148, 148*t*, 149*f*; democracy's principles predicated on, 275; future role of, 269; intentionality in, 22–23; postcolonial states and, 80–81, 85, 221–22, 247–52, 254; right of sovereign states to, 6, 8–11, 33, 35–42, 35n14, 51, 58, 93, 267, 268, 274–75, 277, 280; in US immigration policy, 152, 152*t*. *See also* border fences; Expansion of Closure hypothesis
border fences, 11, 84, 248–49, 255, 255*t*, 259*t*, 260–64, 263*f*, 268; count by region (2014), 255, 255*t*; economic shocks and, 257, 259*t*, 260, 261; and expansion of closure, 29, 86, 87*f*, 252–66; international organization membership and, 250, 251*f*, 256–66, 259*t*, 265*f*, 267; liberal democracies and, 257, 259*t*, 260, 261; militarized interstate dispute (MID) and, 257, 259*t*, 260, 261; symbolic value of, 86, 90–91, 231, 248, 252, 254; terrorism fears and, 257–58, 259*t*, 260; world polity theory and, 248–49, 252–53, 256, 266. *See also* Expansion of Closure hypothesis
Botswana: border controls in, 81; economic development in, 195; political development in, 192
Brazil: economic development in, 78; exploitation of, 186; slavery and, 69
Brexit referendum (2016), 4, 8, 33
Britain. *See* England/United Kingdom
Bunche, Ralph, 25
Burlingame Treaty, 32
Burundi, colonialism's effect on political development in, 192
Buzan, Barry, 45n46, 47

Cameron, David, 5
Campbell, David, 180
Canada: immigration policy changes in, 61, 148–50, 149*f*; racial classifications in, 139
capitalism. *See* free market capitalism
Carter, David B., 254–55
Casablanca group, 238
Catholics and Catholic Church, 44, 51
Center for Systemic Peace's Major Episodes of Political Violence and Conflict Regions dataset, 257
central Asia: border fences in, 249, 255, 255*t*, 260, 261*t*; emigration underflows in, 136*t*, 137

CEPII (French government research center), 126–27
Césaire, Aimé, 19
Chae Chan Ping v. United States (1889), 32–33
charity and moral duty, 39–40, 44
Checkel, Jeffrey, 244–45
Chetail, Vincent, 38
China: economic growth and development of, 75, 75*t*, 78, 196; Han status in, 47; immigration to US from, 31–34, 54–56, 97, 139–40, 280; Western immigration policies toward, 175, 196, 201, 280; Western views of, 105, 196
Chinese Exclusion Act (1882), 31–33, 55–56, 55n75, 139–40, 266
Chinese Exclusion Case (1889), 32–33
The CIA World Factbook, 139
City of New York v. Miln (1834), 52
Clemens, Michael, 273
climate crisis, recognition of, 12–13, 270, 276, 282–83, 285, 287
closure of borders. *See* border control; border fences
collective identity. *See* nationalism
collective intentionality. *See* intentionality
Collier, Paul, 216, 273n15
colonialism, 11, 14, 16, 19–20, 24, 29, 62–63, 67–69, 73, 77–86, 91, 93, 107, 173, 175–76, 186, 177–78, 199–200, 201–18, 266–69, 275; and arbitrary boundaries, 198–99, 222, 236, 247; and indigenous populations, 70, 73; economic consequences of, 193–98, 268; European institutions and, 74–75, 84, 195–96, 229, 266; and exploitation, 72–79, 177, 195, 215; heterogeneous nature of, 194–95; in North America, 51; and perceptions of the non-White world, 76–77; political consequences of, 198–201, 268; psychological impact of, 215; and racial hierarchy, 25, 103, 186–87, 199–200; residual racism and, 4, 7, 8, 10, 29; scientific racism and, 192, 199, 215; and violence, 73, 76, 79, 175, 191, 199–200; Vitoria on, 36, 37n24
Colonial Legacy hypothesis, 89–90, 203–9
color blindness: in Anglo-European and OECD state policies, 91–92, 270; in Australia, 1, 3, 6; ecological fallacy and, 294; effect of, on non-White migrants, 61, 63; false pretenses of, xvii, xvii*n*11, 3, 10–11; and institutional racism, 24, 62, 94, 103–4, 110, 111n42; neutrality of national interest and, 64–67; racism hidden by, 5–7, 9, 12, 23, 27, 62–63, 67, 79, 89–90, 105–6, 108–9, 116, 144, 151, 266–67, 271, 270, 274, 277–79; residual racism and, 4, 5–6, 9, 63, 77, 93, 144, 252, 269; unmasking racial inequality in, 11, 15, 24, 28, 62, 88, 94, 103–4, 110, 111n42, 114, 116–73, 217, 268. *See also* migration bias; national security and national interest; racial bias; residual racism
conflict. *See* violence and conflict
Congo: exploitation of, 195; violence in, 199
conscription rights. *See* taxation and conscription rights of nation-states
constitutive relations of power, 233
construct equivalence, 16. *See also* cross-national measurement of race
constructivism: definition of, 179; on international organizations, 250n108; in international relations theory, 290–92; objectivist, 183; positivist, 180–82; postmodern, 180–82, 198. *See also* racial constructivism
Cook-Martin, David, 55, 279–80
Coolidge, Calvin, xvii
Cornell, Stephen, 16–17
Correlates of War project, 257
corruption, 50, 198, 199, 236
cosmopolitanism, 283, 283n58
COVID-19 pandemic, 182, 201, 284–85
cross-national measurement of race, 16, 112–13, 118, 124
cuius regio eius religio principle, 40

Darwinism, 48
Dawson, Andrew, 199
decolonization and postcolonial world, 7, 28, 79–86; and antagonism toward Anglo-European states, 231; border control as norm in, 80–81, 85, 221–22, 247–52, 254; and border fences, 248–49, 255, 255*t*, 259*t*, 260–64, 263*f*, 268; Colonial Legacy hypothesis in, 89–90, 203–9; correlational aspects of racism in, 108–9; corruption in, 198, 199; creation of sovereign states in, 84–85, 220–23, 234–35, 248, 253; dependency on former colonial powers in, 72, 78–79, 196, 219, 229; despotism and lack of political stability in, 199–201, 215; economic development and, 71, 80–81, 175, 193–98; Expansion of Closure hypothesis, 79, 90–91, 254, 256, 261–62; and exploitation by Anglo-European states, 19–20, 186, 221; and false equality, 10, 219; and former colonizers' restrictive immigration policies, 29, 145–50, 171, 203, 209–14, 210*t*, 212*f*, 216; global society and, 10–11, 219; and intentionality, 23; interventionist world order in, 189–90; nation-state form adopted by, 20–21, 79–81, 80n53, 85, 107, 220–29, 234–37, 243, 247–54, 256, 266–67; political institutions in, 198–201, 228; racial hierarchy of, 185–91; resistance movements and, 237–40; restrictive ideology of sovereignty in, 62, 64, 80, 91, 187–88, 250; viewing other postcolonial subjects through colonizer's lens, 106–7; symbolic reforms and policies in, 229–31, 231n38, 241, 248, 252–54; violence in, 199–200, 215, 257; Western states' acquiescence to, 20, 220, 230; Western views of, 68–69, 72–73, 98–99, 105–6, 161, 186–91, 192, 216; WTO standards reinforcing inequality in, 188. *See also* global South; non-White world
decoupling, 83–84, 85, 227–32
De Haas, Hein, 118n5, 145
DEMIG policy dataset (18th century through 2013), 146–50, 147–48*t*, 149*f*, 154*f*, 156–57*f*, 203, 209
democracy. *See* liberal democracies
Democratic Republic of Congo, violence in, 199
Denmark: colonial history's effect on immigration policies in, 209–11, 213*t*; immigration policy changes in, 148–50, 149*f*, 169–70
dependency theory, 196–98
deportation and exit policies, 148, 149*f*; in US immigration policy, 152, 152*t*
desirable immigrants, 9, 34; high-status workers as, 97; from OECD states, 137; Pufendorf on, 39; Vatel on, 41. *See also* undesirable immigrants
Doty, Roxanne, 26, 27–28
Du Bois, W.E.B.: "The African Roots of War" (essay), 9–10, 69, 177; on colonialism and racial imperialism, 62, 63, 91; compared to Garvey, 238; on colonial world views in twentieth-century politics, 77, 176–77; contributions to international relations theory by, 287; definition of race by, 20; on end of slave trade, 71; and "global color line," 134, 176–77; quantitative study by, 288n79
Duda, Andrzej, 5
Dutton, Peter, 2–3
Duvall, Raymond, 232–33

East African Community, 235
eastern Europe: immigration from (late nineteenth/early twentieth century), 56. *See also specific countries*
ecological fallacy, 106n30, 194, 294
economic development: border fences and, 257, 259*t*, 260, 261; colonialism and, 175, 193–98; education level and, 82, 128; GDP shocks and immigration policies, 163*t*, 164, 166, 204, 304–7*t*; immigration based on perceived economic benefits in

destination state, 128, 161, 286; inflation rates and immigration policies, 163*t*, 164, 204, 304–7*t*; neoliberal model of, 81; as priority for postcolonial states, 78, 80–81; share of world GDP for India, China, and Europe (1700–1952), 75, 75*t*; trade openness and immigration policies, 163*t*, 164, 204, 206*t*, 285, 304–7*t*
economic gravity model, 130–31
economic migrants, 38, 42, 52, 56, 202
education, 82, 128
England/United Kingdom: Aliens Act (1905), 56; border controls in, 36; colonial history's effect on immigration policies in, 211–14, 213*t*, 214*f*; colonial political institutions of, 199; free trade and, 188; immigration policy changes in, 53, 61, 148–50, 149*f*, 169; industrialization and colonial expropriation by, 195. *See also* Brexit referendum
English School scholars, 219, 224, 292
Enlightenment philosophy, 45, 47, 178
entry and exclusion. *See* border control; border fences; state sovereignty
ethnic fractionalization in Africa: due to colonial rule, 199, 215; due to slave trade, 70
ethnicity: definition of, 17; distinct from race, 17; interdependence with race, 17–18; Locke's racial ontology and, 18. *See also* ethnic fractionalization in Africa
ethnonationalistic fervor, 49
eugenics, xv–xvii, 48, 55, 57, 65, 93, 102. *See also* scientific racism
Eurocentrism, 182, 187, 190
European immigrants, 56–57, 108
European Union: 2015 migrant crisis, 254; border fences in, 255, 255*t*, 260, 261*t*; Schengen Area, 281; and Turkey, 285
exclusionary politics, 4–8, 144, 273, 276, 281. *See also* border control; border fences; state sovereignty
Expansion of Closure hypothesis, 79, 90–91, 254, 256, 261–62
explicit racism: chattel slavery and, 69–72, 183; colonialism and, 69–72, 287; color blindness superseding, 6, 61, 95, 97, 108, 116, 172, 271; immigration policies driven by, 6, 23, 63, 97n5, 172, 272; international politics shaped by, 268, 288; as no longer legally acceptable, 63, 77, 150, 277; persistence of, 269
exploitation of non-White world: after decolonization, 19–20, 186, 221; colonialism and, 72–79, 177, 195

failed states, 189
Fair Housing Act (1968), 13
Fanon, Frantz, 19–20, 62, 63, 77, 79, 91, 215
feminism, 292
First Amendment, 66, 66n14
fiscal costs of immigration policies, xvii, 286
Fitzgerald, David, 55, 279–80
France: colonial history and immigration policies in, 209–11; immigration policy changes in, 148–50, 149*f*, 153; integration of immigrants in, 14, lack of racial measurements in, 113, 140
Frazier, E. Franklin, 25
freedom of movement: EU Schengen Area and, 281; in global South, 222, 222n17; Grotius on, 37–38, 40, 42; labor market expansion and, 44; in precolonial period, 43, 50–51, 81, 222, 247–48, 252, 267; Pufendorf on, 38–39; regional zones of, 285; right of natural partnership and communication and, 36–37; Vatel on, 40–41; Vitoria on, 36–38, 37n22, 42
Freeman, Gary, 112
free market capitalism, 5, 105, 110, 233, 293–94

The Gambia, UN membership of, 235
Garvey, Marcus, 238
George III (king of England), 51
Germany: colonial history and immigration policies in, 209–11, 213*t*; immigration to

Germany (*continued*)
US from, 53; language requirement in immigration policy of, 24
Gilley, Bruce, 183n28
globalization: after decolonization, 10–11, 219; and diffusion of hegemonic norms of Anglo-European states, 265–66; first wave of, 52–53, 224; more restrictive immigration resulting from, 281–82
global North: asymmetry in immigration interests with global South, 286; climate refugees coming to, 282–83; color-blind immigration policies of, 91–92; color line along global North–global South divide, 134; economic development of, 134; emigration overflow from, 136*t*, 137; immigration policies, restrictiveness of, 4, 85, 115, 161, 170, 202, 260; migrants from, 29. *See also* Anglo-European countries; colonialism
global South: border fences in, 11, 29, 260–61; climate change's effect on, 282; colonialism's effects in, 175, 216, 219; and color line, 134; and dependency on former colonial powers, 79, 229; dependency theory and, 196–98; effects of European colonialism in, 71, 175, 193–98; emigration underflows from, 136*t*, 137, 171; and hegemonic norms, 265–66; immigration from other states within, 222; immigration to Europe from, 54; presumptions about immigrants from, 78, 201, 204, 269; racial inequality in immigration from, 4, 11, 85, 94, 96–97, 142, 144, 170; racialized countries in, 134; slavery's effect on, 69. *See also* colonialism; decolonization and post-colonial world; non-White world; racial inequality; undesirable immigrants
Global Terrorism database, 258
good governance, setting criteria for, 13
Gramsci, Antonio, 221, 223, 233–34, 236, 237, 241, 243
Great Britain. *See* England/United Kingdom
Grotius, Hugo, 36–38; *Mare Liberum*, 37; Pufendorf compared to, 39; *The Rights of War and Peace*, 37
Group of 77, 239
Grovogui, Siba, 11, 26
guest worker regimes, 285
gun-slave cycle, 70

Hafner-Burton, Emilie M., 229
Hainmueller, Jens, 167
Haitian revolution, 71
Hamilton, Charles V.: *Black Power* (with Ture), 104, 119, 172–73
Harlem Renaissance, 18
Hartmann, Douglas, 16–17
hegemonic stability theory (HST), 234n46
hegemony: Gramsci's definition of, 233–34; within international society, 231–43; resistance movements and, 237–40; of the West, 64, 80, 82, 84–86, 90, 92, 221–22, 248, 253; of world culture, 240–43
Heldring, Leander, and James A. Robinson, 194–95
Henderson, Errol A., 25–27, 102n20, 155n71, 182, 228, 236n52, 238, 241n80, 253, 287n77; *African Realism?*, 246–47
high modernism, 31, 45, 47–52, 55, 58–61
Hindu-Muslim conflict, 200
historical institutionalism, 224–26, 224n20, 227, 231, 232
Hitler, Adolf: *Mein Kampf*, xvi
Hobbes, Thomas, 38, 182
Hobson, John, 78, 182
Ho Chi Minh, 240
Holocaust, xvii, 61
hospitality law and tradition, 36–37, 37n24, 38n28, 39
housing segregation, evidence of, 13, 19, 21–22
Howard School, 25
Huckabee, Mike, 275
Human Genome Project, 13

Hungary, 56, 67
Hunt, Michael H., 106n33

Iceland, immigration policies in, 153, 169, 213–14, 214*f*
Immigration Act (1924), xvi–xvii, 56–57, 108
Immigration and Nationality Act (1965), 66
immigration policies: factors behind, 6–7; in future, 29, 279–83; Grotius on, 37–38, 40, 42; lack of data affecting studies of, 95, 111–13. *See also* quota systems; scientific racism; undesirable immigrants
income and migration bias, 133–39, 135*f*, 136*t*
India: and Bangladesh border, 249; effect of colonialism on GDP of, 75, 75*t*; and Muslim-Hindu conflict, 200
indigenous populations: categorization of, 19, 74, 191, 200; effects of colonialization on, 191
Indonesia: as colonial state, 203; immigration policies of, 211
Industrial Revolution, 44, 75, 224
institutionalism. *See* historical institutionalism
institutional racism. *See* structural racism
integration (postentry rights of immigrants), 146–49, 149*f*; in US immigration policy, 152, 152*t*
intentionality, xvii, 20–24, 94, 99–100, 104, 172
international cooperation: on climate change, 283; on immigration, 285–87; COVID-19 pandemic and, 284–85
international law: and admission of foreigners, 36, 286; colonial biases continued in, 11; and exclusion of foreigners, 28, 33–34, 41–42, 52, 58; Vitoria and, 36
International Monetary Fund (IMF), 242, 248n104
international organizations, 240–48, 248n104, 250, 250n108, 251*f*, 253, 266–67, 268; border fences and, 250, 251*f*, 256–66, 259*t*, 265*f*, 267
international political economy (IPE): British approach to, 289, 290n87; implications for scholarship of, 288–90
international politics: constructivism and, 179–80; future of, 269–70, 278; nation-state as unit of (19th century), 44; study of race and racism in, 22, 24–28, 95, 287–88
international relations scholarship: constructivism and, 179, 182; definition of hegemony and, 234; Eurocentrism and, 182–83; hierarchies in, 186–87, 218; history of, 25–28, 269; paradigms of, 290–92; and study of racial inequality, 109, 269, 287–88; Teaching, Research, and International Policy (TRIP) survey (2017), 291
interventionist world order, 189–90
IPE. *See* international political economy
Ireland, immigration to US from, 53
Israel, 211, 213*t*
Italy: colonial history and immigration policies in, 209–11; immigration policy changes in, 148*t*; immigration to US from, 53, 56

Japan: colonial history and immigration policies in, 209–11; immigration policy changes in, 148–50, 149*f*
Japanese American internment (WWII), 33n8
Jew hatred, xv–xvii, xv*n2*
Jewish immigrants, xv, xviii, 293–94
Jim Crow, 20
Johnson, Boris, 5
Johnson, Simon, 195
Joppke, Christian, 53, 56

Kaczyński, Jarosław, 5
Kant, Immanuel, 16, 47, 182, 183
Kaplan, Robert, 216
Keegan, John, 254
Kendi, Ibram, 184–85
Kenya, 136

Kenyatta, Jomo, 240
Kleindiest v. Mandel (1972), 66n14
Krasner, Stephen, 292
Krishna, Sankaran, 26, 27–28

labor: anti-immigrant policies and shortage of, 280; colonial exploitation of, 72–79; developed states' expropriation of, 197; freedom of movement and, 44; guest worker regimes, 285; hegemony and, 234; and migration of low-skilled workers, 279; and migration of skilled workers, 56, 81, 145, 193; protectionism and, 282; and value of technical vs. nontechnical skills, 95–96, 97
Lake, David, 290–91
Lange, Matthew, 199
Latin America: border fences in, 249, 255, 255*t*, 260, 261*t*; colonial institutions in, 74; corruption in, 236; deindustrialization of, 75; emigration overflow from, 136*t*, 137; immigration policies in, 61; slave trade and slavery in, 69; US immigration policies toward, 137. *See also* colonialism; decolonization and postcolonial world; *specific countries*
Law and Justice Party (Poland), 280
Lawson, George, 45n46, 47
League of Nations, 226
legal entry and stay, 146–49, 149*f*; in US immigration policy, 152, 152*t*
legal positivism. *See* positivism
legitimacy of new nation-states. *See* decolonization and postcolonial world; modern nation-state's rise
Lesotho, UN membership of, 235
liberal democracies: bolstered by and bolstering of racism, 280; border fences and, 257, 259*t*, 260, 261; liberal imperialism of, 291n94; restrictive immigration policies and, 5, 163*t*, 165, 166–70, 168*f*, 204–5, 206*t*, 207–9, 208*f*, 275, 280, 303*f*, 304–7*t*; totalitarianism and, 48n56; trade-off between volume and rights in immigration policies, 145–46; weak vs. strong liberal democracies, restrictive immigration policies in, 207–8, 208*f*
liberalism, 45n46, 178, 275, 280–81, 290–92
Lincoln, Abraham, 184
Ling, L.H.M., 26
Locke, Alain: Howard School and, 25; and international relations theory, 287; and race as social construction, 18, 95, 101–3, 105, 137, 140–41, 141n56, 159–60, 176, 177, 270
Locke, John, 182
Logan, Rayford, 25
Lumumba, Patrice, 240

Machel, Samora, 240
macrophenomenological perspective, 82, 82n61, 227
Malm, Andreas, 282n55
Mamdani, Mahmood, 236
Mangwana, Nick, 249
Manning, Patrick, 70
Mao Zedong, 240
Marr, Wilhelm, xv*n*2
Martin, Philip, 145–46
Marxism, 110, 197, 289, 292
materialism, 181
McKeown, Adam, 9n49, 35n14
Mearsheimer, John, 243–44, 290–91
measurement of racial bias, 28–29, 119–44; Abel and Sander on bilateral flows, 124; ancestral distance measure and, 155–60, 160n80, 162*t*, 164, 166, 168n100, 169–70, 169*t*, 302*f*, 302*t*; anti-Black and anti-African racism in, 160–62, 162*t*; Bayesian approach to counterfactual model, 118; Canadian public health scholars' measurement of race, 139; Colonial Legacy hypothesis, 89–90, 203–9; cross-national, 16, 112–13, 118, 124; dyadic migration deviations for Italy (2000), 122, 122*t*; Expansion of Closure hypothesis, 90–91; graded response model and, 151–53, 152n70, 152*t*, 156–57*f*, 298–99;

migration bias, 120–24; migration flow data, 124–26; need for, 11–15; nonlinear, kernel-based interaction technique, 167–68, 168*f*, 300, 303*f*; pseudoscientific approach to race and, 15, 25, 71n28, 98, 100n11, 113, 139, 141, 159; Racial Bias hypothesis, 86–88, 124; Racial Reaction hypothesis, 88–89, 145; sending-state migration deviations for Italy (2000), 123, 123*t*; strategy for, 117, 121–24; United Nations World Population Prospects (WPP) demographic data (2000–2015), 125, 125*f*; World Bank bilateral migration stocks (1960–1995), 125, 125*f*, 204; zero inflation and, 125–26, 126*f*, 131, 204. *See also* baseline model of migration; racial bias
medical restrictions on immigration, 92
Mexican immigrants, 99. *See also* global South
Meyer, John W., 81, 83, 221, 231
Middle East: border fences in, 249, 255, 255*t*, 260, 261*t*; corruption in, 236; deindustrialization of, 75; effect of racial difference on migration policies in, 160–62, 162*t*; emigration underflows from, 136*t*, 137; undesirable immigrants from, 106. *See also specific countries*
migration bias: definition of bias, 120; in post–WWII era, 133*f*, 142; region and income and, 133–39, 135*f*, 136*t*; trends in, 132–44, 133*f*. *See also* racial bias
Mill, John Stuart, 280
Miller, David, 216
Miller, John Franklin, 31
Mills, Charles, 100, 178
Mkandawire, Thandika, 27, 235
modern nation-states, 28, 223–26; Agamben on, 48n56; and border control, 6, 8–11, 33, 35–42, 35n14, 51, 58, 93, 267, 268, 274–75, 277, 280; decolonization and, 20–21, 79–80, 107, 220–27, 228, 234–37, 243, 248, 253, 266; decoupling and, 83–84, 85, 227–32; high modernism and, 31, 45, 47–52, 55, 58–61; and nationalism, 30–31, 45–46, 49, 58–59, 60, 220, 224–25, 268; in nineteenth century, 44–45, 58, 275; as only legitimate model in international system, 80, 84, 223, 226, 234, 253; popular sovereignty and, 43–46, 50–51, 60, 223; and racism, 28, 30–31, 46–49, 58–59, 268; regulation of movement and, 44; world culture's role in, 83, 226–27, 240–43; world polity (world society) theory and, 9, 81–83, 90, 221. *See also* taxation and conscription rights of nation-states
Monrovia group, 238
Montesquieu: *Spirit of the Laws*, 47
Morgenthau, Hans, 64
Mozambique: border controls in, 81; White settler colonies in, 192
Mugabe, Robert Gabriel, 240
Muslims, 2, 8, 66, 99, 170, 200, 237, 277
Myanmar, 2–3, 2n8

Namibia, border controls in, 81
Napoleon, 71
national interest. *See* national security and national interest
nationalism: colonial powers and, 236; and identity, 45–46, 224; modern nation-state and, 30–31, 45–46, 49, 58–59, 60, 220, 224–25, 268; sovereignty and, 35
National Origins Quota Act. *See* Immigration Act (1924)
national security and national interest: neutrality of national interest, 63, 64–68, 93–94, 281; protection of, 278, 281; in Racial Reaction hypothesis, 88–89; as reasons to restrict immigration, 20, 63–64, 79, 89, 92, 94, 108n35, 202, 273, 274, 276
nation-states. *See* modern nation-states; state sovereignty
nativism, 6, 8, 14–15, 166
natural law, 40, 45, 178
natural selection and Darwinism, 48
Neblo, Michael, 278

Negritude movement, 225
Nehru, Jawaharlal, 240
neocolonialism, 78, 84–85, 196, 225, 289
neopatrimonialism, 236, 253
Netherlands, colonial history and immigration policies in, 211, 213*t*
neutrality, assumptions of. *See* color blindness; national security and national interest
New International Economic Order, 239
New Political Economy special edition on raced markets (2007), 289
New Zealand: immigration policies in, 36, 61; neutrality of national interest in, 67
Nielsen, Richard A., 164, 205
Nigeria: governance institutions in, 229; lack of social cohesion in, 199; undesirable immigrants from, 136
Nishimura Ekiu v. United States (1892), 35
Niyazov, Saparmurat, 249
Nkrumah, Kwame, 80n53, 225, 240
Non-Aligned Movement, 239
nonproductive immigrants. *See* undesirable immigrants
non-White world: adoption of Anglo-European models of immigration by, 20–21; border fences and, 260–61; colonial exploitation of, 72–79, 177, 195; failed states in, 189; global South equated with, 134; perceived inferiority of, 69, 71n28, 98–99, 106, 161, 177–79, 216; postcolonial exploitation of, 19–20, 186, 221; "Third World" narratives of, 76; US admission quotas for, 57; Western views of, 24, 34, 51, 54, 61, 68, 76–77, 100, 170, 200, 201, 216–17, 220, 276. *See also* Africa; global South; undesirable immigrants
norms: hegemonic, 265–66; of nation-states, 80–81, 80n53, 85, 221–22, 228–29, 247–52, 254, 256, 266–67; of state sovereignty, 260
Norway: and climate refugees, 283; immigration policy changes in, 169–70
Nyerere, Julius, 235
Obama, Barack: assimilationism and, 184; immigration policy of, 138
Obasogie, Osagie K, 160n80
objective criteria, use of, 3. *See also* color blindness; national security and national interest; poverty; undesirable immigrants
OECD datasets on immigration policies, 112
OECD states. *See* Anglo-European countries; global North
open economy politics (OEP), 288–89
Orbán, Victor, 5, 67
Organization of African Unity (OAU), 238
Ottoman Empire: dissolution of, 225; exploitation of, 186; governance institutions in, 229; and immigration to Europe, 54
ÖVP (Austrian political party), 276
Oxford University immigration policy dataset, 146. *See also* DEMIG policy dataset

Pakistan, 200
Pan-African Congress (1945), 240, 240n72
Pan-Africanism, 237
Pandya, Sonal S., 27
Pan-Islamism, 237
Paris, Roland, 242
Paris Exposition Universelle (1889), 192
passport and visa systems: creation of, 34, 231; vaccine passport, 284; visa waivers, 92
Peace of Augsburg (1555), 40
Penn World Table, 128, 164
Persaud, Randolph, 26–27
persistence of racial inequality. *See* racial inequality; residual racism
"Peter Pan theory," 78
Peters, Margaret E., 118n5, 151, 152n70, 164, 216
Philippines, 76
Piketty, Thomas, 284
Ping, Chae Chan, 32
plenary power doctrine, 32–33, 66, 275

Poland, immigration policies of, 280
politics. *See* exclusionary politics
popular sovereignty, 43–46, 50–51, 60, 223
populism, 4, 220, 224, 254
Portugal, immigration policies in, 169, 211, 213*t*
positivism, 27–28, 40, 176, 289; positivist constructivism, 180–82
Post, Paul, 254–55
postcolonial world. *See* decolonization and postcolonial world
postcommunist states, emigration underflows from, 136*t*, 137
postmodern constructivism, 180–82
poverty, 8, 51, 68, 73, 76, 78, 108, 201; Colonial Legacy hypothesis and, 90; rich-poor gap, 73, 83–84
Powers, Kathy, 241n80
PRIO armed conflict dataset, 129–30, 165, 204
Pritchett, Lant, 273
Prussia, 53
Pufendorf, Samuel, 42; *The Law of Nature and Nations*, 38–40

Qatar, 193
quota systems, 57–58; Immigration Act (1924), xvi–xvii, 56–57, 108; neoliberal theories on, 88

race: construct equivalence and, 16; correlation with income and region of, 134–35; country of origin and, 139; cultural determination of, 47, 100, 102–3, 106, 160; as distinct from ethnicity, 17; hierarchy of, 25–26, 47, 100; history of term, 16, 102, 114; inherent problems in study of, 27, 109–13, 134, 139; as interdependent with ethnicity, 17–18; as international concept, 20, 99–100; lack of scientific basis for, 15, 17–18, 101–3, 107, 140, 177, 179, 184, 270; Locke and, 18, 95, 101–3, 105, 137, 140–41, 141n56, 159–60, 176, 177, 270; meaning of, 14–15, 16–17, 100–101, 114; Montesquieu's definition of, 47; observable markers for, 47; permanency of, 18; and quotas, 57–58; Theodore Roosevelt and, 55; social construction of, 15, 17–18, 20, 95, 101–3, 105, 107, 137, 140–41, 159–60, 176, 177, 184, 270. *See also* White supremacy
race-neutral laws, 4, 6, 12, 20, 63–64, 93, 104. *See also* color blindness
racial bias, 28, 139–70, 141*f*, 143*f*; color blindess and, 144; definition and use of, 119–21; immigration policies and, 145–55; Racial Bias hypothesis, 86–88, 124, 139; Racial Reaction hypothesis, 88–89, 145. *See also* measurement of racial bias
racial constructivism, 15, 18, 68–69, 98, 101–3, 160, 176, 185; positivist, 182–85
racial contextualism, 94, 99–100, 101
racial eliminativism, 14–15, 94, 97–99, 101, 102
racial inequality, 16–20; in absence of overt racism, 12, 172; border control and, 267; as collective action problem, 12; and Colonial Legacy hypothesis, 89–90, 203–9; and Expansion of Closure hypothesis, 79, 90–91, 254, 256, 261–62; forensic evidence of, 117; future implications for, 270–74, 277–78; globalization and, 10; methods for measurement of, 11–15; and migration within the global South, 11, 85; model for migration in world without, 87–88; persistence of, 9, 28–29, 61, 62n8, 68, 77–78, 88, 91, 93–94, 107, 109, 175, 190–91, 219, 220, 252, 266–67, 271; problems in study of, 13, 109, 138; and Racial Bias hypothesis, 86–88, 124; and Racial Reaction hypothesis, 88–89, 145; responsibility for, 277–78; unmasking of, 11, 15, 24, 28, 62, 88, 94, 103–4, 110, 111n42, 114, 116–73, 217, 268. *See also* racial bias; undesirable immigrants
racial skeptics, 94, 96–97, 101, 120–21, 270
racism: Anglo-European models of sovereignty and, 20–21; in Australian immigration policies, 1–3; contemporary

racism (*continued*)
manifestations of, 270–74; correlational aspects of, 108–9; cultural, 47, 281; definition of, 18–19, 23, 100–101, 177; in post–Cold War era, 5, 13, 144–45; and high vs. low cultures, 53, 56; and housing segregation, 13, 19, 21–22; ideology of, 103–7, 109–11, 116; incentives for, 185, 271; individuals' role in perpetuation of, 271; inherent problems in study of, 27, 109; intentionality and, xvii, 20–24, 94, 99–100, 172; as international concept, 20, 100; in international politics, 22, 24–28, 95; erasure of history of, 25–26; modern nation-states and, 28, 30–31, 46–49, 58–59, 268; principled conservatives and, 278; racial prejudice distinguished from, 177; racism-race reification process, 19, 101, 106, 113; reluctant, 272–73; as social construct, 182; symbolic, 29, 99, 271, 294; types of, 272–73, 278; US foreign policy informed by, 106n33. *See also* color blindness; explicit racism; residual racism; scientific racism; structural racism; undesirable immigrants
rationalism, 28, 31, 35, 47, 82, 179
Real ID Act (2005), 148, 148*t*
realist theories, 82n61, 219, 227, 231, 232, 278, 290–92
realpolitik, 243–44
redlining, 13, 19, 21
Reed, David, 57
refugees, 2–3, 38, 129–30, 145, 148, 252; climate refugees, 282–83
regional trade agreements, 241n80, 285
residual racism, 4, 5–6, 9, 11, 63, 77, 93, 144, 186–91, 252, 269, 271; colonialism and, 4, 7, 8, 10, 29, 266
resistance movements, 237–40
Responsibility-to-Protect Doctrine (R2P), 189–90
Rezai, Mohammad R., 140–41
Roberts, John G., 66
Robinson, James A., 74, 194, 195
Rohingya, 2–3, 2n8
Roosevelt, Theodore, 55, 76
Rudolph, Christopher, 164
Ruhs, Martin, 145–46
Russia, 211

Sander, Nikola, 112n46, 124
Scalia, Antonin, 36
Schelling, Thomas C., 109, 172
scientific racism: anti-Semitism as, xv; colonialism based on, 192, 199, 215; cultural practice and, 18; Human Genome Project and, 13; immigration policies and, 50–58, 279; modern biology and Darwinism associated with, 48, 48n56; modern state's adoption of, 9, 30–32, 35, 46–49, 58–59, 93; in nineteenth century, 45n46, 225; as no longer socially acceptable, 93
Scott, James, 44–45
Second Industrial Revolution, 225
securitization theory. *See* national security and national interest
Sewell, Abigail, 19
Shelby, Tommie, 111n42
Shilliam, Robbie, 26, 270, 289
Sierra Leone: effects of colonialism in, 192, 199; governance institutions in, 229
Slapak, Bluma (Beatrice), xv, xvii
slavery and slave trade, 10, 69–72, 79, 144, 177
Slovak Republic, 211, 213*t*
social class: and capitalist hegemonic order, 233–34; nationalism's effect on, 45–46
Somalia: and anti-immigrant sentiment, 252; effects of colonialism in, 192, 199; governance institutions in, 229
South Africa: border controls in, 81; border fence in, 249; colonial institutions in, 74; as colonial state, 203; economic development of, 78; immigration policy changes in, 148–50, 149*f*; immigration to Australia from, 2–3, 2n8; White minority in, 160
South Sudan, 229
sovereignty. *See* state sovereignty

Spain: colonialism of, 36–37; immigration policies in, 169, 211
Spanish-American War, 76
Spencer, Herbert, 48
Spolaore, Enrico, 164
state sovereignty, 30–59; adaptability of, 292; decolonization and, 220–21; and exclusion of foreigners, 28, 33–34, 42, 52, 58; interventionist world order and, 189–90; norms of, 260; and passport and visa systems, 34, 231; Peace of Augsburg (1555) and, 40; police power of, 51; in postcolonial world, 62, 64, 80, 91, 187–88, 250; and principle of sovereign equality, 188–89; racism and, 8, 28, 50–58; and recognition of new states, 224; reconception of, 269, 277, 292n98; and right to enter/exclude, 28–35, 39–40, 40n34, 42, 52, 54, 58, 64–65, 90, 92, 217, 268; symbolic policies of, 248, 252, 253–54; Treaty of Westphalia (1648) and, 40; Vatel on, 30, 40; White supremacy and, 42–50. *See also* border control; border fences
Statistics Canada, 139
structural racism: collective intentionality and, 22, 24, 94; color-blind immigration policies and, 62; constructivism and, 103–4; future manifestations of, 271; as global ideology, 4, 110–11; need to reveal, 172–73, 288; Shelby on, 111n42
structural realism, 179
sub-Saharan Africa: border fences in, 255, 255*t*, 260, 261*t*; emigration underflows from, 136*t*, 137, 138*f*, 171, 302*f*; lack of economic development in, 194; migrants within, 252
Supreme Court, U.S.: and border control, 35–36; Chinese Exclusion Case (1889), 32–33; and "Muslim ban," 66; and national interest, 66n14; and regulation of entry, 52
Sweden: and climate refugees, 283; immigration policy changes in, 148–50, 148*t*, 149*f*
symbolic racism, 29, 99, 271, 294
Syrian Civil War, refugees from, 283

Tanganyika African National Union (TANU), 235
Tannenwald, Nina, 180
Tanzania, 235
Tate, Merze, 25, 287
taxation and conscription rights of nation-states, 19, 27, 34, 49, 58, 207, 220, 223
terrorism, 257–58, 259*t*, 260
Tilley, Lisa, 270, 289
Torpey, John, 44
totalitarianism, 48n56
Touré, Ahmed Sékou, 240
trade openness. *See* economic development
Treaty of Westphalia (1648), 8, 40
Trump, Donald: on Australian immigration policies, 3; and border wall, 254; immigration policy of, 9, 138; and "Muslim ban," 66
Tsutsui, Kiyoteru, 229
Ture, Kwame: *Black Power* (with Hamilton), 104, 119, 172–73
Turkey: governance institutions in, 229; and Middle Eastern refugees, 285
Turnbull, Malcolm, 2–3
Type I socialization, 244–45, 250
Type II socialization, 245, 247

UCDP/PRIO armed conflict dataset, 129–30
Uganda, 229
Ukraine, 203
underdevelopment, theories of, 193, 196–98, 215
undesirable immigrants: African regions and, 136; Anglo-European designation of, 115; colonialism's role in creating, 20, 24, 62–63, 67–69, 73, 78, 79–86, 89–91, 173, 176–77, 201–17, 218, 266, 268, 275; in Colonial Legacy hypothesis, 89–90, 203–9; color and, 69, 91–92, 177;

undesirable immigrants (*continued*)
criminals as, 37, 51; as dangerous, xvii–xviii, 50, 55, 59, 60, 63, 68, 76–77, 78, 105, 201, 204, 269, 273, 294; European races as, 56; false information about, 23, 105, 175, 181, 191, 201, 272; and group-level screening policies, 55–56, 106; inherent characteristics of, 10, 17, 48–49, 53–54, 73, 76, 97–98, 100, 102, 106–9, 276; non-White immigrants as, 24, 34, 51, 54, 61, 68, 76, 100, 170, 200, 201, 216–17, 220, 276; North American colonies and, 51; in Racial Reaction hypothesis, 88–89, 145; slavery and, 71; sovereign right to exclude, 28–35, 39–40, 40n34, 42, 52, 54, 58, 64–65, 90, 92, 217, 268; unproductivity of, 23, 68, 161, 193–94, 196–98, 202, 215, 273, 286, 294; Western discrimination against, 5. *See also* border control; national security and national interest; poverty
United Kingdom. *See* Brexit referendum; England/United Kingdom
United Nations, 80, 187–88, 226, 234–35, 241: data on global net migration from, 112; International Commission on Intervention and State Sovereignty, 189; Responsibility-to-Protect Doctrine (R2P), 189–90; World Population Prospects demographic data (2000–2015), 125, 125*f*
United States: Black and White as main racial categories in, 99; border wall construction in, 254; immigration policies in, 51, 55, 211, 213*t*; and ethnic cleansing, 55–56; Immigration Act (1924), xvi–xvii, 56–57, 108; Immigration and Nationality Act (1965), 66; immigration policy changes in, 52–53, 61, 148–50, 149*f*, 152–53, 152*t*, 169; Latin American immigration to, 137; Mexican and Muslim immigrants as racial outsiders in, 99; misinformation as basis for anti-immigration policies in, 272; national myths and foreign policy of, 106n33; and the Philippines, 76; political polarization in, 273; Real ID Act (2005), 148, 148*t*; and scientific racism, 52, 56–57, 59

Varieties of Democracy (V-Dem) database, 129, 165, 204–5, 257
Vattel, Emer de, 30, 35–36, 40–41, 42, 52; *The Law of Nations*, 36
violence and conflict: African civil wars, 246; border fences and, 257, 259*t*, 260, 261; colonialism and, 73, 76, 79, 90, 175, 191, 199–200; effect on immigration policies of, 163*t*, 164–65, 204, 206*t*, 304–7*t*; and migration choices, 129–30; in postcolonial world, 199–200, 215, 257; UCDP/PRIO armed conflict dataset, 129–30, 165, 204
Vitalis, Robert, 25–26
Vitoria, Francisco de: on freedom of movement, 36–38, 37n22, 42; "De Indis" (lecture 1539), 36–38; Pufendorf compared to, 39; on Treaty of Westphalia, 40

Wacziarg, Romain, 164
Walker, Rob B. J., 26–27
Walt, Stephen, 290–91
Waltz, Kenneth N., 246, 253
Washington Consensus, 188, 190
wealth gap, 73, 83–84; and migration between high- and low-income countries, 134–35, 135*f*
Weber, Max, 53
Wendt, Alexander, 180–83, 244
Westphalia, Treaty of (1648), 8, 40
Westphalian order, 236, 237–40
White guilt, 99
White supremacy: as global system, 100, 187, 217; in international relations scholarship, 26–27, 287; justification of, 16, 47, 105, 113, 177, 184; connected to racial imperialism and modern capitalism, 71–72, 105, 184; restrictive immigration

White supremacy (*continued*)
policies and, 1n2, 3, 9, 34, 54–55, 144; scientific racism and, 31–32, 46–49, 58–59. *See also* scientific racism
Williams, Eric, 25
Wolff, Christian von, 38, 39–40, 42
World Bank: bilateral migration stocks (1960–1995), 125, 125*f*, 204; and categories of states, 134, 136, 189; conditions for membership and financial aid of, 242; governance indicators of, 14; and trade openness as measure of GDP, 164
world polity (world society) theory, 81–83, 221, 226–27, 230; border fences and, 248–49, 252–53, 256, 266; constitutive relations of power and, 233; restrictive immigration policies and, 81–83, 90, 221; international organizations and, 240; macrophenomenological perspective of, 82, 82n61, 227; nation-state hegemony and, 223–25; shortcomings of, 230–33
World Trade Organization (WTO), 188, 285, 292n98

xenophobia, 46, 166, 170, 207, 220, 225

YouGov, 193
Young, Iris, 278n36

Zambia, 136
Zanzibar, 235
Zimbabwe: anti-immigrant sentiment against, 252; border controls in, 81; colonization in, 74, 192
Zolberg, Aristide, 272

CPSIA information can be obtained
at www.ICGtesting.com
Printed in the USA
JSHW021920100622
26889JS00002B/2